EUROPE SINCE 1914

EUROPE SINCE 1914

THIRD EDITION

Gordon A. Craig

J. E. Wallace Sterling Professor of Humanities, Stanford University

Holt, Rinehart and Winston

New York Chicago San Francisco Atlanta Dallas
Montreal Toronto London Sydney

TO
SUSAN,
DEBORAH,
and
MARTHA
and their families

CONTENTS

Contents

Contents

PART FOUR
1914-1945

GENERAL
OBSERVATIONS

When war burst upon the world in August 1914, a great number of people in every country of Europe comforted themselves with two thoughts. The first was that their country would be victorious in very short order and at very little cost and that life would return to normal very soon. The second was that, by some magic process, the war would solve all outstanding political, economic, social, and even moral problems and purge Europe of its accumulated ills. As one of the characters in Ernst Gläser's war novel *Class of 1902* said:

At last life had regained an ideal significance. The great virtues of humanity ... fidelity, patriotism, readiness to die for an ideal ... were triumphing now over the trading and shopkeeping spirit.... This was the providential lightning flash that would clear the air.... He could see a new world, ruled and directed by a race of aristocrats who would root out all signs of degeneracy and lead humanity back to the deserted peaks of the eternal ideals.... The war would cleanse mankind from all its impurities.

This was, as the English writer C. E. Montague commented sardonically, a "happy vision, beautiful dream!—like Thackeray's reverie about having a very old and rich aunt. But the dreamer awakes among the snows of the Mont Cenis with a horrid smell in the corridor and the hot-water pipes out of order." Some such rude awakening awaited all the participants in World War I. For that conflict was not short, as we shall see in the next chapter; the enemy was not beaten easily and cheaply; and, after five years of desperate fighting in which a generation of young men was destroyed, it was very difficult to differentiate in any meaningful way between the condition of the victors and that of the vanquished.

Moreover, the war seemed to create far more problems than it solved. Friction between nations was so bitter and so continuous after 1919 that the widows of the first world holocaust were soon contemplating the fearful

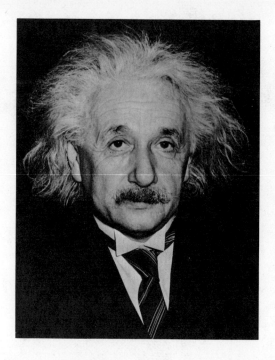

Albert Einstein, 1879–1955.
(Culver Pictures)

probability that their sons would die in a second. Meanwhile, within the different European countries, conflict between parties and social classes assumed an intensity of violence unknown before 1914. Even in a country like England, with a strong tradition of orderly change and respect for law, nothing is more striking in the speeches of government officials, representatives of employers' groups, and labor leaders and in newspaper articles and editorials during the 1920s than the frank recognition that industrial relations had become a running class war. In England, after the general strike of 1926 (see p. 608) had brought the country to its senses, there was a marked diminution in the virulence of this social strife. Other countries, however, were less fortunate; and in many, intestine conflict made orderly government impossible and eventually dissolved the social fabric.

The details of these troubles will fill the chapters that follow. In the appropriate place, it will be seen how they all, in one way or another, stemmed from the losses of the war and the decisions of the Peace Conference, how they were affected by the crippling or actual destruction of the old political hierarchies, how they were influenced by economic dislocations set in train during the long conflict and aggravated by the subsequent depressions and the shrinking role of Europe in the world economy, and, finally, how they were heightened by the rise of totalitarian ideologies with strong national bases.

So much will be said, indeed, in the pages that follow, about the more violent aspects of this quarter of a century that it would be well at the very outset to note that there were other things going on in these years besides external and internal war. The ingenuity of European minds was not directed solely to devising more diabolical weapons or new ways of overthrowing regimes; and it would be a mistake, even in an account that is predominantly concerned with political and social history, to pass over the achievements of Europe's scientists and engineers, its scholars and artists, its writers and musicians. If this was—as it has often been called—an age of conflict, it was nevertheless an age of creative accomplishment as well. How true this is becomes apparent if we think of how greatly our view of the world and the universe of which it is a part has changed as a result of the theory of relativity and the development of atomic research, both essentially products of this period; or of what tremendous advances in medicine, physiology, and surgery have been made possible by the contributions of biophysics and biochemistry to genetics, germ cell and gland research, and particularly by the discovery of vitamins, of insulin (1922) and cortisone (1936), and of such enemies of the virus diseases as penicillin (1929), sulpha pyridine (applied in 1938 in the treatment of pneumonia), and the now familiar and readily available antibiotics, streptomycin and aureomycin; or of how our ability to treat mental disease and to attack certain forms of antisocial behavior has been improved by the development and refinement of clinical neurology and psychiatry; or of how our schools on the one hand and our prisons on the other have benefited from advances in psychology and sociology; or of how many aspects of life, including the political, have been revolutionized by the invention and perfection of such things as the automobile, the airplane, motion pictures, radio, and television.

Not all of these things were, strictly speaking, European in origin; but the part played by European brains and energy in these achievements of pure and applied science was very great. The new physics, which sensibly de-parted from nineteenth-century concepts of energy and mass, received its initial impulse from the German Max Planck's quantum theory of 1900 and found its most comprehensive exposition in the Special and General Theories of Relativity formulated in 1905 and 1915 by Planck's countryman Albert Einstein, who reconciled the apparent contradictions between Newtonian assumptions and the electromagnetic theory of Clerk Maxwell (1873) in a new form of field physics. The development of atomic research began essentially in 1911 with the New Zealander Rutherford's deduction from his studies of radioactivity that the atom, far from being solid, as had been believed since the time of Democritus, was largely an empty structure comprising a minute nucleus (or proton) with a positive electrical charge, surrounded by a shell of negatively charged electrons—in a word, a kind of miniature solar system. With the aid of this explanation and Planck's quantum theory, the Dane Niels Bohr formulated his general theory of atomic structure in 1913; and upon this basis the later work of such distinguished European physicists as Werner Heisenberg of Germany and Erwin Schrödinger of Austria, Enrico Fermi of Italy, and the Englishmen Cockcroft, Walton, and Chadwick was accomplished.

In other sciences, both pure and behavioral, the European contribution was correspondingly great. In clinical and social psychiatry, for instance, the great names were those of the Austrian Sigmund Freud and the Swiss Carl Jung; while in sociology the Germans Max Weber and Karl Mannheim and the Italians Vilfredo Pareto and Gaetano Mosca devised methods of diagnosis that completely superseded the techniques of the older sociology, while their studies of such things as bureaucratic behavior and the role of elites in history made possible a more realistic appreciation of the way society works.

All in all, it must be said that, at a time when Europe's financial and industrial superiority was being lost to the New World, when markets that had once been the preserve of European traders were being invaded by American, Indian, and Japanese goods, and when, despite appearances, Europe's political primacy was already a thing of the past, it retained the scientific leadership of the world throughout most of this period. It was only after 1933, when Hitler's persecution of the Jews and his war against independence of thought led many of Europe's finest scientific minds to go into exile, that the balance began to shift toward the United States and Russia, a develop-ment confirmed by World War II, which left those two countries the best fitted, in financial and other ways, to promote scientific research and development.

In the field of the arts, the same vitality and high achievement were to be noted, although these qualities should perhaps be emphasized less than the spirit of rebellion against the forms and values of the past that characterized them. In architecture, the break with tradition was seen in a marked emphasis upon functionalism—that is, upon the use of new materials and techniques of construction to make the appearance of buildings conform to their use. In cities like Berlin, Vienna, Stockholm, and Helsinki, the new style produced buildings which were perhaps startling to the eyes of those accustomed to regard massiveness and external decoration as the hallmarks of

Cité Radieuse, Marseille. Le Corbusier. (Giraudon)

Walter Gropius: The Workshop Wing, the Bauhaus, Dessau. (Museum of Modern Art, New York)

architectural style but which combined beauty with a cleanness and directness of design that was singularly appropriate to urban industrial society. A fine example was the famous Bauhaus at Dessau, built in 1925 by Germany's leading representative of the new architecture, Walter Gropius. Another pioneer of the modern movement was the French-Swiss architect, Le Corbusier (Charles Edouard Jeanneret-Gris, 1887–1965), a visionary who saw in the revitalizing of urban planning the one hope for the future well-being of western man, and who combatted urban sprawl by preaching that towns should be built upward rather than outward. Le Corbusier's masterpieces in ferroconcrete stand today in Rio de Janeiro, Berlin, Marseille, and Chandigarh in the Punjab. They all illustrate his belief that "the materials of city planning are sky, space, trees, steel, and cement in that order and that hierarchy."

Much of the painting and sculpture of these years was more difficult to enjoy or even to understand, for here the break with the past took the form of a deliberate repudiation of any kind of naturalism. Arnold Hauser has written that the idea that art was supposed to be faithful to nature had never been seriously questioned in principle since the Middle Ages and had remained an article of faith with the impressionist school of the nineteenth century. Postimpressionist art, however, renounced all illusion of reality and set out to "express its outlook on life by the deliberate deformation of natural objects." The expressionist paintings of Chagall, the works of Picasso's cubist period, the surrealist painting of Chirico, Delvaux, and Dali, the sculpture of Epstein and Henry Moore possessed undeniable power; but, in most cases, they portrayed worlds or fragments of worlds not easily recognizable

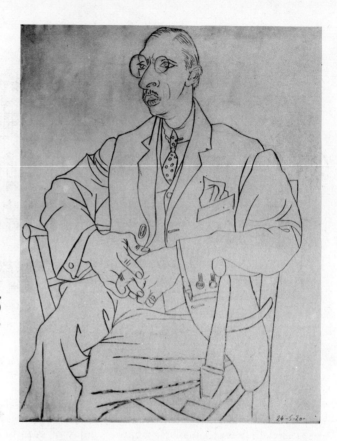

Igor Stravinsky by Pablo Picasso,
1920. (Permission SPADEM 1970
by French Reproduction Rights,
Inc.)

or accessible to the viewer. In some cases, indeed, the artist seemed uninterested in communicating with any audience outside himself, refusing to use accepted methods of communication and inventing a language of his own. This tendency was not confined to painting and sculpture, although it was perhaps most marked there. It also appeared in much of the music of the period and in some of the literature. The road from Stravinsky to Schoenberg was most easily traveled by trained musicians, or mathematicians; the lover of Dickens could find his way through the denser passages of *Finnegans Wake* only with guidebook in hand.

This was a period of literary distinction, and a list of its greatest figures would compare favorably with those of any previous period discussed in this book. It would include, in the field of the novel, Thomas Mann, Hermann Hesse, Alfred Döblin, Marcel Proust, André Gide, André Malraux, Franz Kafka, D. H. Lawrence, and James Joyce; in poetry, A. E. Housman, William Butler Yeats, T. S. Eliot, W. H. Auden, Paul Valéry, Georg Trakl; in the drama, George Bernard Shaw, Paul Claudel, Luigi Pirandello, Bertolt Brecht; in the film, Sergei Eisenstein, René Clair, and Fritz Lang.

In common with the painters and sculptors, most of these men were in revolt against the past, and they showed this sometimes by the choice of radically unconventional style or organization—as in the case of the expressionist dramas and films of the first postwar years (the German film *The Cabinet of Dr. Caligari* would be a good example) and Joyce's *Ulysses* (1922) and *Finnegans Wake* (1939)—and sometimes by a deliberate rejection of commonly accepted values and institutions. The latter tendency took various forms and was to be found in the Fabian frivolities of Shaw, the militant reformism of plays like Ernst Toller's *Man and the Masses* (1920) and *The Machine-Breakers* (1922) and George Kaiser's *Gas* (1917–1920), the cynicism of Brecht's *Threepenny Opera* (1928), and the pronounced pessimism of Housman's poetry and novels like Hermann Broch's *The Sleep-Walkers* (1929) and Kafka's *The Trial* (1920) and *The Castle* (1926). As in the case of the painters also, the writers sought in some cases to withdraw completely from contemporary realities, seeking new inspiration or new values in non-European climes and cultures. Gide looked for inspiration to Africa, and Hesse turned to the East in the conviction that Europe had "fallen finally into a deep spiritual devastation" (*Demian*, 1919), "For us in old Europe," he wrote, "everything has died that was good and unique to us. Our admirable rationality has become madness, our gold is paper, our machines can only shoot or explode, our art is suicide. We are going under, friends." (*Klingsor's Last Summer*, 1920.)

In much of the literature of these years, emphasis was placed either upon the inadequacy of reason to control life or upon the necessity of transcending the limitations of reason in order to attain greater freedom. The latter idea, which was influenced by the Freudian theory that man can be free if he will loose himself from old burdens and repressions, was seen in much of the

Expressionism in the film. *The Cabinet of Dr. Caligari,* 1919, directed by Robert Wiene. (Museum of Modern Art, New York, Film Stills Archive)

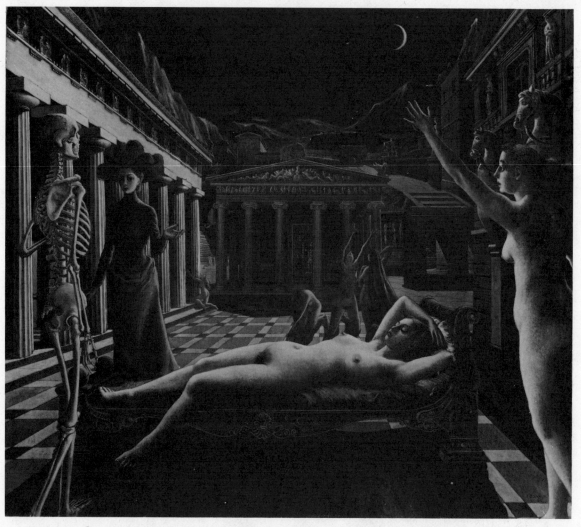

Surrealism in art. "Venus Asleep," 1944, by Paul Delvaux. A meticulous painter, who pays almost excessive attention to detail, Delvaux is nevertheless interested in objective reality only as the framework of dreams. (Tate Gallery, London, and the artist)

work of the expressionist school and was reflected in the widespread popularity, among the postwar youth of Europe, of writers like Dostoevsky and the theologian Sören Kierkegaard, who had emphasized the irrational as a regenerative force and exalted faith over logic. On the other hand, the belief that man's life was determined by external compulsions over which he had no control colored the work of Proust, Joyce, Thomas Mann (especially in works like *Death in Venice* and *The Magic Mountain*) and Alfred Döblin (particularly in his great novel *Alexanderplatz, Berlin,* which appeared in 1930).

The continued vogue of Bergson, the interest in Ludwig Wittgenstein's systematic denial of the possibility of a rational metaphysics, and the development of an increasingly radical empiricism showed that the same reaction against rationalism was important among the philosophers of this period; and, during and after World War II, the growth of existentialism, which stemmed essentially from Kierkegaard and Nietzsche, and was elaborated in Martin Heidegger's *Being and Time* (1927), was to confirm this tendency. This was offset to some extent by the strong revival of Aquinian rationalism, and, under the influence of Étienne Gilson and Jacques Maritain, the scholastic philosophy made a considerable number of converts in this period. In the area of philosophy of history, the work that attracted most attention was Oswald Spengler's *The Decline of the West* (1918), a massive and pedantic book which sought, by biological analogy, to demonstrate that cultures pass through stages from birth to death like living organisms but seemed bent on persuading western civilization to avoid its inevitable fate. More people quoted *The Decline* than read it; and, on the whole, it probably had less influence than Spengler's much shorter essay *Prussianism and Socialism* (1919), which, with its argument that the ideals of Frederick the Great were the real alternative to Marxism, had a profound effect upon the revival of neoconservatism in Germany.

The progress of urbanization, the success of secular religions, and the victory in some countries, particularly the Soviet Union, of governments that were opposed in principle to formal religion raised serious problems for the established churches but at the same time stimulated religious thinkers to rise to the challenge of the times. The tendency of church leaders to adjust themselves to the prevailing materialism and to compromise with popular philosophies of science and the like, which had been reflected before 1914 in the spread of reformism and the avoidance of dogma in Protestantism and Judaism, now gave way to a more stubborn and convincing defense of the elements of religious faith. Roman Catholicism, always less responsive to the forces of appeasement than other religions, had two determined and eloquent spokesmen in these years, Pope Pius XI (1922–1939) and his successor Eugenio Pacelli, who took the title Pope Pius XII (1939–1958). In the person of Karl Barth, Protestantism found its most persuasive enemy of watered-down and rationalistic theology; and, under his leadership and the influence of writers like Albert Schweitzer and Emil Brunner, there was a marked revival of elements in Christianity that had their origin in the teaching of the apostle Paul.

This cursory sketch of the intellectual and artistic tendencies of this quarter of a century may, if it does nothing else, leave an impression of the vitality and the diversity of European thought. The years after 1919 were difficult and perplexing ones, and there was much truth in the words which Paul Valéry addressed to a French audience shortly after the war:

All the fundamentals of our life have been affected by the war and something deeper has been worn away than the renewable parts of the machine. You know how greatly the general economic situation has been disturbed, and the polity of states and the very life of the individual; you are familiar with the universal discomfort, hesitation, apprehension. But among these injured things is the Mind. The Mind has indeed been cruelly wounded; its complaint is heard in the hearts of intellectual man; it passes a mournful judgment on itself. It doubts itself profoundly.

It is true that the confidence that had characterized European thought in the nineteenth century had been weakened by the war; and, when the threat of a new conflict became very real in the late 1930s, that loss made itself felt. But, as we look at the period as a whole, we are apt to be impressed less by the presence of defeatism (that came very late) than by the evidence of a critical testing of old values and an earnest search for new ones. Even in this period when Europe's role in the world was in rapid decline, its spirit was alive and its contributions to the civilization of the Western world very great.

Chapter 20 WAR AND EUROPEAN
SOCIETY, 1914–1918

The onset of hostilities in August 1914 was greeted in many of the cities of the larger countries with an almost carnival gaiety. In London, the mood was one of excitement and enthusiasm; in German towns, reservists on their way to mustering centers were pelted with flowers; in Vienna, crowds promenaded along the Ringstrasse, shouting "Down with Serbia!" with every evidence of happiness. These raptures were of course, the result of ignorance. No one in 1914 had the slightest idea of what the war was to be like; on this score, the generals and the statesmen were no wiser than those who bawled out their enthusiasm in the streets. The operational plans that had been devised by the different general staffs showed that the soldiers believed in a short and mobile war, not essentially different from the brisk conflicts of the 1860s; and the fact that their governments agreed with them was demonstrated by the almost total absence of plans for financing a long war, for producing the munitions or acquiring the strategical materials to support it, or for organizing society in such a way as to prevent the breakdown of normal production and services. No one dreamed that the conflict would last for more than four years and that it would kill two million young Germans, more than a million Frenchmen, almost as many Englishmen and Austrians, half a million Italians, and an unknown number of Russians.

Nor did any of those who shouted in the streets in 1914 realize that the war they were greeting so lightheartedly would destroy the Europe they had known and leave them with sadly depleted physical and psychological resources to face a forbidding future.

THE COURSE OF THE WAR, 1914–1916

The Western Front from Liège to the Marne   From the very beginning the war confounded expectations. The Germans, for example, whose war plans had been reviewed and amended yearly since the days of Schlieffen, had confidently expected that by seizing the initiative they would be able to win a quick and decisive victory in the west that would enable them subsequently to devote their full energies to the slower task of defeating Russia. As it turned out, their most devastating victories in the first months of the war were won in the east, while their western plan came to nothing.

This was partly the result of a German underestimation of their opponents, particularly of the Belgians and the British. The German plan called for a sweep through Belgium, which they did not expect to be opposed, since it was known that the outbreak of war had caught the Belgian army in the middle of a basic reorganization. But the Belgians did fight, gallantly and with such effect that the ring of fortresses around Liège stalled the German columns for four days. When this initial resistance was broken and the Belgian army had been thrown back on Antwerp, the German drive picked up speed, and began the great wheeling movement that was meant to envelop the now uncovered left of General Lanrezac's Fifth French Army, which was holding grimly on the Sambre River. The Germans, however, had forgotten the British or, rather, had supposed that what help the British could send would be late and would arrive at ports remote from the decisive area of operations. Unknown to them, the British had landed one cavalry division and four infantry divisions under Sir John French at Le Havre, Rouen, and Boulogne while the Germans were still being held at Liège. These "Old Contemptibles" were now rushed forward to Mons, where, on August 21, they fell in on the French left and prevented them from being outflanked and overrun.

The battle on the Sambre and the stubborn resistance put up by the British and French armies as they fell back upon Paris slowed the momentum of the German drive, and casualties from battle and fatigue were so heavy that Generals Kluck and Bülow, commanding the German First and Second Armies, began to doubt the feasibility of enveloping Paris in accordance with the Schlieffen plan. After another hard fight with the British at Le Cateau (August 26), Kluck decided to wheel his forces to the east, rather than the west, of Paris, hoping that by so doing they would be able to smash Lanrezac's army, now engaged in bitter fighting with Bülow's forces near Guise. This was a fatal maneuver. The French commander-in-chief, Joffre, a sensible if not brilliant soldier, had been holding his reserves at Paris; now, as Kluck turned, General Galliéni persuaded Joffre to throw everything he had against the German flank and rear. Thus began the battle of the Marne, which put the Germans on the defensive for the first time. The situation might have been retrieved if the German chief of staff, Moltke, had not at this juncture made the mistake of committing his left wing to an offensive against Nancy, thus compounding his fateful prewar decision to increase the numerical strength of the left wing at the expense of the right—a significant departure from Schlieffen's original concept. The result was that the Germans found themselves engaged in two violent and uncoor-

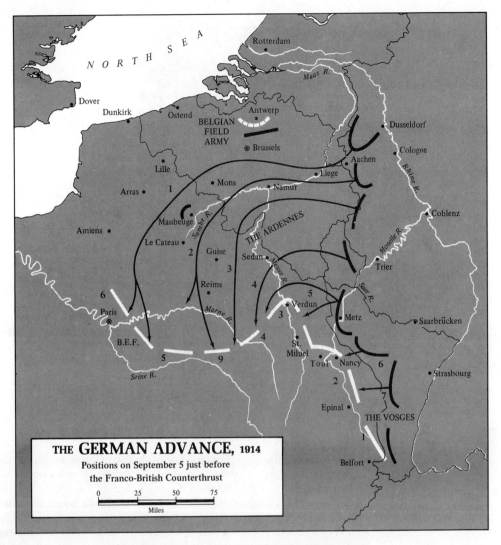

THE GERMAN ADVANCE, 1914

Positions on September 5 just before
the Franco-British Counterthrust

0   25   50   75

Miles

dinated battles, on the Marne and in Lorraine, a situation that proved too much
for Moltke's weak nerves and induced him to leave one of the most crucial
decisions of the war to a subordinate, Lieutenant Colonel Hentsch. This officer,
sent to Kluck's front on September 9 to review the situation, ordered him to
break off hostilities and to withdraw behind the Aisne River. The retreat represented a psychological blow from which the German armies never completely
recovered.

The War in the Trenches   This was not only because it was a clear defeat
and one that marked the definitive failure of the Schlieffen plan, but also because
it turned the war in the west into a kind of struggle for which the German
officer corps, raised in the tradition of lightning, mobile, destructive war, was
not prepared. Even after Moltke was retired on September 14 and replaced by
a more confident and energetic chief of staff, Erich von Falkenhayn, a resumption

"Well, if you knows of a better 'ole, go to it!" This cartoon by Bruce Bairnsfather, which originally appeared in *The Bystander* (London), appealed to fighting men of all nations and won world fame. (© *The Tatler & Bystander.*)

of the German offensive proved impossible. The Germans dug in along the line Noyon-Rheims-Verdun; their opponents followed their example; and the two great armies faced each other in a double line of trenches, each protected by dense barbed-wire entanglements and cunningly disposed machine gun nests and mortar batteries, and backed by a support line and, further back, by heavy artillery. This elaborate underground system soon extended all the way from the Channel ports to the frontiers of Switzerland.

It was to be four years before the deadlock thus created was broken and mobility of operations restored. In the meantime, the youth of England, France, and Germany was squandered on futile assaults upon each other's fixed positions. In this fantastic new form of warfare, men lived like foxes and moles, in burrows that were sometimes only a score of yards from those of their adversaries. By day, they exchanged desultory rifle fire over the parapets, or lobbed grenades into the enemy's trenches, or laid down a systematic pattern of mortar or artillery fire upon his supply lines. At night, small parties crept out into the no-man's land between the lines, their faces blackened so that they would not show in the glare of Véry rockets, and cut their way through the wire, seeking prisoners who might divulge information about the enemy's plans. Periodically, the high command, with an enthusiasm and optimism that never seemed to dim, ordered a general offensive in this or that sector of the front. These big pushes were preceded by a protracted artillery barrage that was intended to flatten the enemy's wire, destroy as many of his strong points as possible, and leave his troops cowering in their trenches in a state of shock. The barrage was frequently preceded by elaborate engineering operations, which dug beneath the enemy's trenches and mined them with explosive charges; and it was sometimes accompanied by the release of chlorine gas, one of the more horrible innovations of the war. When these preparatory steps were complete, the infantry began to go over the top of their parapets in waves and, with fixed bayonets, under a rolling barrage, to walk toward the enemy trenches. All too often it was discovered at this point that the barrage had not been long enough to do what it was expected to do, or that the enemy had withdrawn from the shelled lines and was now fighting back from intact ones, or that the bombardment had turned the battlefield into a swamp that made movement impossible, or that the wind had shifted and was blowing the gas the wrong way, or that some other miscalculation had been made. As a result, the gains were always infinitesimal and the losses tremendous.

During all of 1915, for instance, despite repeated attacks, the British and French did not gain more than three miles at any one point; but the French suffered 1,430,000 casualties. Falkenhayn hammered at Verdun for ten months in 1916 and did not take it, but lost 336,000 men. In the battle of the Somme in the same year, the Allies lost 614,000 men and the Germans 650,000, without any appreciable gain on either side. In the third battle of Ypres in 1917, the British fought for five months and, with casualties of 450,000, advanced less than five miles on a nine-mile front.

The Eastern Front from Tannenberg to Gorlice   In contrast to this situation, the war in the east was marked with great mobility and with considerable gain and loss of territory. The pace was set here at the outset by the Russians, who surprised both the Germans and the Austrians by accelerating their mobilization and throwing two armies into East Prussia and four against the Austrian lines in Galicia.

The advance in East Prussia was in response to the urgent plea of Russia's ally France; and it suffered from overhasty preparation, from grave defects of logistical support, and from lack of coordination at the command level. Since the war against Japan, there had been bad blood between Rennenkampf, the commander of the Russian First Army, and his opposite number in the Second Army, Samsonov; and this and their temperaments (Samsonov was impetuous; Rennenkampf, cautious and slow) made it difficult for them to work together. Their advance into East Prussia had the initial effect of panicking the German corps under Mackensen and making the commander-in-chief in East Prussia, Prittwitz, telephone to Moltke for aid. Cooler heads among the Germans noticed, however, that there was a wide and inviting gap between the two Russian armies; and even before help arrived in the form of a retired general named Paul von Hindenburg, who replaced Prittwitz, and a younger major general named Erich Ludendorff, who had distinguished himself only days before at Liège, plans had been drawn up to exploit the separation. While a single cavalry division was left to face Rennenkampf, a German corps under François moved by rail from

Königsberg around Samsonov's flank to Tannenberg, where it detrained and held his army until two other German corps enveloped it from the rear. The bewildered Russians stumbled into the trap, 90,000 of them surrendering before the fighting stopped on August 30. Their unhappy commander shot himself.

This stunning German success was followed by Hindenburg's victory over Rennenkampf's now isolated force in the battle of the Masurian Lakes. By September 15, East Prussia was freed of Russians, and a legend had been born that was to have profound effects upon Germany's internal politics: that of the military genius and invincibility of the Hindenburg-Ludendorff team.

To place too much emphasis upon the battles of Tannenberg and the Masurian Lakes would be to belittle the important contribution made by the Russians to the Allied cause in the first period of the war. While Rennenkampf and Samsonov were being encircled in East Prussia, four Russian armies under General Ivanov had advanced into Galicia and, between August 23 and the middle of September, a series of hard battles was fought between them and the bulk of the Austrian army, which had, under Conrad von Hötzendorf's direction, taken the offensive in Galicia at the onset of hostilities. The Austrians had initial success at Krasnick and Komarow, but numbers soon began to tell against them; by September 10, with the two forces locked in conflict all along the line, the Russian Fifth Army under Plehve began to creep around Conrad's rear, and a major envelopment seemed in progress. The Russian habit of sending operational orders by wireless without taking the trouble to encode them, however, warned the Austrian chief of staff in time for him to extricate his forces; but he had to withdraw his badly mauled armies to a line 140 miles west of Lemberg, abandoning Galicia to the enemy.

Meanwhile, the Austrians were having trouble in another sector. It will be recalled that the first declaration of war in 1914 had been that of Austria against Serbia, and the Austrians had expected the chastisement of the Serbs to be quick and easy. But the Russian advance into Galicia had forced Conrad to withdraw half of the strength of the Austrian Second Army that was poised on the Save west of Belgrade, and this forced a major alteration of plans for the Serbian campaign. When the Austrian attack began on August 12, it was made by two smaller armies facing east on the Drina, and, to everyone's astonishment, they were promptly thrown back across the river by the aroused Serbians. Dogged seesaw fighting, marked by great atrocities on both sides, followed on the Save, the Drina, and in Bosnia, until both armies had literally marched and countermarched themselves into a state of exhaustion. In December, the Austrians limped back across the Danube, having inflicted 170,000 casualties on the enemy but having themselves suffered 227,000 out of a total force of 450,000 engaged.

In the battles in Galicia and Serbia, and particularly those around Lemberg, the Austrians had lost the flower of their junior officers and their non-commissioned officer corps, a blow from which the Imperial and Royal Army never recovered. As early as the end of 1914, army morale was seriously shaken. Moreover, the Austrian High Command tended to blame its losses upon the Germans. On the basis of rather vague promises made to him by Moltke in 1909, Conrad had expected that the Germans would support his Galician offensive by a threat from East Prussia towards Warsaw. When this did not materialize, he took the line that this was a breach of faith, and he was impervious to the argument that the situation in the west and the Russian offensive in East Prussia made an offensive into Poland impossible. He seemed to believe that, if that was true, it merely indicated that the German army was not as good as he had been led to expect. The German failure in the west, he said, was "a declaration of insolvency" on the part of the German general staff. The Germans on their side were critical of the performance of their allies, although they had themselves encouraged the Austrians to undertake the Serbian and Galician offensives simultaneously, a task beyond their powers. The fact was—and it was now ruefully admitted by the more honest commanders on both sides—that the Central Powers had embarked on a great war without a joint war plan or even an adequate knowledge of the strength, organization, technical equipment, and capacity of each other's forces; and that ignorance and strategical disarticulation had had unfortunate results.

Mutual dissatisfaction and resentment complicated the relations of the allies for the rest of the war. For example, no truly satisfactory solution was ever found for the problem of command, which became acute as the Germans found it necessary to stiffen the shaken Austrian armies with German units. The German preference for mixed armies composed of eight German divisions and three Austrian divisions under German command was resented even when yielded to; and German pressure for a supreme German command over all fronts was resisted by the Austrians (Conrad said that Germans were seeking to make Austria a satellite) until after the great Austrian collapse at Lutzk in 1916.

These differences did not make effective collaboration completely, or even generally, impossible. In 1915, for example, the Austrians had the satisfaction of seeing a great success achieved on the basis of the plans of their own chief of staff. Although Hindenburg and Ludendorff had drafted a plan for relieving Russian pressure by launching an offensive from East Prussia, the German chief of staff Falkenhayn, with his emperor's approval, opted for a plan drafted by Conrad, which called for a combined thrust in the neighborhood of Gorlice and Tarnow in Galicia. Launched on May 2, 1915, this drive hit the Russians at a moment when they were short of shells, guns, and food, and what started as a Russian setback developed into a rout. The disorganized armies fell back beyond Przemysl, Lemberg, Warsaw, and Brest Litovsk until, after six months of desperate rear-guard fighting, they had been pushed behind a line that ran from Riga on the Baltic to the eastern end of the Carpathians. They were 300 miles east of the positions they had held in August 1914, and they had lost 300,000 men and 3000 guns to the enemy. If the pursuing forces had not had to stop from sheer fatigue, the fate of the Russian empire might have been decided in 1915. So tremendous were its losses that it remains a marvel that it could still, in 1916, mount a new offensive strong enough to help relieve the German pressure on Verdun.

The Intervention of Japan, Turkey, and Italy   While these campaigns were being fought, the warring coalitions were making every effort to win new allies. At the very outset, the Triple Entente registered a success when the Japanese government declared war upon Germany. This brought little advantage to the Allies in the theaters in which they were most hotly engaged, for the Japanese were interested primarily in divesting the Germans of their possessions in areas they coveted themselves, like the Shantung peninsula and the islands in the central Pacific which Germany had acquired at the end of the nineteenth century; and they devoted most of their energies to this end.

More important for the conduct of the European war was the position of Turkey and Italy, and in Constantinople and Rome the diplomats of both sides strove to persuade the governments to declare for them or—failing that—to remain neutral. Given the intimacy between the Turks and the Germans in the immediate prewar years, the Turkish decision was almost a foregone conclusion. After some preliminary diplomatic sparring, the Turkish government in October sent a fleet into the Black Sea to harry the Russian coastal trade; and, at the beginning of November, the Entente powers responded by declaring war.

The clarification of Italy's position took somewhat longer. When war broke out, the government in power, which was headed by Salandra, announced that, since Austria's action against Serbia was not defensive in nature, Italy could not consider itself bound by the provisions of the Triple Alliance and that she would consequently maintain a position of neutrality. There seems little doubt that this decision was popular in the country as a whole, and it certainly represented the position of the bulk of the Socialist party, the parliamentary Center, which regarded Giolitti as its leader, and the Italian high clergy, whose acceptance of neutrality was in part dictated by fear that its alternative would be war against that pillar of the church, Austria. The position of the neutralists was complicated by the belief of many of them that Italy should be paid for its neutrality by Austria's surrender of the Trentino and Trieste and perhaps its acquiescence in Italy's acquisition of Albania, but this was not an essential article of their faith.

From the very outset, there was a strong countermovement that favored intervention on the side of the Entente powers. Liberal idealists and republicans who clung to the principles of Mazzini and Garibaldi felt that the cause of England and France was the cause of civilization and that Italy must not be absent from the ranks of its defenders. Intervention was supported also by the Nationalist party, which frankly expected greater gains from it than could be won by remaining neutral; by the Masonic lodges, which were as anti-Austrian as they were anticlerical and had great influence in the political parties, the army, and the press; by influential circles around the king, who was firmly pro-English; and by numerous opportunists, who saw a chance for personal aggrandizement. These last included the Socialist editor Benito Mussolini, who had vigorously opposed the Tripolitanian war but now swung over (apparently because the thought of war appealed to his histrionic temperament and not, as some have said, because of French subventions, although it is true that once his new newspaper *Popolo d' Italia* began to call for intervention, he did receive money from socialist sources in France). More influential than Mussolini was the poet Gabriele D'Annunzio, who appealed to all those who were disillusioned or discontented with the Italian political system. D'Annunzio carried on a remarkable campaign in which he preached that Italy would rise regenerated from war; and his carefully contrived mass demonstrations (from which the Fascists later borrowed many ideas) began to swing Italian public opinion over to war in the spring of 1915.

The Salandra government was meanwhile coldbloodedly bargaining with both the Entente and the Central Powers and was discovering that the Entente was ready to make the more tempting offers. Indeed, any hesitation they may have had was removed by the Entente's promise that, if Italy fought against Austria, it would, at the war's end, receive the Austrian Tyrol as far north as the Brenner Pass, Trieste, part of Albania and other territory at the head of the Adriatic, part of Turkey, and a share in the general war indemnity that would be levied on the beaten foe. These terms were embodied in a secret treaty and signed in London in April 1915.

A last-ditch stand against intervention was made by the man who had been the strongest force in Italian politics since 1903 and who still had the votes to defeat any proposal for intervention that was submitted to parliament. When Giolitti sought to bring parliamentary pressure to bear on the government and the king, however, he had no success. By mid-May excited crowds were prowling the streets of Rome shouting "Death to Giolitti!" and breaking the windows of the Chamber of Deputies; noninterventionists were being beaten up by nationalist mobs; and news from other cities and from the rural villages indicated that the war spirit was strong there also. In face of the violence of this emotion, the Socialist party and the church remained immobile, and parliament allowed itself to be intimidated. On May 18, when Salandra laid a war resolution before the Chamber, it was approved by all but a handful of Giolitti's loyal supporters.

Diplomacy and War in the Balkans   In return for a treaty that was to cause difficulties at the Peace Conference in 1919, the Entente Powers had won an important victory, for Italian adhesion to their cause significantly increased the pressure upon Austria. They were less successful in attaining their diplomatic objectives in the Balkans.

In this area, they were forced, by Turkey's entrance into the war on Germany's side, to try, somehow or other, to prevent her from establishing direct contact with the Central Powers. The best way of doing this was to win the support of the Balkan states that lay between. The key to the situation was Bulgaria, which, because of past Austrian favors, dynastic ties with the German royal family, and enmity for Serbia, could not be expected to be won easily. At the beginning of 1915, Entente diplomats tried to impress the Serbs with the importance of appeasing the Bulgars by restoring to them some of the lands seized during the Balkan wars. The Serbs, already infuriated by what they had managed to learn about Allied concessions to Italy, refused.

Aware that the Central Powers were prepared to promise the Bulgars gains in Thrace and Macedonia if they would enter the war, the Entente governments tried a different tack. They sought the alliance of Greece and Rumania, hoping that this would frighten the Bulgars into continued neutrality. But the Rumanians also wanted territory that the Entente could not promise them, since it, too, belonged to the Serbs; and in Athens, German agents had ingratiated themselves with King Constantine, who was consequently unresponsive to Entente offers.

The attitude of the Rumanian and Greek governments and the whole complexion of the political struggle in the Balkans was determined, in large part, by the most ambitious, and, in the end, most unsuccessful, of the military operations tried by the British in 1915. This was the Gallipoli campaign.

In January 1915, the Russians asked the British to stage some kind of demonstration at the Straits of the Dardanelles that would draw Turkish forces away from the Caucasus, where they were pressing upon the Russian lines. The idea was taken up enthusiastically in London by the First Lord of the Admiralty, Winston Churchill, who was an opponent of the one-front complex of many British soldiers, which, as far as he could see, meant only a continued blood bath in western Europe. Churchill wanted a more open war, with as many fronts as possible; and with respect to the Straits, he had visions of seizing Constantinople and, with one blow, winning the support of all the doubtful Balkan states. After hard fights with the service chiefs, Admiral Lord Fisher being in particular vehemently opposed to risking ships on this enterprise, Churchill won his point.

The Dardanelles campaign was a long series of missed opportunities. In March 1915 the Straits were almost forced by a mixed Anglo-French naval force, but an undiscovered mine field sank three old battleships and disabled three cruisers; and the admiral in command lost heart, and, despite the pleading of his junior officers, called off the attempt. The decision was next made to land the two divisions of the ANZAC Corps (Australians and New Zealanders), with supporting French and British divisions, at two points on the Gallipoli peninsula and to advance overland to positions that would dominate the Straits. Lack of appreciation of what a successful amphibious operation entailed, muddled command relations, and bad intelligence defeated these plans when the original landings were made in April and again in August, when another attempt was made at Suvla Bay. On both occasions, although landings were made successfully, the British failed to get off the beach and seize the high ground behind it when it was open to them; and on both occasions also, the opportunity they lost was exploited to the full by a young Turkish soldier named Mustafa Kemal, who was destined to be the postwar leader of his country. In face of the initiative shown by Kemal and his chief, the German Liman von Sanders, the persistence and valor shown by the invaders did them no good. In December 1915 and January 1916, after months of being raked by Turkish guns, their forces were evacuated, after suffering 252,000 casualties.

Even before the final evacuation, the Balkan countries had seen that the enterprise was bound to fail; and the Greeks and Rumanians had been confirmed in their neutrality. And this, of course, relieved the Bulgars of any further hesitation. In October 1915, they came into the war on the side of the Central Powers and, in conjunction with Austrian divisions, invaded Serbia and, despite stubborn resistance, overran that country before the end of the year.

By the end of 1915, therefore, the Central Powers dominated the Balkans and had a solid connection with the Turks on their southern flank. This did not prevent Allied diplomats from persisting in their efforts in this area. In 1916, indeed, they had two qualified successes. During the great German offensive at Verdun, when there was danger that that hinge of the western front would be broken, the Entente Powers appealed to Russia for a new offensive and

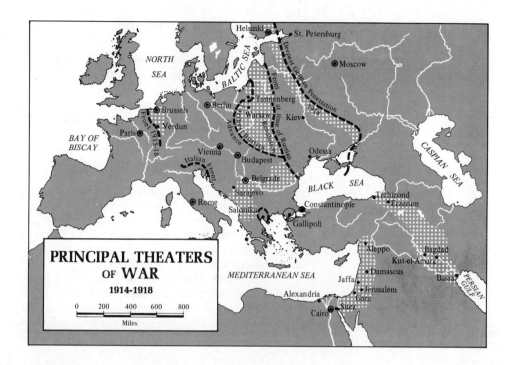

PRINCIPAL THEATERS OF WAR

1914-1918

0   200   400   600   800
Miles

simultaneously bought Rumanian aid with the territorial offers they could not
make while Serbia was still in the war. The great Brusilov offensive of June–July
1916, which broke the Austrian front at Lutzk and took an entire army of 250,000
prisoner with its guns, and the subsequent Rumanian entrance into the war
probably contributed to the German failure at Verdun, by drawing troops away
from that point. It did not, however, permanently alter the Balkan situation,
since Rumania lasted only a month as a belligerent before being overwhelmed
by German armies.

In the course of 1916, also, the Allies won a somewhat tenuous position in
Greece by the use of what today would be called subversive tactics. At the
end of the previous year, in the hope of saving Serbia, the Allies had landed
troops at Salonika, disregarding Greek protests against violation of their soil.
This force did nothing of military importance for the next three years, but its
commander, the French general Sarrail, carried on elaborate and not unsuccessful
political intrigues designed to arouse opposition to King Constantine's policy
of neutrality. These seem to have influenced the thinking of Eleutherios Venizelos,
always a Westerner in sympathy and now anxious to create a Greater Greece
at the expense of Bulgaria and Turkey. In August 1916, when an antiroyalist
revolt broke out in Salonika, Venizelos joined it, formed a provisional government, and was immediately recognized by the Entente Powers. He could not,
however, claim to rule the country as a whole. That was not to come until
mid-1917, when Allied pressure finally proved too much for Constantine and
led him to abdicate in favor of his son Alexander. That act was followed by
Venizelos's appointment as prime minister and by a formal declaration of war
on the Central Powers.

Mesopotamia, the Arab Lands, and Africa   It was not only at the Straits that the British and the Turks clashed in these years. In 1915 a British force under General Townshend advanced from the head of the Persian Gulf up the Tigris toward Baghdad, only to be stopped at Ctesiphon and forced back to Kut el-Amara where it was surrounded and eventually forced to surrender in April 1916. This victory, however, and their exertions at Gallipoli seem to have overstrained Turkish resources, and from this point on their troubles multiplied. While the Russians captured large areas of Turkish Armenia in the first months of 1916, the British resumed offensive operations in Mesopotamia, which were finally crowned with success in the recapture of Kut in February 1917. Meanwhile, by promising support to the cause of Arab independence (the so-called McMahon pledge of October 1915, confirmed and made more precise by the Sykes-Picot Agreement of 1916), the British won the support of the Arabs of the Hejaz, who revolted against the sultan in June 1916 and subsequently played an important role in the British campaign of 1917 in Palestine.

In Africa, a force of South Africans under Botha, using tactics learned in the Boer War, invaded and conquered German South West Africa in a vigorous campaign in the late spring of 1915. The Cameroons fell to French and British troops in the following year. The conquest of German East Africa, on the other hand, proved much more difficult. Here a brilliant soldier, Lieutenant Colonel von Lettow-Vorbeck, severely trounced a mixed Indian-British force when it sought to land at Tanga in 1915 and, throughout 1916, outfought an army composed of South African, Indian, British, Belgian-Congolese, and Portuguese detachments, commanded by General Jan Smuts. Indeed, Lettow remained at large for the rest of the war, although his area of operations was steadily whittled away.

The War at Sea   More decisive, as far as the final result of the war was concerned, were the operations on the high seas, where each side sought to weaken its antagonist by destroying its shipping and, whenever encountered, the naval forces that protected it. In this struggle, the British succeeded during the first year of the war in attaining supremacy, at least on the ocean's surface. The Germans had one spectacular success in November 1914, when their China squadron under Admiral Graf Spee sank two British armored cruisers off Coronel; but, a month later, Spee's force was destroyed in the battle of the Falkland Islands, and by the spring of 1915 there were no German fleet units or merchantmen at large. The High Seas Fleet of which William II was so proud had a brush with the British off the Dogger Banks in January 1915 and then remained at its home bases until May of the following year, when it emerged to fight an indecisive battle at Jutland. In this encounter, the Germans under Admiral Scheer—aided by a British command system that hampered individual initiative, by the breakdown of communications between British fleet units and the flagship and home base, and by clear British inferiority in guns and munitions (a startling commentary upon British technological retrogression in the prewar period)—sank three British battle cruisers, three light cruisers, and eight destroyers at the cost of one battleship, one battle cruiser, four light cruisers, and five destroyers. This could be called a German victory, except for the fact that Scheer himself advised the emperor a month later that England could not be defeated by "battles on the high seas" but only by submarine pressure on its economic life. The German fleet made several not very successful sallies from port after Jutland, but with its best officers and petty officers transferred to U-boats, its efficiency and spirit declined.

The lack of any surface shipping of their own forced the Germans to rely upon neutral ships for their imports, and this in turn led the British and the French, in the interests of imposing an effective economic blockade on Germany, to claim the right to inspect and divert traffic in any goods that might conceivably help the German war effort. This interference elicited strong complaints from neutral countries and most particularly from the government of the United States. Despite his personal sympathy for the Allied cause, President Woodrow Wilson regarded the British behavior as high-handed in the extreme and, with that jealous concern for the interests of his country that was characteristic of him, protested so vigorously on occasion that it was feared that relations between the British and American governments might be broken off.

That matters never got to that point was due in large part to the fact that the Germans were guilty of conduct even more offensive to American feelings. Their inability to match Britain on the surface led them to concentrate on the use of the submarine, which most people considered an even more barbarous weapon that poison gas. American opinion was revolted in particular by the practice of submarine commanders of torpedoing vessels without warning and without any attempt to help survivors; and it was unimpressed by the argument that submarines were frail craft, that many merchantmen were known to be armed, that to surface was always dangerous, and that to remain long on the surface was suicidal.

In Feburary 1915, when the German government announced in a note to the United States government that, within a defined "war zone" which included the British and French coasts, its U-boats would sink Allied ships and ships flying neutral flags that were suspected to be Allied ships, the American attitude was made crystal clear. President Wilson answered with a grave warning that he would hold the Germans to a "strict accountability" for the loss of American ships and American lives. The subsequent sinking of several British ships with American passengers or crew aboard and, especially, the torpedoing of the Cunard liner *Lusitania* on May 7, 1915, with a loss of 1198 lives, including 139 Americans, aroused a storm of indignation in the United States, and the first serious stirrings of an interventionist spirit became apparent.

The intensity of American feeling impressed the Germans; and the fact that they did not, in any case, have enough submarines to be really effective induced them to make concessions to it. The German ambassador informed the American secretary of state that there would be no further attacks on ships like the *Lusitania*. This reassurance and the sharp falling off of submarine attacks of any kind in the fall of 1915 reduced tension.

In the course of 1916, however, the Germans built up their U-boat force swiftly; by January 1917, the naval staff was confident that, if they were allowed to employ it without restrictions, they could starve Britain into submission within five months. At a Crown Council at Pless in January 1917, the sailors and the army high command overbore the doubtful emperor and his chancellor Beth-mann. No concern need be felt, they argued, about that "disorganized and undis-ciplined [country across the seas] which was presided over by a professional crank." Even if the United States should seek to intervene in the war, the chief of the naval staff said flatly, "I give Your Majesty my word as an officer that not one American will land on the continent." In face of this military self-as-surance, the civilians gave way, and the decision to resume unrestricted subma-rine warfare was taken.

By this step, the German government went a long way toward nullifying all of the setbacks it had imposed upon its opponents in the eastern and western theaters of operations and in the diplomatic competition in the Balkans. It strengthened the hands of all those Americans who, because of descent, regard for tradition, economic interest, anxiety about America's future strategical posi-tion, respect for public law, or other reasons, wanted to enter the war on the side of England and France. The German decision went into effect on February 1; on April 6, the United States declared war on Germany.

THE HOME FRONT

Total War   On February 10, 1916, a panic broke out along the east coast of England because of a rumor that a German Zeppelin had appeared over the resort town of Scarborough; and public indignation over this outrage was so great in the weeks that followed that the government found it expedient to appease it by creating ten home-defense squadrons of the Royal Flying Corps.

The incident is worth mentioning because it illustrates the fact that World War I was the first total war in modern history, in the sense that its rigors were apt to be visited upon all citizens of the participating powers, however remote they might be from the battle area. In earlier wars—even in the protracted and enormously destructive wars against Napoleon—it was only occasionally that the average citizen at home felt the war's effects, and, for long periods of time, it was quite possible for him to forget that there was fighting in progress. In the war of 1914–1918 this kind of detachment was impossible. Citizens of northeast France or Belgium or Poland, whose countries were overrun, whose homes were commandeered as billets, and whose friends and relatives were sometimes held by the occupying forces as hostages to assure the maintenance of local order, knew the war as intimately as the troops who passed through their streets. But they were by no means alone. Crofters in the Scottish highlands, businessmen in Leipzig, Russian farmers in the Volga lands were all brushed by the touch of war, even when they did not attract a visit from a Zeppelin or were well out of range of guns like that notorious Big Bertha which the Germans used to shell Paris. The fortunes of war influenced or determined their freedom of action, their employment, their diet, and even what they were allowed to think and to say. It subjected every aspect of their lives to an increasing degree of control and regimentation. And the fact that it did so had effects which persisted even after the war was over.

Only three aspects of this total war need concern us here: the progressive centralization of political authority, even in countries where political central-

"The War in the Air." Fight between German and British units; a painting by an unknown German artist (Erich Lessing from Magnum)

ization had long been suspect; the economic regimentation practiced by all governments; and the tendency toward thought control and restriction of civil liberties.

Political Centralization   In all of the countries that participated in the war, the beginning of the fighting elicited a wave of patriotism and a closing of ranks.

Even political parties and organizations that had been the bitterest opponents of governments six months before the war rallied to the national cause in August 1914. In France, the anarchist Gustave Hervé, who had been the defendant in a sensational trial in 1912 in which he was accused of encouraging mutiny in the French army, now became the most ardent of patriots; and this attitude was symptomatic of the general attitude of French socialism and French labor. In the French Chamber there was a party truce and the creation of what was called a *Union sacrée,* and this situation had its counterpart in Germany, where the parliamentary factions buried their differences and listened with sincere emotion to the emperor's words: "I recognize parties no more. I recognize only Germans!" In Great Britain, although Ramsay MacDonald resigned the leadership of the Labor party rather than support a war for which he believed Great Britain shared much of the responsibility, his action was repudiated indignantly by the majority of his party and by the trade-union movement as well. Similar evidence of political unity was manifest in other countries.

This recognition of the overriding importance of the national interest freed governments from the criticism to which a vigilant opposition normally subjected them and enabled them to indulge in practices and to make claims to authority that would never have been tolerated in time of peace. The result was an increasing centralization of power, which, by the end of war, had assumed the appearance of government dictatorship in more than one of the great European states. It is not too much to say that no country was entirely exempt from this drift toward totalitarian political methods.

It is, of course, not surprising that this sort of thing should have happened in Russia, Austria, and Germany, where the tradition of parliamentary government was weak; and it was, of course, in those countries that the tendency was most marked and most disastrous in its results. In Russia, what progress had been made toward the separation of political power and the sharing of political responsibility came to an end during the war. This was unfortunate, because the vigorous and useful criticisms of the weaknesses of the Russian war machine came from the Duma and from the zemstvos. But, in September 1915, the tsar, who had already assumed over-all command of the armed forces in a quixotic gesture in August, suspended the Duma for the duration. In effect, then, the affairs of a great country were left in the hands of the empress, her favorite Rasputin, and whatever bureaucrats were willing to be their pliable tools.

In Austria and in Germany, centralization was marked by a diminution of parliament's role and an increase of that of the military. Until the death of Emperor Francis Joseph in November 1916, after which time the fabric of the empire began rapidly to dissolve, Austria was held together by the authority of bureaucrats and soldiers. This was even more marked in Germany. At the outset of the war, the new tone was set when the local army commands were given the right to intervene in certain aspects of local government and, in some cases, to supersede local-government authorities entirely. On the national level, military influence was pronounced in 1914 and predominant from September 1916, when Hindenburg became chief of staff, until the end of the war. The team Hindenburg-Ludendorff and the political bureau in the General Staff not only made military decisions but laid down the main lines of economic and diplomatic policy. Backed by a popular support that amounted to adulation, they arrogated to themselves authority that properly belonged to the emperor and the chancellor and, when crossed, won their point by threatening to resign. It was they who were responsible for the decision to resume submarine warfare; it was they who forced the resignation of Chancellor Bethmann Hollweg in July 1917 because he had permitted the Reichstag to debate and pass a vague resolution expressing interest in the possibility of a negotiated peace; it was they who dictated the terms of the treaty of Brest Litovsk, which did so much political disservice to their country. Until the armies collapsed in the summer of 1918, their dictatorship was virtually free of any control.

This degree of centralization was never reached in the countries of the west. It is worth noting, however, that even England was not free from either concentration of power in few hands or the growth of excessive military influence. England started the war governed by a loose coalition government and ended with a small, tight war cabinet dominated by Lloyd George, with powers infinitely greater than those enjoyed by any peacetime government. Moreover, Britain's soldiers, usually silent in peacetime, were far from being so during the war, and some of them showed a dangerous contempt for the "frocks" and seemed to believe that military men could do a better job of directing the war.

In France, the government started the war by declaring a state of siege and, during the first year of hostilities, the major decisions were made by the High Command and put into effect by presidential decree. This was perhaps understandable, given the extent of the threat to France in the first months of the war; but, even after the danger of defeat had receded, the High Command was reluctant to give up the position it had won. Not until November 1917, when Clemenceau became premier, was it reduced to its proper role, for Clemenceau was a man who believed that even war, let alone politics. "was too important a matter to be left to the generals." It should be noted, however, that if Clemenceau restored civilian authority in France, his government, by normal standards, was dictatorial in its own right.

In neither England nor France did parliament, in any sense, abdicate. For reasons of security or efficiency, however, certain areas of action commonly subject to parliamentary decision or review were now handled by administrative or executive agencies. The growth of executive authority and the expansion of government powers in areas formerly considered private did not go as far as it did in the countries of Eastern Europe and was not as disastrous in its results; but it was, nonetheless, marked.

Economic Regimentation   Two stories are often told to illustrate the naive attitude of European governments toward economic matters at the beginning of the war. The first is that the French government permitted the Renault motor works to cease production at the beginning of hostilities because it could foresee no military use for its products. The second is that when the German industrialist Arthur Dix sent a memorandum to Chief of Staff Moltke outlining the need of an economic general staff, he received the answer: "Don't bother me with economics. I am busy conducting the war."

It did not take many months of war to show how unrealistic these attitudes were. One of the rudest awakenings—and it was experienced by all countries—was the discovery that there were not enough shells to keep the war going and no present means of producing enough to keep up with the demand. In September 1914 Joffre informed the French government that he needed a minimum of 70,000 shells per day and that his batteries had less than a month's reserve. At the same time, the British commander, Sir John French, was pleading with his government for more ammunition, and soon ugly hints were appearing in English newspapers about troops having to go over the top with inadequate artillery preparation and being slaughtered as a result. In Russia in 1914 factories were producing only a third of the shells needed at the front, and infantry were forced to rely wholly on night bayonet attacks because the armies had neither artillery shells nor rifle ammunition. In Germany, where the army had been confident that its preparations were sound, experts were appalled at the rate at which ammunition reserves melted away in modern war.

The shell shortage in France was caused by the fact that the enemy's swift advance had robbed the country of its richest industrial areas; in other countries, it was the result of a feckless mobilization policy, which sent skilled workers in industries soon to be discovered as crucial to the front, and by a general failure of imagination. The crisis was too serious to be solved by normal methods. Instead, governments appointed what might be called munitions tsars—the Socialist engineer Albert Thomas in France, David Lloyd George in Britain, men of similar energy in other countries—with extensive control over all branches of production of munitions and related articles, with authority to grant or deny government contracts to private firms, with adjudicative powers in labor-management disputes, and with the right to exempt skilled metal workers from military service and return them to bench and lathe. From this beginning, the European governments gradually extended their authority over all aspects of their countries' economic activity.

In Germany, for instance, Walther Rathenau, the son of the founder of the *Allgemeine Elektrizitäts-Gesellschaft,* persuaded Moltke's successor Falkenhayn that an inventory of Germany's material resources was a prerequisite of any effective war planning. With government authorization, Rathenau established a War Raw Materials Department (*Kriegsrohstoffsabteilung,* or KRA), which conducted an extensive survey and determined that Germany's stocks of essential raw materials would last less than a year and that it was, therefore, necessary to impound and control existing stocks, to eliminate luxury production, to requisition strategically important materials in occupied areas and purchase them from nearby neutral states, to develop new techniques of production, and to encourage the introduction of substitutes and synthetics. Starting with a miniscule staff, the KRA developed into a mammoth organization with subdivisions in all vital industries, each with authority to apportion raw materials to manufacturers with war contracts.

Simultaneously, the German government set up bureaus to control the import and export trade, the most important being the Central Purchasing Company (*Zentral-Einkaufs-Gesellschaft* or ZEG), which had a monopoly of all purchasing abroad, and a War Foodstuffs Office, with subsidiary agencies, to control food supplies, regulate rationing, and encourage the use of substitutes. In November

1916, in order to solve the problems created by a growing labor shortage which had not been alleviated by extensive use of women, children, and foreign laborers (French prisoners, Belgians, and Poles), a Central War Office (*Kriegsamt*) was established under the direction of General Wilhelm Groener, with wide powers to adjudicate between management and labor. A month later, with the inauguration of the so-called Hindenburg Program, a National Service Law came into effect that provided for compulsory employment of all noncombatant Germans between the ages of seventeen and sixty-one, made arbitration of labor disputes compulsory, and made change of employment subject to the approval of boards under the chairmanship of a representative of the local army command.

In the other belligerent nations, similar steps were taken to mobilize economic resources, efficiently in Britain and France, less so in Austria, Italy, and Russia. In most cases, manpower laws were passed and normal labor activity was restricted. In England, for example, the trade unions agreed in March 1915 that there should be no strikes for the duration of the war, that contracts should be relaxed to permit longer hours, speeding up of production, and the employment of women and unskilled labor in the interests of the war effort. The government assured the unions that these concessions would not hurt their postwar position and that the old conditions would be restored with the peace. Even so, as the war proceeded, there was growing suspicion in labor ranks that the concessions had been a mistake and that the workingmen were being asked to make sacrifices not borne by the employers or other classes of society. Something of the same feeling began to permeate labor ranks in Germany and other countries in the last years of the war and was reflected in a rise in the number of strikes, although most of these were unofficial.

Thought Control   The regulation of economic life placed restrictions upon the freedom of citizens to sell their labor or services as they wished and to spend their wages as they would normally have done. But the war placed more serious limitations upon their liberty than these, affecting their rights of assembly and speech, and even their freedom of thought. In all belligerent countries, special laws were passed for the internment of people suspected of being enemy agents or sympathizers, for the prevention of the dissemination of information that might be useful to the enemy, and for the prohibition of activities that threatened to spread defeatism among the population; and, since these laws were administered by tribunals that were not immune to the influence of local hysterias and often openly encouraged tale bearers and self-appointed guardians of the national security, injustice was often committed in the name of the law. The democratic nations were no more enlightened in this matter than the absolute monarchies. In England, the Defense of the Realm Act gave the government the right to do anything it pleased with citizens suspected of sins against the war effort. Houses were searched without warrant; the possession of any literature considered by some overzealous magistrate to be subversive made a person liable to legal action; despite habeas corpus, deportation and internment were not unknown; public meetings were prohibited by police without right of appeal; and speeches held to be unpatriotic were punished by prison sentences.

Newspapers were subject everywhere to a rigorous censorship. Items which might give aid or comfort to the enemy or weaken the population's determination to fight to total victory were deleted. Some of the censorship was private (when Lord Lansdowne sent a letter to *The Times* in 1917 urging the necessity of seeking peace by negotiation, the editors refused to print it), but generally it was imposed by the government, which inserted into the spaces created by its deletions official propaganda that often baldly misrepresented the facts, magnified national successes and depreciated those of the enemy, and recounted atrocity stories designed to arouse hatred of the foe.

Since these practices deprived the reader of any objective presentation of fact, they denied him true freedom of thought and imposed distortions and myths upon his mind. In some cases, official propaganda bred a confidence in victory that was disastrous in its result. The discovery that they were not, after all, going to win the war came with such a shock to the German people that they succumbed to despair and let the tide of revolution sweep over them. In other countries, there can be little doubt that wartime propaganda played a large part in creating the hatreds and the illusions that made the job of arranging a just peace so difficult.

THE COURSE OF THE WAR, 1917–1918

Western Setbacks   For the Western powers, the year 1917 began with two exhilarating events. The first was the overthrow of autocracy in Russia which ended the ideological division within the alliance, and the coming to power of a democratic government that was determined to pursue the war energetically and efficiently. The second was the entrance of the United States into the war.

It was not long, however, before it was seen that the latter event did not mean that strong American armies would be landing in Europe in the near future. Until the United States had time to conscript and train an expeditionary force, the brunt of the fighting would still have to be borne by Britain, France, and Italy. Moreover, since it was soon apparent that the events in Russia heralded not a regeneration but a collapse, the burden of the war promised to be heavier.

Indeed, more troubles were in store for the Allies than they had dreamed even in their most pessimistic moments. The year 1917 was a long series of defeats. In April the Allies launched one more of those big pushes to end the war that have been described above. In the Arras theater the British Third Army under Allenby dented the Hindenburg line, as the German defenses were called, and the Canadians took Vimy Ridge in one of the most brilliant assaults in the war. But to the south, the French offensive in Lorraine under General Nivelle was an unmitigated disaster, with losses in the neighborhood of 200,000 men; and it was followed by a wave of mutinies in the French army that made any offensive action impossible for months, until Nivelle's successor, Pétain, and his chief of staff, Foch, had taken action to improve front-line conditions, increase leaves, and restore morale.

In July, the British commander Haig launched his long-planned drive in Flanders, against the better judgment of Lloyd George, who called it a "wild military speculation," an "insane enterprise," a "muddy and muddle-headed venture." Haig was a stubborn man, and he continued his push until November

20; but, for fifty square miles of wire and mud, he lost 150,000 dead and almost 300,000 wounded or captured. The third battle of Ypres was, like the Somme a year before, a patent revelation of the stupidity of all the talk about "wearing the enemy down," for British losses were almost twice those of the Germans. A brilliant British success at Cambrai in November 1917, when tanks were used for the first time in strength, showed that there was an alternative to this ghastly strategy of attrition; but the soldiers were not yet ready to consider it.

In October it was Italy's turn. In a carefully planned thrust, the Central Powers threw six German and nine Austrian divisions at Caporetto on the Isonzo River and smashed the whole Italian position. The rout that followed has been brilliantly described in Hemingway's *A Farewell to Arms*. In the course of it, two Italian armies were swept all the way back to the Piave River, losing six thousand square miles of territory and 320,000 men. British and French divisions were rushed to the Italian front to stave off complete collapse. They were not, in fact, needed, for the Italians rallied; but for some months the situation was critical.

Finally, to complete the dark catalog, November brought news of the second revolution in Russia, the seizure of power by the Soviets of Soldiers, Peasants and Workers, the elevation of the Bolshevik leaders Lenin and Trotsky to executive authority, their appeal to the belligerents for an immediate peace without annexations and indemnities, and, in December at Brest Litovsk, their conclusion of an armistice with the Germans. These events promised that the Germans would soon be able to throw their full weight against a West seriously weakened by the bloodletting of 1917.

The Weakening of the German Coalition   All was not well, however, with Germany and its allies. The waning of Turkish strength, which has been mentioned above, was far advanced by the end of 1917. In the course of the year, the British General Allenby, fresh from Arras, put new life in the Egyptian Expeditionary Army and smashed his way into Jerusalem, after chewing up the Seventh Turkish Army under Mustafa Kemal. He was now preparing to thrust his way into Syria, while simultaneously other Allied forces were pushing toward Mosul in Mesopotamia and threatening Turkish lines in Macedonia. The Turkish enthusiasm for the German cause, still strong in leaders like Enver Pasha, was no longer shared by the war-weary armies or the people as a whole. Across the straits, Bulgaria was feeling the same pinch. Its armies had, after all, been fighting since the first Balkan war; the constant pressure upon their lines in the Salonika sector was rapidly wearing them down; and German and Austrian support troops had been sharply reduced in the course of 1917. Meanwhile, the country was at the end of its economic tether, for there had been bad harvests. Both army and populace were fast approaching a state of demoralization.

Even more serious was the situation in Austria-Hungary, where any semblance of cooperation between the Magyar oligarchs and the government in Vienna had broken down, and where serious defections were apparent among the subject nationalities. At a meeting of the Austrian Reichsrat in May 1917, both the Czech and the South Slav representatives had demanded far-reaching rights of autonomy; and it was evident that their military contingents were no longer reliable.

In the first months of 1918, the disaffection of the subject nationalities was sharply increased by two things. The first was a series of speeches by the President of the United States, culminating in his address to Congress on January 8, 1918, in which he laid down, in the soon famous Fourteen Points, the principles that he felt should guide a peace settlement, including a promise that the peoples of Austria-Hungary would be assured an autonomous development. The second—in sharp contrast to the Wilson offer—was the nature of the treaties the Central Powers concluded with Russia at Brest Litovsk and with Rumania at Bucharest (March–May 1918). These treaties, which demanded huge territorial and monetary concessions from the defeated states, made it all too clear that a victory for the Central Powers would mean continued Teutonic domination of eastern Europe, with no autonomous development for the subject peoples at all. Nothing did more to sharpen the desire for freedom at the cost of the defeat of Germany and Austria than these punitive settlements.

Germany itself, despite its apparent successes, was at the end of 1917 feeling further from victory than ever before. The promises made by the naval staff in February, about the imminent strangulation of Great Britain by submarine, had come to nothing. It was true that great losses had been inflicted upon Allied and neutral shipping: 2122 ships had been sunk in the Atlantic in 1917 and 844 in the Mediterranean. But their losses had not made the British falter, and now the losses were decreasing and the mortality of submarines mounting fast. What was saving the British was a World War I innovation second only in importance to the tank: the convoy system, in which the supply ships moved to their destination in large numbers under the protection of submarines, surface vessels, and aircraft. The convoy was making nonsense of all of the German calculations at a time when the British blockade was bearing more and more heavily upon the German economy, and when murmurs of disaffection and wildcat strikes were making the first cracks in the nation's solidarity. In July 1917 the passage by the Reichstag of a resolution inviting the government to consider peace by negotiation was, to many Germans, a warning of rapidly weakening will to resistance.

The High Command answered these signs of weakness, however, not by any spirit of concession but by calling for a grand offensive that would end the war with victory in the spring of 1918.

The Collapse   After the war was over, much was written about the criminal stupidity of Hindenburg and Ludendorff's pledging the whole security of their nation on one desperate gamble, when they might have exploited their position of apparent strength to win moderate terms by negotiation. Aside from the fact that there is no assurance that the Allies would have responded to any offer of negotiation, this argument overlooks the fact that neither the High Command nor the economic interests that supported them could afford to accept moderate terms. The most palpable fear in their minds was that of a growth of democracy in Germany, and it was their belief that only a total victory with rich annexations in eastern and western Europe would divert the German people from their desire for self-government. Their objective, as one of their number admitted, was to escape "the democratic swamp into which we should undoubtedly be drawn after a lukewarm peace." The High Command, therefore, suppressed all talk of negotiation, planned its great offensive, and used all of the resources of its propaganda to assure the Germans that it could not fail.

On March 21, 1918, Ludendorff's spring offensive opened with a crash of guns and with the might of the whole German army thrown upon the British front between St. Quentin and Arras. The British Third Army was thrust aside and Gough's Fifth overrun; Bapaume, Peronne, the line of the Upper Somme were lost; and the hinge between the British and French armies threatened to snap and open the way to Paris. But Ludendorff's momentum was slowed down by the lack of fuel for his motorized units and by other logistical faults, and he lacked the reserves to keep up the pressure. When the expected gap did not appear between the Allies (and it was at this time that the British, French, and Americans lessened the likelihood of its doing so by taking the long delayed step of creating a Supreme Command under Foch to coordinate their operations), Ludendorff allowed himself to be diverted from his key objective and shifted his attack to points where it seemed easier to break through. In April, he rolled over the Portuguese in Flanders and retook all of the ground lost to Haig in 1917. But the British held at Ypres, and Ludendorff changed direction again, developing a series of attacks between Soissons and Rheims in May and crossing the Marne in the first week of June. The German thrusts were becoming weaker now and increasingly disarticulated. Within sight of the positions held in September 1914, the great offensive in July began slowly to grind to a halt.

Then, on August 8, General Rawlinson's Fourth Army, supported by French units, struck with dramatic suddenness east of Amiens, and masses of Allied tanks tore the German lines to shreds. This was "the black day of the German army," and it recoiled, never to seize the initiative again. By the beginning of September, the Allied armies were sweeping forward in every sector: the British were through the Somme and hammering at the Hindenburg line; the French were pushing forward in the Champagne; and the Americans, whom the German navy had vowed to keep out of Europe, had won their first fight at St. Mihiel and were advancing in the Meuse-Argonne.

And now, at the other end of Europe, the process of dissolution began. In mid-September, the French commander at Salonika, Franchet d'Esperey (known to all British troops as "Desperate Frankie"), attacked and smashed the Bulgarian lines and began a headlong advance into Serbia. The Bulgars immediately sued for armistice terms and signed them on September 29. Turkey was left at the mercy of converging Allied armies, and its government hastened to follow the Bulgarian example. Even before these events had taken place, the Austrians, whose attempt to break the Piave line in June 1918 had broken on Italian resistance at a cost of 150,000 men, had informed their ally that they could fight no longer and had begun diplomatic exchanges with the Allies.

Even the indomitable Ludendorff could not stem this rush of events. On October 3, his strong nerves snapped, and he frantically informed his government that it must sue for peace. Prince Max von Baden, just appointed chancellor by the emperor, had, like most parliamentarians and the majority of the German people, believed as late as September that victory was certain. He was incredulous at the message from the High Command. He had no alternative, however, to obedience and appealed to President Wilson for terms.

This maneuver the American President defeated neatly by informing the chancellor that he would not even consult his allies until he was assured that the Germans were prepared to lay down their arms, thus rendering resumption of hostilities impossible, and to accept the Fourteen Points as the basis of the peace, and until he was certain, moreover, that the German government truly represented the German people. This last point convinced a lot of Germans that they would secure better terms if they got rid of the emperor and their military masters, and it was from this point on that revolutionary agitation began to mount in Germany. Meanwhile, Prince Max did his best to satisfy Wilson of German compliance with his wishes; Wilson referred the request to his allies; and the armistice negotiations began. By the time the terms were ready, revolution had gripped Berlin, Munich, Hamburg, and other cities, and the emperor had laid down his title and fled across the border into Holland. With their proud empire in ruins, the German representatives signed the armistice terms on November 11, 1918, and the long war came to an end.

CONCLUSION

Some Social Effects   The effect of the war upon the territorial organization of Europe, its economic prospects, and its political future will be best discussed in the next chapter, in connection with the decisions of the Peace Conference. In view of what has been said above, however, about the behavior of governments during the war, two observations are appropriate here.

The first has to do with something we have noticed in several connections in the chapters above: the decline of liberalism and of the liberal attitude in politics and economics. There is no doubt that this decline was greatly advanced by the war. Governments expanded their size and their functions, and people became so accustomed to seeing them do things previously performed by private agencies that they did not protest very loudly when government continued to do them after the war. *Étatisme* had become not only normal but desirable to many people.

In some cases, when governments relinquished powers or gave up functions with the restoration of peace, their doing so was not greeted with universal approbation. During the war, for example, governments had encouraged industrial expansion while at the same time protecting the enterprises affected from the normal risks of such expansion. Nothing could have done more to weaken the competitive spirit and the willingness to accept risk that had been characteristic of liberal capitalism. It is small wonder that, when economic storms began to blow in the 1920s, many European businessmen yearned for the security of the war years, when they were partners of government, protected against bankruptcy if they overextended themselves, assured of big profits, and—not least important—supplied with a docile labor force. Part of the reason why so many industrialists supported men like Mussolini and Hitler was that those political dictators promised to restore the wartime economic relationships.

Finally, in connection with the waning of the liberal attitude in European politics, it should be noted that the war accustomed governments to working in a crisis atmosphere and gave them the dangerous idea that, when things were going to pieces around them, action was always to be preferred to inaction.

As Mendelssohn Bartholdy has written, this amounted to

> a new philosophy of public morals called decisionism. It denounced caution
> as unmanly. It upheld the virtue of courage in the taking of the respon-
> sibility for the rights and wrongs of an ill-considered decision on the
> grounds that actually *taking* it ... even if it proved wrong or unnecessarily
> expensive, is always better than shrinking from responsibilities and losing
> fortune's fleeting moment.

In postwar Europe, in both the democratic and the totalitarian states, this
attitude was productive of much harm.

Lost Generations   The character of postwar politics might have been different and the leadership of the democratic states in particular might have been
stronger if it had not been for the terrific losses suffered by all nations during
the war of 1914–1918. Europe was to pay dearly for the generation of young
men who died in Flanders and Poland and Greece and Palestine.

But it should be noted that the war had made another lost generation. This
was composed of all of those veterans who found, when the fighting was over,
that they could no longer adjust themselves to the requirements of civilian society.
Sometimes this attitude was the result of disenchantment on the part of men
who had gone off to war in the hope that they were creating a better world

"To the Nameless Ones," 1916, by Egger-Lienz. (Erich Lessing from Magnum)

and had come back to find that those who had remained at home had not shared their dreams. These men felt like the returned soldier in Erich Maria Remarque's fine novel *The Road Back,* who says to a friend:

> Ludwig, what are we doing here? Look about you: look how flat and comfortless it all is. We are a burden to ourselves and others. Our ideals are bankrupt, our dreams are *kaputt,* and we wander around in this world of rotten opportunists and speculators like Don Quixotes in a foreign land.

In many cases this kind of disillusionment was overcome or suppressed, but all too often it hardened into a fixed resentment against civilian society and a longing for the comradeship and the sense of shared sacrifice that had been present in the war. Those who felt this way came to idealize the war, to see values in it that might yet save Europe from materialism, and to believe that the soldier—the true soldier, not the brass hat or *Bürogeneral* or staff officer at the rear but the *Frontkämpfer,* the man in the trenches—might lead the way to Europe's regeneration. Ernst Jünger, a front-line soldier himself, wrote in 1920, in a widely read book called *Battle as an Inner Experience:*

> There is the new man, the storm fighter, the elite of Europe. An entirely new race, smart, strong, full of will. What has been revealed here in battle will tomorrow be the axis around which life revolves, more and more swiftly.... This war is not the end, but the chord that heralds new power. It is the anvil on which the world will be hammered into new boundaries and new communities. New forms will be filled with blood, and might will be hammered into them with a hard fist. War is a great school, and the new man will be of our cut.

Here is the authentic voice of the revolution of the right, of the *squadristi* of Mussolini, of Hitler's brown shirts, who rose from the ranks of those whom World War I left disenchanted and alienated, with the war still in their bones.

Chapter 21 THE PEACE TREATIES AND THE SEARCH FOR COLLECTIVE SECURITY

In 1919 there were a good many people in the world who seemed to believe that peace was something you could declare, in the same way that you declared war. They soon discovered that this was not true. In number and complexity, the problems facing the peacemakers of 1919 greatly exceeded those that the negotiators at Vienna had had to deal with in 1814 and 1815, and their deliberations lasted longer than was desired by electorates anxious to return to normal conditions. World War I ended formally in November 1918, so abruptly that the victorious powers found themselves without any clear idea of how to go about making peace. It was four months before serious negotiations got under way, and it was not until June 1919 that the terms of a treaty with Germany, the Treaty of Versailles, had been worked out, submitted to the former enemy, and accepted. This treaty had to be followed by other laborious negotiations and other peace treaties: the Treaty of St. Germain-en-Laye with Austria, September 10, 1919; the Treaty of Neuilly with Bulgaria, November 27, 1919; the Treaty of Trianon with Hungary, June 4, 1920; and the Treaty of Sèvres with Turkey, August 10, 1920.

Long before this last date, the statesmen and the peoples of Europe had learned that the transition from war to peace was not going to be easy. Even in the first phase of the peace negotiations—when Woodrow Wilson, Lloyd George, Georges Clemenceau, and Vittorio Orlando were directing the proceedings in Paris (January-June 1919)—the possibility of new wars was being made evident by Poland's incursions into the territory of its neighbors, by the activities of German freebooters in the Baltic countries, by the establishment of a Soviet in Budapest under Béla Kun, and by serious differences between Italy and

Yugoslavia over the possession of the port of Fiume. Moreover, almost as soon as the various peace treaties were completed, they were challenged in whole or in part by states which felt that they had been unjustly treated; and these challenges were sometimes made with arms in hand. Meanwhile, the machinery that had been devised to meet problems of this nature, the League of Nations, started its existence with the defection of the country under whose aegis it had been founded and with the two other principal Allied powers hopelessly split on the question of how it should be used, as well as on other fundamental problems.

In the circumstances, anything resembling peace was slow in coming to Europe, and it was not until 1925 that there was a general detente and relaxation of tension.

THE PEACE TREATIES

The Paris Peace Conference   The assembly of nations that convened in Paris in January 1919 to begin the task of arranging a general peace settlement was the greatest gathering of its kind since the Congress of Vienna (see pp. 11–19), and its very membership reflected all of the changes that had taken place in the territorial balance of Europe and the world in the intervening century. Of the five Great Powers that had dominated the proceedings at Vienna, only two were present here: Great Britain, represented by her great war premier, Lloyd George, the foreign secretary Arthur Balfour, and a host of able subordinates; and France, whose delegation was headed by Georges Clemenceau and included, among others, the head of the united command that had won the war, Marshal Foch. Of the other Vienna powers, two were excluded from the deliberations because, as defeated powers, they were to be the recipients of the decisions made, and the third, Russia, was absent because its new government was the object of universal detestation on the part of the victors as a result of the separate peace it had concluded with Germany at Brest Litovsk and also, of course, because of its ideological beliefs. (Their absence did not prevent the new rulers of Russia from playing a part at Paris; Arno Mayer has demonstrated that fear of Bolshevism affected all of the delegations and influenced many of their decisions.)

The membership of the conference was swollen by representatives of states whose independence had not been recognized in 1815 or whose potentiality for political growth might have been denied at that time. Chief among these were Italy, which, in the person of its prime minister Vittorio Orlando, occupied a place in the directorate of the conference; Belgium, accorded universal respect for its sufferings during the war; Greece, who, thanks to the political acrobatics of Venizelos (see pp. 378, 471, and 600), had ingratiated itself with the French and British governments; Poland, now resuming independence after more than a century of oppression; the brand new state of Czechoslovakia, still more a concept than a reality when the conference began its sessions.

The most startling difference from the Vienna Congress was the important role played at Paris by non-European states, a sign that the age had passed when it could be claimed—in Mazzini's words—that Europe was "the lever that moved the world" and an intimation that the time had come when Europe could not even solve its own problems without external help. The British dominions were represented by the prime ministers of Canada, Australia, New Zealand, and Newfoundland and Generals Botha and Smuts of South Africa. Marquis Saionji of Japan was not only present but a member of the Council of Ten that directed the conference in its first stages, an honor granted in recognition of Japan's contribution to victory by its naval operations in the Pacific and the Mediterranean. And finally, the center of all attention as the conference opened and, more than any other single individual, its guiding spirit, was the President of the United States, Woodrow Wilson, who had broken precedent by deciding to come to the negotiations in person.

Procedural Questions   From the standpoint of intellectual grasp and general ability, the leading statesmen at Paris were in no way inferior to their predecessors at Vienna. They soon demonstrated, however, that they were somewhat less competent in matters of organization and procedure.

When the war came to an end, the Allied and Associated Powers had reached no agreement concerning their war aims or the procedures to be followed in realizing them. They had all made the mistake that they were to repeat in World War II, of believing that political plans could and should wait until the fight was over; and they had reacted with irritation to suggestions that this might have awkward results. The sudden collapse of the enemy, therefore, found them in possession of neither a philosophy nor a strategy for peace; and, although President Wilson persuaded them, at the time of the German request for an armistice, to accept the Fourteen Points[1] as the basis of their future deliberations, this was hardly a sufficient preparation for the tasks that lay before them.

It seems clear that with the possible exception of the French, the leaders of the Allied nations did not appreciate the importance of procedural questions.

[1] See page 482. President Woodrow Wilson's address to Congress on January 8, 1918, enumerated a peace program based on Fourteen Points, as follows: (1) Open covenants openly arrived at; (2) absolute freedom of navigation alike in peace and war, except as the seas might be closed by international action to enforce international covenants; (3) the removal, as far as possible, of all economic barriers; (4) adequate guaranties that armaments would be reduced to the lowest point consistent with domestic safety; (5) an impartial adjustment of all colonial claims on the principle that the interests of the population must have equal weight with the claims of the government; (6) the evacuation of all Russian territory and the free determination of its own political and national policy; (7) evacuation and restoration of Belgium; (8) evacuation and restoration of French territory and righting of the wrong done to France in the matter of Alsace-Lorraine; (9) readjustment of the frontiers of Italy along clearly recognizable lines of nationality; (10) opportunity for autonomous development for the peoples of Austria-Hungary; (11) evacuation and restoration of Rumanian, Serbian, and Montenegrin territory, together with access to the sea for Serbia; (12) the Turkish parts of the Ottoman empire to be assured a secure sovereignty, but the other nationalities to be given an opportunity for autonomous development, and the Dardanelles to be permanently opened to the ships of all nations under international guaranties; (13) an independent Poland, to include territories indisputably Polish, with free and secure access to the sea; (14) a general association of nations to be formed to afford mutual guarantees of political independence and territorial integrity to great and small states alike.

They might have learned much from a study of the way in which the Congress of Vienna had gone about its business, but Lloyd George was too indifferent to history to bother to read the excellent handbooks on Vienna and other conferences prepared for him by the foreign office, and President Wilson bridled at the very suggestion that a democratic statesman should consult Metternich and Castlereagh. In consequence, they made some unfortunate mistakes.

In particular, they allowed the full conference to convene before the principal Allies had clarified or coordinated their views about the general nature of the settlement to come or devoted any systematic thought to the machinery of negotiation or even prepared a tentative agenda. They began their work with no agreement as to how many treaties they were going to write or with whom. They did not even have a clear understanding on the vital point of whether their decisions at Paris were to be final or tentative. There was a vague idea, to which the representatives of the leading powers referred frequently, that the present meeting was merely a preliminary conference, to be followed by a more definitive one to which the enemy states would be invited, with rights of negotiation on equal terms with the others. But this was never made explicit and precise.

In due course, by a process of trial and error, the conference found a procedure and a workable machinery of negotiation. The organ originally established to direct and coordinate the conference's work—a Council of Ten composed of two representatives of each of the principal Allies (the United States, Great Britain, France, Italy, and Japan) was found to be too rigid and unwieldy and was replaced by a more flexible system. This had two principal organs: a Council of Four (Wilson, Lloyd George, Clemenceau, and Orlando) with powers of over-all direction and ultimate decision; and a Council of Five (composed of the foreign ministers of the five principal Allied Powers), which dealt with special problems assigned to it, especially economic questions rising out of the blockade of Germany, and was the recognized organ for handling the reports of the Territorial Committees. These committees, originally appointed by the Council of Ten, were made up of experts who were given the duty of assigning frontiers to new states like Poland and Czechoslovakia and performing related tasks, in the execution of which they were, unfortunately, handicapped by the lack of clear instructions or until very late, of a central coordinating agency. Finally, there was a Plenary Conference, on which the lesser states were represented, which dealt with the questions of war guilt, reparations, the League of Nations, international labor legislation, and ports, waterways, and railways.

Once this organization had been devised (in mid-March), and it had been agreed that individual treaties should be concluded with all of the former enemy powers, much of the confusion of the first weeks was cleared up and the negotiations fell into a coherent pattern. Unfortunately, by this time there had been so much delay that any thought of making a preliminary settlement with Germany in preparation for more comprehensive negotiations later on was abandoned. This had one deplorable effect. Decisions made by the Territorial Committees in the belief that they were tentative and would be revised now became definitive and were written into the treaties, with much resultant injustice.

One other procedural mistake may be mentioned here, if only because it was repeated in World War II. The Allies made no attempt to make sure that they

The signing of peace in the Hall of Mirrors, Versailles, June 28, 1919. Portrait by Sir William Orpen. Figures in the front are Dr. Johannes Bell (Germany) signing with Hermann Müller leaning over him. Seated at the center of the table: President Woodrow Wilson, Georges Clemenceau, and David Lloyd George. (The Trustees of the Imperial War Museum, London)

retained enough military strength to enable them, if necessary, to impose their will upon recalcitrant enemies or friends. The pressure of public opinion at home led to a precipitous demobilization of American and British troops, beginning almost immediately after the armistice. Demobilization weakened the ability of the Allies to impress people like the Poles, when they began to violate the territory of their neighbors; and it probably contributed to their decision to continue the blockade of Germany as the most expeditious means of preventing any serious German resistance until that country accepted the peace terms. This failure to provide for contingencies that would require the use of force, combined with the delay caused by the procedural errors mentioned above, contributed to the progressive political and economic disintegration of central and eastern Europe.

The German Settlement   In the prearmistice negotiations between the Germans and the Allies, the German government had been given to understand that the future peace would be made on the basis of President Wilson's Fourteen Points, with two reservations: first, that the Allies retained full discretion concerning the freedom of the seas (which meant that the British would refuse to give up their doctrine of the blockade) and, second, that it was to be understood that "compensation will be made by Germany for all damage done to the civilian population of the Allies and their property by the aggression of Germany by land, by sea and from the air." Unfortunately, the Germans were not informed of other more informal concessions made by the Americans to remove their allies' objections to the Fourteen Points; and this put them in the position of being able, in 1919 and for years thereafter, to charge the Allies with bad faith.

It must be admitted that the Germans had a case. Since they were excluded from the negotiations at Paris, Wilson's first point, calling for "open covenants openly arrived at," was certainly rendered meaningless as far as they were concerned. Point two, calling for freedom of the seas, had been eliminated by prior agreement. Point five, which had talked of an "impartial adjustment of all colonial claims," was passed over silently at Paris, and all of Germany's former colonies, disguised as mandated territories, were parceled out among Japan, Great Britain and the Dominions, and France. Point thirteen, which had stipulated that the future independent Poland would be composed of territory inhabited by indisputably Polish populations, was interpreted in such a way as to hand large numbers of Germans over to Polish control. Nor did this exhaust the list of decisions that could be called, and were called by the Germans and others, flagrant violations of Wilson's charter of principles.

This is not, however, a black and white matter. It is true that the colonial question was handled in a manner that flatly contradicted Wilson's principles, because the President, here as on many other points at issue in Paris, felt that he had to satisfy the territorial desires of Japan and the British Dominions in order to make sure of their support of the League of Nations (see p. 502). But other violations were unavoidable. In the Polish question, for example, it was virtually impossible to give the new Polish state access to the sea without including some Germans in the corridor created, unless one resorted to forcible evacuation; and the population of the territory affected was so mixed that it was difficult, even by a process of elaborate fragmentation, to create districts that were "indisputably" either Polish or German.

As far as the territorial settlement was concerned, the final treaty—apart from the colonial clauses—must have contained few surprises for the Germans. Once the war was lost, they knew that they would have to renounce their grandiose plans for the Baltic regions and the Ukraine, the gains they had exacted from the Russians and the Rumanians at Brest Litovsk and Bucharest (see pp. 482 and 519), and their hold over Poland; and it should have been no secret to them that they would also lose Alsace-Lorraine, which they had taken after the Franco-Prussian War. These territorial changes were stipulated in the treaty. In addition. Germany had to cede the towns of Eupen and Malmèdy to Belgium, to place the Baltic port of Memel in Allied hands for future disposal (in 1923 it was taken by Lithuania), to cede the province of Posen and a strip of territory running through West Prussia to Poland, and to allow plebiscites to determine the future possession of Schleswig, which had been seized by Prussia after the Danish war of 1864 (see p. 210), and certain districts of East Prussia and Silesia, which had large Polish populations. These provisions could all be justified by the principle of national self-determination, which the Peace Conference had accepted from President Wilson as one of its guiding principles in territorial adjustment. In some cases German protests were honored and adjustments made in their favor; and, in general, the plebiscites (by which Germany eventually lost Northern Schleswig and part of Upper Silesia) were fair and conducted under impartial auspices.

There were two final territorial clauses that could hardly have been foreseen and were less easily justified. The first was the transformation of the German Baltic port of Danzig into an internationalized free city; the second was the transfer of the Saar coal region to the administration of the League of Nations and the economic control of France for a period of fifteen years, after which time its future would be determined by plebiscite.

This last provision was one of several that aggravated the problems created for Germany by the reparations clauses of the treaty, which were the harshest and most unrealistic part of the German settlement. During the prearmistice negotiations, the principle that Germany must pay for damage to the civilian populations of her enemies had been established and accepted by the Germans themselves. What had not been made clear was that such damage would later, at Britain's request, be made to include not only shipping and property losses but service pensions and allowances as well, an addition that more than doubled the German liability. Nor was it foreseen that Germany's means to pay would be seriously weakened by its forced loss of territory and population, colonies and natural resources, and by the confiscation of practically its whole merchant fleet. Even during the peace conference, this last point was not clear to those charged with formulating the reparations terms, for—and here we come back to the procedural weaknesses of the conference—they worked without any knowledge of the decisions that were being made concurrently with respect to cessions of territory and resources.

The victors decided in the end not to set a total figure for reparations until a later date. In a meeting of the Council of Four, Lloyd George said frankly: "If figures were given now, they would frighten rather than reassure the Germans. Any figure that would not frighten them would be below the figure with which he and M. Clemenceau could face their peoples in the present state of public opinion." Thus, the German people had to wait until 1921 to learn that, in addition to the down payment of five billion dollars, the cessions of shipping and territory, and the coal deliveries to neighboring countries that were required by the treaty, they would be expected to pay thirty-two billion dollars to their former enemies.

The figure was perhaps not in itself important, for long before 1921 the very idea of reparations was anathema in Germany, even to people who might otherwise have admitted the justice of Germany's paying a war indemnity. This was because the reparations clauses of the treaty were prefaced by an article (Article 231) that stated that "the Allied and Associated Governments affirm and Germany accepts the responsibility of Germany and her allies for causing all the loss and damage to which [they] and their nationals have been subjected as a consequence of the war imposed upon them by the aggression of Germany and her allies." Drafted by the young American expert and future secretary of state John Foster Dulles, the clause was intended as a concession to the British and French, who had been persuaded by the Americans not to ask for even larger reparations, but who insisted on some formula that would clearly state their *right* to ask for more even if they did not use it. Unfortunately, it was interpreted by the Germans as an attempt to make them solely responsible for having caused the war; and, as Dulles himself wrote later, "it was the revulsion of the German people from this article of the treaty which, above all else, laid the foundation for the Germany of Hitler."

Equally humiliating to many Germans was the demand that the emperor of Germany be tried by an international court for his offenses against international morality. This forecast of the elaborate trials of war criminals after World War II came to nothing. On November 10, 1918, William II had left his country and taken refuge in Doorn, Holland, where he spent the rest of his life. An attempt by the Allies in 1920 to persuade Holland to surrender him for trial was rebuffed politely but firmly, the Netherlands government expressing doubts about the legality of the proposed procedure and refusing to withdraw their protection from one who had freely sought it.

As was to be expected, the Allies spent much time and effort in drafting the military sections of the treaty, and they imposed heavy restriction upon Germany's future freedom of action in military affairs. In order to deprive it of the means to disturb the peace of the world a second time, they stipulated that the future German army be limited to a force of 100,000 officers and men, without the right to possess military aircraft, tanks, or other offensive weapons, that the General Staff, the War Academy, and the cadet schools, which were supposed to be the breeding places of Prussian militarism, be dissolved, and that the future navy be limited to a token force with no vessels exceeding 10,000 tons and no submarines. Until these provisions were carried out, and the Allies were, in addition, satisfied that all production of war material had been made impossible, the Rhineland was to be occupied by Allied troops, and it was to be permanently demilitarized, together with a strip fifty kilometers wide to the east of the Rhine.

Leaving aside the practical difficulties of enforcing these provisions (and more is known today about the problems of arms control and inspection than was known in 1919), these military clauses turned out to have two weaknesses. The first lay in the Allied insistence that the future German army be made up entirely of long-term volunteers, the officers serving for twenty-five years, other ranks for twelve. The French had been willing to tolerate a larger army based on short-term conscription, but they had given in to the insistence of Wilson and Lloyd George, leaders of countries in which conscription had always been unpopular. Their victory meant that Germany would have an army that was, by its very terms of service, sealed off from civilian life and values and would, moreover, be likely to appeal to those elements that were most devoted to the Germany of the past and least tolerant of progress toward democracy. In the second place, in another example of textual clumsiness, the Allies prefaced the military clauses with a statement expressing the hope that German disarmament would be followed by general disarmament. This unnecessary clause was to be interpreted by Adolf Hitler and others as an Allied pledge to disarm, the nonfulfillment of which justified German violation of the treaty terms.

The Germans might have been treated differently if the fears entertained by some of the delegations with respect to the menace of Bolshevism had had more substance. In March 1919, when the Communist Béla Kun seized power in Budapest (see p. 487), there was a panicky mood in Paris, and Lloyd George was not alone in urging that mitigation of the German terms was necessary in order to prevent the occurrence of something similar in Berlin, where the political situation was highly unstable (see p. 557). But the French held firm, and, since the Bolshevik tide showed no sign of rolling further westward, were able to block any significant appeasement of the Germans.

The Versailles Treaty, which embodied all the terms of the German settlement, might have been an even more severe document than it was if it had not been for Woodrow Wilson's spirited and successful opposition to French desires to detach the whole of the Rhineland from Germany. Even so, when seen in its totality, it was harsh enough to cause misgivings to those who had worked on its separate parts. In the last days of the meetings, Jan Christian Smuts often sat with John Maynard Keynes, the British economist, and they would, in Smuts's words, "rail against the world and the coming flood." And on one of these occasions, Smuts told his friend that he was reminded of the prayer of an old Griqua chief whose village was in peril: "Lord, save Thy people. Lord, we are lost unless Thou savest us. Lord, this is not work for children. It is not enough this time to send Thy son. Lord, Thou, must come Thyself." Yet the terms were the result of so many delicate compromises between the Allies that any serious revision promised to open up innumerable questions and prolong the peacemaking process indefinitely. When the treaty was presented to the Germans in May 1919, therefore, the Allies made few concessions to the objections and the lists of proposed amendments that came back from Berlin. Instead, they made it clear that, unless the treaty were accepted in its entirety by June 23, hostilities would be resumed. Allied firmness was doubtless hardened by German success on June 21 in scuttling their High Seas Fleet, which had been interned at Scapa Flow. Infuriated by what must have seemed a proof that the Germans were unregenerate, they brushed aside the last notes from Berlin and ordered Foch to prepare to begin his advance at 7 P.M. on the 23d. The Germans gave way and, five days later, in the Hall of Mirrors in Versailles, signed the treaty.

EUROPE AFTER **WORLD WAR I**

World War I Losses

by Germany

by Austria Hungary

by Bulgaria

by Russia

0   500

Miles

The Settlement in Eastern Europe   The conferees at Paris were now confronted with what Lord Balfour called "the immense operation of liquidating the Austrian Empire." This had been forecast by the rapid dissolution of imperial unity under the stress of war, a process that had been accelerated on the one hand by the terms of the treaties of Brest Litovsk and Bucharest, and on the other by the encouragement given to the subject nationalities in President Wilson's Fourteen Points address and other wartime speeches (see p. 482). It proved to be an enormously complicated operation that was not complete until three more treaties had been written and signed by former enemy states, and a large number of territorial, commercial, and military conventions concluded with the states that were the beneficiaries of the dissolution of the Hapsburg monarchy.

The main outlines of an Austrian settlement had taken shape before the Council of Four turned the bulk of the peacemaking work over to subordinates and held its last meeting on June 28, 1919, and it was rapidly concluded in the weeks that followed. The resultant treaty was, in the first instance, a recognition of events that had taken place inside the Hapsburg empire since October 1918. In that month, Thomas Masaryk and Eduard Beneš, who had worked tirelessly throughout the war years to win Allied sympathy for the cause of Czech independence, proclaimed the deposition of the young Emperor Charles and the creation of an independent Czechoslovakian republic. In the same month, the Poles of Galicia seceded from the empire, and a diet in Croatia proclaimed the secession of Croatia and Dalmatia from Hungary, thus preparing the way for the fusion of these and other southern Slav provinces of the empire, including Bosnia and Herzegovina, with the kingdom of Serbia a month later. On October 24 also, a liberal government under Count Michael Karolyi had seized power in Budapest, and two weeks later it proclaimed Hungary to be an independent republic. Now, the Treaty of St. Germain of September 1919 required Austria—which had itself become a republic by revolution and the abdication of Emperor Charles on November 11, 1918—to accept all of these losses and to recognize the independence of Czechoslovakia, Poland, Yugoslavia, and Hungary.

Whether what was left of Austria—a trifling territory with a population of six and a half million, a third of whom lived in Vienna—could become a viable state does not seem to have concerned the peacemakers at Paris to any great degree. It was a question that worried the Austrians themselves. On November 12, 1918, when they set up their new regime, they had specifically declared that Austria would be "a component part of the German Republic." This the Allies refused to countenance, and the Austrian Republic was forced to begin a career of reluctant independence, clouded in advance by the prospect of grave economic troubles. This outlook was made more forbidding by the loss of access to the sea, by the cession of part of the German-speaking Tyrol to Italy, and by the treaty's stipulation that Austria would be required to pay an undisclosed amount of reparations. In the circumstances, the provision that the Austrian army must be restricted to 30,000 officers and men was not regarded unfavorably in the republic.

Hungary was treated with even greater severity and suffered in particular from the fact that its new boundaries were drawn by a number of committees (on Czech claims, on Rumanian claims, and so forth) which operated independently and made no attempt to inform each other of their prospective exactions. As a result, the former Magyar kingdom, in the name of national self-determination, lost three fourths of its area—its South Slav lands to Yugoslavia, Slovakia to the new state created by Masaryk and Beneš, and Translyvania to Rumania. The Treaty of Trianon also provided for stringent limitations on Hungary's military establishment.

Peace was made with Bulgaria by the Treaty of Neuilly. The only enemy state whose dynasty survived the war, Bulgaria received treatment no better and no worse than that accorded those who had embraced democracy at the war's end. Its main territorial losses were the cession of its Thracian outlet to the Aegean Sea to Greece, and the transfer of its holdings in Macedonia to Yugoslavia.

What these countries lost was won by the states who had contributed to the victory of the Allies. Nor were their gains made only at the expense of their enemies. Rumania, for example, which acquired former Bulgarian and Hungarian territory, also took Bessarabian districts from its former ally, Russia, a step hardly calculated to make for good relations with that power. Poland, not content with what could be gained in Paris, quarreled with the Czechs over the duchy of Teschen (and eventually gained part of it by Allied award in 1920) and resorted to military means to seize territory from Russia (see p. 524) and to wrest the city of Vilna from Lithuania.

The settlement of the South Slav question was also marked by a dispute between the Allies, which began during the peace conference and was prolonged until 1924. Dissatisfied with the territories promised them by secret treaty when Italy came into the war in 1915, the Italians insisted that their new possessions on the Istrian and Dalmatian coast should include the port of Fiume. Woodrow Wilson's resistance to this, on the grounds that the Yugoslavs had a better claim on ethnic grounds, and his attempt to appeal to the Italian people over the heads of their government caused a major crisis in Paris, marked by temporary Italian withdrawal from meetings of the Council of Four. The unresolved dispute was aggravated when Gabriele D'Annunzio, at the head of an expedition of black-shirted patriots, seized the port in September 1919. His subsequent antics in the town proved as embarrassing to the Italian government as they were instructive to Italy's future dictator, Mussolini, already resolved to out-D'Annunzio the poet-politician; and in the end the Italians found it expedient to strike a compromise. By the Treaty of Rapallo (November 1920) they surrendered to Yugoslavia the whole Dalmatian coast south of Fiume with the single exception of the town of Zara (Zadar). Italy retained most of Istria and four of the Dalmatian islands. Fiume was left as a free city until 1924, when a new agreement ceded most of the port to Italy and its suburbs to Yugoslavia.

Seen in its totality, the settlement of eastern Europe was rather sounder than its critics were willing to admit. By 1919 it was too late to stop the disintegration of the Hapsburg empire. The most equitable guiding principle for the inevitable territorial readjustment was the principle of nationality, and this was followed. Given the mixed state of the populations of eastern Europe, it was obviously impossible to redraw the map in such a way as to eliminate national minorities. All of the new countries had such minorities; and the new Czechoslovakia was made up of peoples with no natural ties, Czechs, Slovaks, Germans, Poles, Hungarians, and Ruthenians—a mixture that spelled future trouble. But, granted the inevitability of minorities, it says something for the peacemakers at Paris that on the whole the boundaries they drew stood the test of time.

The principal weaknesses of the eastern settlement were two. The increased political diversity of the area was destined to cause a high degree of economic instability. This might have been avoided if the succession states had adopted economic policies that reproduced the conditions of interdependence and collaboration that had existed inside the Austrian-Hungarian empire. But the nationalism engendered by their new independence and the suspicions that those who had gained territory entertained toward those from whom they had acquired it prevented this kind of mutual support and led to wasteful economic competition and military spending, which contributed to the general instability of the area. It is difficult to see how this could have been entirely avoided by anything within the power of the peacemakers at Paris.

In the second place, the whole eastern settlement suffered from the failure of the conferees in Paris to come to grips with the Russian problem. The attempts made in the first part of the conference to explore the possibilities of an accommodation with the Bolshevik regime were never pressed, largely because the balance of political forces in the victorious nations had swung sharply to the right at the end of the war, and public opinion would not have tolerated the recognition of the revolutionary power. After the Hungarian coup of Béla Kun, the Western powers stopped temporizing and went over to an openly anti-Bolshevik line, which led to support of the White armies of Denikin and Kolchak and toleration of the Polish invasion of the Ukraine (see pp. 520–525). They seemed to assume that if Bolshevism could not be crushed, it could at least be contained and that they could deny Russia a role in European affairs at the same time that they were barring Germany from the European system by the imposed limitations on its freedom of action and its exclusion from the League of Nations. But Russia and Germany were too large and potentially powerful to become political nullities; and events were to prove that the failure of the peacemakers in Paris to integrate at least one of them into the new European system was to render tentative all of their decisions in eastern Europe.

The Near Eastern Settlement   During the war promises of Turkish territory as compensation for aid to the Allied cause had been made to a number of states and national groups, and an attempt was now made to sort them out and resolve their inconsistencies. This was not easy, but it was attempted by the Treaty of Sèvres, which gave Palestine, Mesopotamia, and Transjordan as mandates to Great Britain, and Syria as a mandate to France, made the Arab state of Hejaz independent, granted Smyrna, Thrace, Adrianople, and Gallipoli to Greece, gave large spheres of influence to France and Italy, and internationalized the Straits. The execution of this treaty was delayed in the hope that the United States might be prepared to accept a mandate over either Armenia or Constantinople itself; and, by the time this hope had proved to be illusory, a revolutionary nationalist movement, headed by the hero of the Gallipoli campaign, Mustafa Kemal, had risen to contest the moribund sultanate and had declared its inflexible opposition to the Sèvres terms.

Kemal was encouraged by the diplomatic recognition and support accorded him by the Bolshevik regime in Russia, and he was greatly aided by deep dissension among the Allies. The French and the Italians, resentful of the gains made by Britain and Greece, soon expressed the belief that the Treaty of Sèvres should be revised and began secretly to supply the Nationalists with arms and ammunition. The Lloyd George government in England completely misread the situation, and the prime minister himself—a great believer in personal diplomacy—encouraged the Greeks to embark on a fatal attempt to suppress the Kemalist movement and enforce the treaty from which they had gained so much. In September 1922, the Greek armies were routed and driven into the sea at Smyrna; and Kemal's armies threatened the small Allied forces upon the Asiatic shores

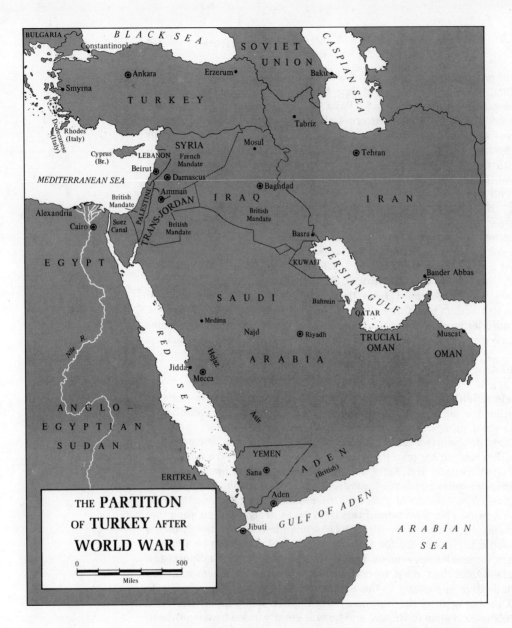

THE **PARTITION**
OF **TURKEY** AFTER
WORLD WAR I

0   500

Miles

of the Straits. At this juncture the French and Italians withdrew, leaving the British to find their way out of an apparently hopeless situation in which one false step might mean a major war. The British, however, held their ground; and Kemal, displaying great qualities of statesmanship, elected to negotiate. Talks at Mudania in October 1922 laid the basis for a new conference at Lausanne in the early summer of 1923, where the Sèvres Treaty was completely rewritten.

Turkish interests were ably defended at Lausanne by Ismet Pasha, a future president of his country; British claims were skillfully presented by the foreign secretary of the new Conservative government, the Earl of Curzon. Britain retained most of the territorial gains made at Sèvres, as did France and the Hejaz. Greece lost to Turkey virtually everything that had been granted it, and even had to turn the Dodecanese Islands, which it had acquired from Italy in 1919 with Turkish assent, back to Italy. Ismet's diplomacy established Turkey's rights over Anatolia, Cilicia, Adalia, Smyrna, eastern Thrace, and Constantinople and complete independence in directing its internal affairs. Freedom of navigation was established in the Straits, and they were demilitarized.

Turkey was thus the first successful revisionist power; but it had accomplished its revision without touching off a major war, and the settlement gained was sounder than the one it replaced.

In the lands that it took from Turkey, the British government tried patiently but with eventual failure to reconcile the promises made during the war to the Arabs and the Jews. The original pledge of support for Arab independence made in 1915 (see p. 472) had, in Arab eyes, been attenuated by the Sykes-Picot agreement of 1916, which provided, it is true, for an independent Arab state or a confederation of states, but also made it clear that there would be large British and French spheres of influence and that Palestine and the holy places would be given a special status. Uneasiness over these provisions ripened into indignation when Lord Balfour declared in November 1917 that "His Majesty's Government view with favour the establishment in Palestine of a national home for the Jewish people." Made in an effort to gain the sympathy and financial support of world Jewry for the Allied cause, and also because of the gratitude that the British government felt for the services to the Allies performed by Dr. Chaim Weizman,[2] the president of the World Zionist Organization (see p. 368), the Balfour Declaration was regarded by the Arabs as a violation of the spirit of the pledges made to them and an attempt to give political control of Palestine to the Jews in defiance of their own historical rights and their services to the Allied cause.

To conciliate Arab nationalism, the British assigned their mandates in the Near East to Arab rulers who would work under their supervision. Thus, Prince Faisal, son of the ruler of the newly independent Hejaz, King Hussein, was installed in Mesopotamia with the title king of Iraq and another of Hussein's sons became the ruler of Transjordan. Agitation for self-government began almost immediately in these territories, as it did in Syria and Lebanon, which passed under French control in accordance with the Sykes-Picot arrangement. Meanwhile, the heavy Jewish immigration into Palestine, while of inestimable value to that land, further incensed the Arabs and led to frequent and bloody clashes between the two contending populations in the postwar period.

Machinery for Revision   Any final judgment of the great peace settlement that followed World War I must take into consideration the fact that the peacemakers created machinery designed to complete the organization of the peace, to carry out special tasks made necessary by the treaties (the administration of plebiscites in disputed areas, for instance, the protection of minorities in

---

[2] In 1914, when Britain was deprived of acetone, which had been imported from Germany, Weizman found a method of synthesizing cordite from wood.

countries like Poland and Czechoslovakia, and the supervision of mandates), and to perform whatever tasks of adjustment, revision, and compromise might prove necessary for the preservation of international order and harmony. In his Fourteen Points address, President Wilson had declared that: "A general association of nations must be formed under specific covenants for the purpose of affording guarantees of political independence"; and, when he came to Paris, the President insisted that this be given top priority among the subjects to be discussed there. So great was the importance that he attributed to this concept that he did not scruple to assent to decisions of the Council of Four of which he personally disapproved, when he felt that this was necessary in order to assure the establishment of the new world organization. It was his fixed belief that the organization would correct any mistakes made and injustices done at Paris.

Largely as a result of the President's insistence, a special covenant was inserted into the major peace treaties that provided for a League of Nations, to which all Allied and Associated Powers, and such other states as were invited, would belong. It would be composed of an Assembly in which all members would be represented, a Council in which the Great Powers would have permanent seats and four seats would be assigned for shorter periods to other states, and a Secretariat composed of international civil servants whose first loyalty was to the League. Provision was also made for the establishment by the Council of an International Court of Justice and for an International Labor Office to further the improvement of conditions of labor by international action.

The organization of these bodies got under way immediately; the British diplomat Sir Eric Drummond was made the first secretary general of the League and charged with the task of arranging for its first meetings; and there was general hope that, once established, the League and its sister bodies would make possible the achievement of peace and security through collective action.

FROM VERSAILLES TO LOCARNO

The Weaknesses of the League   The first Assembly of the League of Nations gathered in Geneva in November 1920. The British delegation, headed by Lord Balfour, took up its quarters in the Hotel Beau Rivage, where they discovered that the management had installed a shiny new slot machine in the lobby for the diversion of the delegates. This device fascinated Balfour, and he rarely passed it without feeding coins into it. One day, however, in an excess of enthusiasm, he pulled the handle too hard; and the machine, after vomiting coins all over the lobby, broke down. The management removed it.

On anyone sensitive to portents, this incident, carefully recorded by Balfour's biographer, must have made a foreboding impression. For the League of Nations was also a shiny new machine, and who could tell how much strain it would be capable of withstanding? Considering the tasks it was created to perform, it began its existence with certain grave weaknesses.

In the first place, although the original membership list was impressive, it was marked by some notable omissions. The annex to the Covenant listed thirty-one Allied and Associated states which had signed the treaties as the original members and thirteen neutral states which had been asked to accede to the Covenant. All of the European Allies, the British Dominions, the succession states of eastern Europe, Japan, China, and Siam in the Far East, all of the Latin American states, and Persia, the Hejaz, and Liberia had been asked to send representatives. But none of the former enemy states was included in the original list and, although Austria and Bulgaria were admitted after the first meeting of the Assembly, Hungary was not a member until 1922, Germany until 1926, and Turkey until 1932. Just as important as the absence of Germany was that of the Soviet Union, which continued until the early 1930s to attack the League as a front for capitalistic imperialism and tried to organize a countersociety of underdeveloped or anticolonial states.

More shattering in its effect upon the mood in which the League began its work was the decision of the United States government not to be represented in the organization for which Woodrow Wilson had fought so hard. This disappointing decision was partly due to domestic political factors and to tactical mistakes made by the President himself during and after the Peace Conference; but its primary cause was certainly a marked change in American public opinion in the months after the end of hostilities. The American people had gone to war in a spirit of idealism and reforming zeal, but this faltered and died in the face of the expenditure of life and resources required by the struggle, the unexpected length of the peace negotiations, the discrepancies between the final peace terms and the original Fourteen Points, the postwar revelations of the secret treaties concluded before and during the war, and, above all, the discovery that "to make the world safe for democracy" would demand continued effort and sacrifice on the part of the United States. By the end of 1919, there were fewer citizens of the United States who desired membership in the League than there were Americans who feared that it would seriously impair American sovereignty or believed that the United States should return to a policy of isolationism or had simply stopped thinking about the problem at all. The United States Senate, under the circumstances, blocked ratification of the Covenant until the Presidential elections of November 1920, in which the Democratic candidate, who had campaigned on Wilson's program, was overwhelmingly defeated. After that, the League was a dead issue in the United States; and the government decided against ratifying any of the treaties, making separate peace arrangements with the former enemy powers in 1922.

The effect of the American decision upon the authority and the morale of the League in its first days need not be dwelt on here, but mention may be made of another of its consequences. In some ways, the most serious result of American abstention was that it left Great Britain and France face to face in the League with no power of equal stature to mediate between them and adjust their views. This vacuum was unfortunate because these two countries had sharply opposed conceptions of what the League should be, and their differences had consequences as serious as the American decision.

Anglo-French Differences   Once the war was over, the British people, in a movement of opinion somewhat akin to that in the United States, reverted to their traditional aversion to continental entanglements. This change of attitude was reflected in the behavior of their government, as was shown by a significant action taken at the end of 1919. During the meetings of the Council of Four in Paris, Woodrow Wilson had persuaded Clemenceau to give up the French demand for cession of the German Rhineland; in return for France's surrender of these claims, the British and American governments had promised to guarantee France against any future German attack. When the United States Senate refused to ratify the Versailles Treaty, it repudiated this pledge too, and the British government decided to follow suit.

This action threw a shadow over relations between Britain and France for at least a decade. Arnold Toynbee, indeed, has written that

> this was, in effect, a dissolution of the Anglo-French Entente of 1904, after the necessity of the Entente for the survival of Great Britain, as well as France, had been demonstrated, in the first World War, by a terrifying practical experience of Germany's military strength. . . . The non-ratification of the post-war British guarantee to France dealt a blow to Franco-British relations from which these never recovered; and, from that time onwards, the two former partners ... fell farther and farther out of step with one another till the eventual tragic parting of their ways in June 1940.

In 1909, the British were not, of course, looking that far ahead. Rather, they were thinking of avoiding undue risks and entanglements in Europe at a time when they had to concern themselves with pressing problems among their own dependencies and along the lifelines of their empire (see p. 611). Moreover, their reluctance to assume responsibilities on the continent was endorsed by the Dominions, who, having fought one major war rising out of European complications, did not want to become involved in another. Since the Dominions now claimed, and received, a voice in the determination of imperial foreign policy, the home government no longer possessed the freedom of action in European affairs that it had had before 1914.

These factors determined Great Britain's attitude toward the League. In that organization's early days, Lord Balfour always seemed to be remembering the slot machine. He insisted that the League's true purpose was to promote international cooperation and that it should avoid assuming tasks that exceeded its powers. It was better designed to serve as a meeting place in which delegates could learn to know and understand each other's points of view than as an organ for taking executive action. Above all, it should avoid being placed in the position of applying, to either members or nonmembers, those military and economic sanctions mentioned in the Covenant as the means to be employed against refractory and aggressive states.

The French, for geographical and historical reasons, took an entirely different view. They were not protected by water from the possibility of invasion, and they had had German troops on their soil twice within half a century. They were aware that their recent victory had been won only with the aid of half the world and that, with a population that was now only two thirds that of Germany, and falling relatively, they would have to supplement their own defensive resources with those of other powers. They had thought that such aid was assured by the Rhineland pledge of the United States and Great Britain; once that evaporated, they had to find a substitute, and they could not regard the League, in its present form, as an effective one. As they read the Covenant, they were, in contrast to the British, particularly interested in the provisions for collective action against aggressors: in Article X, in which the members undertook to "respect and preserve against external aggression the territorial integrity and existing political independence" of all other members; in Article XI, which declared that "any war or threat of war [is] a matter of concern to the whole League" and "the League shall take any action that may be deemed wise and effectual to safeguard the peace of nations"; in Article XVI, which mentioned the economic, financial, and military means which League members might severally employ in case of an act of war. Their principal criticism was that the obligations implicit in these provisions were not binding upon all members and that the actions designed to check aggression would not come automatically into play when the aggression was committed. In their view, steps must be taken immediately to put teeth into the Covenant so that it would become a terror to wrongdoers.

In the first years of the League's operation, the French government sponsored two plans for strengthening the League. The first was the Draft Treaty of Mutual Assistance of 1923, which proposed that, once the Council had declared that a member state was the object of aggression, all other members would be obliged to come to its assistance. The second and more carefully devised proposal was the Geneva Protocol of 1924, which provided for the submission of all international disputes either to the International Court of Justice or to the League Council and declared that refusal to submit would automatically constitute an act of aggression, which each member of the League would be obliged to resist "in the degree which its geographical situation, and its particular situation as regards armaments, allows."

Both of these proposals, and the Geneva Protocol especially, received wide backing among League members. Both failed as a result of the opposition of the British government and the Dominions. In one respect, the British were admittedly in a difficult position, for they had been warned by the American secretary of state, Charles Evans Hughes, that, if they signed the Geneva Protocol and if the United States then became involved in a dispute with a League member and was branded as an aggressor, they might be required to go to war against the United States. But this possibility could have been removed by an amendment to the protocol, if it had been the only thing that stood in the way of its acceptance. The real reason for British opposition was their disinclination to accept automatic obligations in Eastern Europe and other areas in which they had no vital interests—or thought they had none. Besides, as Sir Austen Chamberlain told the League Assembly, the protocol was too logical an arrangement. The British had always distrusted logic in politics and had generally been right!

The French Search for Security   Even before the defeat of their efforts to reform the League had been made definitive, the French had been pursuing other lines of policy that were designed to give them the security they desired. For one thing, they had begun to build up a network of military alliances outside the League of Nations.

In 1920, for instance, the French government concluded a defensive alliance with Belgium and immediately inaugurated staff talks with the object of devising joint plans to make any future German invasion through Belgium impossible. The agreement was a source of satisfaction to French soldiers who remembered how nearly Schlieffen's plan had come to winning the war in 1914; but it was not in itself sufficient. Germany must be made to realize that, in any future war, it would have to fight on two fronts again; and this realization would be forced on it only if France could find allies in Eastern Europe to take the place occupied by Russia after 1891.

France therefore turned to Poland, which seemed potentially the strongest military state in the east and the one least likely to become friendly with the Germans. An opportunity of winning Polish gratitude was found in 1920 when the Poles overreached themselves in an attempt to seize the Ukraine and were pushed back to the outskirts of Warsaw, which seemed in imminent danger of capture by units of the Red Army commanded by Marshal Tukhachevsky (see p. 525). The French helped organize the successful defense of the capital and the subsequent Polish advance that retrieved some of the lost territory. This collaboration led to the conclusion of a formal treaty in February 1921, in which the two powers agreed to "consult each other in all questions of foreign policy so far as those questions affect the settlement of international relations in the spirit of the Treaties" and, in the event of unprovoked aggression upon the territory of either, "to take concerted measures for the defense of their territories and the protection of their legitimate interests."

The first alliance led to others. From a strategical point of view, Czechoslovakia was as useful an ally against Germany, and from a political point of view as natural a one, as Poland. In 1924 France concluded a military alliance with it and in subsequent years, sent French engineers to construct its defensive rampart in Bohemia. But Poland was already allied with Rumania, out of common fear of the Soviet Union; and Czechoslovakia had joined with Rumania and Yugoslavia to form the combination that came to be called the Little Entente and was designed as a means of common defense against a resurgent Hungary. It seemed logical for France to combine with the friends of its friends and, by 1927, it had forged military ties with them as well.

The French alliance system always seemed stronger than it actually was, and the future was to show that the French people were not willing to make the financial and military commitments necessary to hold it together when it was actually needed against Germany in the 1930s. It seems clear in retrospect that eastern Europe could have been made a bulwark of collective security only by a joint Anglo-French commitment in that area. This was always an unlikely possibility, but it was made more so by France's unilateral policy of alliance building, which annoyed the British and made Anglo-French cooperation, in eastern Europe, in the League, and elsewhere, more difficult than before.

Aside from this, it can be argued that the French alliance policy contributed both to the weakening of the League in its formative years and to the general insecurity of the continent. France's alliance ties sometimes placed it in a position in which it felt justified in bypassing the League. Thus, in 1923, when Poland attacked Lithuania for possession of Vilna, the French government blocked

League mediation and arranged a Great Power award of the disputed area to their ally. This sort of thing is likely to invite emulation. In the same year as the Vilna dispute, Italy's new dictator, Mussolini, refused to allow League interference in his dispute with Greece over Corfu and was allowed to have his way (see p. 551). Nor was this the end of Mussolini's experiments in imitation. In eastern Europe, he sought to compete with France for allies, turning his attention particularly to Austria, Hungary, and Bulgaria; and this increased the general unease of the area.

Finally, the new search for allies inaugurated by France contributed to the failure to implement Article VIII of the League Covenant, which provided for the formulation of plans for "the reduction of national armaments to the lowest point consistent with national safety." In the ten years that followed World War I, the only progress made toward such reduction was in naval armaments, and that was not impressive. The Washington Conference of 1921–1922 provided that the United States, Great Britain, Japan, France, and Italy should observe a ratio of 5:5:3:1.67:1.67 in capital ships for a period of ten years; but it was unable to establish any effective limits on cruisers or submarines. Nor were the Geneva Naval Conference of 1927 and the London Conference of 1930 successful in this regard. As for land armaments, there was a good deal of discussion of limitations but nothing in the way of results. By 1929 all powers were arming on a scale exceeding that of the prewar period, with the exception of the former enemy powers, whose efforts in this field were limited by treaty. Even in their case, it was known that illegal arming was going on in Austria and Hungary; and there were secret agreements between the Red Army and that of the German Republic which enabled German soldiers to receive training in weapons denied them by the Versailles Treaty (see p. 562).

Britain, France, and the German Question   Meanwhile, the differences between Britain and France that had begun with the repudiation of the Rhineland pledge and had been aggravated by their failure to agree about the League, their diverse policies in face of Kemal's national revolution in Turkey (see p. 499), and France's alliance policy in eastern Europe were being made more serious by France's German policy.

In large part, this centered on the reparations problem. The French persisted in believing that the Germans should pay on the scale envisaged during the Peace Conference. The British very rapidly came to doubt whether this was possible or even desirable and to suspect that the French were actuated by political rather than economic motives—that their insistence on complete payment was, in fact, merely another aspect of their security policy, designed to keep Germany permanently impoverished.

As if ashamed of having yielded to popular passions during the Paris Conference, Lloyd George undertook the job of persuading the French that it would be to Europe's interest and their own to lighten the burden imposed upon the Germans. His efforts were rendered ineffective by maladroitness on the part of the people he was trying to help. When the British prime minister persuaded the French to allow the Germans to appear at a conference at Spa in July 1920 to suggest how, and how much, they could pay in reparations, the German government sent a delegation that included General von Seeckt, who wore his uniform, complete with iron cross, and the industrialist Hugo Stinnes, who made incoherent speeches in which he accused the French of being "afflicted with the disease of victory" and of wishing to use black troops to oppress Germany and threatened them with a stoppage of all coal shipments. These provocations hardened the French in their attitude. Two years later, when Lloyd George organized a general economic conference at Genoa, which might have done something to alleviate the German economic position, the German delegation, headed by Foreign Minister Walther Rathenau (see p. 478), became nervous because they were excluded from private conferences in Lloyd George's villa. They allowed the Soviet delegation to talk them into a special pact of friendship and collaboration, the Treaty of Rapallo, the announcement of which had the effect of a bombshell, blowing up the Genoa Conference before any consideration was given to Germany's economic difficulties.

The Rapallo Treaty made the British government more eager to secure some reduction of Germany's burdens, lest she slip completely into the Soviet camp. In France, it had the opposite effect, strengthening the resolve to insist upon complete fulfillment of the reparation obligation. Thus, there was a direct causal relation between Rathenau's action at Rapallo and the French invasion of the Ruhr in January 1923. The author of this fateful action was the French prime minister Raymond Poincaré, an inveterate opponent of any concessions to France's former enemy. Taking advantage of a German failure to make certain timber shipments to France in accordance with an agreed schedule of payments in kind, Poincaré insisted that the Reparations Commission declare Germany in violation of its legal obligations. When this was done, over the opposition of the British representative, he announced that France must seek redress and dispatched French troops into the Ruhr, one of the most valuable of Germany's remaining mining and industrial areas.

As a means of attaining security for France—which is doubtless how Poincaré regarded his stroke—this was a drastic blunder. For one thing, as will be indicated below (p. 566), it seriously weakened the prospects of democracy in Germany and strengthened the forces of reaction. The social effects of the inflation brought to a head by the French action were disastrous and permanent, and it is no mere coincidence that Adolf Hitler made his first bid for power during the political confusion incidental to the Ruhr invasion. But even immediately the invasion backfired. When the tottering German economy collapsed under this new blow, it became impossible for the Germans to make any reparations payments; and, when this became manifest, there were serious repercussions abroad, not least of all in France.

The Dawes Plan, Locarno, and After   The critical situation created by these events did, however, elicit an effective response on the part of the Western powers and did something to resolve the Anglo-French differences on German policy. In 1924, under the leadership of the American banker Charles Dawes, an international commission of economic experts worked out a new long-term schedule of reparations payments for Germany, while at the same time laying a basis for foreign loans to that country which would enable it to resume reparations

French cartoon of the German Chancellor Hans Luther, Foreign Minister Gustav Stresemann, and the French Foreign Minister Aristide Briand at Locarno. (Hoover Institution)
"Into the Light," a 1925 commentary on Locarno by the American cartoonist Rollin Kirby
from the *New York Herald Tribune.*

payments during the period when its own currency was being reformed. The
easing of the economic situation encouraged the ablest German statesman of
the interwar years, Gustav Stresemann, to seek a political agreement that would
place Germany's relations with the Western powers, and particularly with France,
on an entirely new basis. Stresemann informed London and Paris that, in the
interests of a general detente and in the hope that it might facilitate the evacuation
of German soil by Allied troops, the German government was prepared to recognize the permanence of Germany's present boundaries with France and Belgium
and to have them placed under international guarantee. Pushed enthusiastically
by the British, this proposal led to negotiations between Stresemann, Sir Austen
Chamberlain, Aristide Briand (Poincaré's successor, a man infinitely more receptive to the idea of Franco-German collaboration in the interest of general appeasement), and other interested parties at Locarno, Switzerland. The negotiations eventuated in a number of treaties and agreements. Germany, France, and
Belgium agreed to respect their common frontiers and to forswear the use of
war against each other except in self-defense or in accordance with the League
Covenant; Great Britain and Italy agreed to guarantee this so-called Rhineland
Pact; Germany agreed to seek admission to the League of Nations, on condition
that it receive a permanent seat on the Council and (in view of its inferiority

in armaments) that it be exempted from certain of the military obligations of the Covenant; Germany also agreed to submit any disputes that it might have with its neighbors to arbitration or conciliation and, while not accepting its eastern frontiers, to seek their modification only by peaceful means. A covering protocol declared that in concluding these agreements the powers were seeking "by common agreement means of preserving their respective nations from the scourge of war and for providing for the peaceful settlement of disputes."

To a Europe tired of the tension and quarrels of the last six years, Locarno seemed to be a hopeful sign that those goals might be attained. The collaboration of Stresemann, Briand, and Chamberlain aroused great enthusiasm on the continent, which saw resulting from it the beginning of a genuine Franco-German rapprochement, and a reinvigoration of the League of Nations and the principle of collective security in general.

These hopes were not wholly groundless. The entrance of Germany into the League in 1926 did bring new prestige and authority to that organization; and, thanks to the earnest efforts of Briand and Stresemann, relations between their countries improved sufficiently to make possible a relaxation of the controls placed upon Germany in 1919, the evacuation of German soil by Allied troops (completed in 1930), and the scaling down of the reparations burden by the Young Plan of 1929—all measures designed further to contribute to the relaxation of European tension.[3]

Nevertheless, with the benefit of hindsight, we can see that the enthusiasm engendered by Locarno was excessive and, in some cases, dangerous.

If the League gained strength from Germany's adhesion, it was nevertheless not the kind of strength that might have been derived from the passage earlier of the Draft Treaty of Mutual Assistance or the Geneva Protocol. In a sense, the enthusiasm aroused by Locarno tended to make people forget that the enforcing machinery of the League and the provisions for action against aggressors were still too weak to be effective in a major crisis. The establishment of a grouping of powers outside the League—the so-called Locarno cabal—did nothing to correct this or to increase the League's prestige.

In the second place, what security the new treaties brought to Europe was rather one-sided and would not be complete until the Rhineland Pact was supplemented by some kind of eastern Locarno. Despite French efforts, this proved to be unattainable, among other things because of British opposition. Although it was not generally appreciated at the time, Great Britain's signature of the Rhineland Pact was not evidence of a new willingness to accept European responsibilities. It was rather a final answer to the Geneva Protocol. In guaranteeing the Rhine boundaries, Britain was expressing its inflexible opposition to commitment on the Vistula, and this meant that an Eastern security pact would be impossible.

---

[3] Another measure that served the same purpose was the Pact of Paris (Kellogg-Briand Pact) of August 1928, by which some 23 nations, including the European Great Powers and the United States, renounced the use of aggressive war. The pact made no provision for sanctions, which prompted a gibe in the French satirical journal *Le canard enchaîné,* "The next last war will be illegal".

Finally, Locarno did not, as some enthusiasts thought, assure lasting friendship and cooperation between its signatories. Germany followed its ratification of the Rhineland and the other treaties by concluding a new treaty of friendship (the Treaty of Berlin, 1926) with the Soviet Union, a power that had done its utmost to prevent the Germans from going to Locarno and was a declared foe of the League system. Italy, despite its collaboration in the work at Locarno, plunged into a new and dangerous rivalry with France in the Danubian area; and Great Britain remained vaguely suspicious and generally opposed to the main line of French policy.

Locarno, in short, was important only as a beginning to the solution of European tensions. It bore some good fruit in the years that followed. But, because it induced a general euphoria, it tended to make the European peoples relax and prevented them from urging their governments on to new efforts in the interests of collective security.

Chapter 22 THE RUSSIAN REVOLUTION AND THE WEST, 1917–1933

In a letter written in March 1868, Feodor Dostoevsky predicted that within a hundred years the whole world would be regenerated by Russian thought. That prophecy has not been fulfilled in the sense that the great novelist meant it; but it is undeniable that the political, economic, and social thinking, and in some cases the system of government and the institutional framework, of many countries all over the globe have been profoundly influenced by Russian ideas, Russian examples, and, in recent years, Russian conquests.

It is hardly likely that this would have been true, or true to the same extent, if tsarist Russia had survived. The impact of Russian thought upon the rest of the world began to become impressive only with the victory of communism in the land of the tsars.

THE RUSSIAN REVOLUTION

The End of Tsardom How long the tsarist regime might have lasted if there had been no world war it is, of course, impossible to say. Considering its inherent weaknesses and its failure of omission and commission after 1905 (see pp. 395–397), it is difficult to believe that its life could have been much prolonged. However that may be, the war threw a glaring light upon its inadequacies, while at the same time exposing the Russian people to hardships and suffering that made them increasingly intolerant of their lot.

Russia was unprepared agriculturally, industrially, or financially to fight a long war. Even after Stolypin's agrarian reforms (see p. 396), Russian agriculture lagged far behind the countries of the west in efficiency, and, once the war deprived it of the manpower upon which it depended in lieu of machines, production fell off precipitously. Russian industry was too backward either to remedy this situation by producing more farm implements or to supply the military needs of the state. In the course of three years of war, it produced hardly more than a third as many rifles as there were men mobilized. These deficiencies were reflected in food shortages that sapped civilian morale and in military weaknesses that made Russian casualties in the field higher than they would have been if the troops had been adequately armed. In the campaigns of 1915, in which the Russian armies were driven out of Galicia and Poland (see p. 467), Russian casualties have been conservatively estimated at more than two million; and in Brusilov's great push in 1916 (see p. 471) his forces lost close to a million men and were left in a state of near-demoralization.

By the end of 1916, these disasters had exhausted the patience even of former supporters of the regime. In November, when the Duma reconvened, Paul Miliukov, the leader of the Constitutional Democratic (or Cadet) party, delivered a furious attack upon the inadequacies of the government's policy and did not hesitate to extend his criticism to the throne itself by intimating that the empress shared the responsibility for them. In December these protests took a more tangible form, when a group of noblemen led by Prince Yusupov invited the empress' favorite, Rasputin (see p. 390), to a private dinner party, fed him cakes and wine liberally dosed with cyanide of potassium, and, when the wine had no perceptible effect, shot him and threw his body into the freezing waters of the Neva. Neither these events, however, nor the reports of bread riots in his principal cities impressed Nicholas II, who, as the crisis of his regime approached, proved his intellectual immaturity by immersing himself in trivialities, relying upon his police and his home garrisons to put down disorders.

But it was now too late for that. At the beginning of March, a series of strikes broke out in the national capital of Petrograd,[1] and on March 8, International Women's Day, demonstrations of housewives touched off attacks on bakeries and other disorders. These became so serious that by March 10 all factories and industrial establishments in the city were closed down and, on Sunday, March 11, troops had to be called out to disperse the crowds, some of which were filled with people carrying banners and signs reading "Down with the German woman!" a reference to the empress. The troops did their duty, so effectively that some sixty people were killed in one of these affrays, but there were some fateful signs of fraternization between the troops and the demonstrators.

On March 12, it became clear that the situation had deteriorated too seriously to be corrected and that the collapse of the regime could not be prevented. On that day, the local garrisons, led by the Volhynian Guard, arrested their officers and joined the revolutionary cause. Simultaneously, factory strike committees met with representatives of the different socialist factions and, as in 1905 (see p. 393), organized a Soviet of Workers Deputies. By the following morning, the Soviet had been recognized by the mutinous garrisons, had taken over direction of all vital public services, and was in complete control of the city.

---

[1] St. Petersburg was renamed Petrograd during the war.

Revolution in St. Petersburg, July 1917: The police of the Kerensky
government firing on a workers' demonstration. (Sovfoto)

The authority of the Soviet did not extend beyond local affairs, but its creation
jolted the Duma into taking more extensive action. Strictly speaking, this national
legislative body had no legal standing, for the tsar had declared it prorogued
on March 11. But it defied that order and established a provisional committee
"to restore order and deal with institutions and individuals." This group was
presided over by Prince Lvov and included members of the nonsocialist parties
from Cadets to Progressive Nationalists, as well as one Socialist Revolutionary,
Alexander Kerensky, serving in his own right rather than as a representative
of his party. On March 14, the committee constituted itself as a provisional
government and, in the hope of restoring order to the country, sent representatives
to the tsar to urge him to abdicate. On March 15, Nicholas II did so, in favor
of his brother Michael, who declined the honor, leaving the succession open
and making Russia a *de facto* republic. There is no evidence that the loss of
his power caused Nicholas II any sorrow or soul searching. His rule had shown
him to be a strangely insensitive person with a warped perspective; and he was
able to write in his diary on the day after the loss of his throne: "I had a long
and sound sleep. Woke up beyond Dvinsk. Sunshine and frost. . . . I read much
of Julius Caesar." He seemed perfectly happy with the prospect of being able
to devote himself entirely to his family. This, however, he was not to be permitted

to do. After months of detention, first at Tsarskoe Selo and then in Siberia, Nicholas and his family were murdered by the Communists in July 1918.

From March to November   The abdication of the tsar left a confused situation in the country, with political authority divided between the provisional government of Prince Lvov and the soviets that had been organized in Petrograd and other cities. On the face of it, these bodies appeared to be natural enemies, since the provisional government, if it represented anyone, represented the middle and aristocratic classes, who had abandoned the monarchy reluctantly and could be counted on to oppose radical social change, whereas the soviets spoke in the name of the toiling and oppressed masses and the soldiers who had made the revolution and would presumably want to carry it further. That there was no open clash between them in the first months was due largely to the fact that the provisional government was uncertain of the resources at its disposal, while the leaders of the soviets, to the growing disgust of their rank and file, were reluctant to claim power for themselves.

The hesitation of the soviet chiefs to assume political responsibility was due largely to the fact that most of them were socialists who desired to make the revolution that had burst upon them accord with their theoretical preconceptions. Aware that Russia was a backward country, they were inclined to believe that the present revolution was the long-awaited bourgeois revolution designed to free it from the bonds of feudalism, and that logically it should be directed by bourgeois leaders (that is, the provisional government). A proletarian revolution would doubtless come some day, but only after a bourgeois regime had created the conditions for it. This kind of doctrinal rigidity produced what Isaac Deutscher has called "the honeymoon" of the March republic, in which the Mensheviks, the Socialist Revolutionaries, and, for a time, even the Bolsheviks agreed to tolerate the Lvov government. Moreover, they carried toleration to the point of supporting the war, which they had once denounced as a reactionary and imperialist venture, on the theory that it had now become a revolutionary crusade which would achieve a democratic peace without annexations and indemnities. They were also hesitant about the advisability of extensive changes in the ownership of land until the war was over.

The end of the honeymoon and of the relative unity of the socialist groups was not, however, long delayed. It came in April 1917 with Lenin's return to Russia from his exile in Switzerland. The acknowledged leader of the Bolsheviks owed his return to Petrograd to the German government, which supplied the famous "sealed train" to carry him across Europe in the hope that his agitations would disrupt the Russian war effort. This hope was fulfilled, for Lenin used his influence to persuade the socialists to terminate their support of the war. In his so-called April theses, he pointed out that the war was still an imperialistic one and that neither it nor the groups profiting from it deserved any assistance from representatives of the people. It was doubtless true, he argued, that the Russian revolution was a bourgeois-democratic one, but it would soon pass on to its next phase, the socialist phase, a transition to be aided by revolutions in central and western European countries. In Russia the socialist phase would be ushered in by the conquest of full political power by the soviets. This should be the objective of Bolshevik policy, Lenin insisted, and to promote it the Bolsheviks should not only strive to gain a majority in the soviets but do everything in their power to transform the imperialist war into a civil war, encouraging the expropriation of the landlords by the peasantry and the assumption of control of the factories by the workers.

Lenin's demand for a more militant program was greeted with misgivings by some of the other Bolshevik leaders, but they were unable to withstand the force of his personality. His views were accepted as the new party line, and the Bolsheviks began a propaganda campaign designed to discredit the provisional government and weaken its authority. From the beginning the campaign was enormously successful with the city masses, partly because of the efficiency of the party organization and the polemical skill of the Bolshevik leaders, but more perhaps because of the essential attractiveness of the picture of the Russia of the future that they held up before the people. In Lenin's own words:

> All power in the state, from top to bottom, from the remotest village to the last street in the city of Petrograd, must belong to the Soviets of Workers', Soldiers' and Peasants' Deputies. . . . There must be no police, no bureaucrats who have no responsibility to the people, who stand above the people, no standing army, only the people universally armed, united in the Soviets—it is they who must run the state.

The masses could hardly foresee that this idyllic future would not be realized in Lenin's time and would recede almost completely from view in Stalin's. They responded to Bolshevik slogans with enthusiasm, so much that they became impatient for their realization and, in July, attempted a rising in Petrograd which was put down by front-line troops summoned to the capital by the provisional government. That body, under fire because of heavy losses suffered in a new Galician offensive that had been ordered by its war minister Kerensky, took advantage of the abortive July rising to blame its defeat in Galicia upon Bolshevik agitators and to accuse Lenin of being an agent of the German General Staff. Bolshevik headquarters were raided by government police and rightist vigilantes; Trotsky and Kamenev were arrested; and Lenin and Zinoviev had to go into hiding, Lenin fleeing to Finland.

This did not affect the steady growth of Bolshevik support in Petrograd and in Moscow; and, in any case, Kerensky found that he could not afford to do without Bolshevik aid. This flamboyant and eloquent figure, whom the Bolsheviks accused of regarding himself as the Bonaparte of the Russian revolution, had become prime minister and minister of war in a coalition government formed in July, when the government of Prince Lvov resigned. Between Kerensky and the commander-in-chief of the army, General L.G. Kornilov, there was much bad blood and the ambitious general made no secret of his lack of faith in the war minister. In September he went further. News of the loss of Riga to the Germans in that month led to charges and countercharges of treason and subversion, the Kornilov withdrew his support from the government and sent troops to take Petrograd. In self-defense, Kerensky freed his Bolshevik captives and urged them to help in suppressing the mutiny, which they did by mobilizing their Red Guards and by sending agitators who succeeded in persuading Kornilov's forces to abandon him. The general's defeat brought little credit to the provisional government, which now underwent another of those reorganizations that were signs of weakness rather than strength—Kerensky now becoming the chief of a five-man directorate. The Bolsheviks, on the other hand, gained prestige and, more important, won a clear majority in the Petrograd and Moscow soviets and in the provincial soviets as well. That was the beginning of the end for Kerensky.

The Bolshevik Revolution   Lenin was still hiding in Finland, but he was able to judge the significance of the shift of power within the soviets. He reacted by sending a message to the Central Committee of his party in which he argued that the time for armed insurrection had come. On October 23, he slipped into the country to urge this in person, and a protracted debate ensued in which he pointed out that revolution by violence was the logical conclusion of the tactics followed since April. His arguments failed to convince Zinoviev and Kamenev, but all of the other party leaders, including Trotsky, Stalin, and Dzerzhinsky, were won over. Thus, in these weeks when Kerensky was trying to maintain order in the face of renewed strikes in the cities, heightened peasant violence, and mass desertions from the army and was discovering that his new government commanded no more support than the ones that had preceded it, the Bolsheviks were methodically making plans for their coup d'état.

The master-mind of the operation was Leon Trotsky (1879-1940), who now demonstrated for the first time the strategical gifts and the tactical virtuosity that were to serve the Bolshevik cause so well during the civil war. Born Lev Davidovich Bronstein, the son of a well-to-do Jewish farmer in the province of Kherson in the Ukraine, the future war commissar became a convert of Marxism and entered revolutionary politics before he was twenty, was arrested by the tsarist police in 1898, and, after two years imprisonment in Odessa, was exiled to Siberia. He managed to escape and to make his way out of the country with a forged passport in the name of the chief jailer at Odessa, Trotsky, a name he used for the rest of his life. Already known for his propaganda work, he became one of Lenin's associates on the editorial board of *Iskra* in London (see p. 391). During the revolution of 1905, he returned to Russia and was the outstanding figure in the Petrograd Soviet, over which he was presiding at the time of the police raid that resulted in the arrest of its entire executive committee (see p. 391). Exiled once more to Siberia, he again escaped to the West, where he worked with socialist groups in Vienna and Paris and—after his expulsion in 1917 by the French government for spreading antiwar propaganda—in New York, where he edited the newspaper *New World*. After the abdication of Nicholas II, he returned to Russia once more and, for the first time, joined the Bolshevik party, having previously been associated with the Menshevik wing of the old Social Democratic party. His prestige within the party is shown by the fact that when the first Politburo of the Bolshevik Central Committee was appointed—at the same meeting in October 1917 at which it was decided to organize an armed insurrection—he was made a member, along with Lenin,

Zinoviev, Kamenev, G. Y. Sokolnikov, A. S. Bubnov, and the man who was to become his most hated enemy, Joseph Stalin.

It was Trotsky who pointed out that a rising against the provisional government would have a greater chance of success if it were made under the auspices of a soviet and in the guise of a defensive action against a counterrevolutionary plot, than if it were undertaken openly in the name of the Bolshevik party. His advice was followed. Working through the Revolutionary Military Committee of the Petrograd Soviet, the Bolsheviks deliberately challenged Kerensky's right to order troop movements in and around the capital. When, as was expected, the premier reacted with a ringing denunciation of their tactics and an ineffectual attempt to arrest their leader once more, they accused him of treason to the revolution and struck back with deadly efficiency. On the night of November 6–7, the Soviet's Red Guards, supported by regular army units, seized every key point in the city and surrounded the Winter Palace, the seat of the provisional government. In a matter of hours, the operation was complete, and the city woke to find the Bolsheviks in control. The coup had been timed to coincide with the opening of the Second All-Russian Congress of the Soviets,[2] and, on the evening of November 7, when that body convened, Lenin appeared before it as the effective ruler of the capital.

The Bolsheviks had a majority in the Congress when it assembled, and it became overwhelming when the Mensheviks and the right wing of the Socialist Revolutionary party walked out in protest against the insurrection. Those who remained approved the formation of an all-Bolshevik government—the Council of People's Commissars, with Lenin as its head, Trotsky as commissar for foreign affairs, and Stalin as commissar for nationalities—and elected a new Central Executive Committee composed of 62 Bolsheviks and 29 left-wing Socialist Revolutionaries. They also passed two decrees laid before them by Lenin: one proposing the immediate conclusion of a peace without annexations and indemnities, the other abolishing private property in land and transferring all private and church lands to land committees and soviets of peasant deputies for later distribution.

Meanwhile, Kerensky had fled to the provinces, where he sought to rally the army against the insurgents in Petrograd. His efforts failed miserably, and he was forced to seek refuge abroad. There was, indeed, little resistance at this stage to the Bolsheviks expanding the authority they had taken in Petrograd. Moscow fell to them after a week's fighting, and, within a month, most of the cities of Russia were in their hands. Their consolidation of power was facilitated by the apparent failure of the other parties to comprehend what the consequence of a Bolshevik dictatorship would be. The parties that might have challenged the Bolsheviks effectively, the Mensheviks and the Socialist Revolutionaries, showed a disinclination to think in terms of power that played directly into the hands of Lenin and his followers. Thus, when elections were held in late November for that Constituent Assembly which the Russian Left had made the object of their hopes for generations and which was expected to make constitutional arrangements for the new Russia, Lenin interfered openly in the electoral

[2] A First All-Russian Congress had met in June.

procedures, arrested some of those who were elected, and outlawed the Cadet party. His own party won only twenty-five percent of the seats in the Assembly, which accounts for the fact that, when that body finally met in January, Lenin had it dissolved by Bolshevik guards after one session. No one was in a position to protest effectively against these measures, because the Bolsheviks by this time had a monopoly of force in the country.

First Decrees and the Peace of Brest Litovsk   The dissolution of the Constituent Assembly was part of a deliberate Bolshevik policy of smashing all institutions that might serve as a rallying point for opposition. The members of the old provisional government were deported; the municipal councils of Petrograd and Moscow, which were anti-Bolshevik, were dissolved; in December, the Imperial Senate was abolished; and, a month later, a Bolshevik decree did away with the zemstvos (see p. 390), which, in the last years before the war, had been centers of liberalism and agitation for moderate constitutional reform. Meanwhile, a series of decrees ordering the election of all officers in the army, changing the rank system, and speeding up demobilization removed the threat of military opposition by causing the army literally to disappear. In February 1918, complete separation of church and state was announced and although no attempt was made to abolish the Russian Orthodox Church, its power and authority were seriously weakened by expropriation of its lands, repeal of the old marriage and divorce laws, and withholding official recognition from any but civil marriage. A potential threat to complete Bolshevik control of the peasantry was removed in December 1917 when clever tactics by Lenin forced a split in a Congress of Peasant Deputies meeting in Petrograd and created an opportunity for effecting a fusion of the Peasant Soviets with the Workers and Soldiers Soviets, thus breaking the Socialist Revolutionary party's power in its last remaining stronghold.

Meanwhile, the sharing out of the great landed estates, which proved to be the measure that generated most popular support for the new regime, was carried out and other steps were taken to transform the national economy. In November, workers' committees were authorized to supervise factory production, and the eight-hour day became universal. In subsequent months, the government created a Supreme Economic Council, nationalized the banks, and, in a step productive of many future complications, canceled the debts of the tsarist regime.

While all this was going on, the national domain was being seriously diminished. Poland's independence had been recognized by the provisional government before its demise; Finland demanded independence immediately after the Bolshevik take-over, and, in a unique example of voluntary surrender of territory by the Soviet regime, this was recognized, in the name of national self-determination, by the commissar of nationalities, Stalin. Between December 1917 and the following February, Lithuania, Latvia, and Estonia all declared their independence and, although the Bolsheviks resisted, they had their way in the end.

The implementation of Lenin's Decree of Peace led to additional losses. Despite the daring improvisations and the skillful tactics of delay employed by Trotsky in the negotiations with the Germans at Brest Litovsk, the German General Hoffmann insisted on sizable annexations and, when these were refused, ordered a new advance which the Bolsheviks were powerless to oppose. Some members of the party's Central Committee believed that a revolutionary war should be resorted to, but Lenin insisted that the German terms be met and threatened to resign if they were not. He was supported by the narrowest of margins, and the Bolshevik regime accepted the peace of Brest Litovsk in March 1918.

By its terms, Russia was forced to accept the loss of Poland, the Baltic states, Finland, large areas of Byelorussia and the Ukraine, and part of Transcaucasia: a total of 1,300,000 square miles and 62 million people, not counting the loss of Bessarabia to Rumania, which was stipulated in Germany's Treaty of Bucharest with that country. The losses were so great in extent that Petrograd was considered too close to the new border to be safe, and the center of the government was shifted to Moscow.

The Civil War   The conclusion of the peace of Brest Litovsk was considered an act of betrayal by the Allied governments, who were still locked in conflict with Germany. It threatened to release an untold number of German troops for action against the weary Allied armies on the western front and to enable the Germans also to lay their hands on the vast quantities of stores and ammunition that the Allies had been sending to Russia as late as October 1917.

To prevent the latter of these possibilities from being realized, the British landed naval units at Murmansk in March 1918; and other landings and occupations followed, made from more obscure motives. The Japanese sent strong forces into Vladivostok, which were followed by British and American units, presumably sent to watch over them. The British occupied Archangel, Batum, and the Baku oil fields. A mixed force under French command took Odessa, and a comprehensive blockade of Russian waters was established.

The broader significance of these military moves was that they gave encouragement and material assistance to anti-Bolshevik and counterrevolutionary movements. Local Allied commands did not hesitate to recognize and supply White governments that grew up in the districts under their authority, and before long there were a score of these dotted around the boundaries of Bolshevik authority from Siberia to the Ukraine. Along the southern borders of the country between the Black and Caspian seas, the leaders of the Don and Kuban Cossacks were opposed to the regime. This area was the base for a White Army commanded first by General Kornilov, who had managed to escape from the detention into which he had been placed after the failure of his coup, and later, after Kornilov's death in fighting around Ekaterinodar, by General Anton Denikin. In south central Russia, from Samara on the Volga to Omsk and Tomsk in central Siberia, a second anti-Bolshevik front was created by the revolt of the Czech Legion. This force, which had fought beside the Russians during the last year of the war, was left without occupation by Brest Litovsk. It obtained permission from the Bolshevik government to leave the country by way of the trans-Siberian railway, with the intention of going around the world and reappearing on the western front. Difficulties with Bolshevik officials en route led it to break with the government and to seize a chain of strong points along the railroad.

The Czech success not only heartened Denikin in the south and encouraged the Allies to increase the scope of their intervention but soon led to a fusion

Leon Trotsky (from *Deiateli Oktiabr'skoi revoliutaii,* Moskva, 1922). (Hoover Institution)

of all anti-Bolshevik groups in Siberia. This was effected in September 1918 at Ufa, where a national government called the Directory was set up with headquarters at Omsk and with the mission of directing the anti-Bolshevik crusade. The effective functioning of this government was hampered by difficulties between the partners, the most troublesome of whom were the Socialist Revolutionaries, whose right wing, it will be remembered, had broken with Bolshevism after Lenin's armed insurrection and whose left wing had been expelled after it reverted to terrorism in protest against the treaty of Brest Litovsk. The trouble with the Socialist Revolutionaries in Siberia was that they hated the bourgeois groups with which they had to cooperate almost as much as they did Lenin's party. In November the conservatives at Omsk tired of their tactics, arrested their leaders, and handed supreme power over to the former commander of the Black Sea Fleet, Admiral Alexander Kolchak.

At the beginning of 1919, the tsarist general E.K. Miller took over power at Archangel from a local Socialist Revolutionary group and placed himself and his forces at Kolchak's disposal, and at the same time a Northwestern White Army was assembled in Estonia by General Yudenich and supplemented by German forces who had been engaged in the Baltic lands and who preferred adventure to the uncertainties of civilian life in a now defeated Germany. Thus, the Bolsheviks were confronted with four sizeable armies of great initial strength.

If the Whites had had the forces in 1918 that they had a year later, they might have destroyed Bolshevism. Their initial weakness gave Leon Trotsky the opportunity to do his greatest service for the state that finally rejected and killed him. In March 1918, Trotsky became war commissar and began to build up the force that became the Red Army. In April 1918, compulsory military service was decreed for all workers and peasants. Rejecting the early revolutionary notion that an army can be run by political committees, Trotsky returned to a more traditional system of discipline and openly relied upon the only trained officers he could find, former commanders in the imperial army. During the civil war,

almost fifty thousand former tsarist officers served with the Red Army, some
rising to the highest ranks, like the young Michael N. Tukhachevsky, who in
1917 escaped from a German prison camp (where one of his fellow prisoners
was a French captain named Charles de Gaulle), made his way home and volunteered for the Red Army, and, by 1920, was commander-in-chief of all Red forces
on the western front.

To watch over the officers and to carry out essential propaganda tasks, Trotsky
appointed political commissars, who were not, however, supposed to interfere
with command decisions. Once the army had taken to the field, desertion and
failure were punished with death; success, with new opportunities to serve the
state. The war commissar himself appeared on every front, hectoring, bullying,
inspiring men who only months before thought they had thrown away their
rifles for the last time. But they fought and fought well, and with their successes
came a pride and *élan* that the Whites could not match.

There were moments in 1919 when the fate of Bolshevism trembled in the
balance. The White commanders slowly tightened their ring around the Bolshevik
center. In October Denikin was in Kiev and Orel, and Yudenich was on the
outskirts of Petrograd. But in the end both those drives failed; and, even before
they had reached their point of greatest promise, Kolchak had been checked
at Glazov by a Red Army under Michael Frunze (whose name today graces the

Lenin during the Civil War (from *Lenin.* Compiled from material in the
Central Lenin Museum, Moskva, 1939). (Hoover Institution)

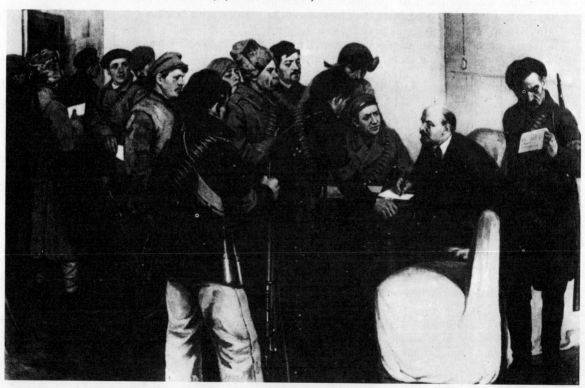

Soviet War Academy) and had been slowly pushed back into Siberia. The Whites suffered from deficiencies that they were incapable of correcting. Their military leadership was, on the whole, of inferior quality. Not until Baron P.N. Wrangel succeeded Denikin in April 1920 did they find a commander of truly outstanding ability, and then it was too late. They received inadequate aid from the Allied governments, who never fully committed themselves to the war against Bolshevism. The various White forces generally failed to coordinate their drives and thus frittered away great opportunities and were defeated piecemeal. Their rule of the areas they controlled was weakened by party squabbling; and they failed to impress local populations with the sincerity of their democratic professions. Finally, the fact that they gave protection to former landlords seeking to regain their estates deprived them of the support of a peasantry that was determined not to allow the old agrarian system to return.

For all of these reasons, the Whites were beaten. Yudenich was driven back into Estonia in November 1919, where his army dissolved; Kolchak was captured by the Reds at Irkutsk in January and shot; Miller was overthrown at Archangel and made his way abroad, where he played a part in refugee politics until September 1937 when he was kidnapped by Soviet agents in Paris and never seen again; Denikin was isolated at Novorossiisk in March and evacuated by the British. Wrangel, after playing a part in the Polish war described below,

The Defense of Petrograd, a Soviet poster. (Hoover Institution)

fell back to the Crimea, where he held out until the end of 1920, when his force was evacuated by the Allies to Gallipoli and a year later to Yugoslavia and Bulgaria. By that time, Russian soil was free of Allied and White troops, with the exception of part of the Maritime Province, which was not evacuated by the Japanese until October 1922.

The Polish War   In the first months of 1920, when the White threat in the north and east was abating, the Bolshevik regime was threatened by a vigorous offensive on the part of the Poles, in conjunction with the Ukrainian nationalists led by Petlyura and the White Army of Wrangel, advancing from the south. The Poles had great initial successes and took Kiev and other centers, but they were soon in difficulties. Their aggression aroused a wave of genuine patriotic enthusiasm in Russia, which gave weight to a powerful counterthrust by the

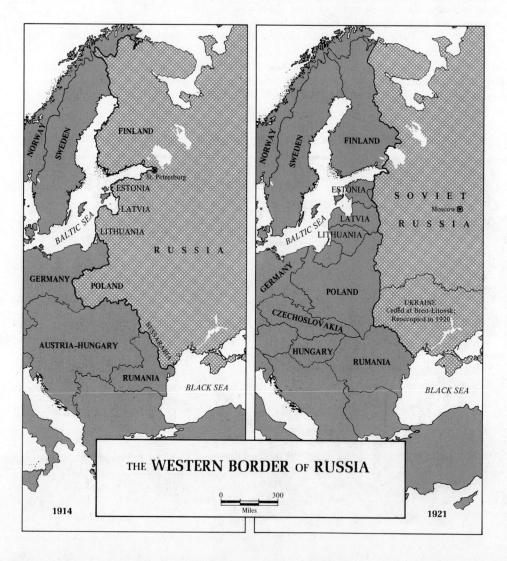

THE **WESTERN BORDER** OF **RUSSIA**

0   300
Miles

1914

1921

Red Army. In June Kiev was retaken, and the Poles began a general retirement. In July Soviet forces under Tukhachevsky advanced to the very walls of Warsaw, and communism seemed about to burst into Europe. But at this point Colonel Aleksander Yegorov, commanding the forces on Tukhachevsky's left flank, decided—perhaps on the advice of his political commissar, Stalin—to march on L'vov instead of backing the main drive against Warsaw. Before the gap created by this decision could be closed, the Polish commander, Joseph Pilsudski, acting in consultation with the French general, Maxime Weygand, struck at the exposed flank and the Red Army broke and retreated.

Both armies were wearied and, when the Bolsheviks sued for peace, negotiations were begun and concluded at Riga in October 1920. The Poles benefited from the mistake in front of Warsaw. They received a boundary well to the east of the ethnic frontier, the so-called Curzon Line laid down by the Allied Supreme Council in December 1919, and with it acquired a Russian minority of four million persons.

THE TOTALITARIAN STATE

The Organs of Power   The Soviet Union, or Union of Soviet Socialist Republics, was formally established in January 1924 when the constitution of July 1918 was replaced by a new one that adopted this name rather than the previous title of the Russian Socialist Federated Soviet Republic (RSFSR). According to the constitution of 1924, the USSR comprised seven republics: the RSFSR, the Ukraine, White Russia, the Transcaucasian Federation (Azerbaijan, Armenia, and Georgia), Turkmen, Uzbek, and Tajik. By the constitution of 1936, the number was increased to eleven, Azerbaijan, Armenia, and Georgia being given equal standing the the others, and Kazak and Kirghiz being added.

Within this vast and variegated realm, power was wielded by four main agencies: the soviets, the party, the secret police, and the military establishment. In all three of the constitutions, pride of place was given to the soviets, as if Lenin's demand that all power be vested in the soviets had become a reality, which was not the case. Even so, the soviets remained of undeniable importance, for they were the link between the new rulers of Russia and the masses; and they were, as Lenin said, "the vanguard and the school of the whole gigantic mass of the oppressed classes which till now have stood outside all political life and all history."

The soviet system was a great pyramidal structure with its base resting on the villages, each of which had a soviet of its own, which elected delegates to the territorial soviets, which in turn sent representatives to provincial soviets, which in their turn elected the soviets of the republics, which finally elected the All-Union Congress of Soviets. All citizens over eighteen were entitled to participate in elections on the local level, provided they did not belong to one of many categories specifically excluded from political life: criminals, mental defectives, priests, members of forbidden parties, officials of the old regime, and whatever other groups were proscribed at any given moment.

The All-Union Congress was composed of about two thousand members, too unwieldy for any real business. In reality, it met only at two-year intervals to hear progress reports from the real rulers of the country and to elect a Central Executive, the name of which was changed in 1936 to the Supreme Soviet and was described then as the highest organ of state power. The Supreme Soviet was composed of a Council of the Union, representing the nation as a whole, and a Council of the Nationalities, representing the constituent republics. Nine members elected by each of these bodies and nine by the two of them acting jointly constituted the Presidium of the Supreme Soviet, whose functions, however, were largely ceremonial. The actual business of the state was in the hands of a ministry called the Council of People's Commissars, which was appointed by the Central Executive Committee and presided over by Lenin from 1917 until 1924.

This system was both logical and impressive, but it obscured the real source of power in the country, which lay in a body not mentioned in the constitutions of 1918 and 1924.[3] This was the party, which in the writings of Marx and Engels had been assigned the role of directing the revolution and ruling during the presumably transitional dictatorship of the proletariat and which had been described repeatedly by Lenin as a body of trained and dedicated professional revolutionaries. The party, which in 1918 took the name the Russian Communist party (Bolsheviks), was obviously designed as an elite, and one without competition, since all other parties were abolished. In 1921 it had 730,000 members, of whom a third were purged before the end of the year; in 1929 it had more than one million members; and in 1939, it had a million and a half. Even if one added to this total the members of the youth groups, who numbered up to five million at the latter date, this was a small percentage of the national population. It was kept deliberately so.[4]

The structure of the party was similar to that of the soviets. There were local cells, urban, provincial, and republican conferences, and, above these, a 3000-member Party Congress that met at Moscow at stated intervals. Each Congress elected a small Central Committee of the party which remained in permanent session and was composed of a Secretariat, an Organization Bureau, and a Political Bureau or Politburo. From the very beginning of the revolution, this last body had been the actual governing body of the country and during the civil war it had been composed of five men: Lenin, Trotsky, Stalin, Kamenev, and Bukharin, to whom Zinoviev and Tomsky were later added. The agenda for the Politburo was prepared by the Secretariat of the Central Committee, whose general secretary after 1922, Stalin, made it an increasingly important post. Without going into details about the complicated shifting relation between the soviet and party structures, it can be said simply that power decisions made in the higher organs of the latter were automatically carried out by the supreme agencies of the former.

Exercising increasing power in the state after the first years, although doing so under the direction of the party chiefs, was the secret police, which had

---

[3] It was formally recognized in the constitution of 1936.

[4] After Stalin's death in 1953 there was a great expansion of party membership and, as of January 1965, there were 10,811,433 members of the party plus 946,726 candidate members. At that time, one twentieth of the population were party members.

Portrait from *Lenin,* Moskva, 1939.
(Hoover Institution)

its origin in the Extraordinary Commission for Struggle with Counterrevolution
and Sabotage (Cheka). This body was established in December 1917 and is
believed to have liquidated as many as fifty thousand persons between that
date and the end of 1922, most of them in the terror that followed the assassination
of its chief Uritsky and the serious wounding of Lenin by Socialist Revolutionary
terrorists in August 1918. Westerners who were anxious to be open-minded about
the Soviet experiment found a variety of excuses for this sort of thing. The
Scottish poet Hugh MacDiarmid wrote, in his "First Hymn to Lenin":

> As necessary, and insignificant, as death
> Wi' a' its agonies in the cosmos still
> The Cheka's horrors are in their degree;
> And'll end suner! What maitters 't
>   wha we kill
> To lessen that foulest murder that deprives
>   Maist men o' real lives?

This proved a feckless rationalization. The Cheka was abolished in February
1922 but was replaced by an even more formidable body, the GPU (later the
OGPU) or Unified State Political Administration. Ostensibly this organization
was under the direction of the Ministry of the Interior, but its leader Dzerzhinsky
and his successor Menzhinsky were always close to Stalin and followed his
orders. Like the Cheka, the OGPU was used to track down counter-revolution-
aries, a term that proved in time to be very elastic; and its duties also included
the apprehension of "exploiters" and "wreckers" and the operation of various
concentration camps, including those for nonpolitical prisoners. In the trials of
the Stalin period, it played a key role, especially after 1936, when (now under
the name Peoples Commissariat of Internal Affairs, or NKVD) it was directed
by N.I. Yezhov, for a time the most feared man in Russia.

Finally, there was the army. In the first years after the civil war, it was able
to maintain a large degree of independence from the party organization. This

was gradually whittled away by the elimination of most of the ex-tsarist officers, by careful indoctrination of new officers and recruits, and, finally, as will be noted below, by the great purge of the mid-1930s. At the cost of some military efficiency, the party assured itself of the political reliability of the army; and this, and the control of its secret police, made it reasonably safe against the internal explosion that refugees and foreign anti-Communists kept hoping would occur in Russia.

From Lenin to Stalin   The first leader of the Russian revolution suffered a stroke in May 1922 and a second one in November of the same year. After that it was clear that the country was going to be caught up in a succession struggle of heroic proportions between his two strongest associates, Trotsky and Stalin. Lenin himself seems to have been disturbed by the prospect of such a conflict and even to have feared what he must have guessed would be its outcome. In a postscript to his political testament, written in January 1923, he expressed strong criticism of Stalin and proposed that the party should remove him from his post of general secretary and appoint a man "more patient, more loyal, more polite and more attentive to comrades, less capricious, etc." Lenin would probably have sought to effect this change by arguing for it personally at the Party Congress of 1923, but he suffered his third stroke before it met and was inactive politically from then until his death in January 1924.

The target of Lenin's suspicion had been born Joseph Vissarionovich Dzugash-vily, near Tiflis in Georgia in 1879. His parents had hoped that he might become a priest, but he was forced to leave the Tiflis Seminary either because of health (as his mother later told newspaper reporters) or because he propagated Marxist doctrines among his fellow students (as he himself insisted was true). He became involved in socialist politics, adhering to the Bolshevik wing after the party division in 1903, and acquiring a reputation for resolution and energy during the revolution of 1905, when he was an agitator in the Baku oil fields. He preferred underground work in Russia to prolonged exile abroad, and carried on a duel with the tsarist police that was marked by frequent arrests and escapes until 1913, when he was exiled to Siberia. He returned in 1917 to play a prominent role in the revolution and the civil war. Scorned by Trotsky as "the outstanding mediocrity of the party," Stalin (as he had called himself since the days in Baku) possessed gifts of bureaucratic finesse and political manipulation that enabled him to defeat and exile his more brilliant rival and to secure a position in which he could indulge what was clearly his strongest motivation, a lust for untram-meled personal power.

Once Lenin's strong hand had been weakened by illness, his authority came to be wielded by a triumvirate within the Politburo, composed of Zinoviev, Kamenev, and Stalin, all of whom were enemies of Trotsky. Their tactics were to weaken the war commissar's position by transferring his closest associates to jobs remote from the center of power while simultaneously giving encour-agement and influence to the many enemies whom he had made in the party organization during his meteoric career. Since brilliance is rarely popular, they succeeded, and, by the time of Lenin's death in 1924, Trotsky's power was in decline, and he was being criticized for "factionalism," a dangerous charge in

Stalin during the Civil War. (From Lenin, Moskva, 1939). (Hoover Institution)

a party already tending toward monolithic unity. In January 1925, his enemies persuaded the Central Committee to dismiss him from the War Commissariat, and, although some of his supporters expected him to resist by calling on the Red Army to support him, he refused to do so. He was too loyal to the party to attempt a coup against it, and his concurrence in his dismissal marked the end of his power. Within two years he had been expelled from the Central Committee and, as a result of street demonstrations in his favor in November 1927 (he was always more popular with the masses than with the party hierarchs), from the party. In 1929 the Politburo authorized his expulsion from the Soviet Union, and the creator of the Red Army was forced to begin that troubled odyssey from one foreign refuge to another which ended in 1940 when he was assassinated in Mexico.

Even before Trotsky's fall was complete, Stalin had freed himself from the embrace of the other original triumvirs by using his authority as general secretary to build up his power at their expense, by using divisive tactics in the Politburo, and by accusing his former partners of deviation from Lenin's views (a useful argument, since Stalin, alone among the Old Bolsheviks, had never opposed Lenin on a serious issue and could claim to be the best judge of orthodoxy). Zinoviev and Kamenev were both expelled from the party in 1927 for association with Trotsky's ideas and, although they were later readmitted, their power was now spent. Similar tactics proved effective against the other Old Bolsheviks in the

Politburo—Bukharin, Tomsky, and Rykov. By the end of 1930 they had been forced out of the Politburo, which thus came to be composed exclusively of Stalin's followers, as did the party organizations of the large cities and organs of central government like the Council of People's Commissars, whose chairman, another loyal Stalin man, Vyacheslav Molotov, had once answered one of Trotsky's gibes by saying, "We can't all be geniuses, Comrade Trotsky, but we'll see who lasts longer."

Economic Regimentation   The ascendancy of Stalin and Russia's progress toward totalitarianism were both advanced by events in the economic sphere. Whatever ideas Lenin and his associates had had about socializing the economic system of Russia had been rendered unrealistic by the chaos caused by the civil war and by the great drought in the grain areas of the Volga and the Don during 1920. By 1921 industry was at a standstill and a fifth of Russia's population was in the grip of famine and cholera. Lenin was hard-headed enough to see that production was more important than theory, no matter how much departure from Marxist orthodoxy might aggrieve the party ideologues. Over the opposition of people like Trotsky, Lenin carried a series of resolutions through the Party Congress in 1921 which laid the foundations for what came to be called the New Economic Policy (NEP). In effect, NEP allowed what Lenin admitted was "a partial return to capitalism" by permitting the revival of private industry and authorizing the peasants to produce and trade for profit. At the cost of tolerating the rise of a new bourgeoisie, the Soviet regime was able to repair the ravages of its first years, and by 1927 industry, with some exceptions, was producing at 1913 levels and agriculture was prosperous once more.

The old dream of effecting the utter destruction of capitalism by transforming the economy remained, and Stalin made it his own with the promulgation of the first Five-Year Plan in 1928. It is likely, nevertheless, that he was less interested in the economic aspects of this plan, which put an abrupt end to NEP and placed the accent once more on orthodox socialist economics, than he was in the political advantages that he suspected would accrue from it. For the successful imposition of a socialized economy upon Russia promised to make the state machine, of which he was now virtually the master, supreme by weakening all the other loyalties that diverted the minds of the masses—loyalty to the soil, to the trade union, to the family—and by giving the state an argument for liquidating those who persisted in holding older values.

The first Five-Year Plan went into effect in October 1928. It set norms for production in all basic industries, calling for increases that ranged from 200 to 400 percent. In agriculture, an increase of 150 percent was demanded, to be accomplished by a policy of collectivizing the peasant farms. Stalin expected some popular resistance to the new policy and the sacrifices it demanded of the workers and peasants, and he was prepared to meet it. Resistance to collectivization by the peasantry was put down with complete ruthlessness, OGPU agents and army units surrounding villages, shooting indiscriminately into crowds, burning down houses, transporting trainloads of men, women, and children to Siberia. Since the troops called upon to do these tasks were often drawn from the peasantry themselves, serious morale problems arose in army units; but no relaxation of the terror was allowed. The desperate peasants fought back by burning their crops and destroying their livestock, with the result that by 1933 there were less than half as many houses in the Soviet Union as there had been in 1928, and it was not until 1937 that over-all production regained the 1928 level. The number of people who died in the collectivization struggle and the famine of 1932–1933 to which it contributed exceeded five million. As against these losses, however, Stalin had succeeded in breaking the will of the peasantry and making it subservient to the totalitarian state.

In the industrial sector also, events encouraged the drift toward totalitarianism. In order to dramatize the economic drive and stimulate effort to meet the assigned goals, a series of sensational state trials were held of people charged with being wreckers, saboteurs, foreign agents, and the like. In these trials, the effects of what has come to be called brainwashing were first revealed to the world, for a high percentage of those tried confessed to an astonishing variety of unlikely crimes and often implicated other people in their confessed conspiracies against the state. The trials created an atmosphere of fear and suspicion in the factories and discouraged the expression of any opinions except those that reflected loyalty and devotion to the regime.

The objectives of the first Five-Year Plan were not met, partly because the industrial goals had been set too high. The state, out of sheer necessity, had to accept a version of agricultural collectivization less extreme than that originally envisaged, and to embark on another Five-Year Plan to stimulate sectors of the economy that had not responded to the first. Even so, the gains were not negligible. It was obvious that Russia was on its way to becoming an industrial power of the first magnitude; and foreign observers, imperfectly informed of the human cost, were impressed by what could be accomplished in a relatively backward country by state planning on a massive scale. Indirectly, therefore, the Five-Year Plans made the capitalist countries, who were about to encounter serious economic difficulties of their own, more amenable to the idea of a planned economy than they had previously been.

The most important result of the Russian "Second Revolution," however, was internal, and it was not economic. It tightened the state's grip on the peoples of the Soviet Union and diminished even further their liberties.

The Great Purges   Stalin's personal autocracy was consolidated and given an almost Oriental character in the mid-1930s, when the instruments of terror that had been used against the masses were turned against the Communist elite itself. The violence and waste of the years 1928–1933 had caused growing opposition in the upper hierarchy of the party and in certain of the army commands (Marshal Blücher, for example, had successfully blocked collectivization in eastern Siberia by warning bluntly that otherwise the area could not be held against possible attacks from the Japanese in Manchuria); and it appears that at least one serious conspiracy was being hatched with the objective of forcing Stalin's downfall. Other evidence indicates that Stalin, while not actually aware of any plots against himself, had decided that the time had come to make a palace revolution impossible by inventing conspiracies and culprits and liquidating them *pour encourager les autres;* and it has been further suggested that he had a shrewd suspicion that totalitarian regimes can only be made to work by terror and fear and that it was up to him to supply these things.

We shall probably never know the whole truth about the party purges of 1936–1938, or even about the event that touched them off: the assassination in December 1934 of Sergei Kirov, Zinoviev's successor as head of the party in Leningrad and, in the opinion of some, Stalin's chosen heir. It is pretty well agreed that Stalin ordered the death of Kirov. It was blamed, however, on a gigantic conspiracy planned by Zinoviev and Trotsky, and arrests of supporters of these former titans began immediately and continued through 1935. These were followed by the arrest and trial of Zinoviev and Kamenev, of lesser lights like Karl Radek, of the most respected generals of the Red Army, among them the hero of the civil war, Tukhachevsky, and his colleagues Marshal Yegorov and the once redoubtable Marshal Blücher, and, finally, of Bukharin and Pyatakov, who had been described by Lenin as "the shrewdest heads among the younger generation," Rakovsky and Rykov, and the former police chief Yagoda. Thousands died without the benefit of trial, including the man who carried out most of the arrests and executions of the first two years of the purges, Yagoda's successor, Yezhov.

As the remorseless process went on, the average party member became almost indifferent, accepting arrest and execution as inevitable. Morbid jokes began to circulate, like the one Wolfgang Leonhard repeats in his memoirs: One morning at 4 A.M., the time at which arrests were usually made, there was a thunderous knock on the door of a house occupied by five families. They arose ashen-faced and trembling but did not dare open the door, until the menacing sound was repeated and one of their number forced himself to answer it. They heard him whispering with a man standing outside. Then he returned to his terrified housemates and said with a relieved smile: "Nothing to worry about, comrades! The house is on fire, that's all!"

This kind of rueful resignation is understandable when one considers the incredible losses suffered by the Soviet Union's ruling elite. According to recent tabulations, as many as 800,000 party members were killed, including six of the thirteen members of the Politburo, ninety-eight of 138 members of the Central Committee, fourteen of the eighteen members of the Council of People's Commissars, and nearly all the premiers and peoples' commissars of the federated republics. In the army, the dead included three of the five marshals, fourteen of the sixteen army commanders, sixty of the sixty-seven corps commanders, 136 of the 199 divisional commanders, and 221 of 397 brigade commanders. About half of the officer corps, some 35,000 in all, were shot or imprisoned.

This was social prophylaxis on a grand scale, something unheard of in the age that preceded this, boldly undertaken despite the weaknesses it imposed on the state in a time of growing foreign peril, in order to eliminate the possibility of an alternate government. With the purges Stalin's totalitarianism was complete.

SOVIET FOREIGN POLICY, 1917–1933

World Revolution as an Objective   The Bolshevik regime began its life by repudiating the traditional framework and standards of international relations

and pledging itself to the overthrow of capitalist regimes everywhere. During
the war, Lenin had said that when his party came to power they would

> systematically start to incite rebellion among all the peoples now oppressed
> . . . all the colonies and dependent countries of Asia (India, China, Persia,
> and others). And we would also raise the socialist proletariat of Europe
> in rebellion against their governments. . . . There is no doubt that the victory
> of the proletariat in Russia would create very favorable conditions for
> the development of the revolution in Asia and Europe.

Once he had assumed power, Lenin put that master strategy into effect, beginning with the Proclamation of Peace, the first formal act of his regime, which
called on the masses everywhere to rise against their rulers. Throughout the
world of 1918, the Bolsheviks did what they could to exploit the unrest caused
by the war in eastern Europe, in the Middle East, and elsewhere; and, in March
1919, with the formation of the Comintern, they institutionalized revolutionary
agitation as a permanent feature of Soviet foreign relations. The Comintern, or
Third (Communist) International, was an agency for world revolution. It was
designed to be a central directorate for Communist parties in other countries;
and its executive, which was headed by Zinoviev and dominated by other
Bolshevik leaders, had the mission of instructing the leadership of those parties
in the tactics of subversion, infiltration, and propaganda best designed to promote
revolution in their countries. In Bolshevik eyes, the Comintern, rather than
traditional diplomacy, would be the chief instrument for carrying out the Soviet
Union's foreign objectives. They placed so much importance on the idea of world
revolution that they saw no reason for any other foreign policy and no use for
any diplomatic machinery other than that provided by the Comintern's network
of agents.

The Bolshevik hope that Europe would succumb to revolution, once the process
had started in Russia, was not fulfilled. There were revolutions in 1918 in both
Germany and Austria, but they merely brought to power moderate Socialist
parties with pronounced bourgeois predispositions. In 1918 and early 1919, Soviets
were established in Bavaria and Hungary but failed to receive mass support
and were quickly suppressed. As for Britain and France, their governments not
only refused to collapse but took the offensive against Bolshevism by intervening
in the civil war and helping check the Red Army's drive on Warsaw. The capitalist
states were, in short, showing surprising resources of strength, while the Bolshevik
regime, on the other hand, was weakened by the rigors of the civil war and
subsequent economic troubles. In the circumstances, while not entirely abandoning their belief in the efficacy of the Comintern, the Bolshevik leaders acknowledged that new tools of foreign policy would have to be devised to deal with
the capitalist states and prevent them from new assaults against Russia. This
meant a reluctant return to traditional diplomacy.

The Uses of Diplomacy   The man who directed this new effort was Georgei
Chicherin, a former archivist in the tsarist Foreign Office, who had been a
Menshevik before the war, had joined the Bolshevik party in 1917, and, in the
following year, when Trotsky moved from the Commissariat of Foreign Affairs

"Chicherin at Genoa." Soviet foreign minister Chicherin being greeted at Genoa by King Victor Emmanuel III. (From the French satirical magazine *Le Rire*, 1922.)

to the War Commissariat, had succeeded him. By temperament a realist, Chicherin was conscious of his country's weakness and felt that the best protection against foreign exploitation was a truce with the capitalist world. If the countries of the West, in particular, could be persuaded to recognize the new Russia as a member of the family of nations and to conclude political and economic agreements with it, the risk of a new attack would be minimized.

The fear of new pressure from the capitalist world was not imaginary. In the years 1920–1922, there was a good deal of discussion in the West of the possibility of arranging an international consortium to exploit Russia's known economic distress in such a way as to compel the Communist regime to repay the tsarist debts that had been repudiated, restore confiscated European property, and even submit to a series of capitulations that would permit European traders to do their business in Russia under the protection of extraterritorial rights. This possibility was eagerly canvassed on the eve of the European economic conference that Lloyd George convened at Genoa in 1922.

It was at Genoa that Chicherin showed what diplomacy could accomplish for his country. Invited to bring a delegation to the Italian city, he made the most of the opportunity to ingratiate himself with the representatives of the smaller powers in the assembly and to exploit their jealousy of the greater ones. The consortium idea he sidetracked by insisting that his country was ready to make arrangements with foreign traders on an individual basis and by portraying the advantages of trade under Russia's New Economic Policy in such a way as to stimulate the competitive instincts of the other powers. He raised issues that were not on the agenda—the need for universal disarmament and for a planned global redistribution of natural resources—which appealed to liberal groups in all countries but which merely served, at the moment, to confuse the Genoa discussions. And, finally, by his sensational coup at Rapallo, where he persuaded the German foreign minister to conclude a treaty forging political and economic ties between Germany and his own country (see p. 508), he caused the Genoa conference to break up in confusion and was able to return home with credit for the only triumph registered there: the termination of his country's diplomatic isolation.

In the years that followed, Chicherin exploited his gains. In the Lausanne conference of 1923 (see p. 500), he won the sympathy of several small nations by championing the cause of Turkey and simultaneously protected Russian interests in the Near East. In the same year, he undermined a recently concluded treaty that promised to subordinate Persia to a large degree of British control and helped alleviate the distress caused in Germany by the Ruhr invasion (see pp. 508 and 564) by sending grain into that country. These evidences of Russian vigor and friendship for weak nations appealed to important groups within many European states and had the result of further relieving the Soviet Union of its former isolation. In 1924, when left governments came to power in both Britain and France, they sought normal relations with the Soviet Union. Indeed, 1924 came to be known as the year of recognitions, because, during its course, the Soviet Union was formally recognized by Great Britain, France, Italy, Norway, Sweden, Denmark, Austria, Hungary, Greece, Mexico, and the Chinese Republic, with Japan joining the impressive list in January 1925.

New Setbacks, 1924–1927   These gains were not permanent. The old Bolsheviks still retained their preference for revolutionary methods and their contempt for traditional diplomacy; and even in the period of Chicherin's greatest success, his delicate maneuvers were handicapped by startling reversions to the early policy. In 1923, for example, the Comintern inspired unsuccessful revolutions in Bulgaria and Germany, which forced the foreign minister to exhaust all of his inventive powers in devising proof that the Soviet Union had not been involved in them. And, after 1924, during the confused power struggle that followed Lenin's death, the coordination between various branches of the Soviet government broke down, and the Comintern became as active in foreign politics as it had in 1919 and 1920, with unfortunate results for the Soviet Union's foreign position.

In October 1924, the British Foreign Office came into possession of a letter allegedly sent by Zinoviev to the Communist party of Great Britain, urging increased agitation and the formation of cells within army and navy units. The question of this letter's authenticity has long been debated and is probably not important. Its text was in line with Zinoviev's known ideas; it was widely believed to be genuine when it was published in the press; and it helped bring the defeat of the first Labour government and a perceptible cooling of Anglo-Soviet relations. In December 1924, Zinoviev inspired an attack by a group of Russian officers, supported by a few hundred Estonian Communists, upon the Estonian port of Reval. It was a miserable failure, and it was publicized all over Europe and lowered Soviet stock even further. Finally, in April 1925, the Comintern was widely believed to have instigated a renewal of revolutionary ardor on the part of the Bulgarian Communist party, the first result of which was the explosion of a time bomb in the Sveta Nedelya Cathedral in Sofia, which killed 128 persons.

From these three events can be dated the Soviet Union's swift decline from the position of relative strength gained for it by Chicherin. Signs of this were immediately apparent. No overtures of any kind were made to the Soviet Union during the Locarno negotiations of 1925 (see p. 509); and these talks were, after all, of vital importance to Russia, since they threatened to detach Germany from the Rapallo line by inclining it to the West and bringing it into the League of Nations.

Against this drift of Germany and against the strengthening of the League, which was always an object of special detestation to the Soviet Union in the 1920s, Chicherin fought a spirited but losing fight. He managed to persuade Germany to balance its Western commitments by concluding a new treaty, the Treaty of Berlin (1926), with the Soviet Union, but his efforts to build up a rival League under Soviet sponsorship attracted favorable response only from Lithuania, Turkey, Afghanistan, and Persia. The fact of the matter was that all the old distrust of the Soviet Union had been reawakened, and it was now deepened by other Soviet actions that countered Chicherin's efforts.

Since 1923, the Soviet Union had maintained formal relations with the Kuomintang, the Chinese nationalist party founded by Sun Yat-sen and led now by Chiang Kai-shek, which controlled south China and was seeking to do the same in the north. They were also on good terms with the Japanese government, which, as before the war, had interests in Manchuria and in Korea. Now, in 1925 and 1926, at a moment when its European contacts were being jeopardized, the Soviet government indulged in tactics that were bound to weaken its position in the Far East as well. Comintern agents became active in all major Chinese cities, as well as in Korea and Japan, and the Soviet government sought simultaneously to play politics inside the Kuomintang, supporting the left wing against the authority of Chiang Kai-shek.

These activities brought the indignation of the powers to a boiling point, and in 1927 disaster fell on Russia from every side. In the spring of that year, Chiang Kai-shek liquidated the Kuomintang's left wing and instituted the anti-Communist policy that he was to follow for the rest of his life. Simultaneously, in Japan, the government was taken over by forces that favored an active Manchurian, and hence anti-Soviet, policy. In May, the British police raided the headquarters of the Soviet trade mission in London and seized its files. On the basis of evidence of anti-British propaganda and subversive activities found in them, the British government severed diplomatic relations. In June there was a flare-up of anti-Soviet feeling in Poland, and the Soviet ambassador in Warsaw was murdered. In October, the French government demanded the recall of the Soviet ambassador. In Germany, evidence of Soviet subversion caused enthusiasm for the Rapallo-Berlin line to wane. In Persia and Afghanistan, Great Britain won back ground that had been lost earlier to Russia. By the end of the year Russia was as isolated as she had been in 1917.

The Soviets and the West after 1927   These setbacks helped discredit Zinoviev and his methods and probably contributed indirectly to Stalin's rise to complete authority by demonstrating the dangers of the policy of world revolution preached by some of his chief rivals and the advantages of his own policy of "socialism in one country." Under Stalin, Comintern adventures went out of fashion, and Russian diplomats were instructed to sell the Soviet Union as a peaceful and cooperative nation. Especially after the threat of National Socialism became apparent, a policy of ingratiation with the West was followed that was to culminate in Russia's entrance into the League in 1934.

To repeat the work that Chicherin had done was not easy, and it was never completely successful. Despite the admiration that existed in western countries for the economic and technological gains of the Soviet Union, accumulating evidence of the internal conditions of that country appalled large sections of the western populations and even dimmed the former enthusiasm of their left-wing and labor parties. At the same time, the Soviet government's tendency to slip from the ways of peaceful diplomacy into the intrigue and violence of revolution was not forgotten in the West. Its bland assurances that the Comintern was an independent organization and that the Soviet Union had not been involved in its activities convinced nobody and deepened the feeling that any real cooperation between the Soviet Union and the West was impossible.

Even when the threat of Hitler became more immediate than that of communism, the Western countries would find it difficult to make common cause with the great revolutionary power in the East.

Chapter 23 THE RISE OF
ITALIAN FASCISM

The victory of communism in Russia and the known desire of Russia's leaders to spread its doctrines to the rest of the world had one effect that was not dwelt upon in the previous chapter. Especially in countries that seemed potentially vulnerable to Communist subversion, it encouraged the rise of totalitarian movements of the right headed by strong men who promised to keep their countries free from Marxist infection. This was the case in Italy, which surrendered itself to the dictatorship of the Fascist party in the first decade after the war.

It would nevertheless be a mistake to regard the emergence of communism as the sole, or even the most important, reason for the victory of fascism in Italy. Fascism was the result of many things, among which the economic and psychological dislocations caused by the war, the resentment of returning veterans over the lack of recognition for their services, the frustrated ambitions of Italian nationalists, and the failure of the Italian party system were fully as important as the fear of Communist infiltration.

THE VICTORY OF FASCISM

The Results of the War The results of World War I in Italy justified all of the doubts and hesitations expressed by those who had resisted intervention in 1915. There were no outstanding victories in the field to look back on, and the clumsy greediness of Italy's negotiators at Paris had left its allies annoyed and its own liberals so ashamed that one of them, G.A. Borgese, wrote that his country had forfeited the opportunity for a future of spiritual greatness and social progess. The most valuable of the territorial gains made as a result of the war—those at the head of the Adriatic and along the northern frontier—would probably have come to Italy even if it had remained neutral, and, in any case, it was doubtful that they were worth the loss of 500,000 men. Aside from this, the war left the country in a state of economic chaos.

All told, the long conflict had cost a sum about twice as large as the total of all government expenditure between 1861 and 1913, and the government had been able to withstand this burden only because of the unlimited credit extended by the Allied governments. As soon as hostilities were terminated, that economic aid came to an end, and Italy found itself with a staggering debt, a great imbalance in foreign trade (imports far exceeding exports), and an inflation that was threatening to get seriously out of hand. This last danger was increased by the continuation of subsidies to grain farmers and to the industries that had converted their production to meet war needs and now expected to be reconverted at government expense.

Meanwhile, other wartime chickens were coming home to roost. To maintain the will to victory, the government had promised that peace would bring a more equitable distribution of land in the interests of the peasants, as well as any number of benefits for the industrial masses. The potential recipients of these promises decided not to wait for their fulfillment; and the result was a number of violent strikes in industry and, in rural areas, a series of spontaneous risings—admirably described in Panzini's novel *Il padrone sono me* (*The Boss Is Me*)—in which the peasants simply took matters into their own hands and seized their landlords' fields. The resultant confusion and dislocation of the economic system was further deepened by the existence of thousands of army deserters, who took to brigandage in order to support themselves, and by the demobilization of those who had fought until the end of the war, which immediately created a serious unemployment problem.

The Failure of the Parties   This situation called for vigorous action by the political parties. Their response was wholly ineffective. In the parliament elected in 1919, the three largest parties were the Socialists, the Catholic Popular party, and the Liberals who recognized Giovanni Giolitti as their leader. The Socialists were both disunited and irresponsible. Their tendency to split into factions was increased by the events in Russia, which caused violent doctrinal debates and, in 1920, led to the secession of the party's left wing, which constituted itself as the Italian Communist party. Those who did not secede seemed more desirous of persuading the departed brethren that they were true Marxists than of playing an effective role in Italian politics, for they refused to collaborate with the parties to the right of them in any program to check social deterioration and went on mouthing revolutionary slogans in which they did not believe. The Catholic Popular party, led by the Sicilian priest Don Luigi Sturzo and some gifted younger men, including a future prime minister (Alcide de Gasperi), also lacked internal cohesion. Although its leaders professed some useful ideas of social reform, the party as a whole was united only on opposition to anticlericalism, and since the majority of its members were suspicious of both Liberals and Socialists and opposed to collaborating with them, the role of the *popolari* was necessarily a negative one. As for the Liberals, they were characteristically opposed to government action in the economic sphere, and their leader Giolitti had, in any case, always believed that problems solved themselves if one was wise enough to leave them alone.

In addition, all three of these political groups had been predominantly anti-interventionist in 1915, when Italy had been jockeyed into war by the maneuvers of D'Annunzio and others (see p. 468). They all suffered from an understandable craving to have their prescience acknowledged by those who had overborne them, and they indulged this weakness to a dangerous degree. In parliamentary debates, they spent more time recalling the past than grappling with the present, and they recognized current social problems only to prove that they were the inevitable result of the victory of their enemies in 1915. There were times, indeed, when it seemed that they actually welcomed every new disaster that befell their country, because it strengthened their case against the interventionists.

In these circumstances, the first postwar governments, loose coalitions of various liberal and right groups with intermittent participation by the *popolari,* headed first by a former professor of political science named Francesco Nitti and then by the venerable Giolitti, accomplished little. They had no constructive policy for checking the runaway inflation or for reducing the government's debts. In the face of continued lawlessness in the countryside and the towns, they recognized no responsibility for government action. Nitti found it expedient to give retroactive sanction to land seizures by the peasants; and, in September 1920, when industrial workers in northern Italy responded to employers' lockouts by seizing several large factories, the Giolitti government followed a policy of strict nonintervention.

The behavior of the government had the result of alienating three important groups in the country. In the first place, the wealthy landowners and the industrialists, whose economic interests were threatened by the continuation of strikes and expropriations, began to cast about for a leadership that would be more responsive to their plight than those of the older parties. In the second place, the nationalist groups that had pressed for intervention in 1915 and still believed that it was Italy's mission to become a great Mediterranean and Balkan power not only resented the drumfire of criticism that the Socialists and Liberals directed against them in parliament but were bitter about what they considered to be the government's blindness to Italy's vital interests. Unlike the Liberals, who felt that Italy had asked for too much at the Peace Conference, these groups thought that Italy had received far less than it deserved. They were unconvinced by the argument that Italy's safety was assured by the breakup of the Austro-Hungarian Empire, and they regarded the constitution of a large Yugoslavia with a coastline on the Adriatic as an Allied plot against Italy. They were enthusiastic about the expedition that D'Annunzio led against Fiume in September 1919 and his subsequent establishment of a "Regency of Carnaro" there which claimed to be an independent state and sent manifestoes to other governments; and they were furious when the Giolitti government signed the death warrant of that adventure by concluding the Treaty of Rapallo in November 1920 with the Yugoslav government and by recognizing Yugoslavia's rights on the Dalmatian coast and in the area surrounding Fiume (see p. 498). These actions and Italy's evacuation of Albania in 1920 seemed to the nationalists to savor of cowardice.

When D'Annunzio, now nearing sixty and worn out by his political and amorous activities, failed them by abandoning his regency at Fiume, they began to look around for a stronger man to represent their cause.

Finally, there were the veterans of the war. Considering the state of Italy's armaments in 1915, which was described by the journalist Prezzolini as prehistoric, they had fought bravely, if not brilliantly; and their gallant stand on the Piave had done much to repair the earlier collapse at Caporetto. They came home expecting to find some sign of gratitude for their service and some evidence that their sacrifices had helped to produce a better Italy. They found neither. Their reward was often the discovery that their former jobs were gone and that to appear in the streets dressed in uniform was to court abuse and assault, since Socialist antiwar propaganda took violent forms. At the same time, as one of their number, Riccardo Bacchelli, was later to write:

> The ex-service men ... found faction and demagogy presenting the war to the people as a monstrous and bloody deception, and the educated classes, with the characteristic insouciance of decadence, using an illusory prosperity to amuse themselves and, one may even say, making it a point of good breeding and *savoir faire* not to play the returned hero.

This was not the Italy they had fought to protect; and some of them—the black-shirted shock troops or *arditi*, in particular, and the younger officers—wanted to do something to change it and were anxious to find leaders who would show them how to do so.

All of these critics of prevailing tendencies in Italian politics found a way of expressing their protests in fascism and in the leadership of Benito Mussolini.

Mussolini and the Fascist Movement   When Mussolini's long-suffering wife was informed in October 1922 that her husband had just been made prime minister of Italy, her first remark is said to have been: "What a character!" There was probably as much astonishment as admiration in those words and, if so, it must have been an astonishment shared by others who had known Mussolini as long as Donna Rachele, and who knew how fluid his principles were and how frequent his fundamental shifts of political position.

Benito Mussolini was born in 1883, the son of a blacksmith, who was an ardent Socialist, and a schoolmistress. Like Stalin (and this was the only thing he shared with his fellow dictator), he was educated at a seminary and expelled from it, apparently for stabbing a fellow student. He taught school for some time but abandoned this career, allegedly because he could not maintain discipline among his students. In 1902 he went to Switzerland in order to escape being drafted for service in the Italian army. After living from hand to mouth for two years, he returned home, performed his military service, and then turned to journalism, the career for which he was best suited temperamentally and which made a decisive impression upon his later political style. In 1909 he was expelled from the then Austrian district of Trent (Trentino) for his violent and subversive articles in the Socialist press, and in 1911 he was jailed by the Italian government for his attacks upon government policy in North Africa. His journalistic prowess brought him considerable reputation in Socialist circles, and in 1912 he became editor of the chief party paper, the *Avanti* of Milan. Yet he was never an entirely orthodox Socialist, being given to the expression of views that bordered on anarchism or seemed to indicate that he was interested in power for its own sake; and there was always more than a suspicion that he was concerned primarily with personal advancement rather than with the causes he advocated.

Having been the most impassioned opponent of the adventure in Tripoli in 1911 and having played a leading role in the excommunication of those party members who had dared support it, Mussolini changed his bearings completely after the beginning of World War I and became an interventionist hardly less insistent than D'Annunzio (see p. 468). This finished his career as a Socialist and left him, when the war was over, with a clouded future. For a time, he considered attempting to outbid the official Socialist party for the support of the working classes, an experiment which, as the elections of 1919 were to show, had no prospects of success; but he soon discovered, through his journalistic activity, that there were better opportunities for personal aggrandizement in other directions. At a time when so many people were saying that the war had been a mistake, Mussolini was perverse enough to say that the war had been one of the finest chapters in Italian history, that Italy had been cheated of the gains won by the blood of its sons, and that those who tolerated the peace of renunciation and traduced the heroism of Italy's dead youth must be driven from power. He was not original in this, but he said what he had to say eloquently and often, and his writings became popular with discontented officers, with perfervid D'Annunzians, and with a younger generation brought up on tales of Garibaldian adventure, balked of the chance of serving their country by accident of age, and disgusted by the flat spiritlessness of their times. It was people like them who joined with Mussolini in the first *Fascio di combattimento,* or fighting group, which he founded in Milan in March 1919 and which was the nucleus of the Fascist party of the future.

About the growth of the Fascist movement there was something adventitious, and there were times in the early days when it threatened to get out of Mussolini's control completely. It started as a loose league of local organizations, some formed in imitation of the Milan *Fascio,* some (associations of veterans, anti-Bolshevik unions, youth leagues, societies for an Italian Dalmatia, and the like) converted from their original purposes. It was aided by the collapse of D'Annunzio's Fiume adventure, for most of the poet's legionnaires became Fascists; but it was also weakened, and even threatened with disintegration, by the individualism of these recruits and of some of its local leaders. Men like Dino Grandi in Bologna, Italo Balbo in Ferrara, and Robert Farinacci in Cremona resisted centralized direction of party activities, partly because they discovered that they could make private profit by hiring their squads out to local businessmen as strikebreakers or to landlords as protectors of property. These *ras* (as the local party chieftains were named, after the tribal chiefs of Abyssinia) were not only capable of resentment of Mussolini's pretensions to over-all leadership but, at times, overruled his views and threatened to repudiate his leadership entirely. It seems clear that it was their influence that made fascism a definitely antisocialist movement, for as late as November 1921, when Mussolini was still thinking of the possibility of a pact between the Fascists and the non-Communist left, the local party chiefs forced him to abandon this idea in favor of continued support of conservative business interests.

On the other hand, Mussolini was indispensable to the local chiefs and, despite their irritation at his radical changes of opinion and his timidity at moments when daring was called for (for the future Duce was never the hero that legend made him), they admitted their dependence on him and, in the end, their subordination. Mussolini had a charismatic authority that none of them possessed; he wielded the pen that won them new converts; and he possessed the ability to speak to the Italian people in ways that could flatter, amuse, and move them. Grandi and Balbo and Farinacci and their like were successful local bosses, but their abilities did not go beyond that; Mussolini made fascism a party with national support.

The Surrender of Italian Liberalism   It is nevertheless doubtful whether the Fascists would ever have come into power if it had not been for the failure of Italian liberalism to carry out its political responsibilities and to remain true to its principles. It was the refusal of Giolitti's Liberal government of 1920–1921 to interfere in the serious industrial and agrarian disorders that gave the Fascists the chance to pose as the guardians of public order against Communist attack; and it was the willingness of distinguished liberal institutions like the great Milan newspaper *Corriere della Sera* to condone the violence and the terroristic methods used by Grandi's thugs and Farinacci's goon squads that gave fascism an aura of respectability, won it a position in parliament, and commended it to the middle class as their natural protector.

By November 1921, when the Fascist party was formally established, it had only thirty-five seats in the Chamber of Deputies, but it had a national membership of close to 300,000 and its ambitions had grown commensurately with its numbers. It had learned, during the elections of May 1921, that neither the government's prefects nor the police would interfere if its *Squadristi* used force to intimidate voters. It had learned that Socialist clubs and trade unions would not even unite to resist attacks upon their headquarters, a sign that they were incapable of action for other purposes. It had learned that parliamentary parties of the center and left found it difficult to cooperate on any issue and that the formation of a vigorous ministry with strong parliamentary support was unlikely. It had detected sympathy for fascism both in the army command and at the royal court. In view of these discoveries, there was every reason to believe that an all-out drive for power would be successful. Mussolini openly hinted to parliament that this was now his intention when he said, in the spring of 1922, that he would start a full-scale revolt if any prime minister were appointed who stood for "anti-Fascist reaction."

Even this threat did not convince the Liberal and Socialist parties to join forces against what was clearly an imminent revolution of the right. The Socialists, instead, indulged in a wholly suicidal maneuver by declaring a general strike in August 1922. The strike was so badly prepared that it was bound to fail, as it did. But the very fact that it was tried exasperated the general public, which was tired of strikes and agitations, and gave the Fascists an excuse to declare open war on socialism, to destroy all Socialist and union headquarters in Livorno, Genoa, and other key cities, to smash the presses and burn the building of Mussolini's old paper, *Avanti,* in Milan, and actually to depose the Socialist government of that city. When the public did nothing about this and the conservative and liberal press commended the action, the Fascists were emboldened to go further, and in the weeks that followed, they took over the town councils of Ferrara, Cremona, Parma, Ravenna, and Livorno as well.

This last step was a necessary preliminary to the national coup that was now in preparation. In September and October delicate negotiations were entered into with royalist and church circles, designed to avert possible interference from either direction. Meanwhile, Mussolini appointed a small general staff to make an operational plan for the seizure of power, and, on October 27, 1922, he ordered the mobilization of his Black Shirts and the beginning of a general advance on Rome. He was not entirely sanguine about the results of the projected coup and stayed carefully in the vicinity of the Swiss border, lest he find it advisable to flee. That necessity never arose. The one possibility of resistance evaporated when King Victor Emmanuel III refused to sign a declaration of martial law demanded by the current prime minister, Luigi Facta. A Fascist mission headed by Grandi then persuaded the king that Mussolini was the only possible premier, and the king agreed to appoint him. Once that decision had been made, Mussolini felt it safe to make his personal march on Rome, arriving by sleeping car from Milan on the morning of October 30, looking a not very martial figure in morning coat and white spats.

The Consolidation of the Revolution   In his first major address to the Chamber, Mussolini told the curious deputies that he had refused to "overdo the victory."

> With 300,000 youths, fully armed, fully determined, and almost mystically ready to act at my command, I could have chastised all those who have defamed and tried to injure fascism. I could have made of this sordid, gray assembly hall a bivouac for *Squadristi,* I could have kicked out parliament and constructed a government exclusively of *Fascisti.* I could have done so, but I did not want to, at least not for the present.

This speech had the effect of lulling its auditors into the drowsy assumption that the new premier would be no different from those of the past and that, if he became fractious, they could always get rid of him later on. They were reassured also by his willingness to head a twelve-man ministry that had only three Fascist members; and they had no objections whatsoever to conferring "full powers" on him for the period of one year.

Mussolini took advantage of this mood to take over the administration of the state by slow degrees. During his first year of power, the prefectures, the offices of police, and the key positions in the national bureaucracy were filled with new Fascist appointees, and simultaneously the appointment of a large number of new Fascist senators gave the party the control of the upper house. More daring strokes followed. The first, and the one that opened many eyes to Mussolini's real intentions, was the transformation of his *Squadristi* into a national party militia paid by the state and the simultaneous abolition of the Royal Guards (a supplementary police force created by Nitti), which were now declared to be superfluous. The second was the proposal at the end of 1923 of the so-called Acerbo electoral bill.

This proposal stipulated that in national elections the party or coalition winning the largest number of votes, provided it received at least twenty-five percent of the total votes cast, would automatically receive two thirds of the seats in the Chamber. One might have thought that memory of Fascist tactics in the elections of May 1921 would have been enough to warn the other parties of the probable consequences of the passage of such a measure. There was, indeed, opposition on the part of the *popolari,* the reformist Socialists, and the left Liberals, but the center and right, including such dignitaries as Giolitti, Orlando, and Salandra, voted for the bill and assured the consolidation of the Fascist dictatorship.

In the elections of April 1924, there were, despite Fascist violence at the polls, two and a half million votes cast for non-Fascist parties. But Mussolini's party got four and a half million and received two thirds of the seats in the Chamber. Immediately it began to bring pressure to bear upon the opposition parties and the press, and the drift toward totalitarianism became evident. The clearest sign of this was the liquidation of the new regime's most dangerous foes, which began with the brutal murder, in June 1924, of Giacomo Matteotti, a leader of the moderate Socialists and an unflinching critic of Mussolini's policies.

The news that this courageous and widely admired man had been kidnapped and left dead in a ditch caused a national revulsion so strong that the whole Fascist organization was shaken, and Mussolini felt it necessary to dismiss his chief of police and make other concessions to the national temper. It is barely possible that the Liberal and Socialist parties might have taken advantage of this popular mood to curb Mussolini before it was too late, but this possibility was never tested. After waiting in vain for the king to discipline his new premier's party, the opposition deputies made a tactical mistake of the first order, taking their key from Filippo Turati's speech in memory of Matteotti, in which he referred to the last stand of Caius Gracchus and his followers on the Aventine Hill and said:

> The only real representatives of the people are those who now stand on the Aventine of their own conscience, whence no wiles shall move them until the rule of law is given back and the representation of the people ceases to be the ghastly jest to which it has been reduced.

In this spirit, they absented themselves from the Chamber of Deputies. This "Aventine secession" meant, in reality, that the opposition had abandoned the only arena in which they might have fought fascism before the eyes of the whole nation. They had surrendered the field to their enemy.

Mussolini himself realized this, and he recovered from his momentary loss of nerve. In January 1925, in a dramatic speech in the Chamber, he declared:

"I alone accept the political, moral and historical responsibility for everything that has happened." Simultaneously, he ordered new attacks upon the opposition, which wilted before them. In the course of 1925, the non-Fascist members of the ministry lost their posts; all other parties were dissolved; censorship of the press was tightened, and owners of newspapers like *Corriere della Sera* were persuaded to dismiss independent-minded editors; the take-over of the bureaucracy and local government was completed; and a secret police (OVRA) was established. Italy had become a totalitarian state.

THE INSTITUTIONS OF FASCISM

The Machinery of Government   No immediate attempt was made by the Fascists to do away with the governmental machinery that they had inherited. Mussolini had at one time flirted with republicanism, as with every other shade of political thought, but he saw no advantage to making Italy a republic in a formal sense. Victor Emmanuel III remained on the throne, although it must have been difficult at times in the years of Mussolini's glory for the Italian people to remember that they had a king. The bicameral legislature was permitted to continue to function also, although it too had suffered a sea change, for both houses became exclusively Fascist, and neither had much contact any longer with the Italian people. After 1928, the election of the Chamber was carried out on the basis of an approved party list of candidates for which the voters could vote either yes or no—a method that eliminated both campaigning and free choice. The powers of the Chamber were nominal and limited for the most part to hearing and obeying. The prime minister (Mussolini) was given the right to initiate all legislation and to govern, when he wished, by decree. He had extensive rights of appointment, and all appointees were responsible to his person, including the other department heads and ministers of state.

As in the Soviet Union, the party was the source of real power in the country. Small in relation to total population (it came to number about a million members or 2.5 percent of the population), it was the guardian of the regime throughout Italy. It was organized on a local basis and was ultimately composed of about 10,000 *Fasci,* grouped into provincial federations. At the head of the party pyramid was the Fascist Grand Council, a body of about twenty men that included the leaders of the March on Rome and several other officials. The Grand Council was supposed to rule the party and shape its policy and to be consulted in all constitutional matters, changes in the royal succession or in the powers of the prime minister, and other important issues. In reality, it never seems to have had much to do—at least not until 1943 when, to everyone's surprise, it deposed Mussolini—and real authority was wielded by its chairman (Mussolini) and the party's secretary general.

Party membership was a prerequisite for a political career, and it brought certain advantages in other forms of employment as well. It was therefore—at least until the depression years, when there were more party members than jobs—eagerly sought, and the party was able to be selective and to insist that candidates meet certain standards. After 1927, for example, no one could hope for admission who had not passed through the graded youth organizations of the party: the *Balilla,* the *Avanguardia,* the *Giovani Fascisti.*

Anti-Fascist cartoon from *Il becco giallo,* an Italian émigré journal, Paris, December 21, 1924.

The party controlled the other agencies of power within the state by infiltration and parallelism. That is to say, there were many devoted Fascists within the hierarchy of the regular army and the national and local police organizations; but the party also maintained a police force of its own and, as a possible check on the regular military establishment, a large and well-armed party militia.

With one other powerful institution the Fascists found it expedient to make a truce. In 1929, after prolonged negotiations between Mussolini and Pope Pius XI, the Treaty of the Lateran brought to an end the long feud between the Vatican and the kingdom of Italy (see p. 312). The Italian government now recognized papal sovereignty within Vatican City and St. Peter's in return for papal recognition of the kingdom of Italy and renunciation of claims to former papal estates. Supplementary agreements provided for a financial settlement and gave the pope the right to appoint all bishops in Italy after consulting the Italian government to see whether there were any political objections. The state continued to pay the salaries of churchmen and exacted an oath of loyalty from them. These Lateran Treaties removed a perennial source of friction between church and state and diminished the possibility of church opposition to Fascist policies. They were perhaps the most popular of Mussolini's actions and certainly the most substantial, for they survived his fall and were written into the constitution of the new Italian Republic.

The Corporative State   One of the most advertised aspects of Fascist rule was corporativism, which was designed ostensibly to do away with the harsh individualism of the liberal state, to promote mutual understanding between capital and labor, and to eliminate class conflict. These purposes were sought by the dissolution of the older trade unions and the abolition of strikes and lockouts, and the subsequent organization of a good part of the population into syndicates or corporations of employers, employees, and professional men, under whose joint auspices labor courts were established to deal with disputes. This system was supplemented by codes of fair practice, guaranteeing working conditions and providing social insurance. In time, the various corporations were given the right to suggest to the Fascist Grand Council the names of people who should be parliamentary candidates and, as the system became more involved, to send delegates to a National Council which was meant to advise parliament on economic matters. In 1939 it was announced that a Chamber of Fasci and Corporations would actually supersede the Chamber of Deputies, but the war made this final elaboration unrealistic.

The corporative system aroused much interest abroad, and the English conservative John Buchan (Lord Tweedsmuir) was probably thinking of it when he said, rather incautiously, in 1929, that "but for the bold experiment of Fascism, the decade [had] not been fruitful in constructive statesmanship." In reality, corporativism was a fraud, which never worked in practice as it seemed to do on paper. For the Fascists, it served three purposes. It drew a veil over the harsh outlines of their totalitarianism and permitted foreigners to think that Italy was devising a new and more equitable social system which gave full expression to the people's will. In the second place, it satisfied the most important supporters of the Fascist movement, the industrialists and landlords, by eliminating the possibility of effective labor organization. By the Palazzo Vidoni agreement of October 1925, the industrialists were, in effect, assured that they would no longer have to worry about strikes. In the third place, it supplied a great number of jobs for party members.

Wiser than Lord Tweedsmuir, the London *Economist* pointed out in 1935 that

> the new corporative state only amounts to the establishment of a new and costly bureaucracy, from which those industrialists who can spend the necessary amount can obtain almost anything they want and put into practice the worst kind of monopolistic practices at the expense of the little fellow who is squeezed out in the process.

Economic and Social Policy   The institutions of corporativism helped eliminate the social disorder that had characterized the years immediately before the march on Rome, but they did very little to improve the working of the Italian economy or the conditions in which the Italian people lived. It has indeed been argued that what prosperity Italy had in the 1920s was due to the governments of the pre-Fascist period, and that it was shortened in duration and Italy made more vulnerable than it might have been to the shock of the world depression by Mussolini's policies.

Possessing no coherent economic ideas of his own, Mussolini was fascinated by the spectacular and the unattainable. He weakened the financial structure of the state by elaborate public works programs and overambitious transportation schemes (which did, nevertheless, as was always pointed out by his admirers, make the trains run on time and give Italy some of the best roads in Europe) and by the establishment of an army, navy, and air force that far exceeded Italy's needs and in the end proved to be luxuries, better designed for show than for use. More dangerous was his insistence that Italy follow the road of autarchy, which, given its resources and geographical position, was illogical and imposed a heavy strain on all aspects of its economy. Mussolini's desire to make Italy self-sufficient led him to inaugurate a "battle of wheat," which succeeded in producing large quantities of that commodity at uneconomic prices and at the cost of taking land away from olive culture, pasturage, and fruits, with resultant disruption of the economy. It led him to indulge in grandiose but impractical schemes like the one that was supposed to make the country self-sufficient in oil and gasoline by 1938. It persuaded him, in a much-publicized "battle for births," to subsidize matrimony and award procreation with medals and prizes and to announce that his goal was to increase the population of the country to sixty million.

What this would have done to the standard of living in Italy if Mussolini had succeeded it is not difficult to predict. Already in 1930, a report of the International Labor Office pointed out that real wages in Italy were lower than in any country of western Europe, including Spain. This did not seem to bother Mussolini, who said publicly in 1936 that the goal of fascism was *not* to restore prosperity and that Italy was probably moving to a permanently lower standard of living, which would nevertheless be healthier morally and physically for all.

In the field of popular education, fascism registered some progress, at least in increasing attendance and reducing illiteracy. The problem here was a formidable one, for as Ignazio Silone pointed out in the introduction to the English edition of his brilliant anti-Fascist novel *Fontamara,* there were villages in which the peasants did not even speak Italian, let alone read or write it, and the gulf between them and organized society was complete. The Fascists increased attendance in elementary schools from three million to four and a half million in the first decade of their power and reduced illiteracy to about twenty percent of the national population.

On the other hand, the content of elementary education left much to be desired, since time was devoted to inculcating military virtues and "Fascist culture" that might better have been spent on basic disciplines. The mind did not, after all, derive much sustenance from pabulum like the following excerpt, which Denis Mack Smith has culled from a Fascist text for eight-year-olds.

> A child who, even while not refusing to obey, asks "Why?," is like a bayonet made of milk. . . . "You must obey because you must," said Mussolini, when explaining the reasons for obedience.

All things considered, as one looks at the economic and social achievement of the Fascist regime, the impressive thing is not what was accomplished (for that would probably have been achieved by any regime) but what was not done at all. Certainly, all the really hard problems were left untouched—the social and political backwardness of the south, the problem of banditry, the Mafia, the prevalence of malaria, the unequal distribution of income, and much else. Luigi Barzini has written that, in face of all this, one wonders what Mussolini did with his time; and that the sad answer is that he devoted it not to constructive work but to putting on a good show for the Italian people, which, it must be admitted, they gave every evidence of enjoying until the war years.

Fascist Doctrine   The official doctrine of the Fascist movement was as fraudulent as the concept of corporativism and as disorganized as the mind of its leader. Mussolini, as we have noted, had no firm principles of his own, and, at the beginning of his career in power, was given to boasting that fascism needed none either, that the Fascists were "the gypsies of politics," and that action was more important than philosophy. It was only when the world began to take an interest in his movement and when foreign pundits began to write pieces about its philosophical foundations that he thought it necessary to oblige them with doctrinal statements of his own.

Since he was always against more things than he was for, these were rich in negatives. Fascism was always declared to be the antithesis of liberalism and democracy and socialism, but anyone who desired to know why this should be considered a recommendation, or what fascism gave to the individual that these philosophies did not, found it very difficult to get a straight answer, either from Mussolini or from the man officially appointed to explain fascism in philosophical terms, Giovanni Gentile. In general, the line taken was that those older philosophies sacrificed the ideal of the community and the nation to a false conception of freedom and destroyed man's essential nobility by promoting individualism, materialism, and cold-blooded rationalism. Fascism, on the other hand, brought freedom through authoritarianism, and heroism and nobility through discipline and sacrifice. This could not be proved; it had to be felt. As Gentile wrote:

> We all participate in a sort of mystic sentiment, [in which] we do not form clear and distinct ideas, nor can we put into precise words the things we believe in, but it is in those mystic moments when our soul is enveloped in the penumbra of a new world being born that creative faith germinates in our hearts. . . . The fascist spirit is will, not intellect.

Intellect failing, it was necessary to fall back on incantation. The doctrinal statements of Fascist leaders are for the most part rhapsodic and incoherent glorifications of the state and the heroic virtues, in which the words power, courage, blood, sacrifice, discipline, victory, and especially will appear and reappear with monotonous regularity, as if the authors hoped by incessant iteration to give them reality. Italy's greatest philosopher of this time, Benedetto Croce (1866–1952), the only man whom Mussolini did not dare try to silence, was properly scornful of this ragbag collection of ideas. In a statement signed by dozens of anti-Fascist intellectuals on May 1, 1925, he declared that it was "an incoherent and bizarre mixture of appeals . . . flight from culture and sterile reachings toward a culture without a basis, mystical languors and cynicism."

Croce's emphasis upon the last quality was not misplaced. The most striking thing about what passed for Fascist philosophy was that the values it invoked were not very evident in the actual practice of fascism or in the lives and behavior of Fascists. In the remarkable pictures of Fascist reality that we find in the novels of Alberto Moravia (especially *The Indifferent Ones*), there is precious little power or courage or heroism, and, after the devastating record of graft and corruption that Mussolini's police chief Senise has left to the world in his memoirs, all the proud talk of sacrifice and discipline sounds ludicrous.

The Cult of the Leader   If the corporative state and the philosophy of fascism were taken more seriously than they deserved to be, this was largely due to the respect and fear in which the leader of the party came to be held in Italy and in the rest of the world. The Duce's imposing stature was in large part the creation of his controlled press. This is not to say that he did not possess natural talents. He had an animal vitality that impressed both men and women, a bluff and bullying manner that overbore people weaker than he, an incurable habit of self-dramatization that helped him dominate any situation, a flair for the sensational that came from his journalistic past, a not inconsiderable fund of peasant shrewdness, and oratorical gifts of the first order. But he was also timid, ill-educated, ignorant of foreign affairs, bereft of administrative ability, and too self-indulgent to repair his deficiencies, and it is a pity that Italy and the world did not appreciate these weaknesses sooner than they did.

Instead, thanks to Fascist censorship and control of the means of mass communication, Mussolini was presented to his people and the world as the *Übermensch* for whom they had long been waiting—the man of inflexible resolution, the soldier of experience and genius (he had, like Hitler, been a corporal, but without Hitler's long front-line service), the devoted public servant who labored day and night for his people, the man of strong passions but ascetic discipline, and the political genius whose predictions had an uncanny accuracy. The countryside was filled with signs reminding his subjects that "*Mussolini ha sempre ragione*" ("Mussolini is always right!") and gigantic pictures showing him in commanding poses—the calm and confident leader, sure of his course and its ultimate success.

It is perhaps understandable that the unlettered peasants and workers of Italy should have been taken in by this, but it is still hard to believe that so many Italian intellectuals and foreign statesmen were impressed by qualities that the Duce did not really possess. The acceptance of the legend of Mussolini by people like Austen and Neville Chamberlain, and their willingness to take his boasts and his threats at face value, had the long-run effect of convincing Mussolini himself that he possessed the qualities and the power they thought he had. And this had tragic results for Italy and for the world.

THE EARLY FOREIGN POLICY OF FASCISM

First Steps: Corfu   During the years before the March on Rome, Mussolini had repeatedly attacked the "peace of renunciation" and insisted that Italy under Fascist leadership would refuse to be bound by its terms. Over and over again he asserted that Italy must be an expanding power and that "imperialism is the basis of life for every people which tends to expand economically and spiritually." To the extent that the peace treaties stood in the way of Italian expansion, they must be revised; and Italy would not be balked of its just deserts either by the letter of the law or by the procedures of the new League of Nations. For this organization Mussolini professed to have the greatest scorn. "Fascism," he said in 1921, "does not believe in the vitality and the principles of the so-called League of Nations. It is a kind of Holy Alliance of the plutocratic nations of the Franco-Anglo-Saxon group, to guarantee to themselves the exploitation of the greater part of the world."

Once he had come to power, the Duce seemed to have felt it necessary to demonstrate that these were not idle boasts. In his first speech to parliament, he sternly warned Europe that Italy had no intention of maintaining the status quo just for the sake of peace, although he rather weakened the effect of this by intimating that he could be bribed into remaining quiet.

> We cannot afford the luxury of a policy of foolish altruism or of acting entirely in the interests of others.... My formula is simple: *Niente per niente.* Those who wish to have concrete proofs of friendship from us must give us concrete proofs of friendship in return.

When no one rose to this suggestion, Mussolini undertook to prove it was dangerous to disregard him. In August 1923, an Italian general and his staff were killed on the Greco-Albanian border, probably by Albanian bandits. Without waiting to discover who was responsible for the deed, or even on whose soil it was committed, Mussolini sent an ultimatum to the Greek government, demanding any number of apologies and compensations and, when they were not immediately forthcoming, bombarded and occupied the Greek island of Corfu. When Greece appealed to the League of Nations, the Duce was contemptuous. "In case the Council of the League declares itself competent in this matter," he said loftily, "the question whether to remain or resign from the League arises for Italy. I have already voted for the second alternative." The Western powers were not particularly impressed by this, but they decided not to force the issue and referred the dispute to the Council of Ambassadors in Paris, who arranged the return of Corfu to Greece in return for the payment of damages to Italy. Thus, Mussolini won a cheap triumph and aroused the first serious doubts about the efficacy of the collective security system.

Corfu, however, seems to have exhausted his inventiveness, and his energies were in any case absorbed for the next two years by pressing domestic problems. He was content to leave the management of foreign affairs for the most part in the hands of professionals, who toned down ideological matters and sought to win the confidence of Italy's traditional friends and to contribute to the general appeasement of Europe. Under their direction, Italy, as we have seen (pp. 498, 509), not only adjusted its relations with Yugoslavia but also participated in the negotiations at Locarno and guaranteed the Rhineland Pact that was concluded there.

Toward Revisionism and Imperialism　　　　Mussolini was not incapable of being flattered by opportunities to play the guardian of order and public law and, as Stuart Hughes has pointed out, he was never able to refrain from putting his signature on any treaty placed before him. Even so, a conciliatory foreign policy was not congenial to him and seemed contrary to the "Fascist style" which he was always talking about and which he equated with courage, resolution, action, forcefulness, and dynamism. The satisfactions to be gained from collaborative diplomacy did not seem to him to be worthy of Fascist Italy, which must dazzle the world with spectacular triumphs of its own.

His prejudices in this regard were shown clearly in the policy he followed in the late 1920s in the Danubian area. Here real statesmanship might have garnered economic advantage and personal prestige, while at the same time contributing to the general security of eastern Europe. Mussolini seemed less interested in these things than in carrying on a pointless competition with France in that area, seeking first to detach the Little Entente powers from its security system and, when that failed, to build up a rival bloc under Italian leadership. In pursuance of this second objective he made secret agreements with Austria, Hungary, and Bulgaria and had no hesitation about violating the military clauses of the Versailles Treaty when this promised to serve his purposes. In January 1928, Italian agents were caught red-handed shipping five carloads of machine guns into Hungary, and a little later the Italian government was involved in a scheme to send large numbers of rifles and machine guns to Fascist elements in Austria. These actions could not help but awaken lively fears in the other Balkan nations, and the resultant insecurity weakened the cause of peace.

This was a matter of no very great concern to the Duce. The deterioration of economic conditions at the end of the 1920s and the consequent disruption of European power relations opened new vistas to his eyes and made him impatient of old restraints. In 1932 he dismissed his foreign minister Grandi and assumed his functions, a sign that the reign of the professionals was over and that the *tono fascista* would be stamped on all future foreign policy. Even before this, he had announced a large increase in the Italian navy and given the first intimation of the future program of imperialism by announcing that Italians would not remain prisoners in the Roman sea. "Words are very fine things," he told his Black Shirts in 1930, "but rifles, machine-guns, warships, airplanes, and cannon are still finer things. They are finer because right without might is an empty word."

Unprincipled opportunist that he was, he was still uncertain as to his future course, but he sensed that something would turn up. He had predicted some years earlier that Europe would pass through a major crisis between 1935 and 1940 and that Fascist Italy must be prepared to act then. By 1930 he was saying confidently that "in 1950 Europe will be wrinkled and decrepit. The sole country of young men will be Italy.... Either we or they! Either our ideas or theirs! Either our State or theirs!"

Chapter 24 THE REPUBLICAN EXPERIMENT IN GERMANY

While totalitarian regimes were consolidating their power in Russia and in Italy, an experiment was being conducted in Germany to determine whether a democratic republic could be made to work in that country. After fifteen years of trial and crisis it failed, and the ultimate consequences of that failure were a second world war and the death of millions of men, women, and children.

If some benevolent spirit had granted the peoples of Germany and the neighboring European states even a fragmentary glimpse of what lay in store for them in the 1940s, it is impossible to believe that they would not have made every possible sacrifice to maintain the Weimar Republic against its enemies. But that kind of foresight is not given in this world, and the German republic always lacked friends and supporters when it needed them most.

THE FOUNDING OF THE REPUBLIC

The Revolution   The German revolution of 1918 was not the result of planning but the offspring of confusion. The abrupt announcement that the military effort had collapsed and that the government was requesting an armistice stunned public opinion, paralyzed the wills and energies of the governing class, and created a situation in which war-weariness, fear, hunger, disillusionment, and social resentment exploded into violence, which spread with frightening rapidity from one locality to another. At the end of October, the rumor spread in the naval base at Kiel that the German High Seas Fleet was going to be ordered to take to sea to make a last stand against the British. Protests by the men against this suicidal gesture led to arrests, which resulted in further demonstrations, until finally, on November 4, workers in the town established a Workers and Soldiers Council on the Soviet model. The Kiel example was imitated in other coastal towns—Lübeck, Hamburg, Bremen; and movement then spread rapidly to Hannover, Magdeburg, Braunschweig, Oldenburg, Schwerin, Rostock, Cologne, Dresden, and Leipzig.

In all cases, the councils seized control of the local government but confined their efforts for the most part to formulating demands for an end to the war and for the abdication of Emperor William II, whose continued rule seemed to them to jeopardize the chances of peace. In South Germany, however, events took a more serious turn. On November 8, a Constituent Soldiers, Workers, and Peasants Council was established in Munich under the leadership of the Independent Socialist Kurt Eisner, and it immediately proclaimed the establishment of a Bavarian Democratic and Social Republic. It was this action—which seemed to forecast the imminent dissolution of the Bismarckian Reich—that finally sealed the doom of the monarchy by forcing the national government in Berlin, against its will, to take the republican road.

On the morning of November 9, Prince Max von Baden, who had been made chancellor by the emperor at the end of September and had been engaged in armistice negotiations ever since, laid down his seals of office. In doing so, he declared that it was the intention of William II and the crown prince to relinquish their rights to the German and Prussian thrones, and that he himself was turning his office over to Friedrich Ebert, the head of the Majority Socialist party, who would serve as "Reich chancellor." Ebert immediately announced that the new government would be "a people's government" and that its goal would be "to bring peace to the German people as soon as possible, and to establish firmly the freedom which it has achieved."

He said nothing, however, about a republic; and, had he had a free hand, he would certainly have left the decision as to whether Germany should change its basic form of government to a later date and to a constituent assembly representing the whole of the German people. But Eisner's action in Munich was now known in Berlin, and the tide seemed to be running so heavily in the direction of republicanism that Ebert's colleagues felt it necessary to make that cause their own, lest they be anticipated by parties to the left of them. Thus, at 2 P.M. on November 9, 1918, Philipp Scheidemann ended a speech to a mass demonstration in front of the Reichstag building by shouting: "The Hohenzollerns have abdicated. Long live the great German Republic!"

Throughout the country, this announcement was accepted calmly. There were no anguished protests and no signs of a Vendée-an rising by embittered royalists. The monarchical system and the political and military hierarchy that supported it had been so completely discredited by the war that no one was prepared to fight for them. And this very fact might, if conditions had been different, have eased the transition from the old to the new and facilitated the laying of solid foundations for a democratic Germany.

What prevented this was the disunity of the Socialist party. The greater part of this—the Majority Socialists, led by men like Ebert and Scheidemann—were revisionists (see p. 283), who had long since given up any belief in the necessity of violent revolution and, now that power seemed within their grasp, wished to proceed by orderly methods towards the consolidation of democracy and the inauguration of a program of social development. They were disinclined to attempt too much in the way of social reform until certain urgent tasks—the restoration of normal food supplies to the population, for instance—had been carried out. Ebert himself, a patriot and a realist, was aware that an excess of revolutionary zeal might promote social disintegration and make the country vulnerable to separatist ambition and the depredations of the Poles and others. His desire was to restore order and then to proceed as quickly as possible to elections for a National Assembly which would draw up a new constitution for the country, give it a government with a clear mandate, and make orderly progress possible. He fully agreed with Friedrich Stampfer, the editor of the Socialist newspaper *Vorwärts,* who wrote at this time: "Socialism is organization. Disorganization is the worst enemy of socialism."

The views of the Majority Socialists were contested by two groups. The first of these, led by Karl Liebknecht, the son of the founder of the Social Democratic party, and by the gifted Polish Jewess, Rosa Luxemburg, called itself the Spartacist Union and (after January 1919) the German Communist party. It was an internationalist party, seeking to emulate the success of the Bolsheviks in Russia. Luxemburg held that "the role of the working class is to be realized only through the path of an armed workers' revolution"; her associates agreed that a National Assembly would be a bourgeois and counter-revolutionary body; and their objective was to prevent the meeting of that body by seizing power in the state before it could convene.

The Spartacists were too few in number to take effective action by themselves, but they were always able to count on considerable support from the third socialist faction, the Independent Socialist party, which had broken away from the majority in 1916 in protest against further support of the war effort. A heterogeneous and disorganized group, which nevertheless had considerable popular backing, the Independents were never as radical in their views as the Spartacists; but, like the Socialists in Italy (see p. 539), they seemed in their dealings with the Communists to have an inferiority complex and to feel the necessity of proving their common Marxist faith. Thus, in effect, in most disputes with the Majority Socialists, they lent their support to the radical wing.

The Days of Spartacus   These Socialist divisions had two results. In the first place, they threatened to defeat Ebert's efforts to restore public order. The Majority Socialist leader had sought to promote this by establishing a provisional government of three Majority Socialists and three Independent Socialists with authority to conduct necessary state business; but the effectiveness of this body was hampered by attempts of the Independents and Spartacists to subordinate it to control by the Workers and Soldiers Councils, as well as by continual strikes, demonstrations, and armed *Putsches* openly encouraged by the Spartacists. In the second place, they led Ebert, because of his concern for public order and his justifiable fear that the Spartacists would attempt a major rising in the near future, to look for aid to groups to which he might not have turned in other circumstances. As early as November 9, for instance, he felt it necessary to conclude a gentlemen's agreement with General Wilhelm Groener, Ludendorff's successor at the Supreme Army Command, which called for a policy of mutual support against the danger of Bolshevism. Later, as the threat of a Spartacist insurrection became more palpable, he authorized his Majority Socialist colleague Gustav Noske to build up volunteer forces to protect the state in an emergency; and Noske, finding little enthusiasm for such service among members of the Socialist party or the trade unions, was forced to rely upon bands of ex-soldiers which had been forming in various parts of Germany in response to appeals from their former officers. These free corps, as they were called, were much like the original *Squadristi* in Italy (see p. 542). Some had come into existence to cope with local disorder; others had been formed to fight communism or to guard the eastern frontiers; some had been fighting the Reds in the Baltic lands (see p. 521), and had just got home. They were all composed of trained soldiers—*Frontkämpfer* of the most hardbitten variety—and for Noske's purposes they were ideal. Their political convictions, however, left much to be desired, and it was not hard to imagine them being as willing to fight against democracy as against Bolshevism.

Ebert's arrangement with Groener robbed him of much of his future freedom of action in military affairs, and his reliance upon the free corps in 1919 made it difficult for him to disband them later on, even when they had revealed their basic antirepublicanism. The Reich chancellor's justification for assuming these liabilities was that his fears of new attacks upon the shaky republican state were well-founded. In January 1919, the Spartacists did attempt an armed insurrection in Berlin and for four days Ebert and his colleagues were isolated in a city that, for all intents and purposes, had fallen to communism. But Noske's work had been well done, and, on January 10, the free corps began their advance into the city. The Reinhard Brigade (named after its commander) drove the Spartacists out of the munitions plant at Spandau; and Stephani's Free Corps, using flame-throwers, machine guns, mortars, and artillery, attacked the Belle-Alliance Platz and forced the Spartacists in the *Vorwärts* building to capitulate. Other bands sought out and liquidated the remaining centers of resistance. By January 15 the action was complete; Rosa Luxemburg and Liebknecht had been brutally murdered, and Berlin was free of Reds. The government was firmly in control.

Spartacist week ended the possibility of a Bolshevik revolution in Germany. The government, still relying on the free corps, built their strength up rapidly. By the end of January, they were strong enough to begin operations against the provincial cities, and a systematic elimination of subversive elements in all the former revolutionary centers began. In February, Bremen, Wilhelmshaven, Halle, and other towns were pacified; in March, a second Spartacist rising in Berlin was crushed, with 1500 deaths; in April and May, Magdeburg, Dresden, and Leipzig were purged of Spartacists; and in June order was restored in Munich, where conditions had steadily deteriorated since February, when Kurt Eisner had been murdered and where, in recent weeks, Comintern agents had been active. The violent phase of the German revolution was now over.

The National Assembly   The removal of the threat to the government's authority in Berlin had meanwhile enabled Ebert to attain his most cherished objective: the calling of a National Assembly. Elections for this body were held on January 19, 1919, and, on February 6, the deputies gathered in Weimar. The composition of the Assembly showed that the non-Socialist forces in the country had recovered from the paralysis that seemed to affect them in November and December, for, of the 423 deputies, only 187 were Socialists (165 Majority; 22 Independents). On the other hand, the Catholic Center party had won 91 seats; the new Democratic party (which took over from the prewar Progressives) had won 75; 44 deputies described themselves as Nationalists; a new People's Party (which inherited the remains of the National Liberal cause) had 19; and there was a smattering of others. It was apparent that in the future the Socialists could not expect simply to have their own way.

The National Assembly had three tasks to perform. It had to establish a legal government, to conclude peace with the Allies, and to write a constitution for the new republic. It completed the first of these with dispatch. When Friedrich Ebert surrendered the powers of his government to the Assembly, it elected him to the post of Reich president and authorized his party to set about forming a new cabinet, which, in view of the election returns, would necessarily be a coalition cabinet if it were to expect majority support. After trying to persuade the Independent Socialists to collaborate (an effort that failed because of their resentment over Ebert's use of the free corps against fellow Marxists), Philipp Scheidemann formed a coalition cabinet in which half of the ministers were Majority Socialists and the other half were drawn from the Center and Democratic parties. This was the original Weimar coalition, and its members were to prove to be the most loyal supporters of the Republic throughout its career.

The task of concluding peace was more difficult, and, indeed, subjected the new governmental machinery to an almost intolerable strain. The first reaction to the peace terms that were forwarded to Berlin in mid-May (see p. 495) was one of incredulity, and this was succeeded by an indignation shared by all parties. "What hand would not wither that would sign such a treaty!," cried Scheidemann passionately. It was nevertheless soon apparent that blind rage would serve no useful purpose. The Allies made it clear that they would renew hostilities if the terms were not accepted; and no responsible German statesman could permit that to happen. Yet it was not easy to accept the inevitable, for it was precisely at this juncture that Germany had its first taste of the irrationalism of the right from which it was to suffer so grievously later on. In mid-June, the war minister Reinhardt called a meeting of leading generals at Weimar, informing General Groener beforehand that the meeting was intended as a council of war and that, if the cabinet decided to accept the peace terms, he intended to repudiate the action and lead an insurrectionary movement in eastern Germany, regardless of Allied action.

Nothing came of his fantastic scheme. The enthusiasm of the generals evaporated when Groener demonstrated to them that neither troops nor munitions would be available for a new war and that no support could be expected from the civilian population of the East Elbian districts. A memorandum spelling out these military realities, which he prepared at Ebert's request, succeeded also in persuading the majority of the National Assembly to drink the bitter draught prepared in Paris. During the impassioned debate that raged over the peace terms, the Scheidemann government had resigned; but a new one was formed under the Socialist Gustav Bauer, and, on June 28, two of its members signed the treaty.

The crisis over the peace terms had ominous results. The memories of the extreme conservatives and the superpatriots were notoriously short. They had already forgotten how decisively Germany had lost the war; and it was in these very months that the *Dolchstoss* legend was being born—the myth that the invincible German armies had been defeated not by the enemy but by "a stab in the back" inflicted by pacifists, socialists, and defeatists on the home front. They found it equally easy to forget that a renewal of hostilities was completely beyond Germany's capacities in 1919; and they were to claim repeatedly in the years that followed that the Socialists and other supporters of the Republic had willingly accepted a shameful peace, when they might have resisted it successfully with arms in hand.

The third order of business for the National Assembly was the drafting of the constitution, and this occupied the delegates until August 14, 1919, when the new charter was proclaimed to the German people. The constitution that resulted represented an impressive attempt to do what the members of the Frankfurt Assembly had sought to do in 1848: to reconcile liberty with national unity and strength.

The first article stated: "The German Reich is a republic. Political authority derives from the people"; and the powers and rights of the people were stressed throughout the document. While executive authority was vested in a Reich president with broad prerogatives, serving for seven years, that officer was to be elected by secret, direct, and universal suffrage. The constitution provided for a bicameral legislature, but the upper chamber or Reichsrat, which represented the member states, had only nominal powers; all real authority was centered in the Reichstag, the members of which were elected by popular vote with proportional representation. In this people's chamber all legislation originated, and before its members the chancellor and the other cabinet ministers had to defend their policies. Besides providing in this way for the expression of popular sovereignty, the Weimar constitution guaranteed to all Germans such fundamental rights as equality before the law, freedom of speech and association, and freedom of belief. Church and state were separated, and the education of the young was placed under the supervision of the state.

One of the most striking features of the Weimar constitution was the attempt made in it to correct some of the weaknesses of the Bismarckian Reich. The central government was no longer made dependent upon the financial contributions of the separate states but was granted the right of direct taxation, which the imperial government had never possessed. The national government was given exclusive jurisdiction over foreign and colonial affairs, citizenship, travel and residence, national defense, currency, customs duties, posts, and telegraphs and telephones, and it assumed ownership of the railway system. Its laws were given priority in matters in which the separate states had the right of concurrent legislation—civil and criminal law, judicial procedure, social welfare and insurance, expropriation and socialization, press laws, and the like. The national government also claimed the right to lay down normative regulations concerning religion, education, and housing.

If the drafters of the constitution had had their way, centralization would have been carried even further; but the Assembly yielded to the strong protests of southern Germany and left extensive rights of local government to the separate states. It was stipulated nevertheless that they must all recognize republican principles and use universal suffrage and proportional representation in their elections; and, in general, the diminution of their authority greatly reduced the forces of particularism in the country.

In two respects the enthusiasm for the utmost in democratic method shown by the framers of this constitution caused future trouble. Proportional representation is doubtless the best method ever devised for seeing that all shades of opinion are represented, but it works best in times of political and social peace and in situations in which there is a general acceptance of certain basic values. Neither of these conditions obtained in postwar Germany, and the use of proportional representation in Reichstag elections complicated the legislative process by increasing the number of parties, thus making it difficult for any single one to get a majority. This made coalition government inevitable and also jeopardized the security of the Republic by giving representation (and an opportunity for publicity and growth) to antirepublican splinter groups that might otherwise have died from lack of attention.

Another evidence of the anxious deference paid to popular sovereignty was the provision made for initiative and referendum. Perhaps because this was not accompanied by adequate safeguards against misuse, it too had unfortunate results. The conditions for making a referendum necessary on any public issue were so easy to fulfill that enemies of the Republic used it as a means of obstructionism, as they did, for example, during the debate over the Young Plan in 1929.

Finally, events were to prove that the extensive powers granted to the Reich president could be misused. The president was given the right to command the armed forces, to appoint and dismiss the chancellor, to call for a national plebiscite in certain contingencies, and, in time of emergency, to suspend the constitution. This last right was laid down in Article 48, which read: "Should public order and safety be seriously disturbed or threatened, the President may take the necessary measures to restore public order and safety; in case of need, he may use armed force . . . and he may, for the time being, declare the fundamental rights of the citizen wholly or partly in abeyance." This was the article that, in the last stages of the Republic, was to be used to undermine its foundations. Its authors were doubtless intent upon giving the government sufficient power to deal with renewed Communist disorders; and, given the state of Germany while they were completing their work, they can perhaps be forgiven for failing to foresee that the real danger was to come from a president under reactionary influence.

Antirepublican Forces   The Weimar constitution did everything that a piece of paper could do to create the conditions in which a democratic republic could grow and attain strength. What the Republic really needed now, however, was time and friends—a period free of crisis in which to consolidate itself and a large group of dedicated republicans in parliament, the civil service, and the general public. It got neither. The four years that followed the promulgation of the Weimar constitution were years of continual crisis, caused for the most part by external events and pressures; and, even after the dangers of the year 1923 were passed, the public was allowed no real alleviation of the tensions that plagued it.

At the same time, there were always fewer devoted friends of the Republic than there were enemies and neutrals. At both extremes of the political spectrum stood inveterate foes, who would do everything in their power to destroy the republican experiment. On the left were the Communists, supplemented by the left wing of the Independent Socialists, who believed that the Majority Socialists had betrayed the revolution. On the right were the Nationalists, for the most part unregenerate monarchists and landowners and industrialists who regarded the Majority Socialists as being as dangerous as the Bolsheviks; and, even further to the right, the welter of anti-Semitic, anti-Bolshevik, antidemocratic splinter groups that would eventually coalesce and form the National Socialist party. In the political groups nearer the Center, open opponents of the Republic were rarer, but there were many in the People's party and even in the right wing of the Center who maintained a studious neutrality toward the regime and who could not be counted on to support the new system in a real crisis.

This was true also of departments of the public service upon which any regime must depend for support of one kind or another: the universities and schools, the bureaucracy, the courts, the police, the army. The revolution of 1918 had not been carried to the point of driving all public servants whose democratic sentiments were not unimpeachable from their jobs. To have attempted to do this would, for a period at least, have invited chaos. All branches of the public service, therefore, were staffed for the most part with their prewar incumbents. All too often their attitude toward the new regime was one of tolerance, broken not infrequently by revelations of latent or open hostility. There were many different manifestations of this. It was to be found in the way in which school-teachers glorified the past. It was seen in the contrast between the "boys-will-be-boys" attitude taken by the police toward the hooliganism of nationalist thugs and the stern treatment they meted out for violations of the law by socialist organizations. Similarly, it was evident in the light sentences that magistrates imposed upon men charged with desecration of the symbols of the republican regime or even with the murder of its leading statesmen. Readers of Lion Feuchtwanger's remarkable novel *Success*, which deals with the situation in Bavaria between 1919 and 1923, cannot fail to be impressed by his well-documented description of the perversion of justice by the courts for political purposes.

A crucial question throughout the history of the Weimar Republic was that of the reliability of the army. Here again the natural unwillingness of the Ebert government of 1918 to court chaos had prevented the raising of a truly republican force; and the 100,000 man *Reichswehr* authorized by treaty (see p. 494) came to be filled with royalist officers and former members of free corps, who were not sympathetic to the Republic, and with long-term volunteers who could hardly expect to learn devotion to the Republic from these leaders. About the patriotism of the upper hierarchy of the army, there was never a suggestion of a doubt, but their allegiance was paid to the German Reich rather than to any particular government or regime, and they had a tendency to arrogate to themselves the right to determine what was the best interest of the Reich they served. This meant that in any crisis their attitude was ambiguous, and there was always a real possibility of their withdrawing their support from any government whose policies did not accord with their views.

To a much greater extent than was true in imperial Germany, the army became a state within the state. Claiming to be the best judges of what was good for Germany, its leaders had no hesitation about inaugurating policies of which the government was either ignorant or imperfectly informed. Thus, General Hans von Seeckt, chief of the Army Command from 1920 to 1926, entered into secret agreements with the Red Army, providing for technical assistance to that force and for German use of Soviet tanks and air facilities for training purposes; and he also made other financial and administrative arrangements designed to strengthen the German army in defiance of the military clauses of the Versailles Treaty.

It was against Seeckt and men like him that the satirist Erich Kästner lashed out in his bitter parody of Goethe:

> Kennst du das Land wo die Kanonen blühn?
> Du kennst es nicht? Du wirst es kennenlernen.

But poems could not stop them. The chief of the Army Command's greatest ambition was to be able one day to destroy Poland, with or without active Soviet aid, and to revise the eastern frontiers. To accomplish that he needed cannon, even if they had to bloom, temporarily, unseen.

Seeckt felt justified, again on grounds of national interest, in carrying on a subterranean campaign of opposition to Stresemann's Locarno policy; and he found nothing unseemly about giving information to the Russians which he hoped would help them defeat it. Seeckt finally lost his job in 1926, partly because Stresemann and other republican leaders could no longer tolerate his political pretensions, but his fall did not make the army an entirely reliable body in the hands of the Republic, and during the final crisis of the Weimar regime, his successors gave aid and comfort to its enemies.

THE CRISIS YEARS, 1919–1923

The Kapp Putsch   Nothing did more to harden the opposition of the Republic's enemies and increase their number than the efforts made by its leaders to carry out the terms of the Versailles Treaty. These also led to the first serious attempt to overthrow the Republic from the right, the so-called Kapp Putsch of March 1920.

This affair arose out of the Allied demand that the German army be reduced to 100,000 officers and men and that no supplementary forces be allowed to exist. In accordance with this, the German government felt compelled to begin the dissolution of those free corps that had fought the Spartacists in 1919, as well as those that had returned from the Baltic lands. This led to resentment, secret conferences between the officers affected, and the elaboration of a plot

"Kapp's Menagerie," a contemporary comment (1921) by the German artist George Grosz. (From *Das Gesicht der herrschenden Klasse* by George Grosz. Malik-Verlag, 1921)

against the regime. In March 1920, when the government ordered the demobilization of the Marine Brigade of Captain Hermann Ehrhardt and the Baltikum Brigade of the Iron Division (both back from the Baltic lands and both stationed outside Berlin), the commandant of Berlin, General Walther Lüttwitz, defied the government and ordered Ehrhardt's brigade to advance on the capital. At 6 A.M. on the morning of March 13, the troops entered the city and were met by Lüttwitz, General Ludendorff, and a not very distinguished East Prussian politician named Dr. Wolfgang Kapp. They immediately proclaimed a new government under Kapp's leadership.

The Kapp *Putsch* illustrated the ambiguous attitude of the army toward the Republic. When an agitated cabinet met with President Ebert on the night of March 12 to decide what should be done about the threat to Berlin, Defense Minister Noske and War Minister Reinhardt both argued for military resistance to Ehrhardt's advance. They were balked by the then chief of staff, Seeckt, the most influential of the army's commanders, who icily pointed out that "troops do not fire on troops. . . . When *Reichswehr* fires on *Reichswehr,* then all comradeship within the officer corps has vanished."

Since Seeckt's attitude made it clear that support of the local garrison could not be counted on, the government had to flee the city, and the Kapp *Putsch* was put down not by the action of a loyal army but by the crippling effects of a general strike called by the Socialist party and the trade unions. This paralyzed the Kapp "government" in Berlin, which did not, in any case, possess a very clear idea of what it intended to do with the power it had seized. On March 17, Lüttwitz and Kapp fled the city, and the Ehrhardt Brigade—after firing one sullen volley into the crowd that came to watch its departure—withdrew also.

The republican government might very well have visited pains and penalties upon the army that had failed them if the Kapp *Putsch* had not had an awkward sequel. The general strike gave new life to the Communists, who operated under its cover to start disorders in Berlin and Münster, and especially in the Ruhr, where a "Red army" whose strength was put as high as 50,000 men captured several industrial towns and by the end of March dominated the whole area around Düsseldorf. In face of this new threat from the left, Ebert and his colleagues gave up any plans they may have had to punish the army and authorized Seeckt, now raised to the position of chief of the army command, to restore order in the Ruhr. This he did with severity, using some of the same free corps whose insubordination had caused the Kapp *Putsch*.

The Inflation   These scenes of violence were trifling in comparison with those that were to come as the republican government wrestled with the problem of reparations. The main outlines of this question have been given above (pp. 493, 507), where it was pointed out that the failure of the powers to agree at an early date on a sum to be paid by the Germans that would satisfy the Allies but also be within Germany's capacity to pay was due to Anglo-French differences of view and German lack of tact at the Spa Conference of 1920. The total German liability was set by the Allies in May 1921 at the sum of 132 billion gold marks (roughly 32 billion dollars). The German government (still a coalition of the Weimar parties and now headed by a Center deputy named Joseph Wirth) announced that it would follow a "policy of fulfillment," and this policy was loyally followed by the governments that succeeded Wirth's until the beginning of 1923. But they did not have the political courage to attempt to raise the sums due to the Allies by taxation. They knew that such taxation would be resented by all classes and would force a reduction of social services that would cost them the support of their own followers. This perhaps understandable reluctance to invite new social and political troubles led them to rely upon borrowing and upon the printing of new money.

This process started a disastrous inflationary spiral. Foreigners lost confidence in German currency, and the mark, which had stood at 4.2 to the dollar in 1914 and 8.9 in 1919, began to depreciate in value on the international exchange. This had immediate repercussions at home, where people began to try to turn their money into goods. Prices began to rise and soon were rising faster than the exchange rate was declining, since owners of goods were reluctant to exchange them for currency of dubious value, and more money was printed to take up the slack. Continued differences between the English and the French prevented timely foreign intervention in the form of a reparations moratorium; and the French seizure of the Ruhr in January 1923 (see p. 508) turned the steady decline of values into a raging avalanche. It did so because the German government answered the French action with a policy of passive resistance that was enormously expensive and had to be financed by more printing. By the end of 1923, 133 printing offices with 1783 presses were turning out currency at top speed; the mark stood at 25 billion to the dollar; and one German statesman pointed out that the annual profit of the Darmstädter Bank would now be insufficient to buy a tramway ticket. The hero of Remarque's novel *Three Comrades* describes what this meant by saying: "In 1923 I was advertising chief of a rubber factory ... I had a monthly salary of 200 billion marks. We were paid twice a day, and then everybody had half an hour's leave so that he could rush to the stores and buy something before the next quotation on the dollar came out, at which time the money would lose half its value."

In the midst of the resultant chaos, there were some Germans who profited, for the inflation provided many opportunities for gifted speculators. Exporting industries, whose expenses were paid in depreciated currency while their income was in stable monies, made great profits, and by creating subsidiaries abroad they were able to manipulate fluctuations to their advantage. Some of the largest of Germany's industries became larger as a result of the inflation, by absorbing competitors with fewer reserves than their own and taking advantage of the decline of labor costs to enter upon ambitious programs of construction and

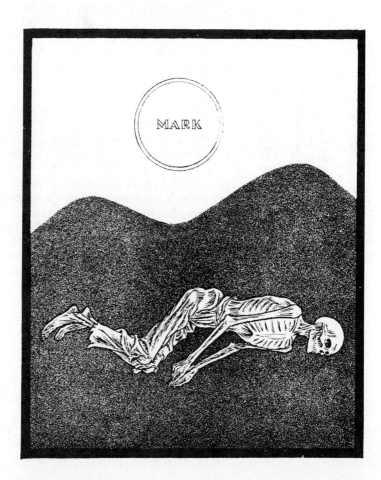

"The New Currency Comes Too Late." The revaluation of the currency at the end of 1923 was powerless to help many whose resources had long been exhausted. From *Simplicissimus,* October 29, 1923.

plant expansion. Some of the objections raised by industrial magnates to the government's termination of the policy of passive resistance to France in the Ruhr were due less to outraged patriotism than to the realization that the action forecast the end of the conditions that had brought them so many profits.

To the working classes, on the other hand, the inflation meant lower wages, longer working hours, and a decline in real income that brought hunger and sickness to their families. The chief mayor of Berlin reported in 1923 that twenty-two percent of the boys and twenty-five percent of the girls in elementary schools were below normal with respect to height and weight, and that thirty-one percent were incapable of doing their assigned work for reasons of health. The plight of the working classes was aggravated by the fact that the inflation wiped out the reserves of the Independent Trade Unions, making it impossible for them to pay benefits to their members or to pay their employees. Because of this and the fact that wage agreements negotiated by the unions became meaningless during the inflation, millions of workers left their unions, thus weakening a movement that had been potentially one of the strongest bulwarks of German democracy.

Even harder hit were those members of the middle classes who had fixed incomes or lived on savings or pensions. Men who had spent a lifetime accumulating enough savings to pay for the education of their children or to provide for their own old age now saw the result of their thrift melt away before their eyes. The psychological effect was shattering and explains why so many decent and respectable people turned for salvation to demagogues whom they would ordinarily have shunned.

The Culmination of Violence   These economic conditions weakened the authority of the government and threatened to cause the overthrow of the Republic. All of the ills of the time were blamed by the extremists of the right on the Republic's acceptance of the peace treaty and the inauguration of the policy of fulfillment. Fanatical rightists regarded it as an honor to belong to organizations whose purpose was to eliminate the persons responsible for what they considered to be treason to the Reich. In August 1921, Matthias Erzberger, the outstanding leader of the Center party and one of the signatories of the armistice of November 1918, was murdered while walking in the Black Forest; and in June 1922 a band of young men shot and killed Walther Rathenau as he drove to work one morning, because this brilliant man—who had been the author of Germany's wartime plan for economic mobilization (see p. 478) and who, as foreign minister, had concluded that Treaty of Rapallo which rescued Germany from complete diplomatic isolation (see p. 508)—was considered by them to be the embodiment of the policy of fulfillment. Other republican leaders were targets of attacks and murder attempts, and the government seemed powerless, and the courts unwilling, to check the progressive breakdown of law and order.

The year 1923 brought attacks not only on individuals but against the very structure of the state. One of the effects of the French invasion of the Ruhr was to stimulate attempts by groups of separatists in Düsseldorf and Aachen to set up an independent "Republic of the Rhineland." This movement was soon discredited by the known fact that it was encouraged by the French, but more

"Walther Rathenau," a drawing by the Berlin artist Max Liebermann, a leading member of the impressionist school and the Berlin Secession. (From M. Friedlander, *Max Liebermann,* Propyläen-Verlag, Berlin)

serious troubles arose in the east and the south. In Saxony and Thuringia, for instance, there was a marked resurgence of communism, and a "united front" of Communists and left Socialists took over the state government at the beginning of October. Using tactics that have since become familiar, the Communists attempted to get control of the police and, when this was resisted by their Socialist partners, tried a *coup de main* in Saxony that failed but caused a deterioration of the public order. These circumstances gave the Berlin government an excuse to intervene; Saxony and Thuringia were placed under martial law; and *Reichswehr* units deposed the government that had caused all the trouble.

The government found it much less easy to deal with the dangerous situation in Bavaria. The state government there had been dominated since 1920 by Gustav von Kahr, a man of inflexibly reactionary views who made himself the head of an antirepublican conspiracy that included Bavarian separatists, supporters of both the Hohenzollern and Wittelsbach dynasties, anti-Semites, and men who wanted to do to Germany what Mussolini was beginning to do to Italy. Kahr had attracted General Ludendorff to his side, a dubious advantage, since the wartime hero's megalomania was now approaching madness; he had won the confidence of General von Lossow, commander of the *Reichswehr* units stationed in Bavaria; and he had entered relations with a young man named Adolf Hitler.

Born in Austria in 1889 and still a citizen of that country, Hitler had come to Munich from Vienna in 1913. He served in a Bavarian unit of the army during the war, attaining the rank of corporal, being twice wounded, and winning the Iron Cross First Class, a distinction rarely bestowed on common soldiers. He had returned to Munich when peace was restored and joined a small racist, militarist group founded by Anton Drexler and called the German Workers party. He soon showed that he possessed remarkable talents as an orator, and his fulminations against the Versailles Treaty, the crimes of the Republic, the evils of Marxism, the unwholesome influence of the Jews, and the necessity of a national regeneration won a wide following in Munich and rural Bavaria. The party's membership increased rapidly; its name was changed in 1920 to the National Socialist German Workers party (NSDAP); and in 1921 Hitler was given unlimited powers as its leader or Fuehrer—a party decision that gave birth to "the leadership principle," about which Nazi propagandists later on had much to say. At about the same time Hitler created a private army called the *Sturmabteilung* (storm troopers) or S.A.—a body of brown-shirted thugs whose job it was to protect the Fuehrer at his own meetings and then, as their numbers and discipline grew, to prevent (and these are Hitler's own words) "all meetings or lectures that are likely to distract the minds of our fellow countrymen." It was the support of this body that Kahr was seeking when he approached Hitler.

The precise objectives of the Kahr movement were not known, but its preparations were ominous enough to indicate that it was probably going to attempt a major blow against the Reich government. That government, however, showed none of the determination it had displayed in dealing with the situation in Saxony and Thuringia. This was partly because it was always more difficult in the Weimar period to win popular support for a blow against "national elements" than it was to take action against threats from the extreme left. It was also the result, once more, of the position taken by the chief of the Army Command, General von Seeckt. Since the commander of the Bavarian army group was one of Kahr's allies, action to nip Kahr's plot in the bud might cause a situation in which *Reichswehr* would have to fire on *Reichswehr*. Seeckt was so opposed to this that he actually suggested to President Ebert that the time had come for "a reconciliation with the right" and intimated that the present government was losing the confidence of the army.

The situation was saved for the Berlin government, however, by Hitler. On the evening of November 8, 1923, when Kahr was holding a meeting of his supporters in the *Bürgerbräukeller,* the Fuehrer broke into the hall at the head of a detachment of his storm troopers, climbed on a table, and fired a shot into the ceiling, declaring that both the Reich and Bavarian governments were deposed and that the "National Revolution" had begun. He herded Kahr, Lossow, and their associates into a side room and made them pledge their support for his government, granting them offices in his cabinet in return.

The demonstration of the art of political hijacking was too much for the Bavarian leaders. During the night, while Hitler planned his campaign against

Berlin, they publicly repudiated their agreement with him and declared that they would defend the constitutional order against his attack. In response, Hitler decided to rally the city to his defense by a show of force. On the morning of November 9, the storm troopers, led by the Fuehrer and by General Ludendorff, marched from the *Bürgerbräukeller* across the river into the heart of the city. At the opening to the Odeonsplatz they were met by a force of police and army troops. There was an order to halt, a sharp fusillade, and a confused melée. Ludendorff was captured; Hitler and his chief lieutenants fled (to be apprehended two days later and jailed); and fourteen storm troopers were killed. They were the first Nazi martyrs, and from 1933 to 1945 a plaque to their memory was fastened to the wall of the *Feldherrnhalle* where they fell, guarded by two burly sentries who made passersby lift their arms reverently in the Nazi salute.

The Beer Hall *Putsch* of Adolf Hitler completely destroyed the Kahr conspiracy and eliminated the last serious threat to republican authority and Reich unity. It was now possible for the Berlin government to breathe more easily and to push ahead its plans for recovery.

THE STRESEMANN ERA, 1923–1929

Toward Financial Security   The first steps toward recovery had already been taken before matters in Bavaria came to a head, and the man who had had the courage to take them was Gustav Stresemann, who in August 1923 had become chancellor of a coalition of all the moderate parties from the Socialists to his own People's party.

Stresemann had been in German politics since 1907, when he became a member of the National Liberal party and, shortly thereafter, one of its most prominent spokesmen in the Reichstag. In the years before the war, he had been known for his extreme nationalism, his uncritical support of imperial foreign policy, and his advocacy of imperialism and navalism. During the war he had been an uncompromising supporter of the military and an opponent of all suggestions of negotiations with the enemy. In a speech in 1917 that is reminiscent of one of Bismarck's most famous speeches, he had declared that the war would be won "not by the speeches of statesmen, not by diplomatic negotiations, not by diplomatic notes, not by Reichstag resolutions, but by Ludendorff's hammer, the strength of our army, the power of our might." He wrote later "Until 1 October 1918 I believed Germany invincible." The discovery that it was not was a blow from which he recovered painfully and which forced a reorientation of his ideas.

Although many National Liberals entered the Democratic party after the war, Stresemann refused to do so and was one of the leading spirits in the formation of the German People's party, which he hoped would become the true middle party, attracting the liberal middle classes who were repelled by communism and socialism on the one hand and by reactionary nationalism on the other. Although he remained a monarchist at heart and believed that monarchy was the form of government best suited to the German people, he set his face against attempts to restore it by illegal *Putsches* and persuaded his party—which he hoped would be a bridge between the old Germany and the new—to accept the Republic as the legitimate form of government.

Stresemann's nationalism had remained undimmed by the defeat of his country, and it was his ambition to restore Germany to its place among the leading nations of the world. Unlike the reactionaries, however, he knew that this could not be accomplished by defying the Allies or making threats that could not be carried out. The Nationalists, he once said, would "not learn that you can get nowhere by saber-rattling, especially when you have no saber in your scabbard." He was realistic enough to see that Germany's recovery would necessitate sacrifice and even surrender, and he was willing to take responsibility for what he knew was sure to be labeled by the right as cowardly behavior.

When Stresemann took office, the policy of passive resistance to the French invasion of the Ruhr, which had led to a complete work stoppage in the area, was depriving the government of desperately needed revenues while at the same time costing it 350 million gold marks a week in subsidies to the resisters. In what was one of the most courageous decisions of his career, Stresemann terminated the policy, although he was violently denounced for it. It was quite clearly a surrender to the French; but it strengthened the hands of those abroad who wished to persuade them to temper their German policy, and it was, in any case, the only step that could avert a total economic collapse in Germany. Once this plunge had been taken, Stresemann went to the Reichstag and asked for a grant of plenary powers to take any and all measures considered necessary in the financial, economic, and social sphere. This law, passed over the objections of the Nationalists and the extreme left, gave the government the authority to pass a series of drastic measures designed to stop the inflation.

These were worked out under the supervision of Hjalmar Schacht, the president of the Reichsbank, and Hans Luther, the minister of finance. They included a cessation of all note printing, the withdrawal of the old currency and the issuance of a new one, the so-called *Rentenmark,* and a number of innovations (new taxes and reductions of state expenditures) that were designed to balance the budget. The new currency had no gold basis and was not convertible, being issued, in theory, against a mortgage on all the land and real estate in the country. In reality, of course, the basis of the currency was the confidence of the German people in it, the result of the vigor and resolution with which the government attacked the economic problem.

While terminating the policy of the passive resistance, Stresemann had appealed to the Western Powers for a new approach to the reparations problem and had won the support of the British and the United States governments. When France finally agreed, two committees of experts began to meet in Paris. One of them, under the chairmanship of the American banker Charles G. Dawes, formulated the plan that was to regulate German reparations payments for the next five years. Germany undertook to make annual payments, beginning at 250 million dollars and rising over a four-year period to a standard annuity of 625 million dollars. Variations from this payment would thereafter be determined by the index of German prosperity. Foreign credits were advanced to speed German recovery and make possible speedy resumption of payments—and in the end a total of 25 billion marks was pumped into Germany in foreign loans, largely from the United States.

The introduction of the Dawes Plan was attacked by the Nationalists in the

Reichstag as a surrender to foreign domination and as acceptance of what Hitler called "interest slavery." Ludendorff shouted from his seat in the Chamber: "It is a shame for Germany. Ten years ago I won the battle of Tannenberg. Today you have made a Jewish Tannenberg." In reality, the plan was the necessary foundation for recovery, and it made possible the remarkable progress of German industry and commerce and the steady rise of living standards and real wages that took place between 1924 and 1929. In 1928 Germany's national income was fifty percent greater than it had been in 1913, and per capita income had increased by the same proportion. The recovery was almost as spectacular as that which followed World War II and which then gained for the Bonn Republic the name of "the economic wonder."

Stresemann's Foreign Policy   Stresemann's chancellorship lasted only one hundred days, and he fell from office when the Socialists withdrew their support from his cabinet in protest against the difference of treatment accorded by his government to Saxony and Thuringia on the one hand and Bavaria on the other. He was never to be chancellor again; but, in every succeeding cabinet from the time of his fall until his death in 1929, he occupied the post of minister for foreign affairs. It was here that he accomplished his greatest work and, in the words of the British ambassador in Berlin, "raised Germany from the position of a stricken and disarmed foe into that of a diplomatic equal."

The first stage in that accomplishment—the negotiation of the Locarno treaties and the admission of Germany into the League of Nations—has already been described (p. 508); but two additional points may be made with respect to it. First, while proposing and accepting a guarantee of Germany's western frontiers, Stresemann refused to make any pledges concerning the boundaries in the east, which he hoped one day to be able to change in Germany's favor, although by peaceful means. Second, he refused to be deterred from concluding the Rhineland Pact and entering the League by the formidable campaign of threats and blandishments waged against him by the Soviet Union. Stresemann understood the advantages of Germany's ties with the Soviet Union; and in 1926 he was willing to conclude a new pact of friendship, the Treaty of Berlin, with Moscow. But he distrusted the motives of the Soviet government and, basically, his orientation was always toward the West.

Once Locarno was concluded, Stresemann's main objectives were to secure the removal of Allied missions and troop contingents from German soil and to win a further reduction of the reparations burden. His first victory in this respect came in 1927 when the Inter-Allied Control Commission, which had been sent to Germany in 1919 to supervise the reduction of the army to the treaty limit and the elimination of war industries, was finally withdrawn. He found it harder to persuade the Allies to evacuate their troops from the Rhineland. Despite his excellent relations with Aristide Briand, Stresemann could not convince the French statesman that speedy evacuation might accomplish more than the policy of cautious delay that Briand favored. Briand was worried by the presence in Germany of private armies like Hitler's Brownshirts, disciplined veterans' organizations like the *Stahlhelm,* and other irregular forces and insisted that France must not withdraw its troops until they were dissolved. Stresemann argued—wholly sincerely, since he was no admirer of the forces in question and their *Maulheldenthum* (mouth-heroism)—that their growth was encouraged by the continued presence of the Allied troops. It is impossible, in retrospect, to tell which of the two views was correct. The British thought that Stresemann's was, and they applied all possible pressure on the French to make them agree.

The question was finally resolved at the Hague Conference of 1929. At this meeting, the powers drew up the so-called Young Plan, a new arrangement for alleviating the pressure on the German economy by scaling down the schedule of payments set by the Dawes Plan five years earlier. Stresemann's success in persuading the powers that this new adjustment would benefit the European economy in general was in itself a major diplomatic success. But he also convinced them that any agreement on reparations—even one that lightened past burdens—would be unpopular in Germany and that national support for the Young Plan would be easier to attain if a simultaneous announcement were made that Allied evacuation of the Rhineland would be completed by 1930. The French remained doubtful but finally gave way under British pressure. Thus, when Stresemann died in October 1929, he knew that his dearest desire was going to be accomplished and his country was going finally to be freed of foreign occupation.

After Stresemann's death, the French writer Jacques Bainville said that his diplomatic achievement had been greater than that by which Bismarck had brought Prussia from Olmütz to Sedan, for, unlike Bismarck, Stresemann did not have great military power at his disposal. Stresemann's own estimate of his performance was more modest. In an interview with the British publicist Bruce Lockhart shortly before his death, he talked, indeed, as if his work had been a failure, noting that the benefits which might have been gained by a more conciliatory Allied attitude on reparations and evacuation could hardly be gained at this late date and that the mood of reconciliation prevailing at the time of Locarno had been dissipated by the long delay in exploiting it.

Signs of Continued Weakness   The years in which Stresemann pursued his diplomatic effort to restore Germany's full sovereignty and position in the world were good years for the German people economically and were filled with impressive achievements by German writers, artists, and scholars. There is no room here for an intellectual history of these years, and it will perhaps be enough to note that a period which saw the best work of men like Thomas Mann, Kurt Tucholsky, Erich Kästner, Albert Einstein, Paul Hindemith, Oskar Kokoschka, Gottfried Benn, and Friedrich Meinecke hardly deserves the label of decadence that was fastened upon it later by the Nazis.

But if there were many signs of intellectual vigor, there were few of political vitality—or, at least, the vital political forces were not on the side of the democratic Republic. Although the Socialists possessed many able theorists and publicists, they produced few who aroused much interest or enthusiasm among the rising generation. This was true also of the other republican parties. In contrast, neoconservatives like Spengler, who scoffed at the revolution of 1918 and preached that the true socialism was Prussian (see p. 459), Arthur Moeller van der Bruck, whose book *The Third Reich* proclaimed a new and better order, and Ernest Jünger (see p. 486), who called for a return to the heroic virtues of the war years, were read eagerly by young Germans, who also displayed a not inconsiderable interest in the preachments of the German Communist party. One of the most disturbing signs of political weakness in the Republic was that the republican parties did not make an effective appeal to the postwar generation, that the median age in the membership of the Socialist party, for instance, crept gradually upward, and that German youth, as the crisis of Weimar democracy approached, seemed disposed to obey the command of the young conservative newspaperman Hans Zehrer—*"Draussenbleiben!,"* which may be translated as, "Remain uncommitted!"

Stresemann's impressive diplomatic achievements brought little prestige or domestic strength to the Republic. One sign of this, perhaps, was the fact that in 1925, when Friedrich Ebert died, the man who was elected to succeed him as Reich president was not a known republican but Field Marshal von Hindenburg, despite the fact that he was already 77 years old and the additional fact that he had displayed little political wisdom during the war. Another disturbing omen was that every diplomatic success won by Stresemann had to be followed by a bitter domestic struggle before it was approved by the parties and the public. This was true of the Dawes Plan and also of the Young Plan, which, thanks to the Nationalists, became the subject of a public referendum which was held among scenes of violence and hooliganism.

One of the greatest sources of weakness in the Republic was the operation of the party system. It has been noted that the use of proportional representation multiplied the number of national parties and made coalition government necessary. The effectiveness of coalition ministries, however, was always hampered by another feature of the system: Reichstag deputies were not elected from single-member constituencies but on the basis of party lists drawn up by the party organizations. Thus, if a party's national vote entitled it to thirty seats in the Reichstag, the top thirty men on its list become deputies automatically. This system not only prevented the emergence of deputies with strong local roots but tended to make a fetish of party discipline and to stifle individual initiative.

These weaknesses had unfortunate effects on the working of government. The parties participating in any given government never allowed the ministry to forget that its existence depended on their forbearance. They kept their own representatives within the ministry on the tightest possible rein and had no hesitation about commanding them to resign, or to threaten to resign, on questions of no more than tactical importance. Keeping a coalition intact was always difficult, and keeping it intact and working was often impossible. Thus between February 1919 and January 1933 there were twenty-one different Reich cabinets, and there was a growing interest in the possibility of establishing a cabinet of "experts" who would stand above the existing parties and not be controlled by them—an experiment tried with unfortunate results in 1930, when the Bruening government was formed (see p. 576).

In view of the existence and growth of extremist parties dedicated to the destruction of the republican regime, the parliamentary habits of the moderate parties bordered on irresponsibility. Throughout his career, Stresemann devoted the portion of his time and energy that was not absorbed by foreign affairs to the task, first, of convincing the parties to show more understanding of the requirements of coalition government and, second, of creating a "great coalition" of the moderate parties which would resemble Cavour's *connubio* (see p. 194) and serve the same purpose of containing and defeating extremism. Such a coalition had existed during Stresemann's 100 days in 1923 and had been broken up by the doctrinaire tactics of the Socialists. In 1928, Stresemann's efforts helped piece together a new one, combining ministers of the Socialists, the Democrats, the Center, and his own People's party.

Old habits, however, die hard. Stresemann's own party had never been willing to accept his views about ministerial autonomy, and its members were, moreover, becoming increasingly conservative in their views about social and economic policy. On their side, the Socialists were no less uncompromising on matters of economic principle than they had been in 1923. Even in the best of circumstances, cooperation between these partners would have been difficult. As it was, the formation of the great coalition anticipated the onset of the world depression by only a few months, and, when that set in, the differences between the parties became irremediable and the coalition collapsed.

This manifestation of the basic weakness of the party system was a clear sign of the impending end of the German democracy. As the depression deepened and the extremist parties grew in strength and militancy, the republican forces presented to the country an uninspiring picture of confusion and disunity.

Chapter 25 THE CRISIS OF DEMOCRACY: CENTRAL AND EASTERN EUROPE

On Wednesday, October 23, 1929, after a month of nervous fluctuations, the stock market in New York suddenly collapsed. When trading began next morning, it did so in panic conditions and, before "Black Thursday" was over, more than 12,895,000 shares of stock had been sold and values had tumbled to levels so low that some of the most respected banking houses in the city were forced to close their doors and tens of thousands of small investors were wiped out. Desperate attempts were made in the days that followed to shore up the market, and state and national officials tried to rally public confidence by statements that were, unfortunately, robbed of conviction by their frantic optimism. None of this helped. By the end of November, when the market began to make a spotty recovery, irreparable harm had been done to the confidence of the country. When the Hoover administration did nothing to correct this, markets shriveled and disappeared, production faltered and stopped, manual laborers, salesmen, clerks, technicians, and junior executives began to receive notices of dismissal, breadlines started to form, and the United States entered the greatest economic depression in its history.

The causes of the stock market crash of 1929 have long been the subject of heated debate, and they need not concern us here. It is more important to consider its consequences. Thanks to the spread of industrialism and capitalism, the world had become so integrated in an economic sense that the collapse of what had become in 1919 the financial capital of the world inevitably had profound repercussions in every part of the globe. This was particularly true in Europe, where many important national industries had an intimate connection with American firms and where, in addition, a great amount of American capital was invested.

One of the first effects of the New York crash was the calling in of short-term loans and the virtually complete halt in new lending; this had a depressing effect on the economy of European countries, especially in central Europe, which had depended heavily on American credit. Throughout 1930, governments in this area sought strenuously to stave off trouble by programs of retrenchment and fiscal stringency; but trade and production declined with ominous steadiness and, even before the end of the year, thousands of people in Germany and Austria were feeling the pinch of hunger. The first six months of 1931 saw the failure of both the great Viennese bank the *Creditanstalt für Handel und Gewerbe* and one of Germany's three largest joint-stock banks, the *Darmstädter und National-bank*. The shock caused by these crashes not only deepened the distress of central Europe but was communicated to Great Britain and to France, the last remaining stronghold of prosperity. The depression now became general.

The depression subjected democratic institutions, wherever they existed, to a rigorous trial. In some countries, notably the United States and Great Britain, they survived the test and, indeed, were strengthened by the revelation of weaknesses that could be corrected. But this was not true of central and eastern Europe, where democracy's roots were not deep enough to survive a storm of this magnitude and where one country after another sought security in dicta-torship.

The most important country in this part of the world was Germany, and it was here that the collapse of democracy was most complete and most tragic in its results.

THE VICTORY OF NATIONAL SOCIALISM IN GERMANY

The Bruening Government   At the end of 1929 the chancellor of Germany was the Social Democrat Hermann Mueller, presiding over that government of the great coalition which Stresemann had helped create the year before (see p. 574). One of the first effects of the coming of the depression to Germany was to destroy the internal cohesion of this government and, in March 1930, to force its resignation.

The question that broke the coalition up was whether the government, with its already unbalanced budget, could afford to make the heavy outlays in unem-ployment insurance necessitated by the sharp increase in the numbers of the jobless. This insurance was provided from funds to which labor, employers, and the state contributed, but the state's share was much heavier than it had been in the case of Bismarck's nineteenth-century social welfare laws and, in the opinion of those parties representing the business community, would become insupportable in a long depression. Therefore, the People's party, a member of the government coalition, demanded that unemployment payments be reduced and in some cases (like domestic and seasonal workers) eliminated entirely. Mueller's own party protested that this would simply increase suffering and, while expressing a willingness to approve a slight increase in the assessments levied on employed labor, refused to support any reduction of benefits. The issue was one on which compromise should have been possible, but the worst features of the German party system asserted themselves, and parochialism and intransigence brought the cabinet down. Many of those who contributed to this result were later to curse their own shortsightedness, for their action opened the door to those who were to destroy the Republic.

It was pushed open further by the army, which, from this point on, played an unhappy role in German politics. The defense minister in Mueller's cabinet was Wilhelm Groener, the same general who had succeeded Ludendorff in 1918 and had made the bargain with Ebert in November of that year (see p. 556). Groener had served the Republic loyally since that time, but he was worried about the failure of the parties to provide effective government, and he feared that, in depression times, this would be dangerous to the national security. He was, therefore, responsive to a plan suggested by his most intimate adviser, General Kurt von Schleicher. Scheicher's proposal envisaged the formation of a cabinet composed of men who would be unhampered by any narrow conception of party loyalty but would govern from the standpoint of the nation alone, and in case they encountered parliamentary difficulties, would rely upon the emergency powers of the Reich president. To head such a cabinet, Groener and Schleicher favored the appointment of Dr. Heinrich Bruening, a member of the Center party, whose distinguished war record they felt would appeal to President von Hindenburg and whose sound financial views would assure him of support from parties to the right of his own. On the first score, at least, they were correct. The president authorized Bruening to form a cabinet in March 1930.

The new chancellor proved to be a man of great energy, intellectual power, and courage, but these qualities were offset by an arrogance that made enemies and a willfullness that gave them opportunities to do harm. To deal with the economic plight of the nation he had a program rigidly deflationary in nature and emphatic on the score of government economy and retrenchment; and he was unwilling to countenance either opposition or amendment to it. When he took office, he warned the Reichstag that his ministry represented "a last attempt to achieve a solution of the nation's pressing problems in conjunction with the people's legislature" and that, if the parties would not cooperate, he would look elsewhere for support. This was hardly language calculated to win supporters, and the Reichstag refused to accept his financial proposals. Bruening immediately appealed to the president and received authority to put them into effect by emergency decrees under Article 48 of the constitution. To Socialist charges that this represented a dangerous step toward dictatorship, the chancellor answered, quite sincerely, that, on the contrary, it was designed "for the education of the German people to political thinking." When the Reichstag expressed its dissatisfaction by passing a vote of no confidence in his policy, Bruening dissolved it and ordered new elections to be held on September 14, 1930.

The chancellor and his military backers were confident that this energetic behavior would impress the voters and create a workable Reichstag majority. They paid no attention to those people who warned that elections held during the depression could help no one but the parties on the extremes. But the warning voices were correct. When the vote was counted, Bruening's party had gained six seats, while the Socialists, the People's party, and the Nationalists had all declined in strength. But the Communists had increased their Reichstag representation from fifty-four to seventy-seven, and—most amazing of all—the National

Socialists had increased theirs from twelve to one hundred and seven and had become second only to the Social Democrats in strength.

The Growth of National Socialism   The Nazis had had some lean years following the debacle in Munich in 1923. While Adolf Hitler served his reduced sentence[1] in the fortress at Landberg-on-the-Lech, whiling away the time by dictating his book *Mein Kampf* to Rudolf Hess, his party had fallen to pieces, its leaders had scattered, and its members had drifted away to other messianic cults and sects of salvation. A new beginning had to be made, and Hitler was resolved to make it, but in a different way. While in prison, he told a friend:

> When I resume work, it will be necessary to pursue a new policy. Instead of working to achieve power by an armed coup, we shall have to hold our noses and enter the Reichstag against the Catholic and Marxist deputies. If outvoting them takes longer than outshooting them, at least the result will be guaranteed by their own constitution. Any lawful process is slow. . . . Sooner or later we shall have a majority—and after that, Germany.

Although forbidden by law to speak in public for two years after his release from prison in 1925, Hitler set about reconstructing his party with great energy. Through the pages of the *Völkischer Beobachter,* a newspaper acquired by the party in 1920, he carried his antirepublican, anti-Marxist, anti-Jewish views to the public and attracted new dues-paying members. Growth was slow, but even in those days of republican consolidation, steady; the party rolls swelled from 27,000 in 1925 to 178,000 in 1929. More important was the creation of an effective and surprisingly elaborate party structure. For electoral purposes, the country was divided into districts or *Gaue* that corresponded roughly with the Reichstag electoral districts, and each of these was divided into circles or *Kreise* and these, in turn, into local groups or *Ortsgruppen.* The leaders of these divisions—the *Gauleiter, Kreisleiter,* and *Gruppenleiter*—were the hard core of the party and carried its message to the remotest corners of the country. *Gaue* were created also for Austria, Danzig, the Saar, and the Sudetenland of Czechoslovakia—a plain hint that Hitler was deadly serious about the views of foreign policy expressed in *Mein Kampf* (see p. 630).

In looking to the future, Hitler said later, he had realized that it was "not enough to overthrow the old State, but that the new State must previously have been built up and be practically ready to one's hand." Thus, the party structure included a number of organs that paralleled the ministries of the legitimate government. The party's Political Organization, for example, had departments of foreign affairs, labor relations, press affairs, agriculture, justice, and national economy. There was also a separate propaganda division, in which Hitler took a very direct interest, a *Wehrpolitisches Amt,* to study defense questions, and a youth organization with various divisions that was to be of great importance later on. The party's private army was composed of the *Sturmabteilung,* which

---

[1] After the Beer Hall *Putsch,* he had been sentenced to five years' detention but served less than a year.

was expanded in size and given a more effective organization by Ernst Roehm, a soldier of fortune who was one of the oldest members of the party and who, after a temporary break with Hitler and some years of freebooting in Bolivia, took over the direction of the S.A. in 1930. There was also a second elite force, which was destined to become the most fearsome organization in Germany, the *Schutzstaffel* or S.S. This body was designed originally as a personal bodyguard for Hitler and had various leaders until 1929, when it found its permanent chief in an unimpressive looking chicken farmer named Heinrich Himmler.

At the head of the elaborate party organization stood Hitler himself, with the title supreme leader of the party and the S.A., chairman of the National Socialist Labor Organization. His personal authority stemmed from a party decision of July 1921, but it was maintained essentially by the compulsive power of his personality and the shrewdness with which he handled his subordinates. His control over the organization enabled him to deal with potential rivals by appeasing them with new jobs or undermining their strength by detaching their supporters from them. While Hitler was in prison, Gregor Strasser, a former druggist who had joined the party in 1920 and was always very popular with the rank and file, had taken over the leadership of the party, made alliances with other nationalist groups, and collaborated with them in the Reichstag elections of 1924. Strasser, after all this, was reluctant to submit to "the Leader"; but Hitler reduced him to subordination, first, by seeming to give him a free hand in directing party affairs in northern Germany and, then, by rendering this meaningless by winning to his own side and appointing to the post of *Gauleiter* in Berlin Strasser's chief aide, Paul Joseph Goebbels, a stunted little man with a club foot and a genius for propaganda.

In the last analysis, Hitler maintained his control over the motley assortment of nihilists, disinherited intellectuals, and *condottieri* by sheer strength of will. Men like Strasser and Roehm might complain bitterly to their own underlings about his decisions; but they rarely made the same complaints in Hitler's presence, and, when they did, they were either browbeaten or charmed into acquiescence with the Leader's point of view. Most of Hitler's closest associates—men like Hess, Goebbels, and the former war ace Hermann Goering, who had fled to Sweden after the *Putsch* of 1923 but returned to duty in 1927—regarded him with an attitude that bordered on reverence. This was true of lesser lights like Himmler, Alfred Rosenberg, the confused and turgid philosopher of Nordic supremacy, Walther Darré, the party's expert on agriculture, Hans Frank, the head of its legal division, and Baldur von Schirach, the Reich youth leader. The fact that Hitler was able to inspire and awe these often gifted but self-centered and cynical men, as well as the habitual drunkard Robery Ley, the future labor boss, and the perverts Roehm and Julius Streicher, *Gauleiter* of Nuremberg, helps to make less mysterious his later success in impressing the generals, the industrialists, and the press, as well as any number of foreign statesmen, including Lloyd George, Neville Chamberlain, Benito Mussolini, and Joseph Stalin.

If the party grew slowly during the years 1925–1929, its rate of growth in both membership and popular support after 1929 was tremendous. The reasons for this lay, of course, in the depression, which brought back to Germany all of the suffering of 1923. One index of its seriousness was unemployment, which increased sharply from 1,368,000 in 1929 to 3,144,000 in 1930 and then went on rising to 5,668,000 in 1931 and 6,014,000 in 1932. What this meant in human terms has been described by German novelists of this period: the plight of the white collar worker most poignantly perhaps in Hans Fallada's *Little Man, What Now* (1932) and the collapse of normal values of political and social morality very effectively in Erich Kästner's *Fabian, The Story of a Moralist* (1932). In the foreword to a new edition (1950) of his novel, Kästner recalled the conditions that did so much to bring victory for National Socialism:

> The great unemployment, the spiritual depression that followed the economic one, the craving for oblivion, the activity of thoughtless parties, these were the storm signals of the coming crisis. Even the frightening calm before the storm was not absent—the laziness of the spirit that resembled an epidemic paralysis. Many were impelled to stand against the storm and the calm, but they were shoved aside. People preferred to listen to the circus barkers and the drummers who recommended their own mustard plasters and poisonous patent medicines. People ran after the pied pipers, down into the abyss where we now are, more dead than living. . . .

During the good years of the Republic, the NSDAP had been supported for the most part by superheated patriots, fanatical anti-Semites and social misfits. Once the depression had set in train the progressive demoralization of society, the party appealed to a much wider audience; and Hitler saw to it that special messages and promises of salvation were carried to unemployed manual workers, to agricultural laborers and small farmers who had been hit hard by the fall of prices, to industrialists whose markets had disappeared, and to other special economic groups. The messages were sometimes carefully reasoned and based upon work done by the separate sections of the party's Political Organization, but party orators had no compunction about directing their appeal to the prejudices of their audiences or to the willingness to repudiate reason that often overcomes people in extremity. Peter Drucker has written of hearing a Nazi spokesman shout to a wildly cheering crowd of farmers: "We don't want higher bread prices! We don't want lower bread prices! We want *National Socialist* bread prices!" This sort of thing was especially popular with audiences of the lower middle class—that sector of society whose security was always provisional, whose members were the first to be affected by depression and the least well prepared to resist it, since they had neither the reserves of the upper middle class nor the organization of the working class, and which had been, throughout German history, a hotbed of social resentment. It was here that Hitler had least trouble in persuading audiences to believe that Jews, plutocrats, and socialists were the cause of all their woes and that only the destruction of the Republic by a Nazi party victorious at the polls would save them.

Bruening and his supporters failed either to pay sufficient attention to the strength of Hitler's party organization or to imagine how effective its propaganda might be in conditions approaching economic collapse. They were completely unprepared for Hitler's victory in the elections of September 1930, when six and a half million Germans voted for the NSDAP.

"New Types: The Racial Man (or The Man of Breeding)". In July 1924, in *Simplicissimus,* Karl Arnold portrayed the anti-Semites who flocked to Hitler's support with this drawing, entitled ambiguously *Neue Typen: Der Rassemensch.*

Schleicher's Maneuvers and the Appointment of Hitler   Bruening's position after September 1930 was one of mounting difficulty. The Reichstag was more unmanageable than ever before, with the Communists and the Nazis indulging in continual obstructionism and disorder. Bruening was able to stave off votes of no confidence only by a slim majority that depended on the willingness of the Social Democrats to tolerate him because they feared what might happen if he fell. For the carrying out of his economic program—which was so Spartan in its character that it had earned him the name the 'Hunger Chancellor'—this was not enough, and he had to rely on the continued authority of the president exercised under Article 48.

It was the chancellor's hope that he would be able to strengthen his position by winning a resounding foreign success that would impress public opinion at home; and he set his mind on such things as a complete termination of reparations and the concession to Germany of equality of status in armaments. Throughout 1931 he sought to convince the other powers that it would be to their interest to make concessions to a democratic Germany rather than to have to deal with a Communist or Nazi one. The British proved amenable to this sort of argument, but Bruening's success in winning over his other neighbors was handicapped by a series of impolitic speeches by members of his government, in which they alluded to the necessity of correcting the eastern frontiers and talked querulously about the restrictions on Germany's freedom of action in the Rhineland. The Bruening government also hit on the idea of seeking to improve economic conditions in central Europe by creating a customs union between Austria and Germany but, instead of consulting the other powers first, made the mistake in March 1931 of announcing the new *Zollunion* as a *fait accompli.* The results of this lack of tact were shattering. France, supported by Italy and the Little Entente, protested that the union was incompatible with the peace treaty and other agreements; the plan had to be submitted to the World Court at The Hague, which eventually set it aside; and what had seemed a promising gain for the Bruening government was transformed into a humiliating diplomatic defeat. Moreover, it had economic effects as well, for it was one of the reasons for French delay in accepting President Herbert Hoover's proposal, in June, for a one-year postponement of all intergovernmental debt payments. The French delay robbed the Hoover moratorium of much of its potential effect, and it had no success in checking the deepening depression in Germany.

As 1932 opened, Bruening had two new problems. Despite Hitler's decision to seek power by legal means, which he had declared publicly in a court trial in 1930, his Brownshirts were indulging in acts of violence and terrorism all over Germany. Several of the state governments wanted federal action against Nazism, and the Social Democratic party was intimating that, unless Bruening agreed, their support of him in the Reichstag would stop. In the second place, President von Hindenburg's term of office expired in the spring of 1932 and, unless the parties agreed to a prolongation, there would be elections that would almost certainly disrupt the economy and the public order. Bruening wished to avoid this and, because he hoped to persuade all the parties to agree, refrained from any action against the Nazis.

This did him no good. Hitler refused to assent to Bruening's plan for prolonging Hindenburg's term and put himself forward as a candidate. The elections were conducted in conditions that justified all the chancellor's fears. The first polling was indecisive, Hindenburg receiving 49.6 percent of the vote, Hitler 30.1 percent, the Communist candidate Thaelmann 13.2 percent, and the National candidate Duesterberg 6.8 percent. In the second poll, held on April 10, 1932, the old field marshal, thanks to Duesterberg's withdrawal from the race, received 53 percent of the vote to Hitler's 36.8 percent and Thaelmann's 10.2 percent and was declared elected.

On the eve of the first election, the S.A. had been mobilized and had thrown a cordon around Berlin. The purpose of this exercise was not clear, but it alarmed the government, as did materials discovered in police raids on Nazi centers, which seemed to indicate that a *Putsch* was being planned. On the advice of Defense Minister Groener, the chancellor decided to strike out at Hitler and, on April 14, decreed the suppression of the S.A. and the S.S.

What appeared for the moment as a sign of strength was soon revealed, however, to be the cause of Bruening's downfall. The agent of this was Groener's friend and subordinate, Schleicher, who had originally supported the ban on the S.A. but now reversed himself. In Schleicher's view, Bruening, who he had hoped would lead Germany out of the swamp of party politics, was now proving himself to be merely a pawn of the Socialists. It was time, he thought, to try a new political combination whose first order of business would be to reduce the Socialists to impotence, so that, if it were necessary to use force against the Nazis later on, there would be no doubt that such action was taken in the national interest rather than for the benefit of the left. Schleicher does not seem to have believed that a blow against the Nazis would be necessary. He hoped to persuade Hitler to accept political responsibility under conditions that would

A prophetic cartoon printed in *Simplicissimus* (July 3, 1932) shortly after Heinrich Bruening's dismissal. Here the departing chancellor is saying to President von Hindenburg: "And sometime write me a post card from the Third Reich."

keep him under restraint or, failing that, to split his party and detach important groups from it.

Immediately after the promulgation of the ban on the S.A., therefore, Schleicher used his influence with the president's son, Oskar von Hindenburg, to persuade the old man that the decree had alarmed and offended the army. There was some truth in this. National Socialism was beginning to attract the junior officers of the *Reichswehr* and, even among senior officers who disliked Hitler and his opinions, there was admiration for the spirit and energy of the movement and respect for the military potential represented in it. Several retired generals wrote letters to the president expressing concern over this blow to Germany's military resources. Hindenburg was impressed by these complaints and felt he had been insufficiently informed by his chancellor; and, once the seeds of suspicion were planted, it was easy for Schleicher, Oskar von Hindenburg, and others in the president's entourage to nourish them. Although Groener tried to protect Bruening by attempting to assume responsibility for the ban and resigning as defense minister on May 13, the chancellor himself lasted only till the end of the month, when Hindenburg made it clear that he would no longer support him.

The politics of the next eight months were so complicated that it is impossible to give more than the barest outline of them in a brief account. They were dominated by the figures of three arch intriguers: Schleicher, who sought to carry out the policy sketched above; Baron Franz von Papen, former Guards officer, military attaché in Washington during World War I whence he was expelled for espionage, and now member of the Center party; and Hitler. Papen was the man selected, and sold to the president by Schleicher, to replace Bruening and give Germany the authoritarian government that Bruening had failed to create. To give Papen a fair start, Schleicher made a secret agreement with Hitler in which the Fuehrer apparently promised to tolerate Papen in return for a promise that the ban on the S.A. would be lifted and new Reichstag elections would be held at the end of July. Armed with this equivocal pledge, Papen—at Schleicher's bidding—struck out at the main center of Socialist power in Germany, the Social Democratic government of Prussia. Taking advantage of a street battle between Nazis and Communists in Altona, near Hamburg, on July 17, in which seventeen persons died, he accused the Prussian government of being incapable of maintaining public order and secured a decree from President Hindenburg appointing him national commissioner for Prussia and authorizing him to dismiss its government, which he did on July 20. The Prussian ministers yielded without resistance, and it is difficult to see what else they could have done. General von Rundstedt had been ordered to back up Papen's action by force if necessary, and the ministers did not believe that their police force would resist the army even if authorized to do so, particularly since the president's decree would have made such action seem illegal. Nor could the ministers rely upon the unions to make use of the strike weapon against Papen, as they had against Kapp in 1920 (see p. 563); given the high rate of unemployment, workers with jobs were not anxious to give them up temporarily lest they be filled with blacklegs. Economic want is a great dissolvent of class solidarity. In view of these facts, the Prussian ministers capitulated, inevitably giving an impression of weakness and lack of conviction that was not lost on Hitler.

Neither the Prussian coup nor Papen's energetic foreign policy—his success at a conference at Lausanne in freeing Germany from the reparations burden and his temporary withdrawal from the Geneva disarmament conference in protest against Germany's unequal status—won him any appreciable success with middle class or conservative voters or had any effect on the Nazis at all. When Reichstag elections were held at the end of July, the only two parties that gave Papen any considerable support lost forty-four seats between them, whereas the Communists gained twelve seats and the Nazis doubled their representation, becoming the largest Reichstag party with 230 seats. To stave off a vote of no confidence supported by the two extremist parties, Papen had to dissolve the Reichstag immediately and call for new elections in November; but, when they were held, the results from his standpoint were even worse, 90 percent of the vote being clearly against the government.

At this juncture, Papen seems to have decided that, if a pledge of support could not be secured from the parties, the constitution must be dispensed with, the Reichstag, the parties, and the trade unions dissolved, and the cabinet, backed by the president and the army, must rule by decree. It says much for his powers of persuasion that he had the president convinced that all this was necessary when Schleicher intervened. The general pointed out that the result of Papen's projected action would be joint Nazi and Communist risings, complicated in all probability by border forays by the Poles. The army, he said, was not strong enough to maintain public order and national security in those circumstances. Considerably set back by this confession, Hindenburg had no recourse but to refuse Papen the dictatorial powers he had requested and to accept his resignation. He insisted, however, that Schleicher now assume responsibility for the government and appointed him chancellor on December 2, 1932.

Schleicher was not displeased by these events. To him the most interesting feature of the November elections had been the sudden fall of Nazi strength—a loss of two million votes and thirty-four Reichstag seats. If the Nazis were now past their peak strength, if the public was beginning to be revolted by the rapine and plunder and political murder that had been practiced by the Brownshirts for the last year, then perhaps the time had come to force Hitler to compromise or to split his movement. Schleicher knew that Gregor Strasser was worried by the election returns and thought that he might be willing to enter a new government, bringing people like Roehm with him. It was, indeed, because he saw this possibility that Schleicher had brought the chancellor down by giving Hindenburg a deliberately pessimistic army report.

Alas for Schleicher's hopes! His estimate of the situation was right as far as it went. The Nazi party was in difficulties; it was short of funds; and several of its leaders wanted to take office before it was too late. But Schleicher had not counted on Hitler's political shrewdness or his ability to keep his lieutenants in line. Some secret sense told Hitler that to accept a share of political responsibility on Schleicher's terms would be disastrous. When Schleicher offered Strasser the post of vice chancellor in his cabinet and Strasser urged the party to consent to this, Hitler vetoed the suggestion. Strasser then resigned from the NSDAP, although he did not immediately attempt to start a defection toward Schleicher. In any case, Hitler soon made this impossible by abolishing the Political Organization that Strasser had dominated and setting up a new central party organization under Rudolf Hess that assured him of the support of a united party.

This solution of the crisis in the Nazi party doomed Schleicher. He tried desperately to win strength in the Reichstag, actually promising fundamental agrarian and social reforms in an attempt to win Socialist support, but the Socialists remembered his role in the dissolution of the Prussian government and were unsympathetic. He turned to the president and asked for the same dictatorial powers that Papen had requested, but the president, who was fond of Papen, remembered the arguments Schleicher had used against him and declined. Hindenburg's attitude was doubtless influenced by the alarm that Schleicher's talk of land reform had aroused in the agrarian circles in which he moved, and he let his chancellor know that unless he could find a Reichstag majority, he would have to go.

There were now only two possible successors, Papen and Hitler. Out of resentment over Schleicher's tactics, Papen had been instrumental in easing Hitler's financial troubles by procuring support for him from some prominent Rhineland industrialists. He was now discussing the possibility of a new Papen-Hitler government with the Fuehrer, who, on his side, was holding out stubbornly for the position of chancellor in any such combination. It was rumored in Berlin that if an attempt were made to make Hitler chancellor, the army would intervene to block it. In reality, there was no possibility of this. Schleicher, the man in the best position to call for army intervention, was more fearful of a Papen chancellorship than of a Hitler one. Moreover, there is reason to believe that in the last days of January, when Berlin was filled with rumors of imminent coups d'état, Schleicher was secretly intimating to Hitler that the army would support him if its own interests were protected—that is, if he himself received the position of defense minister in Hitler's cabinet. The attempt of the army chiefs to cure Germany of the ills of parliamentary government, inaugurated with the appointment of Bruening in 1930, had thus been transformed by January 1933 into an attitude of resignation. A Hitler government seemed to them to offer better prospects of order than a return to Papen, and they stifled their doubts about the Austrian corporal by telling themselves that they would be able to control him.

Thus, the army remained neutral and, by its neutrality, assured Hitler's successful acquisition of power. On January 30, 1933, Papen's negotiations reached their conclusion. The president was persuaded to overcome his former antipathy to Hitler and accept him as chancellor of a coalition cabinet with Papen as vice chancellor, Hugenberg of the Nationalists as minister of economics, Seldte of the Stahlhelm as minister of labor, General von Blomberg (instead of Schleicher) as defense minister, the Nazi Frick as minister of interior, and Goering as minister without portfolio. Although there were only three NSDAP members in the predominantly Nationalist cabinet, the crowds of jubilant Nazis that swarmed through the streets of Berlin on the night of January 30 acted as if they were the new rulers of Germany. They were justified by the result.

The Consolidation of Nazi Power   For a few weeks at least, the new chancellor had to move with caution. The president had not given him emergency powers, and, even with the support of the Nationalists, he did not command a majority of the Reichstag. But new Reichstag elections were scheduled for March, and the Fuehrer was counting on the efforts of his lieutenants to make the most of them. Goering, whom he had appointed as minister of interior in Prussia, showed that his confidence was not misplaced. Goering used his position to legitimize assaults on the political meetings of other parties by supplementing the regular police with an auxiliary force of 50,000 men, four fifths of whom were recruited from the S.A. and the S.S. and spent most of their time hounding enemies of the party. Men like Bruening and Stegerwald, the head of the Catholic Trade Unions, found it virtually impossible to make public speeches, and Communists did so at the peril of their lives.

This campaign of intimidation was not in itself enough. Hitler needed an event that would frighten the parties into giving him powers to deal with what he called the Bolshevik menace. He got it on the night of February 27, 1933, when the Reichstag building was gutted by fire. A half-witted Dutch Communist named Marinus van der Lubbe was arrested in the building and confessed to the crime. The fire was in all likelihood planned and laid, if not actually ignited, by Nazi agents (Goering is reported to have boasted in 1942, "The only one who really knows about the Reichstag is I, because I set it on fire!"), although this is still a matter of dispute. However that may be, it was enough to give Hitler solid cabinet backing for a request for a presidential decree "for the protection of the people and the state." This document, signed by Hindenburg on February 28, suspended those sections of the constitution that guaranteed civil and individual liberties and authorized the government to use any methods it desired, including house search and arrest, to guard against "Communist acts of violence endangering the state."

Armed with this decree, truckloads of storm troopers roared through the streets of Germany arresting Communist, Socialist, and liberal leaders, entering homes and carrying persons off to S.A. barracks, smashing newspaper presses, breaking up opposition meetings, and generally terrorizing the country. Meanwhile, the government radio poured out a constant stream of revelations about Communist conspiracies against the state. In face of all this, it is surprising that, when the elections were held on March 5, 1933, 56 percent of the voters still opposed Hitler, the Socialists holding their own, the Center increasing its strength, and even the Communists managing to poll 4,848,058 votes. The Nazis, with 288 seats, and the Nationalists, with fifty-two, had a bare majority in the Reichstag, but no more.

But Hitler still had the powers granted by the decree of February 28, which gave him the right to arrest enemies of the Reich at will; and by holding these over the head of the Reichstag he now got what he wanted. On March 23 he laid before the Reichstag the so-called Enabling Act, or "law for relieving the distress of the people and the Reich." This gave the cabinet full legislative and budgetary powers, including the right to initiate constitutional amendments, for a period of four years, and thus called for a complete abdication of power by the Reichstag. In the tense debate in the Reichstag, only the Socialists spoke and voted against the bill. The Center party played the key role at this crucial moment in German history. In its caucus earlier, its leader, Monsignor Kaas, argued that if Hitler did not get full power this way, he would get it another. The Center decided to vote as a bloc for the bill but to seek assurances from Hitler that the president's right to veto would be observed and other constitutional safeguards provided. Such assurances were not received, but the Center voted for the bill anyway and—since there were no Communists present—their action was decisive. By a vote of 441 to 84, the Reichstag made Hitler a dictator.

Gleichschaltung   There followed the process called by the untranslatable German word *Gleichschaltung*—the systematic smashing, or taming, or "coordination" of all independent agencies or organizations. One of the first steps in this direction was the abolition, in March and April 1933, of the historic rights of the separate states of Germany, the dismissal of their governments, and the appointment of Reich governors, responsible to the chancellor, with extensive powers. The process thus begun was completed on the first anniversary of Hitler's assumption of power by the Law for the Reconstruction of the Reich (January 30, 1934). The popular assemblies of all states were abolished, their sovereign powers were transferred to the Reich, their governors were put under the authority of the Reich Ministry of the Interior, and Germany was completely centralized for the first time in its history.

Long before this law had been promulgated, the parties that might have objected to it had all disappeared. The Communists had been outlawed in February; in June the minister of the interior declared that the Social Democratic party was subversive and must be dissolved; in July the two Catholic parties, the Bavarian People's party and the Center party, announced their own dissolution; the Democrats and Stresemann's People's party yielded to pressure and did the same. Hitler's partners in the cabinet of January 30, 1933, the Nationalists, had seen the light even earlier, although only after their offices were occupied by the police and the S.A. and they had been invited to leave. The whole process was legitimized by a law of July 14, 1933, which declared that the NSDAP was the only political party in Germany and that attempts to found or maintain others would be punished by prison sentence.

The weakness revealed by the trade unions during Papen's coup in Prussia in July 1932 did not persuade Hitler that it was safe to leave them unreconstructed. As long as they existed independently, there was a possibility that they might become centers of subversion or conspiracy against the state, and Hitler was never one to take chances. On May 2, 1933, police and S.A. units raided the headquarters of all of the Independent Trade Unions, arrested their leaders and seized their funds, and ten days later all of their property was attached. On June 24 the Catholic Trade Unions were crushed in the same way. To replace the union structure, a Labor Front was created under the leadership of the perpetually intoxicated *Gauleiter* of Cologne, Robert Ley. This body, which eventually embraced all gainfully employed persons outside of the civil service, had no genuine political or economic functions and nothing to do with the regulation of wages or working conditions (which was left to specially appointed labor trustees, who were supposed to "regulate labor contracts" and "maintain labor peace"). The Labor Front administered the taxation of the working class and performed certain tasks of stewardship and definition of rules of labor, but its essential job was to keep labor in an atomized and powerless condition, with no leaders or representation of their own, and to extirpate from their minds the last traces of Marxism by an incessant process of indoctrination.

No one recognized better than Hitler that the permanent civil service could effectively sabotage the work of a regime, and he was determined that what had occurred under the Weimar regime would not be repeated under his own. Within two weeks of the passage of the Enabling Law, Hitler decreed a "law for the restoration of the professional civil service" (April 7, 1933), which called for the elimination from the service of all non-Aryans and people who were "no longer prepared to intercede at all times for the National Socialist State." This was soon extended to the judiciary and the universities. In a purge that in some ways resembled that of Bismarck in the 1880s (see p. 351), twenty-eight percent of the higher members of the Prussian civil service, including all potential dissidents, were dismissed or demoted. A more thoroughgoing combing out was not necessary, for the psychological results of the first dismissals were pervasive.

Aside from applying the law of April 7, 1933 to the judiciary, no very energetic attempt was made to coordinate the majority of the German courts. But the decision of the *Reichsgericht* or Supreme Court to acquit three of the four defendants in the Reichstag fire trial led to the establishment of a new court,

The result of *Gleichschaltung:* Tyranny enthroned. Hitler and his minions at the Nürnnberg party congress. (The Trustees of the Imperial War Museum, London)

the People's Tribunal, to deal with cases of treason; and, after March 1933, cases of political crime were tried before the *Sondergericht* or Special Court, where defense attorneys had to be approved by Nazi officials. It is, moreover, impossible to appreciate the true nature of Nazi justice unless one realizes that Hitler and, for a time, Goering had the right to terminate criminal proceedings of which they did not approve and that Rudolf Hess, the Fuehrer's deputy, was authorized to take further action against defendants who in his opinion had been treated too lightly. In addition, the Gestapo or Secret Police, established by Goering in April 1933, and the S.D. or Security Service of the S.S. did not hesitate to inflict arbitrary arrest, imprisonment in concentration camps, corporal punishment, and death upon thousands of Germans and, by the decree of February 1936, were declared to be above the law when carrying out "the will of the leadership." They could, as Arnold Brecht once wrote.

> arrest persons and extend the time of detention indefinitely. They could leave the relatives without any information regarding the prisoner's whereabouts and fate. They could prevent any lawyer or other person from visiting him or from looking into the records. They could treat him as they saw fit, for example, overload him with work unsuited to him, feed him and house him badly, force him to say formulae or sing songs he detested, maltreat him in order to get him to confess or to divulge the names and acts of others, and . . . whip him or shoot him. . . . They could do all this, provided only that their superiors allowed them to do so.

Shortly after his appointment as chancellor, Hitler talked of his desire to maintain "a peaceful accord between church and state" and to improve relations with the Vatican. In July 1933, he actually concluded a concordat with the papacy that guaranteed the freedom of the Roman Catholic religion in Germany and the right of the church to regulate its own affairs. The ink was hardly dry upon this treaty when systematic attacks were launched against the Catholic Youth League and other church organizations, upon the Catholic press, and upon the persons of leading churchmen. These were intermittent, but, as the years passed, their number became too great to be ignored, and the church found it impossible to close its eyes any longer to other features of the Nazi system—its brutal persecution of minorities, its callous indifference to normal processes of law, its introduction of legislation calling for the sterilization of undesirables, and much more. In March 1937, Pope Pius XI, in the encyclical "With Burning Sorrow," protested eloquently against infringements of the concordat; and, if this had little effect upon the direction of Nazi policy, it influenced many Catholics to enter the resistance movement against what was clearly, as the pope noted, an attempt to exterminate their faith.

Meanwhile, the Lutheran and Reformed churches were being subjected to a state-backed campaign by a group called the German Christians, who wanted to unite Protestantism in a Reich church, which would incorporate the Nazi racial doctrine and the leadership principle into its body of belief. Despite its long history of being more than eager to render unto Caesar what was Caesar's, German Protestantism found it difficult to agree that the Fuehrer should supplant

Jesus Christ; and hundreds of pastors resisted and were sent to concentration camps for their resistance. As in the case of the Catholic Church, Hitler was able to break overt opposition by force and to exact from churchmen an oath of allegiance as the price of keeping the churches open. But the ranks of the underground resistance were swollen by loyal Protestants who felt they could not tolerate the abuses of the regime.

Gleichschaltung did not stop with these organizations. It was extended to all agencies that could affect the minds of Germans for good or evil. The Reich Press Law of October 4, 1933, stipulated that all newspaper editors must be German citizens, Aryan, and not married to Jews and laid down censorship laws of the utmost rigidity. In the years that followed, some of Germany's oldest and most respected journals—the *Vossische Zeitung,* for instance, which had been founded in 1704—were forced out of existence, and those that were kept for show were mere shadows of their former selves. The radio was already a state monopoly and had become a mere voice of the party, controlled by Joseph Goebbels. Goebbels's Propaganda Ministry also controlled all aspects of the film industry, including production. The most conspicuous result of this control of the means of mass communication was that their intellectual level fell to abysmal depths and their dullness became apparent even to the most loyal Nazi. What happened to German culture may be illustrated by an incident that occurred in 1943 when Germany's largest film company, UFA, celebrated its twenty-fifth birthday. Thanks to Goebbels's ministrations, UFA had so few talented artists by this time that, in making the commemorative film *Münchhausen,* it had to get government permission to employ Erich Kästner, whose books had been banned since 1933, as script writer, Hans Albers, a known opponent of the regime, in the title role, the Hungarian Josef von Baky as director, and the Russian Irmen Tschet as cameraman for special effects. Needless to say, only Albers's name appeared in the credits, and then only because he could not be hidden.

The flight of talent and its proscription for reasons of politics and race also affected the German educational system. All teachers at whatever level were subject to the racial laws and had to take an oath of allegiance to Hitler, and the subject and content of their courses and the books they could use were prescribed by people chosen for their political orthodoxy rather than their pedagogic skill. Thousands of great scholars and teachers lost or left their positions, and those who remained watched, willingly or unwillingly, as learning was distorted to serve the ends of the Nazi state. Hitler boasted that his new Reich would "give its youth to no one, but itself take youth and give it its own education and its own upbringing." It succeeded perhaps in the task it considered most important—in making a large proportion of youth loyal Nazis—but it did not give them a good education. By 1939 German industry was complaining of the shortage of well-trained chemists, engineers, and technicians, and both the economy and the state services were beginning to feel the effects of an educational system that regarded its chief aim as political and racial indoctrination.

The Subordination of the Party and the Armed Forces   By the methods described above, Hitler succeeded, in the words of Franz Neumann, in annihilating "every institution that under democracy preserves remnants of human spontaneity." His tyranny was not complete, however, until he had eliminated two possible threats to his power: that from his own party and that represented by the armed forces.

Hitler never felt the necessity of conducting a party purge on the scale of the purges of Joseph Stalin (see p. 531); but he nevertheless demonstrated, in June 1934, that he was capable of it by eliminating some of his oldest comrades and most outspoken party critics. The essential reason for what came to be known as the Night of the Long Knives was the dissatisfaction felt by many of Hitler's followers with what they considered to be the conservative turn of his policy after March 1933. These people—many of them former followers of Gregor Strasser—had taken the Socialist part of their party's title seriously, and they expected the Enabling Act to lead to expropriation of the wealthy few and distribution of goods to the deserving many. Instead, they saw Hitler on the most cordial terms with the industrialists and the great landowners and the generals and the old elite. Criticism of Hitler was particularly vocal in the S.A., whose commander Ernst Roehm was a genuine revolutionary who wanted, as he said, "to lift the world off its hinges" and who thought of the S.A. as the true revolutionary army that would replace the old *Reichswehr*. Roehm's grumblings were reported to Hitler by malicious colleagues. They also came to the ears of the leaders of the army, who, jealous of their own monopoly of power and fearful of a possible coup by the S.A., urged Hitler to deal with his unruly private army.

Whether the leaders of the S.A. were actually considering a blow against the Fuehrer is still not clear. Hitler, after long hesitation, decided to act as if they were and, with that shattering speed which always characterized his actions once his mind was made up, struck in the predawn hours of June 30, 1934. Detachments of S.A. troops and Gestapo agents snatched Roehm and other S.A. leaders from their beds and shot them without hearings of any kind. Meanwhile, other murder gangs took advantage of the occasion to dispose of prominent anti-Nazis and to pay off old grudges. General von Schleicher and his wife were shot down in their home; General Kurt von Bredow, an associate of Schleicher's, suffered the same fate; Gustav von Kahr, who had broken with Hitler in 1923, was hacked to death and thrown into a swamp near Dachau; two of Papen's closest aides were shot, as a warning to the vice chancellor. All told, hundreds of people met their deaths (at one of the postwar trials the number was set at more than a thousand), and the memory of this night of terror was enough to discourage serious dissension within the party until Hitler's death.

One of the reasons for Hitler's decision to purge the S.A.[2] was his desire to please the army, and this stemmed from a special circumstance. It was known in mid-1934 that Hindenburg's health was failing rapidly, and Hitler intended to take over the powers of his office when the president died. He wanted no interference from the army when that happened, and, as a result of his elimination of the army's chief rival, he met none. When Hindenburg died on August 2,

[2] The organization continued to exist under new leadership but with greatly reduced prestige. Its survival was attributed by some to the fact that it was mentioned in the Horst Wessel song, the party hymn. This would have made its elimination awkward.

1934, it was immediately announced that the offices of chancellor and president had been combined and that Hitler would rule as head of state (Fuehrer and Reich chancellor) and commander of the armed forces. All officers and men in those forces were required to take a special oath of allegiance to the Fuehrer, pledging unconditional obedience to him.

The acceptance of this oath by the armed forces—and there were no open objections to taking it—was the second step in the subjection of the army to Hitler's domination. The first, which had irretrievably weakened the army's moral position, had been its acquiescence in the murders of June 30 and its failure to protest even against the deaths of Generals von Schleicher and Bredow. Henceforth, the army's independence would be progressively sapped.

The senior officers of the army might continue to delude themselves with the belief that, if necessary, they could control Hitler, or depose him; but, as the years passed, the likelihood of this tended to disappear. Especially after March 1935, when breakneck rearmament began (see p. 636), the army grew so enormously in size that the inner homogeneity of the officer corps dissolved, and the older, more conservative officers could no longer speak for the whole. After 1936, the new officer candidates and the new conscripts tended to be boys who had already been indoctrinated in Nazi-controlled schools; and, even among more mature officers, old values began to disintegrate under the pressure of ambition, jealousy, and opportunism in the expanding service. In the air force and the navy, loyalty to National Socialism paid dividends in the form of quick promotions; inevitably, junior officers in the army began to seek the same road to the top.

Hitler's respect for the senior army officers, which had been strong in the beginning, began to wane when he found them raising objections to the pace of the rearmament program and the adventurousness of his foreign policy (see p. 638). When the time came for him to launch his all-out drive to dominate eastern Europe, he felt confident enough to "coordinate" the army as he had the trade unions. At the beginning of February 1938, taking advantage of a scandal arising from the second marriage of his defense minister, General von Blomberg, and professing to believe fabricated charges of moral turpitude against the chief of Army Command General von Fritsch, he dismissed both of those officers—and a number of others whose views he suspected—and reorganized the armed forces completely. Henceforth, all of the services were to be subordinate to a new Supreme Command of the Armed Forces (OKW), under Hitler's immediate command, with General Keitel, a complete admirer of Hitler, as his deputy. The army command and its famous and once all-powerful General Staff were thus demoted, having henceforth to submit their views to Hitler's personal military staff. This outraged the senior commanders, but they did not resist; and the last limits to Hitler's absolute power in Germany were removed.

The War Economy   Under Hitler, Germany emerged from the depression with a speed that amazed the world. Unemployment sank from six million in 1932 to less than one million four years later; the gross national product doubled in the same period, as did the national income. Government pump-priming, expanded public works programs, tax relief for industry, and financial juggling by the capable Dr. Schacht, now serving Hitler more loyally than he had the Republic, all played their part in this. Essentially, however, the stimulus to recover came from the rearmament program, and the whole economy came to be a war economy, predicated on the assumption that war was coming and making the necessary preparations in advance. The Four-Year Plan inaugurated in September 1936 was designed to make Germany self-sufficient and hence invulnerable to a blockade like that of 1914–1918. Accumulation of strategic materials, development of synthetics, mobilization of war industries, all began under its aegis; and all made for employment and prosperity.

To Germany's neighbors, who did not realize the end objective of Hitler's policy, this economic recovery was most impressive, and it helped to make totalitarianism seem attractive, and friendship and collaboration with Nazi Germany desirable.

This was particularly true in the countries to the east, where the trend to dictatorship had already been noticeable before Hitler came to power.

THE RETREAT OF DEMOCRACY IN EASTERN EUROPE

Poland and the Baltic States   The postwar history of Poland afforded a good illustration of the difficulties of making democracy work in eastern Europe. The Poles, whose qualities of courage and chivalry had always made them popular in the West, were treated generously at Paris, and the new Republic started its existence with geographical advantages and economic resources that were superior to those of its neighbors and with reasonable assurance of continued support by the Allied powers. These initial advantages were offset, however, by territorial ambitions that created difficulties that might have been avoided and by political practices that made the solution of internal problems virtually impossible, and consequently destroyed the people's confidence in democratic institutions.

Much of Poland's trouble stemmed from its attempt to expand its territory by assaults upon its neighbors in the immediate postwar years. These aggressions have been described above, and it has been noted that they were not entirely unsuccessful (see pp. 506, 524). Even so, they left behind them a legacy of bitterness and tension, and gave Poland frontiers that were less secure than those originally authorized at the Peace Conference. The fear of future attack from neighbors they had despoiled and the knowledge that one of the results of their aggression was the acquisition of disaffected national minorities convinced all postwar Polish governments that a large military establishment was essential to national security. In effect, despite French encouragement and aid, Polish military expenditures were so heavy that they constituted a strain on the budget and contributed to the steady deterioration of the financial situation that took place in the postwar years. Thanks to the war against Russia, the budget deficit for 1920 was 50 billion zloty; and the zloty dropped from 120 to 500 to the American dollar in the course of the year. By 1922 it was closer to 3000 to the dollar, and by 1923 inflation had gone so far that Poland had to go through an experience similar to that of Germany in the same year—abandoning the old currency and starting all over again on the basis of foreign loans.

Poland did not, however, have anything like the economic resurgence that took place in Germany after 1923. The key to economic growth in Poland was agrarian reform, and the need for expropriation and redistribution of large estates and the modernization of agricultural methods had long been recognized. But, although the Polish parliament discussed and passed several partial reforms, the landlord class was always strong enough to prevent any fundamental change; and the country muddled on in the old way until it was engulfed in the world economic depression, which snuffed out what little economic progress had been made.

The failure to deal with basic economic problems was the result of the nature of Polish parliamentary practice. The Polish constitution, which had been accepted in March 1921, exalted the legislature at the expense of the executive. The powers of the president, who was elected by the two legislative houses (the Sejm and the Senate), were rigidly delimited; the two houses, which were elected by universal, direct, secret, and proportional vote, were not even restricted in their actions by the possibility of presidential veto. At the same time, they soon showed that they could make no effective use of their extensive powers, for they became battlegrounds for the too numerous parties and splinter groups that Polish individualism seemed to demand. Joseph Pilsudski (see p. 398) described the Sejm as "a sterile, jabbering, howling thing that engendered such boredom that the very flies on the walls died of sheer disgust"; and, by the mid-twenties, as one coalition government succeeded another without noticeable accomplishment (there were thirteen such governments between 1919 and 1926), many Poles agreed with him and urged him to change the situation.

In May 1926, Pilsudski yielded to their pleas. He marched upon Warsaw at the head of a mixed force of volunteers and mutinous government troops, and, at the end of three days' fighting, forced the parliament to capitulate. Although he preserved the external forms of the republican government and even refused to accept the presidency, Pilsudski was from this time on the real force in Polish politics, and he and his "colonels" monopolized the premiership and other important offices and systematically reduced the powers of the legislature, having no compunction about arresting political opponents and trying them on charges of subversion and conspiracy.

This change to dictatorship did perhaps moderate the tendency to political anarchy that had at times seemed present in the activities of the Sejm, but it did not make the political system work effectively enough to improve the country's economic condition, to relieve the plight of the depressed working class and peasantry, or to satisfy the grievances of the national minorities. Pilsudski's financial reforms had only short-term effects and did not prepare the country to withstand the shock of the world depression, which greatly increased the already heavy incidence of unemployment and complicated other social problems.

Perhaps the most unfortunate result of Pilsudski's coup of 1926 was that it gave power to a military elite which carried its contempt for democracy over into foreign affairs and pursued a policy marked by such a degree of irresponsibility that the hope of an effective collective security system was weakened. Increasingly after 1926, the colonels were critical of the League of Nations, resenting that body's legitimate interest in the minorities question and the administration of the Polish Corridor. Increasingly, they showed a desire to assert their independence of France, and this led to a fatal strain of opportunism in their policy decisions. Thus, when Adolf Hitler took power in Germany, the Polish government gave him his first victory in foreign policy by concluding a pact of friendship with the Nazis in January 1934. It is clear that the colonels, already fascinated by the aberrant notion that Poland could be a great power in its own right, believed that, in the new and confused state of international affairs, they had a chance to play power politics on a grand scale and that the German pact gave them an advantage over both France and the Soviet Union. Time was to show that this was the purest dilettantism. In reality they had played into Hitler's hands by starting the dissolution of France's security system in eastern Europe and leaving its members to be absorbed by Germany one by one.

The political evolution of the Baltic countries was much like that of Poland. Lithuania, Latvia, and Estonia started their existence with democratic institutions that proved to be ineffective because of the inexperience of those using them, the violence of factional strife, and—in the case of Lithuania, which quarreled incessantly with Poland over Vilna (see p. 506) and incurred lasting German enmity by seizing the former German area of Memel in 1923—the financial and political costs of overambitious foreign policy. In all three countries, strong men eventually took over. In the same year that Pilsudski marched on Warsaw, a group of army officers, industrialists, and landowners seized power in Lithuania and formed a one-party state with a strong similarity to Mussolini's Italy, including the existence of a Fascist militia called the Iron Wolf. Estonia and Latvia followed suit, as the progressive incompetence of democratic government was speeded up by the problems caused by the depression. Dictatorships were established in Estonia in 1934 and in Latvia in the following year.

Czechoslovakia   Events took a different course in the country that been created as a result of the efforts of Thomas Masaryk and Eduard Beneš. Superficially, the Czech parliamentary system worked much like Poland's: there was the same multiplication of parties and the same swift succession of coalition governments. But, in contrast to its northern neighbor, Czechoslovakia's constitution had a better balance between the legislative and executive branches, and the country had the benefit of the continuity of policy made possible, first, by the continuous service of Masaryk (president, 1918, and 1920–1935) and Beneš (foreign minister, 1918–1935, and president, 1935–1939) and, second, by the inheritance from the Austrian empire of a competent civil service. In contrast with Poland also, the Czech state did not handicap its future progress by an adventurous foreign policy and, although its military expenditures became heavy, especially after it began the construction of the so-called Little Maginot Line around its western borders, it paid its way by a careful financial policy based upon equitable but heavy taxation.

Economically, Czechoslovakia solved the problem that was never met in Poland by expropriating the former crown lands and the large private estates (the latter with compensation) and distributing them on easy terms to small holders. Agricultural production increased until the country was virtually self-sufficient in basic foodstuffs, although it had to import nonessentials and raw materials for industry. The general prosperity of the country depended essentially on its great industries: munitions, glass, porcelain, brewing, and the like. In general, its economy was better balanced than other countries of eastern Europe, and it suffered less than they from the economic results of the breakup of the Hapsburg empire. Like all eastern European countries, however, it was less prosperous than it might have been if it had not been for the economic nationalism and protectionism that characterized the policies of the former Hapsburg states.

All of the conditions described helped make democracy a going concern in Czechoslovakia. Even so, it was never completely secure because of the minorities question. The country was, essentially, an artificial creation, composed of bits of other states; and in result it was filled with people who were never entirely satisfied with their new status. This was particularly true of the 747,000 Magyars in the eastern part of the country and the 3,123,000 Germans in the western fringe, called the Sudetenland; but germs of separatism were present also in the minds of many of the 2,190,000 Slovaks, whose union with the Czechs had given the country its name.

Throughout the 1920s, the disaffection of the minorities was kept within bounds by the economic prosperity of the country and the liberal nationalities policy of the government, which permitted the different national groups to have their own schools and use their own language for official and legal business in areas where they predominated. This relative peace came to an end, however, with the coming of the world depression, which because of the country's dependence on foreign trade hit Czechoslovakia particularly hard, and with the rise of Adolf Hitler. The misery caused by the depression produced a desire for change; National Socialism offered a means of effecting it. The Sudeten Germans were naturally the first to pin their hopes on Hitler, forming a National Socialist party of their own (the Sudeten German party of Konrad Henlein) and beginning a campaign for special privileges, which, in reality, cloaked the intention of seeking fusion with Germany. But it did not take long for the other nationalities to begin to wonder whether they too might not gain a better status by appealing to Hitler to save them. These speculations led, as we shall see (see p. 647), to the destruction of the only country in eastern Europe that remained true to democracy throughout the whole of the interwar period.

Austria   The destruction of democracy in Austria came sooner, as the result of a dramatic series of events in which the two most prominent European dictators had parts to play. Austria, as we have seen, started its existence as a new state in highly unfavorable circumstances, deprived of most of the provinces that had assured its greatness in the past and doomed to a future of continual economic and political crisis. Kept afloat by League loans throughout the 1920s, the Austrian republic was denied an opportunity of improving its economic condition by the World Court's veto of the Customs Union Plan of 1931 (see p. 581). This setback completed the collapse of Austrian morale and made the impact of the world depression in Austria greater than in any part of the troubled continent.

Politically, the country was divided between the Social Democratic party, whose greatest strength was in Vienna, and the Christian Socialist party, which was supported by the majority of the rural population, although there was always a small but vigorous Nationalist party which advocated fusion with Germany. Throughout most of the 1920s, the Christian Socialists were the government party and were led by the able Catholic priest Ignatius Seipel, who was chancellor from 1922 to 1924 and from 1926 to 1929. Seipel's government had a decided authoritarian cast, and this was even more true of that of his disciple and successor, Engelbert Dollfuss.

Dollfuss came to the fore at a time when the depression was destroying the last remnants of social stability and political extremism was on the upgrade. Communism was exercising a perceptible influence on the left wing of the Social Democratic party, while, on the other hand, the old Nationalist party had become National Socialist in sympathy and tactics and was not only obviously working for union with Germany but actually following orders laid down in Berlin. Dollfuss, a diminutive but energetic man, with a high regard for his own political wisdom (he was called Millimetternich and does not seem to have disliked the title), thought he could contain both movements and elected to do so by a policy of secret collaboration with Mussolini, which was intended to convert Austria into a Fascist state on the Italian model.

Dollfuss's strong right arm inside Austria was Prince Starhemberg, the scion of a decayed Austrian family, who had been building up a private army of *Squadristi* called the Home Guard (*Heimwehr*). In these efforts he had, even in the 1920s, been aided by arms shipments from Italy, and, once Hitler came to power, they increased. Mussolini was worried by the possibility of an *Anschluß* of the two German states which would bring the Nazis to the Brenner Pass. He told Starhemberg on one occasion:

> Pan-Germanism is extending its tentacles toward the Adriatic. Italy has as little use for Pan-Germanism as it has for Pan-Slavism. That is why Austria is so important. If Austria ceases to exist, there can be no more order in Central Europe. Great dangers will then threaten Italy.

There was much truth in these words, and Mussolini would have been well advised to remember them in later years. But the force that the Duce helped to build up in Austria was not used primarily to guard against the dangers of a National Socialist conquest of the country. Dollfuss and Starhemberg were more immediately impressed by what they considered to be the danger on the left and with Mussolini's approval—indeed, at his insistence—they proceeded to make the same mistake that Schleicher and Papan had made in July 1932; they set out deliberately to smash Austrian Social Democracy, the trade unions that supported it, and the defense force (*Schutzbund*) that had been built up to protect its meetings from *Heimwehr* attacks.

Throughout 1933, the strength of the *Heimwehr* was increased, until, in the opinion of one competent observer, it had enough arms and munitions, including tanks and howitzers, to have equipped an army of 500,000 men for a campaign of moderate length. When these preparations were made, Dollfuss dissolved the parliament and announced, in September 1933, that it was his intention to form a new corporative state. These measures aroused the Socialists, and there was much talk of a general strike and other forms of resistance, none of which came to anything because of differences between the left and right wings of the movement. The chancellor, on the other hand, was ready and eager to act against the left and, at the beginning of 1934, *Heimwehr* squads began to round up political opponents and to occupy Socialist and trade-union headquarters. Open fighting began in the provincial towns but was quickly suppressed and, on February 12, the *Heimwehr* advanced into the working districts of Vienna, using artillery against the *Karl Marx Hof,* an extensive block of workers' tenements whose construction had been one of the triumphs of Austrian socialism, ruthlessly slaughtering knots of resistance and arresting the last of the Socialist leaders.

Once order was restored, Dollfuss promulgated his corporative constitution, convened the parliament for the last time so that it could vote its own dissolution, and, with Starhemberg and Major Emil Fey (one of the *Heimwehr's* original founders) as his vice chancellor and minister of public security respectively, began to rule Austria as a dictator. His reign, however, was short. The Austrian Nazis had also been building up their strength, and on July 25 they tried a *Putsch* of their own, confidently expecting to be supported from Berlin. Their coup was a miserable failure and German aid never materialized, but for a few hours the rebels held the chancellery and in that time they shot Dollfuss and allowed him to bleed to death.

In the days that followed, Mussolini mobilized four divisions of troops and stationed them near the Brenner Pass, announcing simultaneously that Italy would defend Austrian independence. Hitler disavowed any complicity in the rising (and saw to it that those German Nazis who had encouraged it disappeared from sight). Dollfuss's position was assumed by Kurt von Schuschnigg, a devoted follower of the dead chancellor and a supporter of his policies. But the July *Putsch* was a forecast of what was to come four years later. Schuschnigg was to discover then that the armed attack upon the working class organizations in February 1934, of which he had approved, had destroyed the only force capable of resisting National Socialism, for, as Germany became stronger and more popular, while Austria remained sunk in depression, the middle classes became increasingly receptive to the idea of *Anschluß.* The Dollfuss-Schuschnigg authoritarian state was thus a mere way-station on the road to absorption by the more brutal totalitarianism of Germany.

The Middle Danube and the Balkans   The prevailing tendency toward dictatorship was apparent in all of the states of the middle Danube area and the Balkans and was encouraged by the depression and by the apparent success of the Italian and German dictators. In the case of Hungary, democracy never had an opportunity to take root at all. After the suppression of the Soviet dictatorship of Béla Kun in November 1919 (see p. 533), the government had been organized as a kingdom without a king but with Admiral Horthy, the liberator of Budapest, as regent. From 1921 to 1931, the Hungarian premier was Count Bethlen, a complete reactionary who did everything in his power to restore the feudal rule of the Magyar notables, progressively restricting the suffrage and setting his face against agrarian or other reform. The world depression, a series of fiscal troubles, and a bad harvest finally brought Bethlen down in 1931; but he was succeeded by Julius Gömbös, an anti-Semite and Fascist, who tightened the authoritarian regime further. When Hitler came to power in Germany, Gömbös was one of the first leaders of a foreign government to court his favor, and from 1933 on Hungary was a German client state responsive to suggestions from Berlin.

The other countries of this area were all subject to royalist dictatorship. In Yugoslavia, conflict between the Croats, who were Catholic in religion and federalist in politics, and the Serbs, who were of Orthodox faith and firm believers in centralized government, led to a wave of disorders and assassinations and the establishment in 1929 of a dictatorship under King Alexander (see p. 377). Although this was modified in 1931, the king continued to command the state bureaucracy and the armed forces and, indirectly, to control elections to the Chamber of Deputies. In foreign politics, Alexander remained true to his tie with France; but, after his assassination at Marseille in 1934 (see p. 635), the regency that ruled during the minority of his son Peter II tended to flirt with both Mussolini and Hitler. At the time of the outbreak of war in 1939, the country was well on its way to being absorbed in the German economic system and seemed ripe for membership in Hitler's New Order.

Until 1930, Rumania maintained at least the appearance of parliamentary government; and, under the leadership of Maniu's Peasant party from 1917 to 1921 and from 1928 to 1930, and the Liberal party in the intervening years, accomplished a measure of agrarian reform and nationalization of natural resources. In 1930, however, Prince Carol, who had been forced to renounce the throne in favor of his son because of his liaison with a woman of unsavory reputation, deposed the young king and took his place. Henceforward, as the depression deepened, as anti-Semitism grew, and as politics came to be dominated by Fascist murder gangs like the Iron Guard, parliamentary institutions were increasingly restricted, until in 1938 a royal dictatorship was proclaimed. After that, the loyalty of Rumania to the Little Entente and the system of collective security was dubious.

In Bulgaria, the fortunes of democracy were affected by a high incidence of political assassination (which claimed among its victims the ablest of the country's postwar premiers, Alexander Stambuliski), and a policy of active subversion on the part of the Bulgarian Communist party, whose outrages—notably the bombing in the cathedral in Sofia in 1925 (see p. 536)—encouraged the rise of Fascist fighting groups. There were rightist *Putsches* in 1934 and 1935, and in the latter year a royal dictatorship was established under Boris III. In Albania, democratic beginnings were snuffed out by an army coup d'état in 1925, the leader of which, Ahmed Zogu, was subsequently proclaimed king. Not even Greece, the ancient home of democracy, escaped the general trend. Although parliament expelled King George II at the end of 1923 and established a republic, the disorder that had accompanied Greek politics throughout the nineteenth century continued; and a seesaw struggle between royalist forces and groups supporting Venizelos (see pp. 378, 471) led to bloody fighting in 1935, the restoration of the king, and, in 1936, the establishment of a dictatorial regime headed by General Metaxas.

Even during the few years when democracy was the prevailing form of government in eastern Europe, there had been few signs of cooperation among the various states to solve their common economic problems and the growth of dictatorship heightened the corrosive economic nationalism and promoted the political atomization of the area. At the same time, the kind of opportunism that we have noted in the case of Poland came to characterize the foreign policies of all of these states, with the exception of Czechoslovakia and, perhaps, Greece. Thus, when Hitler came to power and began to menace the whole system of collective security, the majority of the eastern European governments yielded to the temptation of seeking material advantage from collaboration with him. In the end, this cost their peoples the remnants of their freedom.

Chapter 26 THE CRISIS
OF DEMOCRACY:
WESTERN EUROPE

To the prevailing tendency to prefer dictatorship to democracy, western Europe was not, of course, immune. All of the forces that produced fascism in Italy and national socialism in Germany were present in the countries west of the Rhine in the postwar years: economic distress, parliamentary incompetence, heightened class conflict, middle class fear of communism, and the existence of large numbers of unreconstructed war veterans, disenchanted intellectuals, and misfits who would rather parade in colored shirts than try to find a place in civilian society. Even a country like Great Britain, with a tradition of parliamentary government that was centuries old, experienced moments when the whole system of inherited law was subjected to serious challenge; and, while Britain survived these crises without sacrificing its democratic institutions, some of its closest neighbors were not so fortunate when their moments of testing came.

GREAT BRITAIN AND THE EMPIRE

Postwar Troubles   The poet Louis MacNeice once expressed the feelings of what was probably a not inconsiderable number of war veterans and other Englishmen after 1918 in the words:

> All we want is a bank balance and a bit
> of skirt in a taxi

But he added sadly:

> It's no go, my honey love, it's no go, my poppet,
> Work your hands from day to day, the winds will
>   blow the profit.
> The glass is falling hour by hour, the glass
>   will fall forever,
> But if you break the bloody glass, you won't
>   hold up the weather.

Certainly nothing seemed capable of holding up the foul economic storms that swept over England in this period. Everything seemed wrong in the economic sphere. The country's foreign trade had been ruined by the war, and when attempts were made to revive it, it was discovered that many of Britain's prewar markets had been taken over by the Americans or had simply disappeared because of the rise of new manufacturing in the British dependencies. The shipping industry was equally hard hit and was not helped by the confiscation of the German merchant marine, which merely denied contracts to British firms, so that, by 1921, two thirds of the men normally employed by British yards were out of work. The backbone of the British economy, the coal industry, was menaced by increasing continental competition (spurred on by German reparations payments in coal, which made it possible for France to sell German coal to former British customers like Italy and the Scandinavian countries), as well as by the increasing use of oil and electricity in place of coal power. The scientific techniques that made coal production profitable in the United States were virtually unknown in England; the organization of the industry was highly inefficient; and the resistance of the coal producers to basic reform kept the industry in a state of depression throughout the whole interwar period. In addition to all this, the economy of the country was strained by the loss of its prewar foreign investments, the fiscal dislocations caused by the war, and the large debt owed to the United States.

Although it was not immediately perceived, Britain's old supremacy as a manufacturing and commercial power had gone for good. There was a brief postwar boom, but it was an artificial one that stopped as soon as other countries resumed production and began to compete with British goods. After that, the long period of stagnation began and unemployment began to mount. At the end of 1920, 690,000 of those workers registered under the National Insurance Act of 1911 were unemployed; by June 1921, this number had increased to 2,171,000; and, although it sank in the following year, it varied between one and one and a half million for the rest of the decade and doubled as soon as the great depression of the 1930s arrived.

The first postwar government, that of Lloyd George, tried to deal with this problem by passing tariff and other measures to protect key industries from competition and by placing obstacles to prevent countries with depreciated currencies from invading British markets. It also increased the government's contribution to the national insurance funds and thus made possible small relief payments to those out of work. But these were palliatives rather than cures;

and "the dole," as the relief payments came to be called, gave the jobless sustenance without hope and, when it became a permanent feature of English life,
as it did, tended to kill the spirit. The novelist J.B. Priestley wrote angrily in
the 1930s: "The dole is part of no plan; it is a mere declaration of intellectual
bankruptcy.... Nobody is getting any substantial benefit, any reasonable satisfaction, out of it.... The Labour Exchanges stink of defeated humanity."

Rather than this sort of thing, what England needed was a thorough-going
reorganization of its industrial plant. This was quite apparent to leading economists, who pointed out that the fundamental weakness of the British economy
lay in the fact that productive capacity had fallen off as a result of worn-out
techniques, reliance upon man-power rather than machine-power, duplication
of services, and uneconomic competition in the domestic market. The cotton
industry, for instance, quite apart from its technical backwardness, suffered from
uneconomic competition. Some 700 spinning and 1200 weaving firms were competing with each other, oblivious to the fact that their failure to consolidate
placed them at a marked disadvantage in comparison with more efficiently
organized foreign industries. The same was true of the coal industry, where
1400 independent producers vied with each other, many working mines too poor
for efficient production. Consolidation here might make possible lower production costs and the introduction of much needed machinery. Without those im-
provements, Britain's share in the world market promised to decline even further.

Instead of being willing to make basic changes, the industrialists generally
preferred to rely on government subsidies and, for the rest, to keep wages as
low as possible. This was perhaps understandable. Less so was the toleration
of this attitude by Parliament, which did not speak well for the quality of political
leadership in this period. Commenting on this in one of his most biting essays,
George Orwell suggested that the British ruling class had begun to decay; that,
living as they did on the profits of firms run for them and on the returns on
investments made for them by specialists, its members had lost any real function
in society; and that, realizing this in a vague sort of way but wishing to retain
both their position and their self-esteem, they had taken refuge in stupidity:
"They could keep society in its existing shape only by being *unable* to grasp
that any improvement was possible." There may be truth in this, although it
is probably safer to say merely that England was now beginning to suffer from
the loss of almost a whole generation of talent at Ypres and on the Somme.
But, whatever the reason, it is undeniable that the general level of political
intelligence and behavior in the interwar Parliaments was far below that of
Parliaments of the nineteenth century, and there were few leaders of outstanding
quality.

The Course of Politics   The prime minister in 1918 was still David Lloyd
George, a man who, in contrast to his successors, did possess qualities of political
genius and deserves to be ranked as a war minister with Pitt and Churchill.
But the "Welsh wizard" had no spells with which to ward off Britain's postwar
troubles. His economic program, as Sir Llewellyn Woodward has written, was
"a handful of amateur notions picked up at random." He was responsible for
the dole but, aside from that, had little constructive to offer. His attention was,

in any case, largely engrossed by foreign affairs and by the political troubles that his conduct of them brought down upon his head. Lloyd George was still nominally the leader of the Liberals, but he no longer represented the party majority—Sir Robert Horne once referred to their growing distrust of Lloyd George by saying in Parliament, "For their prayers they say, 'We err and stray like lost sheep and the Leader of the Liberal Party is our Shepherd and our Crook' "—and depended, as prime minister, upon the support of the Conservatives. By 1922 they had grown tired of his leadership, and the crisis in the Near East (see p. 499), which they attributed to his alienation of the French and his irresponsible encouragement of the Greeks, exhausted what was left of their patience. At a meeting of the Conservative party, the majority of those present voted to break the connection with Lloyd George, after listening to a speech by Stanley Baldwin, in which he acknowledged that the prime minister was a dynamic force but added that "a dynamic force is a very terrible thing." Lloyd George resigned immediately, and never held office again.[1]

In the elections of October 1922, the Conservatives won a clear majority and formed a government under the ailing Andrew Bonar Law, who was succeeded six months later by Stanley Baldwin. An earnest and patriotic man who retained the leadership of the Conservative party until 1937, Baldwin possessed few of the qualities that one expected to find in a prime minister, for he had neither knowledge of nor interest in foreign affairs, and his economic and social ideas were even more rudimentary than those of Lloyd George. A modest man, he was always the first to admit his mistakes, and this endeared him to large sections of the British electorate, despite the fact that the faults confessed were sometimes very serious indeed, as was true, for instance, of his miscalculation of the rate of growth of Germany's air strength in 1935.

Lloyd George once said that Baldwin was "honest to the point of simplicity." The remark was unkind, but it has some relevance to his approach to the pressing problems that faced his government. He believed that economic recovery would be best promoted by a demonstration of Britain's reliability as a debtor. After some complicated talks in Washington at the beginning of 1923, while he was serving as chancellor of the exchequer, he accepted terms for the payment of Britain's debt to the United States that his own colleagues thought could have been improved by shrewder negotiation and were certainly less generous than those that the United States government subsequently granted to France and Italy. As a means of restoring international confidence in Britain and attracting trade, this had little effect, and it imposed a considerable strain on Britain's fiscal position for the next ten years.

If the Conservative party had no formula for relieving economic distress except this, the Labour party was no better. It is true that when the first Labour government was formed, after the elections of November-December 1923, the party had only 192 seats in the House of Commons to 258 for the Conservatives and 158 for the Liberals. It had to rely on Liberal support, and the price of this was the

---

[1] On his last day of office, he gave his secretary Thomas Jones a photograph of Mazzini, inscribed "From one admirer of Mazzini to another." It has been suggested that it was the conspiratorial side of Mazzini that appealed to him.

abandonment of any attempt to realize a truly socialist program. Even if Labour had had a majority, however, it is doubtful whether the party would have adopted a radically new approach to the economic problem, for neither Ramsay MacDonald, the prime minister, nor his chancellor of the exchequer, Philip Snowden, were socialists in any systematic sense, and they were quite happy to follow the economic policies of the previous government, even to the extent of backing Baldwin's fiscal policy. This led some of their supporters to moan:

> Oh, Ramsay dear, and did you hear
> The news that's going round?
> They're cutting down our wages
> For the saving of the pound.

It is not easy to understand why MacDonald, with his upper class tastes and admiration for the aristocracy, his fundamental lack of sympathy for organized labor, and his preference for foreign rather than domestic affairs, retained the leadership of his party so long. He did so because he possessed the charismatic quality necessary to leadership, always looking and acting like a great man, even though he was not one, and because he was adroit in manipulating the rival groups within his own party. In addition, as D. C. Somervell has written, the emotional idealistic oratory for which he was known appealed to a people that had stopped going to church but still craved sermons. Read today, these speeches show a remarkable emptiness of content.

> My friends, I see no end of the journey. We have come, we shall journey, and we shall go on, and our children coming after us will go on with their journey, and their children will go on with theirs. But, my friends, what you and I have to take care of is that the journey is both onward and upward.

This sort of thing may have given little intellectual sustenance, but, delivered with conviction by this strikingly handsome man, it at least left its hearers in a state of comfortable befuddlement and made many of them followers of Mac-Donald simply because he was so sincere.

The principal efforts of the first Labour government were in foreign policy, where the negotiations were inaugurated that eventuated in the Dawes Plan (see p. 570) and a treaty was concluded by which Great Britain accorded recognition to the Soviet Union (see p. 535). Despite the fact that the Anglo-Soviet treaty was little more than a formalization of relations established in the field of foreign trade in 1921, it led to a withdrawal of Liberal support from the MacDonald government, which therefore appealed to the country in new elections. The publication of the so-called Zinoviev letter (see p. 535) in the middle of the campaign scored heavily against Labour, and the Conservatives came back to power with a commanding majority. Baldwin once more became prime minister and, by resuming his policy of fiscal conservatism, proceeded to demonstrate that his year out of office had brought him no new ideas.

Indeed, he and his chancellor of the exchequer, Winston Churchill, accentuated it, for in 1925 they returned to the gold standard at the prewar parity of the pound to the dollar. The economist John Maynard Keynes immediately accused the government of subordinating the true interests of British industry to the desires of the Bank of England and the Treasury in order to restore the prestige of the City of London as a financial center. The pound, he argued, was overvalued by at least 10 percent, and revaluation meant an immediate rise in the price of British exports sold abroad. Unless they wished to lose their share of the foreign market, the export industries, already hard hit by the trade slump, would have to reduce their costs, and the only way they could do this was by driving down wages. Events soon proved that Keynes's argument was sound.

The General Strike   It was perhaps inevitable that the failure of the postwar governments to make a constructive attempt to deal with the continuing depression would lead, sooner or later, to some form of violent protest on the part of the working class, especially since the syndicalist philosophy of direct action (see p. 281) was still influential in many of the large unions. But the return to the gold standard was perhaps the chief reason for that protest taking the form it did. No industry was affected more deleteriously by this step than the coal industry, which, after an artificial spurt in 1923 caused by the stoppage of coal production in the Ruhr during the French occupation (see p. 508), was now suffering from the effects of the resumption of German coal exports in 1924. The added shock of the revaluation of the pound led the mine owners to announce, in June 1925, that previous wage agreements must be terminated and that wages must be reduced and working hours lengthened immediately.

It was this decision that led, by slow degrees, to the general strike of 1926. The Miners Federation refused to accept the owners' proposals or even to discuss a new agreement until they were withdrawn, and in July 1925, with the backing of the General Council of the Trades Union Congress (TUC), they threatened comprehensive strike action. To avoid this, Baldwin persuaded the mine owners to postpone their intended changes pending an investigation of the industry by a royal commission and agreed to support them in the interim by renewed government subsidies.

This action was widely criticized by the Conservative and Liberal press as a capitulation to blackmail and Bolshevism, and one of Baldwin's ministerial colleagues warned that the nation would have to decide whether it was to be "governed by Parliament and the Cabinet or by a handful of trade union leaders." The union leaders would have been well advised to take note of the hardening of middle class opinion after July 1925. They did not do so, and while their more irresponsible members alienated moderate opinion by making triumphant speeches about the imminence of the victory over capitalism, they adopted a position in the pending dispute that made a reasonable solution impossible.

This became clear when a commission, headed by Sir Herbert Samuel, was appointed to investigate the industry and made its report in March 1926. It recommended a basic reorganization, to start with the cessation of subsidies, the closing down of pits that could not pay their way, and a temporary reduction of wages until the effects of reorganization took hold. To people outside the industry these proposals made sense, and even some labor leaders—notably Ernest

Bevin, the head of the Transport and General Workers Union—felt that the temporary sacrifices might be worth making to secure the long-needed reorganization. But the Miners Federation proved to be as opposed to basic change as the mine owners themselves. While the owners were reluctantly constrained to accept reorganization in principle, the miners refused to commit themselves to it unless they were assured in advance that there would be no departure from current rates of pay.

When matters came to a head at the end of April 1926, the government proved less than effective in mediating the dispute. The intransigent statements of the miners and the renewal of the strike threat convinced a sizable group in the Conservative party and the ministry that the time had come to put an end to union threats, and Baldwin did not dare defy this by taking any action that could be interpreted as another capitulation. On the other hand, the General Council of the TUC, while often irritated by the high-handedness of the miners, was too devoted to the principle of labor solidarity to break with or restrain them, and in any case felt that the government showed too little understanding of the merits of the miners' case. The leaders of the parliamentary Labour party played an ineffectual role throughout the last critical negotiations. Thus, the

The British general strike of 1926. Here London policemen rescue a food van after strikers had tampered with the engine. Many trucks were marked "food only" in the hope that they would not be attacked. (Wide World)

strike, which began on May 3, 1926, was the result of the rigidity and lack of statesmanship of all the interested parties.

The general strike of 1926 involved one sixth of the working population of England, Scotland, and Wales, including mining, all forms of transport, iron and steel, metals and heavy chemicals, building trades, and electric and gas power. Considering the prevalent unemployment, the risks taken by those who walked out in sympathy with the miners were great; and, as Alan Bullock has written, the response to the strike call was a remarkable demonstration of working class unity. The strike was, nevertheless, ill-planned, and the leaders had not thought out the consequences of their action.

Since the previous fall, the government had had plans for the protection of necessary services and supplies, worked out by the able permanent under secretary in the Home Office, Sir John Anderson; and it had foreseen the necessity of using the Emergency Powers Act to take what other action was needed to protect the national interest. When the strike came, the flow of supplies was maintained; Hyde Park was closed and turned into a milk depot; volunteers were recruited to run trains and buses; and communications and public information were assured by the publication of a government broadsheet called the *British Gazette*, edited by Winston Churchill, and by the continued operation of the British Broadcasting Company, which was government-controlled. In contrast, the unions had no scheme of organization that provided liaison between headquarters and the local strike committees. Since they had called out the printers, they had no authoritative organ to keep their members informed and to counteract the influence of the Churchill sheet and the *Daily Mail*, which, printed in Paris and flown to England, was filled with articles purporting to prove that the strike was controlled by Soviet agents.

The union leaders were appalled by the discovery that, outside of the working class and left intellectuals, there was virtually no sympathy for their cause. In their desire to demonstrate their power, they had failed to realize that their action would be interpreted by the great majority of the British people as an attempt to substitute direct action for parliamentary government. When this was brought home clearly to them, and when they saw, after the first week, that the government was not only determined to resist them to the end but, thanks to the volunteers, showed every indication of being able to succeed, their resolution began to wane. Strike funds were approaching exhaustion, and reports were beginning to trickle in of clashes between workers and the police that led them to fear that their membership might get out of hand and provoke the government into using more forceful countermeasures. In consequence, the General Council of the TUC seized upon a new formula suggested by Sir Herbert Samuel, which called for the establishment of a National Mines Board to settle disputes and a general agreement that there would be no reduction of wages until measures of reorganization had been agreed upon. The TUC asked the miners to accept this as a new basis for negotiations. The Miners Federation, consistent to the last in its resistance to *any* wage cuts, refused; and the TUC called off the strike. The miners remained out for another six months but finally had to capitulate in December.

In a speech in Commons, the prime minister said that he would not countenance attempts to exploit the collapse of the strike in order to force down wages or destroy unionism. Thanks to this and a general feeling of relief that the strike had passed without a major explosion of violence, there were few reprisals. The miners were the hardest hit, having to go back to work at longer hours and lower pay in an industry that had, as a result of the long interruption of production, lost markets it would never regain.

Perhaps the true importance of the general strike lies in the fact that it alleviated the tendency toward class conflict which had been growing in the first half of the decade. Thanks in part to the revolution in Russia, the middle classes had begun to be almost afraid of the common people; the uproar over the Zinoviev letter was a symptom of that fear. The strike helped put matters in their proper perspective and, once broken, left the middle classes less susceptible to the scare stories of the right-wing press than they had been earlier. Thus, they never responded to the future growth of the labor movement with the exaggerated fear and resentment shown in other countries, including France.

The failure of the strike also contributed to better relations among the classes by discrediting Marxist and syndicalist theories about the inevitability of class conflict. Henceforth, wild talk about revolution was unpopular in labor circles; and, although the unions did not abandon the strike weapon, they kept it as a last resort and no longer thought in terms of concerted strike action, preferring to rely on other means, notably parliamentary ones, to gain their objectives. They therefore tended to follow the advice of their party rather than to dictate to it, and, since the Labour party always sought to widen its appeal beyond the working class, this too made for more understanding among the classes.

The Impact of the World Depression   All this was to the good, and it perhaps helps to illustrate the fundamental stability of Great Britain, which was able to withstand the fiercer storms that lay ahead during the world depression and the war.

It is nevertheless true that the failure of the general strike allowed the mine owners, other producers, and the government to relax, with the result that plans for basic industrial reorganization were dropped. In the long run, this obtuseness, and the parallel attempt of big business to seek protection by turning increasingly toward cartels and trusts, played into the hands of the Labour party and helped it to persuade a growing audience that productive inefficiency coupled with monopoly was not to the public interest and must be corrected by nationalization of key industries. But it was not until after 1945 that Labour had an opportunity to realize its objective. Meanwhile the English economy continued to stagnate until it was overwhelmed by the world depression.

Six months before the stock market crash in New York, Parliament reached its statutory term and new elections were held. The Labour party received 290 seats, not a clear majority; the Conservatives, 260; and the Liberals—the last time that this riven party appeared in significant strength—60. MacDonald once more became prime minister and Snowden, chancellor of the exchequer, with J. H. Thomas appointed to deal with the problem of unemployment, a task in which he was aided by Sir Oswald Mosley, one of the most brilliant of the younger men, who was soon, however, to break away and set himself up as head of the British Fascist party.

The efforts of the government to alleviate unemployment and other problems proved ineffective in face of the avalanche that fell on them at the end of 1929; and during the next two years matters deteriorated steadily. By 1931, the Unemployment Insurance Fund was running in debt at the rate of one million pounds a week. Destitution was wide-spread, especially in the so-called distressed areas in West Cumberland, South Wales, and Tyneside, while the fiscal position of the country was threatened by heavy withdrawals of gold from the Bank of England. Snowden's answer to all this was a program calling for rigid economies designed to balance the budget, and it was hinted that the sacrifices called for might soon include a cut in the unemployment benefits.

These suggestions the bulk of the Labour party and the TUC rejected angrily; and, on August 24, 1931, the government resigned. When King George V asked MacDonald to head a new national, or nonparty, government, however, he agreed to do so, forming a ministry of four Labourites, four Conservatives, and two Liberals. When it became clear that he intended to carry out the kind of program that they had just repudiated, the Labour party read him and the other Labour ministers (Snowden, Thomas, and Lord Sankey) out of the party and went almost solidly into opposition.

The National government came to be dominated by the Conservatives, under the leadership of Baldwin and the rising man in Conservative ranks, Neville Chamberlain. This was especially true after the elections of 1931, in which 558 National Government candidates were elected (471 Conservatives. thirty-five National Liberals, thirty-three Liberal Free Traders, thirteen National Labourities) against an opposition of only fifty-six Labour and five Lloyd George Liberals. Being a government of national concentration, it gave a sense of purpose which helped bolster up confidence in the country, and it showed itself capable, at least sporadically, of determined action. Its first act was to correct the mistake that had been made in 1925 by abandoning the gold standard and allowing the pound to find its own level, which turned out to be thirty percent below parity. It also granted subsidies to shipping and tried to solve the problem of the distressed areas by relocating the unemployed; and in 1932 it brought eighty years of free trade to an end by going over to protectionism.

Even so, there was no large-scale comprehensive plan for recovery, nothing like the New Deal in the United States; unemployment remained high (2,000,000 in 1934 and 1,600,000 as late as 1936); and recovery did not get under way until the country began to rearm.

Ireland, the Near East, India, and the Commonwealth   Throughout this period, the British government was constantly preoccupied with imperial problems and with the rising tide of nationalism in certain of the British dependencies. Ireland was a center of particular unrest, for the decision to postpone the implementation of home rule (see p. 300) exacerbated anti-British feeling and led to the rise of extremist groups, notably the Sinn Fein ("Ourselves Alone") party. In Easter week of 1916, these groups staged a violent revolution, which was put down with much bloodshed and had tragic after-effects. When elections for the British Parliament were held in Ireland in 1918, seventy-five percent of the constituencies elected Sinn Fein candidates. They immediately announced their refusal to go to Westminster and organized a separate parliament (the Dail Eireann) in Dublin, which proclaimed the Irish Republic, with Eamon De Valera as president.

The British government, not unnaturally, resisted; and there followed three years of violence, marked by outrages committed by the self-styled Irish Republican Army against police stations and military garrisons, and reprisals by a British auxiliary force, the "Black and Tans," recruited from former army officers. Lloyd George's plan to end these troubles by permitting the establishment of separate parliaments for Ulster and Southern Ireland was rejected outright by the Republicans, who aspired to a free and united country. But he persisted, and in December 1921 persuaded the southern leaders to sign a treaty that provided for an Irish Free State as a self-governing Dominion and left Ulster the option of belonging to the Free State or having a separate status. This was accepted by both Parliament and the Dail, but was fought bitterly by the left wing of Sinn Fein under De Valera until the end of 1922, when William Cosgrave became president of the Free State. Under his quiet but capable leadership, the disorders came to an end, the boundary with Ulster, which had decided to remain apart, was defined, and the terms of the treaty of 1921, including those requiring allegiance to the king and granting naval and harbor facilities to Britain, were observed.

In 1932 De Valera was elected president and ended ten years of exile. His policy at first was one of whittling away the terms of the treaty without completely severing the tie with Great Britain; but, in May 1937, he piloted a new constitution through the Dail that made no reference to the treaty of 1921 or to the king and the Commonwealth. A year later, by concluding certain financial and tariff agreements and surrendering its port facilities, the British government recognized the independence of Southern Ireland. The North remained true to the crown.

In several of its other dependencies, Great Britain had to make similar concessions to rampant nationalism. In Eygpt, for instance, the movement for independence was so vigorous that it seemed expedient to yield to it; and, in February 1922, the government announced that the protectorate was at an end and that Egypt was an independent sovereign state. To this grant there were reservations, for the British claimed the right to appoint a high commissioner to supervise the new Egyptian king's policy, to garrison the Suez Canal, to protect Egypt against foreign aggression, and to protect foreign interests and minorities. These limitations were unpopular with the Egyptian Nationalist party (Wafd), which became the majority party in Egypt in 1924 and carried on a constant campaign against the 1922 proclamation, using terrorism and political murder as its weapons. British patience and the threat posed for Egypt by Italy's invasion of Abyssinia in 1935 (see p. 636) tempered these excesses sufficiently to make possible an Anglo-Egyptian Treaty in August 1936, which gave Egypt complete independence on terms the British considered reasonable and gave Britain the right to station troops at the canal and to use the naval base at Alexandria.

In the mandates taken over by Britain in 1919, there were also independence movements of varying strength (see p. 501). In 1930 the Labour government concluded a treaty with Iraq, recognizing its independence and agreeing to sponsor its admission into the League of Nations and to surrender its mandatory rights when this was effected. This promise was fulfilled by the National government, and the last British garrisons were withdrawn from Iraq in 1935. Britain also extended limited self-government to Transjordan, while maintaining supervisory and military rights. The problems of these two countries paled into insignificance beside those of Palestine, where the British were engaged continually in efforts to keep the Arabs and the Jews from each others' throats and where their plans for a Palestinian parliament or, alternatively, for partition were rejected by both sides.

During the war, the secretary of state for India had announced that it was the intention of the British government in India to follow a policy of "increasing association of Indians in every branch of the administration, and the gradual development of self-governing institutions with a view to the progressive realization of responsible government in India as an integral part of the British Empire." In the years that followed, however, progress toward the execution of this admirable program was too deliberate to please Indian nationalists, and the agitations of the All-India Congress, the organization that had been working for self-government since 1885, became increasingly radical throughout the 1920s.

The acknowledged leader of the Congress after 1921 was Mohandas Gandhi, a lawyer who had been educated in England and had worked for twenty years in South Africa, protecting the rights of Hindu immigrants. After his return to India in 1914, he had thrown himself into the fight for independence, urging his followers to rely upon the tactics of civil disobedience, passive resistance, nonviolent sabotage, and boycott of British goods. By sheer force of personality, Gandhi was able to create a movement that attracted world-wide attention and sympathy; but in India itself he was unable to overcome caste differences or the gulf between Hindu and Moslem, nor was he able to restrain those of his followers who periodically resorted to acts of terrorism against the British authorities.

Violence became the rule on both sides once the world depression began to be felt in India, for this led on the one hand to agrarian revolts and the murder of British officials and on the other to police brutality, the attempted suppression of all nationalist organizations, and the imprisonment of Congress members. The prospect of an indefinite continuation of these conditions was too much for Englishmen, who remembered how ineffective repressive measures had been in Ireland; and, in 1935, despite the opposition of convinced imperialists like Winston Churchill, Parliament passed a new India Act that provided for a federation of all the provinces of British India and the Indian native states (that is, those ruled by Indian princes who had alliances with the British crown), with a constitution similar to those of the other British Dominions. Executive power was vested in a governor general appointed by the crown and responsible for national defense, external affairs, fiscal and tariff policy, and supervision of the civil service. The legislature was bicameral, and its members were appointed by the native princes or elected by indirect methods to represent communities. The provinces were granted rights of autonomous self-development and government, but their governors were appointed by the crown. The franchise for provincial and national elections were restricted to about fourteen percent of the population.

This constitution was more popular with the native princes, whose extensive powers were left undiminished, and with the Moslem League, which believed in local autonomy and had always limited its end objective to Dominion status, than with the Congress, whose leaders now wanted outright independence. Gandhi's leading disciple, Pandit Jawaharlal Nehru, said of the new act, "We will resist it, we will break it, we will tear it, and we will burn it!" Hindu agitation, therefore, continued to be a source of concern to the British government in the years before the war.

Among the other British Dominions, it was only in South Africa that there was serious trouble. Despite the statesmanship of men like Botha and Smuts, Boer nationalism had continued to smolder, and, in the 1920s, General Hertzog's Nationalist party, while denying any desire to break the connection with Britain, agitated for "sovereign independence." Elsewhere, the growth of nationalism strengthened rather than weakened the ties between Great Britain and the Dominions, while at the same time changing the nature of their relationship.

The nature of the change was defined when Parliament passed the Statute of Westminster in December 1931. This act recognized that Canada, Australia, New Zealand, South Africa, and the Irish Free State were independent states on a footing of legal equality with the mother country, and that, while freely united in common allegiance to the crown, they were subject only to those laws passed by the British Parliament to which they expressly assented, while their own laws could not be vetoed by the home government. By this act, the British Commonwealth of Nations came into being.

Britain and Europe   The gravity of economic problems at home and the complications of the Palestinian, Indian, and other colonial situations left the British Parliament with little energy or desire to concern itself with other foreign problems. This should be borne in mind when one considers the reluctance of the British government to intervene when Japan invaded Manchuria in 1931 or when Hitler and Mussolini began their depredations in 1935 (see p. 636).

Even if the governments of the early 1930s had shown a greater willingness to support collective security than they did, they would have had difficulty in persuading the public to give them the arms to make this possible. The general feeling in England throughout the postwar period was that money should not be spent on armaments when it could be devoted to the easing of social distress, and this belief was supported by a doctrinaire pacifism, which held that the best way to avoid war was to prevent the accumulation of new weapons. The navy, since it was considered to be a defensive force, was least affected by this and was allowed to maintain parity with the United States, which proved to be an expensive business. But during the 1920s the army was cut to a level barely commensurate with Britain's imperial needs, and it was kept there. All branches of the service that were considered nonessential were cut to the bone or liquidated entirely. The tank corps was particularly hard hit, with the result that while the country possessed, in J. F. C. Fuller and Basil Liddell Hart, the most distinguished theorists of armored warfare in the world, it was the Germans rather than their own countrymen who studied their teachings and were ready to put them into effect in 1940. Similarly, the air arm was kept on such short rations that practically all experimentation stopped during the 1920s, and ardent pacifists went so far as to call for a boycott of the annual Hendon Air Show.

As long as there was any hope of general disarmament, this policy could perhaps be justified. After the virtual collapse of the Geneva Conference in 1933 (see p. 633), this was no longer true. Yet for some years it remained difficult to persuade the British people that the time had come to start building up their armed strength. "The whole country," Stanley Baldwin wrote to Conservative candidates in 1933, "irrespective of party, is solidly united in favor of peace and disarmament." In 1934, when the National government took the first hesitant steps toward increasing defense expenditures, it was attacked by Labour M.P.s who claimed that rearmament was "neither necessitated by any new commitment nor calculated to add to the security of the nation." (Neither they nor the ministers they were attacking had any way of knowing that two of the steps taken in 1934—the decision to double the armament of the new Hurricane and Spitfire fighter planes and the beginning of the construction of a radar warning system—would save the country from defeat in the Battle of Britain in 1940.) So heavy were the attacks on the government at the time that Baldwin, who was always responsive to the popular temper, postponed the bulk of his program, with the result that serious rearmament did not get under way until 1936 and did not become effective until 1939.

The policy of appeasement, which will be discussed in the next chapter and which contributed to the collapse of democracy in Europe, must be considered in connection with the relative weakness of Britain's armed strength. In the last analysis, this was the result of the economic troubles through which Britain had passed since 1919, troubles that had not succeeded in shaking the British people's faith in their own democracy but tended to make them inattentive to the threats to European democracy as a whole.

THE FRENCH REPUBLIC

Economic Recovery   The postwar history of France presents an interesting contrast with that of its neighbor across the Channel. In recovering from the physical damage wrought by the war, the country showed a remarkable resilience and achieved a degree of prosperity that could not be matched by Britain. Hidden beneath this surface well-being, however, were those serious social cleavages and political resentments that had never died since 1870 (see p. 337); and, when the storms of the 1930s swept over France, these proved to be strong enough to destroy the foundations of the French democracy.

No country had suffered more heavily during the war than France. Its casualties had been in the neighborhood of four million, of whom 1,300,000 had been killed and 120,000 permanently disabled; and its material losses had been greater even than those suffered by Belgium, Poland, and Russia, to say nothing of those belligerents whose soil had been spared the physical impact of the fighting. Battles like those for Verdun and the Somme had taken place in its most populous and industrialized departments, and the resultant damage to the nation's economic potential was enough to make the strongest heart quail.

Yet, within a few years, France had removed most of the ravages of the war and seemed in a fair way to complete recovery. The government threw all its resources into the task of clearing away the rubble that covered the northeastern part of France, restoring the five million acres of devastated farm lands to cultivation, rebuilding the 800,000 houses and farm buildings that had been destroyed, dredging the damaged canals, and repairing the 600 miles of railroad that had been made inoperable in the department of the Nord alone; and by 1926 it had completed a job of reconstruction that was described by D. W. Brogan as "the greatest economic achievement of postwar Europe."

The very necessity of reconstruction from the ground up brought unexpected advantages. In contrast to British industry, which resisted basic reorganization and modernization, French industry had no choice. It had to rebuild completely, and it did so with modern equipment and techniques, with the result that French textile mills, steel plants, and coal mines were soon operating on a level of technological skill unsurpassed by any of France's competitors. Industry was supplied, moreover, with important new resources. The reacquisition of Lorraine gave France one of the great iron fields of the world and enabled it to become a very considerable steel exporter; and the recovery of Alsace so strengthened the textile industry that France soon became the third largest of the world's producers of cotton goods. Since the markets of the world were also clamoring once more for French articles that defied competition—the wines of Burgundy and Beaune and the products of Chanel and Mainbocher—French trade revived with gratifying swiftness.

The full effects of this recovery were not felt until an answer was found to the difficult financial troubles of the first postwar years. These stemmed from the aversion of the typical Frenchman to paying taxes and the tendency of French politicians to defer to this feeling. As a result, France had entered the war with a heavy debt and had come out of it with a greater one, since no new taxes had been imposed during the conflict except a levy on excess profits and a tax on luxury goods, neither of which was very effective as a means of raising revenue. In 1918 the government had debts in the neighborhood of 150 billion francs, and these were increased rapidly by the costs of reconstruction. It had, of course, been expected that the Germans would pay all the costs of the war; but, before the first reparations installments had been received, the government had to borrow money for its ordinary, as well as its extraordinary, expenses. Moreover, since the Germans never lived up to the unreasonable expectations of their victors (and could not be compelled to do so by maneuvers like the invasion of the Ruhr [see p. 508]), it had to continue to borrow until investors began to show reluctance to lend, which did not take long. At the beginning of 1924, a government loan yielding 6.29 percent actually failed to find enough takers; after that the franc began to slip rapidly in the world market.

Parliament was slow in dealing with this problem and spent perhaps an excessive amount of energy in cabinet-making and cabinet-wrecking (there were six cabinets and seven different ministers of finance in the twelve months following June 1925), but in the end they did solve it. In July 1926 a cabinet of all the parties to the right of the Socialists was formed under the leadership of Raymond Poincaré, whose extreme nationalism and rigid legalism had been responsible for the Ruhr debacle. His long experience in French politics and his always abundant energy served the country well at this critical juncture, for, within thirty-five days, he had carried through a program of basic reform that saved the nation from what had appeared for a time to be possible bankruptcy. He increased taxation of all kinds and improved the system of collection; he imposed a series of administrative economies; he did away with the former system of several different budgets and unified the accounting system; and he negotiated a new loan with the Bank of France that enabled him to balance the budget and drive the value of the franc up to about one fifth of its prewar value, where it was pegged by France's return to the gold standard in 1928. This amounted, in effect, to a capital levy on the rentier class, who were deprived of four fifths of their savings and, in a sense, made to pay for the war. But it relieved the government of most of its capital charges and enabled French industry, for a time, to undersell its competitors in foreign markets; and the very vigor of the government's actions bolstered confidence in the parliamentary system.

The five years that followed were years of solid prosperity. Industry and agriculture flourished; and small businesses and services profited from the yearly discovery, by thousands of happy and financially solvent tourists, of the delights of the Côte d'Azur, the rich beauties of Chartres, and the heady excitement of Paris. There was no unemployment problem and no other social problems serious enough to inflame political tempers; and the avowed enemies of the regime had few issues to exploit. There had been a Communist party in France since 1920, when the left wing of the United Socialist party seceded during the party conference at Tours; and in 1922 the *Confédération Générale du Travail* (see p. 281) had also suffered a split, which resulted in the founding of a Moscow-oriented *Confédération Générale du Travail Unitaire*. Neither of these organizations waxed fat in the years following Poincaré's reforms. Nor did the inveterate foes of the republic who stood on the right. The *Action Française* (see p. 337) was still alive, but no one regarded it as a serious threat to French democracy.

The Colonial Empire   France's possessions, like Britain's, girdled the globe and, in addition to old settlements like St. Pierre and Miquelon in the Gulf of St. Lawrence, Martinique and Guadeloupe in the West Indies, the island of Réunion, and various stations in India, included Algeria, the protectorates of Tunis and Morocco, Equatorial and West Africa, Somaliland, Madagascar, New Caledonia and islands in the Pacific, and the greater part of Indochina. To these were added, at the war's finish, the mandates of Togo and Cameroon in Africa and Syria in the Near East.

During the war, nearly two million troops had been raised by the colonies, including 680,000 fighting men, and this aroused new hopes that union between the homeland and the colonies would be useful in maintaining France's postwar power position, while at the same time forming a great economic community, the parts of which would have specialized functions and would be mutually interdependent. In general, French imperial policy, especially in Africa, was well designed to produce the native confidence that was necessary for any such development. French investors, however, were slow to support the policies that would have given a real push toward modernization of the more backward colonies, and they were discouraged further by the heavy expenses of colonial administration in the more unsettled dependencies.

The showcase of French imperialism was Algeria, which had been French since 1830 and had gradually been made an integral part of the home country, so that it was now considered to form three departments of France and was entitled to send ten deputies to the Chamber. In 1919 native Algerians were offered citizenship, and two years later they were given a share of local government. Throughout the 1920s, this policy of integration showed every sign of working, and the country, despite some economic setbacks, was generally prosperous and satisfied. This was true also of the neighboring protectorate of Tunisia, thanks to careful concessions made by French officials to nationalist groups and the institution of collaborative economic enterprises. Morocco, on the other hand, despite the tremendous achievements of the great soldier-administrator Lyautey in pacifying the tribes, instituting basic agricultural reform, and transforming Casablanca into a modern port, continued to represent a heavy financial burden throughout the 1920s. This was largely due to the rising of the tribes in that part of Spanish Morocco called the Riff. Under a tough and tenacious leader, Abd-el-Krim, the Riffi drove the Spanish garrisons out of their own part of Morocco and then, growing more ambitious, extended their operations into French Morocco as well. The French phase of the Riff war consumed much of 1925 and 1926 before Abd-el-Krim was forced to surrender, and its costs hurt all of the other French colonies.

Morocco was not the only French dependency that was the scene of native war. In Syria, Arab nationalism was as potent as it was in neighboring Iraq, and none of the administrative schemes introduced by the French blunted it. In 1925 rioting in Damascus and a simultaneous revolt on the part of the Druses placed local French garrisons in serious jeopardy, and the danger was not relieved by the bombardment of Damascus by General Sarrail, which simply made the insurrection general. Sarrail was recalled and a new commissioner sent to the area, but it was not until 1927 that even relative calm was restored, and there were frequent clashes in the years that followed.

On the other side of the world, Indochina represented an enormously rich area where French colonial administrators had followed a policy of frank exploitation to a much greater degree than was true in colonies closer to home. This had unfortunate results. Throughout the postwar period, the younger generation in all parts of Indochina found inspiration in the Chinese revolution and in the teachings of communism, especially the propaganda beamed by the Soviet Union to the underdeveloped areas. Nationalism on an organized scale was slow to grow, but it was able to take advantage of peasant unrest when the world depression forced prices down in the early 1930s. In Annam, Tonkin, and Cambodia there were outbreaks of violence in the decade before World War II.

When the Popular Front government was formed in France in 1936, its leader Léon Blum warned that there would be more risings throughout the colonies unless positive steps were taken to conciliate nationalist feeling. By that date, however, Frenchmen were too preoccupied with troubles closer to Paris to give much of their minds to the colonies.

The Impact of the World Depression   It is perhaps a sign of the solidity of Poincaré's reforms that France was the last country in Europe to be affected by the storm that had started in New York in 1929. But the curtailment of the tourist trade, the cancellation of orders for luxury goods, and the tendency toward economic nationalism on the part of countries already suffering hard times eventually eroded the bases of French prosperity. Since France remained on the gold standard even after Great Britain and the United States had abandoned it, the prices of its goods were soon too high for effective competition and exports fell off rapidly. By 1932 the country was in the same desperate position as its neighbors. Unemployment and social distress made their appearance; and, as they did so, the people looked to their government for the kind of effective corrective action that had solved the crisis of 1926. When it was not forthcoming, their faith in parliamentary government began to weaken, and the extremists gained a new hearing.

The French Chamber proved incapable of taking determined action, largely because of unbridgeable differences of principle between the government parties. The elections of May 1932 resulted in a victory for the parties of the left, the strongest of which were the Radical Socialists, led by Édouard Herriot, and the United Socialists, led by Léon Blum. Effective collaboration by these parties proved impossible because the United Socialists' prescription for the depression was a program that included nationalization of key industries and the Bank of France, increased taxation on the upper brackets, introduction of the forty-hour week as a means of reducing unemployment, and extensive government pump-priming in the form of public works. The Radicals, on the other hand, represented the interests of small businessmen, holders of government obligations, and middle class farmers; and they considered all the above ideas reprehensible, preferring to rely upon a program of rigid governmental economy. This incompatibility led to a degree of ministerial instability (there were four ministries in little more than a year) that irritated the public and led to mounting criticism of the political system.

This was reflected in the rapid growth of communism but also, and more spectacularly, in the revivification of antirepublican organizations of the right, which now took on a distinct Fascist tinge. In addition to the old *Action Fran-çaise*, which now spawned an auxiliary organization of young thugs called the *Camelots du Roi*, the most important of these was the *Croix de Feu*, which had been founded in 1927 as a society of war veterans but had now become, under the leadership of Colonel de la Rocque, a militant group of young conservatives. In addition, there were the *Jeunesses Patriotes*, which had been founded to carry on the tradition of Déroulède's League of Patriots (see p. 328) but bore a marked similarity to Mussolini's *Squadristi*; the *Solidarité Française*, founded by the perfume manufacturer Coty, which was violently anti-Semitic and professed a preference for government by dictatorship; the *Francistes*, who dressed like Hitler's S.A.; the Neo-Socialists of Marcel Déat, who were ideologically indistinguishable from the National Socialists; and others—all with not inconsiderable numbers of members.

Like the British Fascist party, to which fleeting reference has been made above (and which never attained any significant strength), the rise of these groups was stimulated by the contrast between the apparent inefficiency of parliamentarianism and what seemed to be the vigor and purposiveness of the totalitarian regimes of Italy and Germany. Their arguments appealed to many respectable and responsible Frenchmen who were concerned about the inadequacies of the present political system. But they also grew as a result of encouragement and support given them by selfish interests—by the heavy industries represented in the *Comité des Forges* and the banking groups represented in the Bank of France, who were alarmed by the strength shown by socialism in the elections of 1932 and by Blum's projected program of nationalization and heavy corporate taxation. Anthony Eden was later to write, with reference to France's failure to respond vigorously to the Nazi threat, "The *Comité des Forges* was so anti-Blum that it had scarcely time to be anti-German."

In 1934 the Republic experienced another of the scandals that seemed to stud its history, and it proved, before it was over, to be more serious than the Panama scandal of 1892 (see p. 331). A stock manipulator named Serge Stavisky was arrested for having issued some fraudulent bonds and committed suicide to escape imprisonment. It was soon discovered that he had been arrested for fraud in 1926 but had never been tried, thanks to repeated postponements of his case, which were due, it was alleged, to the intervention of republican politicians. The conservative press, financed by the same interests that supported the Fascist Leagues, began to trumpet that the government had been involved in a conspiracy with Stavisky and his kind to defraud the French people and that the police had "suicided" Stavisky in order to prevent his revealing the names of his accomplices. The failure of the government to investigate the matter promptly and to take vigorous action against people found guilty of laxity lent an air of veracity to the charges; and, since the economic slump had been in no wise relieved, popular indignation was intensified. On February 6, 1934, in response to a call for direct action issued by the whole of the rightist press, the Royalist and Fascist Leagues, supported by thousands of students and by some Communist groups, assembled in the Place de la Concorde and tried repeatedly to storm the Chamber of Deputies. They were dispersed with great difficulty and only after the police had used fire hoses and small arms against the crowd. The night's rioting caused twenty-one deaths and 1600 other casualties. More important, it led to the resignation of the cabinet then in power, despite the fact that it could claim the support of the majority of the Chamber. It appeared, in short, as if action on the street was on the point of supplanting rule by law and parliamentary procedure.

The Decline of the Republic   For the next two years—more precisely, until the elections of May 1936—French affairs were directed by a series of emergency cabinets, which did not represent the will of the people as it had been reflected in the last parliamentary poll of 1932 and which often included men who were, overtly or secretly, opponents of the republican form of government (like Pierre

Léon Blum, 1872–1950. (Brown Brothers)

Laval and Philippe Pétain, to name only two). Whether their political sympathies had anything to do with their lack of vigor in pushing the French armament program and in showing resistance to the first aggressive moves of Hitler and Mussolini would be difficult to prove conclusively; and, in any case, there were other reasons for these deficiencies. The French people were as reluctant as the British to support heavy military expenditures in time of economic depression, and they were no more perceptive than other people when it came to discerning Hitler's true objectives. The fact remains, however, that the first significant victories of the dictators were won while France was ruled, as a result of the disorders of 1934, by stopgap governments.

During these two years, the Fascist Leagues grew in strength and activity, and their imitation of the street tactics of their German predecessors stimulated the growth of a militant countermovement of the left, in the shape of the Popular Front, which was formed by the beginning of collaboration between the Radicals, the Socialists, and the Communists in 1935. In the 1936 elections, these parties won a great victory and formed a government under the leadership of the Socialist Léon Blum, one of the most courageous and capable republican figures of this period.

When Blum took office, the fiscal stability of the state was threatened by a flight of gold from the country, and industrial production was seriously handicapped by a wave of sit-down strikes. Blum sought to check the first of these dangers by reorganizing the Bank of France and bringing it under government control and by negotiating international agreements for monetary cooperation;

La Grande Illusion, directed by Jean Renoir, 1938. A powerful antiwar film that deals incisively with the conflict between nationalism and class solidarity. Here, on their way to a German prison camp, a French mechanic (Jean Gabin) and a French aristocrat (Pierre Fresnay) are searched by their captors. Museum of Modern Art, New York, Film Stills Archive)

he tried to cope with the second by introducing the forty-hour week, by establishing labor's right to use collective bargaining in making contracts, and by promising annual holidays with pay. These and other government measures—the nationalization of the arms industry, for example—further stimulated the suspicion and hatred of the right and led it to accuse the Republic not only of being corrupt but of falling under the influence of communism.

Although Blum's opposition to fascism at home and abroad did not seem vigorous enough for his Communist partners, who soon withdrew their support from his government, it seemed dangerously impolitic to people who, as Hitler grew in strength, remembered the losses of the last war and feared the results of another.

Shortly after the outbreak of the civil war in Spain (see pp. 627,639–645), the novelist Roger Martin du Gard wrote to a friend:

> I am hard as steel *for neutrality.* My principle: anything, *rather* than war! Anything, anything! Even fascism in Spain . . . even fascism in France! . . . Anything: Hitler, rather than war![2]

[2] Martin du Gard's feelings about the essential futility of war may have been reinforced, a little later, by Jean Renoir's film *La Grande Illusion,* which was released in 1938.

Blum's opponents exploited this fear, arguing that his tactics would, unless checked, precipitate a conflict that would ruin France and benefit only Soviet Russia. The more reactionary newspapers began in 1936 to make a point of explaining to their readers the horrors of modern warfare and the inadequacy of French armaments, while repeating that the Soviet Union was seeking to involve France in wars for its own advantage. As the foundations of collective security were systematically undermined by the dictators, this argument was used against anyone who suggested resistance. "French intervention in the Spanish war," *Le Candide* explained, "would be the beginning of the European conflagration wanted by Moscow." "France's present condition, its prestige, its authority are not increasing in strength," argued the *Revue de France* in 1938, "the facts, alas, prove it," and hence opposition to the dictators would be foolhardy. During the Czechoslovakian crisis (see p. 647), the *Action Française* argued that any attempt to save the imperiled democracy would lead "to an absurd objective and a disastrous result."

Propaganda like this was the end result of the series of events set in train when the world depression destroyed the foundations of the economy, revealed old habits of parliamentary inefficiency, revived antirepublican hatreds, and led inexorably to a dangerous bipolarity of political life. In these circumstances, which encouraged the growth of defeatism, the possibility of French democracy withstanding an all-out offensive by the dictators was dubious.

THE LESSER STATES

The Low Countries and Switzerland   Despite economic troubles and some trying political disputes, neither Belgium nor the Netherlands showed any strong symptoms of political weakness in the period under review. Belgium came out of the war and the long German occupation with a problem of reconstruction and industrial reorganization similar to that of France but smaller in scope, and with troubles caused by the decline of Antwerp, which was suffering from the diminution of German trade and the transfer of the overseas trade of Alsace-Lorraine to French ports. Thanks to planning and hard work, however, recovery was steady; and the worst of the problems of adjustment to new conditions were eased by the passage of social-insurance legislation which was actively promoted by the growing labor movement. On the political side, the Belgian government had to deal with the old tension between the Flemings and the Walloons, which the Germans had made more serious by encouraging the hope of Flemish separation. In 1921 the country was divided along language lines into two administrative sections, and later laws divided the army in the same way and made other concessions to the Flemings, notably in the field of education.

Loyalty to the existing regime was assured by the popularity of the wartime king, Albert I, who continued on the throne until his death in 1934; and political extremism made little headway in the country. It was not, however, entirely without influence. In the 1930s a Fascist movement, the Rexists, was organized by Léon Degrelle and received active support from Hitler and Mussolini; and, by working in cooperation with the extremist wing of the Flemish nationalists, it helped effect an important change in Belgium's foreign policy, one that was disadvantageous to the cause of democracy in Europe.

At the Peace Conference of 1919, Belgium had been freed of the restrictions placed upon it by the treaty of 1839 (see p. 30) and was allowed to pursue an independent foreign policy. The postwar governments elected to ally with France and, after 1920, to collaborate with it in a common defensive system (see p. 506). In 1936, after the German military occupation of the Rhineland, King Leopold III announced to his Council of Ministers that Belgium must follow an exclusively national policy and, the next year, both the British and French governments, acting presumably on Belgian insistence, released the country from its obligations under the Locarno Treaties (see p. 509). This retreat to neutrality, doubtless taken to still the nationalist anti-French agitations of the Flemings and the Rexists, did not protect Belgium in 1940.

The domestic politics of both Holland and Switzerland remained calm throughout the period. In Switzerland, the notable tendencies were an increase of the powers of the national government at the expense of the cantons and a further extension of state socialism and government responsibility in the fields of agriculture and industry. The use of the instruments of direct democracy in politics was continued and widened. In Holland, politics had a more conservative cast. The most pressing problems for the Dutch government proved to be colonial rather than domestic ones. Throughout the 1920s, there was unrest in the Far Eastern dependencies, with riots in Java and Sumatra and, by the beginning of the next decade, a growing nationalist movement in all parts of Indonesia. In Europe, as the conflict between the democracies and the totalitarian states loomed up, both countries tried to preserve their traditional neutral position.

Northern Europe   In a period in which democracy was retreating in many parts of the continent, it made solid gains in the Scandinavian countries. The newest of these, Finland, started its life with a tumultuous period in which Red formations supported by the Bolshevik regime in Russia and White Guards led by General Mannerheim and backed by the German General von der Goltz's Iron Division fought for control of the country. By May 1918 the last Red units had been defeated and, after the armistice, the Germans were withdrawn; and the country could think about organizing itself. In the middle of 1919 a democratic constitution was adopted and the first president was elected. Finland had rich timber resources and a flourishing paper industry; and, thanks to agrarian reforms begun in 1922, one person in three owned his own land. The country prospered throughout the interwar period, and its economic and political health was shown by the pride the Finns took in their institutions and in their graceful capital, which has some of the finest public buildings in Europe. Its faith in democracy was shown also in the stern laws passed against political extremism (forbidding, among other things, the maintenance of political fighting groups) and the bravery with which its citizens defended their system when it was attacked in 1940 (see p. 661).

In the kingdoms of Denmark, Norway, and Sweden, prewar progress toward democracy was carried further in this period. A new Danish constitution of 1915 brought universal suffrage and liberal reform to that country; and here, and in the two neighboring states, there was a notable growth of Socialist and Labor parties that remained true to the revisionist ideal of peaceful evolution by parliamentary means. Communism made little headway in Scandinavia. In all three countries progress toward economic democracy was steady, and there were strong cooperative movements.

The Iberian Peninsula   The story of southwestern Europe was a less happy one. Portugal, weakened by a gallant but costly participation in the world war, was afflicted by grave economic dislocations that were in no way relieved by the incompetence and corruption of its politicians. In 1926, the government was overthrown by a military coup, and General Antonio Carmona became president and dictator, legitimizing his power in 1933 by promulgating a new constitution. In 1928, this strong man appointed Professor Antonio de Oliveira Salazar as his chief aide, investing him with greater and greater power as his administrative and financial gifts became apparent. In 1932 Salazar became prime minister and, in the following year, supervised the adoption of the new constitution. In subsequent years, he assumed dictatorial powers, and if he employed them for the material improvement of his country, it remains true that his regime was not characterized by respect for civil liberties. Free party development was not permitted in Portugal, and the government intervened with a stern hand when signs of opposition appeared.

Finally, in neighboring Spain, the first decade after the war saw the gathering of forces for what promised to be a great victory for democracy but led in the end to one of democracy's most dramatic and fateful defeats.

During World War I, Spain remained neutral, but its internal history continued to be plagued by the turbulence and the ministerial instability that marked the prewar period (see p. 309). Conditions deteriorated further as a result of colonial troubles; and the disastrous war in the Riff in particular seriously weakened public confidence in the monarchy, especially when it was discovered that King Alfonso XIII had taken a personal hand in planning the offensive that led to the battle of Anual (July 1921), in which 10,000 Spaniards were killed and 15,000 taken prisoner. To save his throne, the king connived in a plot by which the captain general of Catalonia, Don Miguel Primo de Rivera, seized power in September 1923. The regime that he proceeded to establish bore a marked similarity to the one currently being consolidated in Italy; and, indeed, both Alfonso and Primo de Rivera showed the utmost cordiality toward Mussolini. Inside Spain, opposition parties were banned, and the press and the universities were subjected to new controls. On the other hand, the government showed a new vigor in dealing with old problems. An extensive public works program was instituted; the transportation net was modernized, with resultant benefits to the economy; and, in 1926, in collaboration with French forces, the army was able to end the war in Morocco.

Despite its initial successes, Primo de Rivera's dictatorship soon began to show signs of weakness. It never developed any mass support and never appealed, as Italian fascism did, to the intelligentsia or to youth. Men like Miguel Unamuno and José Ortega y Gasset, who during the war years had called for a national regeneration, turned away in disgust from the brutalities, the thought control, and the crude materialism of Primo de Rivera's dictatorship; and even the army, which had put him in power, began to defect. The coming of the world depression exhausted what was left of his reputation, and the king hastened to disembarrass himself of his presence by asking him to resign in January 1930.

The sovereign had outlived his usefulness by this time also; and, as republican agitation grew in every part of the country during the next year and began to make inroads in the armed forces, Alfonso XIII decided to go into exile. On April 13, 1931, he fled, and the Republic was proclaimed, amid widespread jubilation during which 200 churches were burned to the ground.

The constitution of December 1931 declared that "Spain [was] a workers' republic" and sought to lay the foundations for economic as well as political democracy. Legislative power was vested in a single chamber or Córtes, to which the ministry was responsible. Alcalá Zamora was elected president, and the veteran republican leader Manuel Azaña became prime minister. The new government immediately launched a program that was designed to destroy the old ruling forces of the country: the church, the plutocracy, and the army. The Jesuit order was expelled, state schools were established to diminish the church's role in education, large estates were confiscated and a beginning was made toward a more equitable distribution of arable land, railroads were nationalized, as was the Bank of Spain, the eight-hour day and social insurance were introduced, and, finally, the officer corps of the army was reduced by almost half.

Some of these measures were clearly unworkable. The Jesuits had to be allowed to continue to run some schools, otherwise there would not have been enough teachers. The plans for industrial and agricultural reorganization had to be decelerated in order to prevent the total breakdown of the economy. Thus, the old governing forces were weakened but left with enough power to do something about their grievances, while the beneficiaries of the revolution began to feel that the pace of change was not fast enough.

The result was that the new republican regime was soon confronted with peasant rioting, military plots, anarchist outrages, monarchist agitations (encouraged by the elections of November 1933 in which the left parties received severe setbacks), separatist movements, labor strikes, and the beginning of a new Fascist movement, the Falange, led by one of Primo de Rivera's sons. In October 1934, a revolt of the miners of the Asturias all but destroyed the city of Oviedo and caused 3000 deaths before it was suppressed.

At the beginning of 1936, the moderate Republicans joined with the Socialists, the Catalan and Basque Nationalists, the Anarcho-Syndicalists, and the Communists to form a Popular Front on the French model and, in the elections of February, won an impressive victory. A government was formed under Azaña, and the program of 1931 (which had been in abeyance since the elections of November 1933) was pushed ahead once more. The rightist parties began a bitter campaign in which they claimed that the government was directed from Moscow (although there were at this time no Communists in the cabinet, only fifteen in the Córtes, and only a few thousand in the country); and the Falange, in particular, resorted to acts of terrorism that soon provoked reprisals. On July 12, 1936, Falangists murdered a young lieutenant of the Republican Assault

Guards. The next day, Calvo Sotelo, finance minister during Primo de Rivera's dictatorship, was shot and killed in retaliation.

It was this last bloody act that served as a signal for the army coup that had long been in preparation. On July 18, 1936, General Francisco Franco flew from the Canary Islands to Morocco and raised the flag of revolt. Ten days later, using German planes, Moroccan troops began to cross to the mainland, and there now began the civil war that was to destroy Spanish liberty and bring the international conflict between democracy and dictatorship to a new pitch of intensity.

Chapter 27 THE ROAD TO WAR, 1933–1939

Distracted by the rigors of the depression and the internal political problems caused by it, the democratic nations reacted slowly and with little urgency to the beginning of a new era of aggression by the totalitarian states. Their leaders were facile in inventing excuses both for the lawless acts committed and for their own disinclination to do anything about them, and they were supported for years by their peoples, who wanted to be assured that foreign affairs would not add to their troubles.

The first example of this blindness to reality came in 1931–1932, when the Japanese government, under the influence of its military leaders, created an incident in Manchuria and used it to begin the systematic conquest of that Chinese province, actually placing a puppet ruler on its throne in February 1932. Although the League of Nations appointed a commission to investigate, which subsequently recommended the censure of Japan, the democratic states failed to agree to apply sanctions against the aggressor or to try by any other means to make it withdraw from Manchuria. Their parliamentarians and editorial writers in their newspapers vied with each other in citing economic and military arguments to prove the inexpediency and probable ineffectiveness of sanctions, as well as elaborate proofs that forbearance and understanding would in time solve the dispute to everyone's satisfaction. The ordinary citizen, if he thought of the matter at all, accepted these arguments and took comfort in the thought that what happened in a place as remote as Manchuria could not possibly affect him. This attitude merely encouraged more flagrant assaults on the public law so that, in the last analysis, the failure to stop Japan in Manchuria led inexorably to its attacks in 1940 and 1941 upon French, Dutch, and British possessions in the Far East.

Is It Beginning To Dawn upon the Diplomats? "Entirely between us, Messieurs, a new peace should really be created; the old one doesn't seem to be capable of living." This pregnant comment by Karl Arnold appeared in *Simplicissimus* in the year 1932, which saw the collective security system gravely shaken by the Manchurian crisis.

It is perhaps not hard to understand the slowness of the democracies to appreciate what was at stake in the Far East in 1931; but it is more difficult to explain their fatal failure to respond to the danger posed by the rise of Adolf Hitler to power in 1933. The brutalities of his storm troopers in his first months of office might have been expected to warn the West that a regime whose domestic practices were so contemptuous of law would probably have a foreign policy with the same characteristics. But they did not see the connection between Hitler's foreign and domestic policies, nor did they for years understand the end objectives of his activity in the foreign sphere. Meanwhile, they deluded themselves with the notion that what Hitler really wanted was merely a revision of the Versailles Treaty and the restoration of Germany's 1914 boundaries, and that he would become a law-abiding citizen as soon as he was satisfied on these points. Their delusions helped make another war inevitable.

HITLER'S FOREIGN POLICY

Hitler's views on foreign policy were largely formulated under the shock of Germany's collapse in 1918. What thoughts he had had about the subject before that time were incoherent and disjointed. While he was a schoolboy in Linz, he seems to have become a Pan-German nationalist. This tendency was strengthened after 1909 when he lived in the slums of Vienna in close proximity to hundreds of rootless and impoverished wanderers from the Slav lands of the east, all of whom he came to detest and to regard as a potent threat to Germanic civilization which must be resisted. The war in its turn made him a convinced militarist with a preference, which never left him, for military solutions to political problems. But the basic ideas that guided his future foreign policy were not worked out systematically until 1918, when, in the face of a defeat that dumbfounded him, he began to analyze the reasons for it.

William II's foreign policy had ended in disaster, Hitler convinced himself, because both its objectives and its methods were mistaken and because inadequate efforts had been made to assure it of public support if and when it got into difficulties. The emperor had been an expansionist, but the expansion he sought had taken the form of foreign trade and colonial acquisition. Hitler was convinced that heavy reliance on trade was to the benefit only of the Jews who, in his opinion, controlled it, and that annexation of areas like South West Africa brought no tangible national benefits but merely helped to disperse Germans and to divert their strength from greater aims. William II's tactics in pursuing these objectives were equally faulty and alienated all the powers with a reputation for strength and reliability, leaving Germany with only Turkey and the decaying "mummy state," Austria-Hungary, as allies. When Germany finally had to go to war, these countries were of little help to it. Germany was handicapped further by the fact that the government had not taken care to suppress or render harmless those elements within the country—moderates, internationalists, pacifists, Marxists, Jews—who could not be counted on to fight till the end. As a result, these groups stabbed the German army in the back and imposed upon their country a shameful peace.

From the beginning of his career as a popular tribune in the postwar years, Hitler made attacks upon the peace settlement a constant ingredient of his speeches and propaganda. Since this emphasis was later to confuse Western statesmen, it is well to note that Hitler never regarded the Versailles Treaty as an unjust one. He wrote shortly after the war, "If I were a Frenchman, and if the greatness of France were as dear to me as that of Germany is . . . I would not act differently than Clemenceau did [in formulating the peace terms]." The settlement was a natural penalty of defeat; and Hitler fulminated against it not because it was unjust but because it was inconvenient. He was always infuriated by people in his audience who answered his attacks on Versailles by shouting "Brest Litovsk!" failing to see that Brest Litovsk (see p. 482) had been a "good" peace because it was to Germany's advantage, whereas Versailles was a "bad" peace because it prevented bigger and better Brest Litovsks. "One could," he wrote, "have crushed one's head against the wall in despair about such a people."

But even worse than these moralists were those Germans who seemed to believe that because he attacked Versailles. Hitler was arguing for a restoration of the frontiers of 1914. When he wrote *Mein Kampf,* Hitler said (in one of those passages not read soon enough in London and Paris):

> The demand for the re-establishment of the frontiers of the year 1914 is political nonsense of such a degree and consequences as to look like a crime. Entirely aside from the fact that the frontiers of the Reich in the year 1914 were anything but logical, they were in reality neither complete with respect to the inclusion of people of German nationality, nor intelligent with respect to geo-military appropriateness. They were not the result of considered political action, but momentary frontiers of a political struggle in no way concluded.

Implicit in this cloudy statement was a rejection of mere treaty revision and the announcement of a future program of expansion that promised to be much more ambitious than anything dreamed of by William II. It would, moreover, involve a fundamental departure from the main line of imperial policy. Hitler wrote:

> A policy of land acquisition cannot be carried out in a place like the Cameroons, but is today almost exclusively possible only in Europe.[We must think in terms of] winning land which increases the area of the motherland itself and thereby not only keeps the new settlers in the most intimate community with the land of their origin but insures to the total area those advantages deriving from its united magnitude.

This meant that Germany must expand eastward, effectively removing the Slav threat by doing so, and bringing under control the most fertile and the strategically most secure land in Europe. In a significant passage in *Mein Kampf* Hitler wrote:

> We National Socialists consciously write FINIS under the aims of the foreign policy of our prewar period. We start where an end was made six hundred years ago. We stop the everlasting German movement toward the south and west of Europe and turn our eyes towards the land in the east. . . . When in Europe today we speak of new territory, we cannot help thinking in the first instance of Russia and the border states that are subject to her.

If not in his speeches, then at least in *Mein Kampf,* Hitler made it clear that unless the other powers submitted cravenly to his will, German expansion could not be effected without a new war. The idea of war ran like a red thread throughout the book, and its author constantly reiterated the principle that all foreign policy must be predicated on the assumption that war was coming. Indeed, William II's failure to act on that assumption was one more reason for his downfall.

In the post-Versailles world, Hitler believed that war was made inevitable by France, for no matter who ruled that country, "whether Bourbons or Jacobins, Bonapartists or bourgeois democrats, clerical republicans or red Bolshevists, . . . France relentlessly throttles us." The projected *Drang nach Osten* could not begin until this threat was removed, and it could in all probability be removed only by war.

To prepare for that, the mistakes made by William II must not be repeated. This time the home front must be prepared for war, and this preparation would involve basic political changes. Instead of the welter of parties that existed before and during World War I, all political parties must be subordinated to, and coordinated by, the state—as must all other independent organizations, whether political, economic, religious, or purely social. All potential dissidents—especially Jews and Marxists—must be liquidated; and, in accomplishing this task, "all humanitarian and esthetic considerations become absolutely meaningless." Hitler admired the way in which Mussolini had dealt with such groups and wrote of "the great man south of the Alps who, in his hot love for his people, did not make pacts with the domestic foes of Italy but strove to destroy them by every means wherever he found them." Germany must act in the same way so as to be able to pursue its foreign aims with a united will and determination. The future *Gleichschaltung* (see p. 587), in short, was the prerequisite of a successful expansionist policy that would probably have to be effected by war. This was the connection between foreign and domestic policy that the Western powers failed to perceive when the Nazi domestic purges began in 1933.

The second step preparatory to war was the acquisition of more efficient allies than "the putrid state corpses" with which Germany had been allied in 1914. Fascist Italy would be one such ally. But more important, if its collaboration could be won, was Great Britain—the most valuable of allies, Hitler wrote, "as long as its leaders and the spirit of its masses permit us to expect that brutality and toughness" which had characterized Britain's policy in the past. To gain an alliance with Great Britain, Hitler was willing to make great sacrifices—the sacrifices that should have been made before 1914. He was willing to renounce colonies and sea power and even, apparently, industrial challenges in the markets of the world in order to bring Britain to his side and, thus, to isolate and make possible the destruction of France.

But the crushing of France was not to be regarded as an end in itself but rather as "a means of subsequently and finally giving our nation a chance to expand elsewhere." And that elsewhere, of course, was eastern Europe.

These views, formulated immediately after 1918 and elaborated in many speeches, put down in cold print in *Mein Kampf* in 1924 for all the world to see (and repeated in a second book that Hitler wrote in 1928 and decided not to publish but to keep under lock and key in the party printing offices) determined the main line of Hitler's foreign policy after he came to power in 1933. But, as Hermann Rauschning warned, in a passage written in 1938 to people in the West who were belatedly beginning to take *Mein Kampf* seriously, Hitler was greater than his book, which must not therefore be taken as an exact blueprint. If Hitler followed the pattern laid down in *Mein Kampf*, he was not bound by the details and was perfectly willing to adjust them according to circumstances. It should be remembered also, Rauschning pointed out, that Hitler had "carried to a pitch of virtuosity the pursuit of tactical elasticity."

HITLER'S POLICY IN ACTION

The First Years, 1933–1935   Tactical elasticity was the hallmark of Hitler's foreign policy in the first years of his power, when a misjudgment or a false step might have been fatal for him. He had three things that he wished to accomplish in this first phase. He wanted to complete domestic preparations for a dynamic foreign policy by *Gleichschaltung,* by ordering affairs in his own party, by beginning to build up his armed forces. He wanted to regain Germany's freedom of action in foreign affairs by withdrawing from engagements entered into by Stresemann and Bruening. And he wanted to test the other powers' will to resistance in order to calculate the speed with which he might move toward his objectives when he had accumulated appreciable armed strength. Hitler had his setbacks in these years, but he did not expose himself to any serious danger, and what he learned about the other powers encouraged him to believe that he would achieve all he desired.

Nothing better illustrates the technique with which Hitler advanced his objectives than his withdrawal from the Disarmament Conference and the League of Nations in 1933. Hitler had inherited the disarmament negotiations from his predecessors. In the negotiations that began in Geneva in 1932, German negotiators had already won a significant victory by persuading the other powers at long last to grant Germany equality of status in armaments. This concession did not particularly please Hitler; nor was he interested in obtaining other concessions, for these might deprive Germany of a grievance that he wanted to exploit. After all, if the Disarmament Conference should succeed in devising a new arms-control plan acceptable to all other powers, Germany would have no excuse for refusing to abide by it and would be subjected to continued controls. This Hitler was determined to avoid.

He did so by using tactics that foreshadowed those he would employ in the Sudeten affair of 1938: he made demands that he was reasonably sure the other powers could not accept. He insisted that equality of status was not enough but that, since the other powers were reluctant to reduce their forces to Germany's level, all controls on its military establishment must be lifted so that it could seek actual equality in its own way. Needless to say, the French government blocked all attempts to yield to this point of view. In October 1933, Hitler withdrew from the Disarmament Conference and, for good measure, from the League of Nations as well.

Before taking this daring step, Hitler appealed, in a number of effective speeches, to the guilt complex of all those in the West who felt that the Versailles Treaty had not treated Germany fairly and that France was stubborn in seeking to hold to the letter of a settlement that should have been revised long ago. He also stated repeatedly that Germany would adhere to any mutual agreements for total elimination of offensive weapons and was prepared to enter pacts of friendship with anyone who desired to conclude them. This left the other governments with the feeling that if he were treated adroitly and not threatened with sanctions or reprisals, he would return of his own accord to the League and to the disarmament discussions. The persistence of this idea was remarkable, especially in England, where, as late as the spring of 1939, Neville Chamberlain told reporters that he thought there was still a good chance of a reopening of the Disarmament Conference, with German participation.

In reality, the Fuehrer had broken once and for all with the disarmament talks and with all kinds of collective-security arrangements. He continued to affirm his faith in international collaboration; but whenever a concrete proposal was made for realizing it, he sidestepped it or refused it by indirection, insisting that he was quite willing to enter agreements for the maintenance of peace, provided they were bilateral agreements. The other powers were so anxious to believe that Hitler was a man of peace that they dropped their more comprehensive projects and, in two notable cases, made the kind of agreement he preferred—forgetting that bilateral pacts could be broken whenever Hitler wished to break them.

Hitler's first success was his conclusion of a nonaggression pact with Poland in January 1934. The Fuehrer's withdrawal from the League and the Disarmament Conference had worried some of his advisers, for—coupled with the progressive cooling of relations with the Soviet Union and the breaking of the old tie between *Reichswehr* and the Red Army—this seemed to indicate that Germany was headed for a dangerous isolation. The Polish pact, the possibility of which occurred to Hitler as early as April 1933, at least reduced the potential danger of trouble on Germany's eastern flank while simultaneously driving a wedge into the French security system in eastern Europe (see p. 596).

What was gained here was lost almost immediately by the unfortunate impression created by the Blood Purge of June 1934 and, more important, by the Vienna *Putsch* of July 1934, in which Dollfuss was killed (see p. 599). Despite all of Hitler's disclaimers, it was well known that he had supplied arms to the Austrian Nazis, permitted them to broadcast their propaganda from a station in Munich, and allowed the formation on German soil of an Austrian Legion, whose apparent mission was to invade Austria. Momentarily, it appeared that Italy, at least, might be ready to take military action against Germany; and, even when this did not materialize, it seemed possible that the powers would work out an effective policy of isolating and containing Hitler. This, at least, was the hope of the vigorous French foreign minister Jean Louis Barthou, who, throughout 1934, traveled indefatigably from capital to capital promoting the idea of a regional security pact that would embrace all the states of eastern Europe and be guaranteed by those of the West—an eastern Locarno supplemented by a network of mutual defense treaties. An additional feature of the Barthou plan was the active participation of the Soviet Union, which was expected also to enter the League system and lend its strength to the common effort to restrain the German dictator.

The Barthou plan represented a serious threat to Hitler, but he was saved from its restrictions by friction between the Czechs and the Poles and the unwillingness of the latter to enter into any defensive arrangements that included the Russians, as well as by the disinclination of the British to make commitments in eastern Europe. By the fall of 1934, the chance of the plan's winning general acceptance was very slim, and in October its author was dead, assassinated by Croat terrorists in Marseille along with King Alexander of Yugoslavia on the occasion of that ruler's state visit to France.[1]

Once his strong leadership was removed, the Western powers abandoned his containment policy and decided instead to try to civilize Hitler, not by pressure but by persuasion and concession. After consultation with the Italians, the British and French governments devised a plan in which Germany was to be offered complete equality in arms if she would adhere to certain arms-control conventions, would cooperate in new mutual assistance pacts designed to give security to eastern and central Europe, and would consider returning to the League.

This comprehensive set of proposals was drawn up in February 1935, and the British foreign secretary, Sir John Simon, and Anthony Eden made prepara-

[1] Anthony Eden has described the results of this tragic affair by writing: "Neither country was to know such decisive leadership again. It is inconceivable that Barthou would have been equivocal to the point of horse-trading over the Italo-Abyssinian conflict or that Alexander would have compromised with Hitler or, from overconfidence, have allowed his air force to be destroyed on the ground when the attack came."

Prosit! Herr Hitler: "The more we arm together, the peacefuller we'll be!" Sir John Simon: "Well-er-up to a certain point—and in certain cases—provisionally—perhaps." From *Punch,* March 27, 1935. © Punch.

tions to go to Berlin to discuss it in the first week of March. Hitler had other ideas. He contracted a diplomatic cold and asked that the British visit be postponed for three weeks. Then, on successive Saturdays, he made two announcements that made the Anglo-French proposals pointless. On March 8, 1935, he let it be known that Germany had a new military air force (it soon transpired that the air force was not, as a matter of fact, new but was already, or so Hitler claimed, as large as Britain's). Then, on March 15, he announced that he no longer intended to abide by any of the military clauses of the Versailles Treaty and that he was expanding the German army from its legal size of 100,000 officers and men to a 36-division force of 550,000.

Hitler calculated that the very effrontery of these actions would confuse the other powers and make effective counteraction impossible; but, in order to make sure of this, he intimated to the British government that he was prepared to make a separate naval agreement with them. The British proved more receptive to this than to suggestions that Hitler be forced to withdraw his unilateral repudiation of the arms clauses of the treaty. Immediately after the announcement of March 15, the governments of Britain, France, and Italy sent representatives to a conference at Stresa to discuss countermeasures, and the Western press talked of a Stresa Front that was preparing to take punitive action. But the essential artificiality of this "front" was shown in June, when the British, without consulting the other partners, concluded an agreement with the German government that gave Germany the right to build a fleet thirty-five percent as large as Britain's and also to construct as many submarines as it desired.

The motives of the British are still somewhat murky, although it is probably true—as Sir Samuel Hoare has written—that they saw in this arrangement a good bargain: a guaranteed superiority over the German fleet that was twice as great as the one they had had in 1914. But the solidity of this advantage depended, of course, on Hitler's good faith, which, even in 1935, there was plenty of reason to distrust. Aside from this, there was no avoiding the fact that the Anglo-German Naval Pact had, in a real sense, legitimized Hitler's repudiation of the arms clauses of the Versailles Treaty by being in itself a violation of those clauses.

Abyssinia and the Rhineland   What was left of the Stresa Front after this body blow disappeared in October 1935 when the Italian member of the combination invaded Abyssinia. Italy had long been interested in this sprawling semifeudal country and on two occasions (see pp. 412 and 418) had paid for its interest with humiliating military defeats. Mussolini seems to have regarded the domination of Abyssinia as the first step toward the creation of a colonial empire that would make Italy the most powerful state in the Mediterranean and the Near East. Since the beginning of his term of power, he had engaged in negotiations with other Near Eastern powers and with local rulers to advance this end. He was no more successful than Crispi had been before him (see p. 418) in winning his way by diplomacy and treaty arrangements, and he decided that he could do so only by military means. He did not believe that the Western powers would interfere with his plans, because they were distracted equally by the depression and by the problem of the new Germany. In any case, he seems to have received secret intimations from the French foreign minister, Pierre Laval, that France would give Italy a free hand in the area. Fortified by these assurances, the Duce seized upon an incident that took place in December 1934 at Walwal on the border between Abyssinia and Italian Somaliland, in which fighting between Ethiopian and Italian forces led to thirty Italian deaths. He charged Abyssinia with aggression and started preparations for war.

Under the energetic leadership of Haile Selassie I, who had ruled the country since 1917, Abyssinia had made a considerable amount of political and social progress, and, as early as 1923, it had been admitted to membership in the League of Nations. The League now used all its resources to adjudicate the dispute, in the hope of maintaining peace; and most of 1935 was given over to attempts to appease Italy by offering it territory and economic rights at Abyssinia's expense. All of these Mussolini rejected, meanwhile pushing ahead his military plans, and in October he inaugurated hostilities.

This action threatened to elicit more determined counteraction from the West than Mussolini had imagined. It is true that the French government was unenthusiastic about resistance to the Duce's plans, for they wished to reserve what energies the depression left them for opposing Hitler. The British people, on the other hand, were furious over Mussolini's callous indifference to the public law; a wave of genuine enthusiasm for the League was sweeping the country; and the government, in response to this, showed every indication of giving material support to Abyssinia, even at the risk of war with Italy. British fleet units were concentrated in the eastern Mediterranean; pledges of support in the event of an Italian attack upon these forces were solicited and received from Yugoslavia, Greece, Turkey, Czechoslovakia, Rumania, and—albeit reluctantly—France; and, on October 11, 1935, under British leadership, the League Assembly—in the first example of such action—voted economic sanctions against Italy. These went into force on November 18.

The crucial commodity in the conflict in Abyssinia, however, was oil and, unless this was cut off, Italy would not be seriously inconvenienced. To avoid so drastic a blow to Italy as would be represented by oil sanctions, Pierre Laval made one more attempt to find a compromise solution, and he persuaded the British government to cooperate. The proposal was worked out in December between Laval and Sir Samuel Hoare, the British foreign secretary; it was supposed to be secret, but someone leaked the details to the French press, which published them. The revelation that the two statesmen were apparently prepared to give Mussolini very extensive tracts of Abyssinia and virtual control over its trade and resources caused a sensation. Alfred Duff Cooper wrote later: "During my experience of politics I have never witnessed so devastating a wave of public opinion." Hoare was forced to resign and the plan was jettisoned, but the incident had unfortunate effects. It compromised the Western cause, at least in the eyes of the United States, whose cooperation in economic sanctions was vital if Italy were to be stopped; and it caused a period of mutual recrimination between London and Paris that necessarily postponed effective action.

All this worked to Mussolini's advantage. He proceeded with his campaign, inspiring his armies with a grandiloquent statement in which he attacked his Western critics for their voting of sanctions. He said:

> The Italian people is capable of resisting a very long siege, especially when they are certain. . . . that right is on their side and wrong on the side of a Europe that does dishonor to itself. The war we have begun on the soil of Africa is a war of civilization and liberty. It is a war . . . of the poor, the disinherited, the proletariat. Against us is ranged the front of conservatism, selfishness and hypocrisy. . . . It is a trial . . . which is a test of our virility.

The references to civilization and liberty rang decidedly false in the ears of Europeans who noted with disgust that the Italians, whose troops outnumbered the Ethiopian forces and were vastly superior to them in the quality of their hand weapons and artillery, were not content with these obvious advantages but felt called upon to attack spear-bearing tribesmen with military aircraft and—despite international conventions forbidding its use—poison gas.

Even with these means, the war was not an easy one. There was bitter fighting throughout the winter months and, despite a series of Italian victories in the first months of 1936, the Abyssinian emperor still had a large undefeated army under his personal command. This heartened those in the West who continued to work for the imposition of more stringent economic limitations on Italy; and Anthony Eden carried on extensive negotiations with other League members with the objective of winning assent for oil sanctions against the aggressor. At the beginning of March it appeared as if these talks might have a fruitful result— but at the crucial moment this hope was dashed by the third of what came to be called Hitler's "Saturday surprises." On March 7, 1936, Hitler marched troops into the Rhineland, simultaneously repudiating the Locarno Treaties and those clauses of the Versailles Treaty that stipulated that this area must be kept free of military garrisons or installations.

This was the most daring of Hitler's actions to date, and he had had difficulty in persuading his generals of its wisdom. They felt that the French would resist and that, if they did, they would have no difficulty in expelling the Germans, who were few in number (the troops that crossed the Rhine, for instance, being only in battalion and company strength). Reason was on the side of the generals; but Hitler, who relied not on logic but on what he called his *"schlaf-wandlerische Sicherheit"* (sleepwalker's assurance), proved more realistic than they. However surprised the public might have been by Hitler's abrupt action, the French and British governments had long expected it and had—as the published documents now show—resigned themselves to it. In January 1935, Anthony Eden had asked Prime Minister Flandin how important the demilitarization of the Rhineland was to France and how far the government was prepared to go to defend it. Flandin was evasive and his language was not, Eden reported to the cabinet, that of a man "determined to fight." Some thought was given on both sides of the Channel to the possibility of anticipating Hitler and offering him a lifting of the restrictive clauses of the treaty for whatever concessions they might get in return. But nothing was done until March, and when Hitler struck, the result, in Paris at least, was general dismay and flabbiness. The government at this time was one of those emergency cabinets described above (p. 620), lacking homogeneity or unity of view, and it was badly split on what should be done about Hitler's action. When the prime minister, Albert Sarraut, called in the military chiefs to help clarify the situation, he was dismayed—as he later wrote—to find that they lacked "that *élan*, that tautening of the muscles, that combative feeling" which had always characterized the French army. The commanders seemed to have an inflated conception of German strength, to be unwilling to act without general mobilization, and to be unenthusiastic about action in any circumstances. This attitude had a dampening effect on the cabinet. They now put the thought of military action out of their minds—although, as Winston Churchill wrote later, a clear request for British military support of a Rhineland operation could hardly have been refused and although the Polish government had intimated that it would support such action. Instead, they entered upon a fruitless exchange of diplomatic notes that let Hitler get away with his breach of treaty law.

It is impossible to overestimate the importance of the Rhineland coup. By virtually destroying the Locarno Treaties, it lowered the stock of all international conventions and brought further discredit on the Geneva system, which had been already seriously weakened by the Manchurian and Abyssinian crises. This increased general insecurity and led the smaller states to revise their commitments—Belgium, for instance, decided in the wake of the Rhineland coup to withdraw from the French security system (see p. 624). All of France's military alliances suffered from Hitler's action, and even the strength of its eastern border defenses, the much-advertised Maginot Line, seemed diminished now that German troops were once more poised west of the Rhine. The French themselves seemed to feel their stature had been reduced, and it is from this point that the defeatism which was to be so significant a force in 1938 and 1940 began to grow.

Finally, the Rhineland coup put an end to any serious attempt to apply oil sanctions against Italy. Mussolini was able to finish his military operations without interference and to announce in May, when his troops entered Addis Ababa, that "Ethiopia is Italian—Italian in fact, because occupied by our victorious armies, and Italian by right because, with the sword of Rome, civilization has triumphed over barbarism."

The Spanish War and the Axis   There had been moments during the Abyssinian war when Mussolini had fallen prey to doubts and hesitations; but, as his troops mopped up in Abyssinia, these fleeting apprehensions gave way to a new excess of confidence. The thought of making the Mediterranean a Roman lake appeared to him now to be within the range of possibility; and, when the Spanish Civil War erupted in July 1936, he saw in it an opportunity for promoting his ambition. He decided to intervene on the side of the rebels.

It was this decision that led him finally to make a deliberate attempt to seek closer relations with Hitler. Up to this time he had watched the rise of his fellow dictator with mixed feelings and, although he was one of the chief beneficiaries of Hitler's Rhineland stroke, he was reported to have been angered by it and to have sat at his desk furiously twisting and untwisting paper clips as the news of it was received. Now he felt it expedient to court Hitler's favor, and thus began that fateful series of events which led to his complete subordination to Hitler's will.

It is significant, for instance, that in the same month that marked the beginning of the Spanish war Mussolini advised the Austrian chancellor, Schuschnigg, to seek an improvement of Austro-German relations. This Schuschnigg did, signing an agreement that, although it was not widely realized at the time, significantly advanced the cause of *Anschluß*. For a cessation of German attacks upon his government and a spurious promise that Germany would not interfere in Austrian internal affairs, Schuschnigg engaged to follow a foreign policy that would "always be based on principles which correspond to the fact that Austria acknowledges itself to be a German state." In a world in which Hitler claimed to be the judge of what was true German-ness, this was a perilous admission. Equally dangerous was Schuschnigg's promise to permit German social and cultural organizations to have branches in his country and to give a greater share of political responsibility to "representatives of national circles" (that is, Nazi sympathizers).

Despite his previous statements about the importance of Austrian independence, Mussolini not only approved of these terms but claimed, in conversation with German representatives, that he had inspired the Austrian request for an agreement with Germany. He used the Austrian agreement, in short, as a proof of his good intentions in his attempt to win German friendship. For his own reasons Hitler received these overtures graciously and, in October—in conversations with Mussolini's son-in-law and new foreign minister, Count Ciano—agreed that Germany and Italy were natural allies against the democracies and that he was prepared to support Italy's policy in Spain. Mussolini was gratified and, on the afternoon of November 1, 1936, from a balcony on the Piazza del Duomo in Milan, announced that the Berlin conversations had resulted in a comprehensive understanding and created a new "Berlin-Rome line . . . not a diaphragm but an axis, around which can revolve all those European states with a will to collaboration and peace."

Meanwhile, the emphasis on peace in these words was being belied by his intervention in Spanish affairs. The background of the Civil War has been touched on above (p. 627). The point that must be made here is that, without foreign aid, the rebel cause might have collapsed before the end of 1936. Although part of the Spanish army went over to General Franco at the outset, he was unable to get control of either the navy or the air force, and this would have proved to be a serious deficiency had not Italy, and to a lesser extent Germany, come to his aid. In a conversation with Hitler in 1940, Ciano recalled that at the beginning of the war "Franco had declared . . . that, if he received 12 transport or bombing planes, he would win the war in a few days. Those 12 planes had grown into more than 1000 planes, 6000 dead, and 14 billion lire." It has been estimated that Italian pilots flew 135,265 hours in Spain; while, in the battle of Brihuega in 1937, four Italian infantry divisions supported the Franco forces. The fighting quality of these "volunteers" was not always high, and there was occasional suspicion that Mussolini was attempting to solve his economic problems by sending his unemployed to Spain; but the total Italian contribution to the Franco cause was impressive, in size at least.

General Franco by Cabrol in *Le canard enchainé* (Paris).

The German contribution was smaller but no less important. In addition to weapons shipments that were heavy enough to worry the army staffs at home, the Germans sent the Condor Legion, which comprised four fighter-bomber, four fighter, one reconnaissance, and two seaplane squadrons, all of which were detached from the new *Luftwaffe;* these were of inestimable value to Franco's operations. Germany also sent one tank battalion under General von Thoma, who used it for training purposes and, by skillful dilution of German personnel, created an armored corps that fought 192 engagements for Franco, plus thirty antitank companies. Some elements in the Nazi party advocated a greater commitment than this, but Hitler seems to have been more interested in seeing that the Spanish war was prolonged than in trying to end it, for its continuation was sure to keep Mussolini involved and might also create crises of which he could take advantage.

The Spanish Republic found it more difficult to get material aid, even though it was the legitimate government of Spain. Much was later made of the fact that it received assistance from the Soviet Union, which was held up by the Republic's enemies as proof that Spain was a potentially Communist state. Yet, as the Germans themselves admitted privately, the Russians intervened reluctantly and only because they dared not lose face with the Communist parties of the West; their help was limited to advisers, technicians, some aircraft, and supplies, which had to be carried to Spain by merchant ships, and their aid

"Guernica," 1937, by Pablo Picasso. The painting was inspired by the German Condor
Legion's ruthless aerial bombardment of a defenseless town during the Spanish Civil War.
(On extended loan to the Museum of Modern Art, New York, from the artist)

was not continuous, stopping a full year before the end of the war. Hugh Thomas,
who has analyzed all available evidence, has written that "the number of Russians
in Spain was certainly under 2000 and probably never exceeded 500 at one time."
Both the Soviet government and the Soviet people were more intent upon the
purges that were taking place in Russia at this time than upon the far-away
conflict in Spain. When Ilya Ehrenburg, an inspired fighter for the Republican
cause, returned to Moscow in December 1937, expecting to find Spain on
everyone's lips, one of his friends said to him: "Here's the latest anecdote for
you. Two Muscovites meet. One says: 'Have you heard the news? They've taken
Teruel!' The other asks, 'Oh, and what about his wife?' " Ehrenburg didn't find
that funny. Nor was it, in all probability, intended to be.

The Republican fighting forces, composed of loyal army and navy units, plus
contingents from trade unions, universities, and the Catalan and Basque nationalists, were supplemented by brigades of international volunteers, among which
were the Abraham Lincoln Brigade and the *Thälmann Colonne,* named after
the German Communist leader.[2] These brigades were not large and their equipment was sometimes scant. The Republican government had hoped for assistance
from the Popular Front government in France (see p. 623); but of the three
government parties there, only the Communists advocated aid, and Blum, while
sympathetic to the Republican cause, could overcome neither the opposition
of the Radicals nor the pacifism that now became dominant in his own party.
Moreover, after the Rhineland, France was more dependent than ever before
on British backing for its policies, and the British government set its face against
any intervention in Spain.

[2] It is significant of the Soviet reluctance to frighten the British and French by appearing
to have too prominent a role in Spain that they did not sponsor a Lenin or a Stalin Brigade.

Throughout 1936 the British people were occupied with pressing domestic matters that made concentration on foreign affairs difficult. In January King George V died, and the subsequent months were given over to preparations for the coronation of his successor, the popular Edward VIII. Before the coronation, however, it was discovered that he desired to marry Mrs. Wallis Simpson, an American divorcée. When efforts to dissuade him failed, a constitutional crisis of first importance arose. It was settled in the end by the king's abdication and the accession of his brother as George VI, but not until the winter of the year, months after the onset of hostilities in Spain.

Through this crisis, which if badly handled might have destroyed the monarchy or seriously weakened the unity of the Commonwealth, the country had been piloted with skill and patience by Stanley Baldwin, who succeeded Ramsay MacDonald as head of the National Government in 1935. In 1937, he retired in favor of Neville Chamberlain, and this event soon brought about an important change in foreign policy. Whereas Baldwin was frankly uninterested in foreign affairs, Chamberlain had decided opinions in this sphere. Specifically, he believed that the time had come for a new realism that would seek to stop the deterioration of international affairs not by repeating old shibboleths but by trying to discover the real grievances of the dictators, to correct them, and to attain a general appeasement. Enunciated by Chamberlain, a confident and forceful man, these views appealed to many people, who failed to note that collective security and support of the League were among the ideas that he considered outworn, and who also failed to reflect that, since the things which the dictators wanted all belonged to other nations, the appeasement policy could probably be made to work only at their expense.

With respect to Spain, the British had taken the initiative in September 1936 in organizing a Committee on Non-Intervention, with twenty-seven participating nations, including Germany, Italy, and the Soviet Union. The ostensible purpose of the committee was to prevent the shipment of men, war materials, and munitions to the belligerents in Spain and to withdraw any volunteers already there. The German delegate to the committee wrote home that, as far as he could see, the real purpose of the committee was the task "of pacifying the aroused feelings of the leftist parties in France and England by [its] very establishment" and that neither the British nor the French government would allow it to take any real action. This proved to be all too accurate a forecast. The Italians and the Germans not only continued their aid to Franco but advertised it. In August 1937, for instance, the news associations printed a telegram from Mussolini to Franco in which he openly mentioned the role of Italian troops in the battle of Santander and promised that "this brotherhood in arms, already close," would continue. The committee proved ineffective in stopping this sort of thing; and, when questions were raised in the House of Commons about similar incidents, government spokesmen took the line that even to try to prevent them might result in more serious conflict.

By the time Chamberlain became prime minister in May 1937, it was evident that the rebels would win the war in Spain if things continued as they were. The new prime minister was apparently willing to accept this outcome. He was anxious to inaugurate his appeasement policy by reaching a new understanding with Mussolini. He soon made it clear that it was time for Britain to recognize the Italian conquest of Abyssinia formally and to accept Mussolini's assurances that he would recognize British interests in the Mediterranean and would withdraw his volunteers from Spain *after* the Civil War was over. Chamberlain's foreign secretary, Anthony Eden, pointed out that this policy would betray the principle of collective security and give Franco and Mussolini a victory that might bring grave strategical disadvantage to Great Britain. But Chamberlain was a self-confident man who had always felt that his foreign minister was prey to idle fears—"The Prime Minister adjured me to go home and take an aspirin," Eden has written of a brush in November 1937—and he was now thoroughly tired of Eden's brand of diplomacy. "Anthony," he said on 18 February 1938, "you have missed chance after chance. You simply cannot go on like this." Eden got the point and, a week later, resigned his office. After that, there was little possibility of any interference with the dictators' designs in Spain. Even those Englishmen who had advocated aid to the Republic earlier were distracted by a new eruption of violence in the Far East. In 1937 Japan inaugurated the second stage of its drive to dominate all Asia by launching a full-scale attack against China, which promised, before it was finished, to affect British Far Eastern interests; and in November, when the Japanese joined Germany and Italy in the so-called Anti-Comintern Pact, Chamberlain was given one more reason for wishing Spain out of the way so that he could concentrate on reaching an understanding with the head of that combination, Adolf Hitler. Finally, the attention of both the British and French peoples was soon completely absorbed in central European affairs, so that the last stages of Franco's victory went almost unnoticed.

The war in Spain was fought with great bravery, much savagery, and tremendous destruction on both sides. By the spring of 1939, when Franco's armies finally broke Republican resistance in Catalonia and advanced on Madrid, Spain's condition was pitiable. It will never be possible to provide even approximately accurate figures for deaths attributable to battle, air raids, disease, and political repression; but it has been estimated that the total stands somewhere between 500,000 and 800,000; thousands, in addition, had gone into exile. Every part of the country showed the wounds of war. The words of the poet Lorca, himself a victim of the first stages of the war (he was killed in 1936) seemed to have come true:

> *las lágrimas amordazan al viento,*
> *y no se oye otra cosa que el llanto*[3]

The end of the war led to the establishment of a new one-party dictatorship in Spain, which immediately (in April 1939) adhered to the Anti-Comintern Pact and began a tub-thumping campaign for the return of Gibraltar to Spain. It weakened France's strategical position in any dispute with Germany by placing a potential enemy on its flank. It deepened the tendency toward defeatism in

[3] "Tears muffle the wind,/and nothing else is heard but the weeping." "Casida del llanto" from *Divan del Tamarit* (1936).

the democracies and carried the principle of collective security closer to bank-ruptcy. And it strengthened the suspicion that already existed between the Western democracies and the Soviet Union. Stalin, a supporter of collective security at the beginning of the war, said at its close:

> Far be it for me to moralize on the policy of nonintervention, to talk of treason, treachery, and so. . . . It must be remarked, however, that the big and dangerous political game started by the supporters of the policy of nonintervention may end in a serious fiasco for them.

The Anschluss   On November 5, 1937, in a secret conversation with his service chiefs and his foreign minister, Adolf Hitler informed them that the time was coming for Germany to solve its problem of living space (*Lebensraum*). The first stages of the solution were to be the acquisition of Austria and Czechoslova-kia. The exact date for the beginning of the drive would depend upon the political events in the next months and years (the state of relations between Italy and the Western democracies being particularly important in this connection), but he made it clear that "if the Fuehrer was still living, it was his unalterable resolve to solve Germany's problem of space at the latest by 1943–1945." He urged the service chiefs to speed up their current programs but—in answer to a direct question from General von Fritsch—indicated that he still thought the time of action reasonably remote.

Two weeks later, however, the new British foreign secretary, Lord Halifax, talked with Hitler, and the result of this visit was to make Hitler revise his timetable. According to Baron von Neurath,

> Halifax admitted of his own accord that certain changes in the European system could probably not be avoided in the long run. The British did not believe that the *status quo* had to be maintained under all circum-stances. Among the questions in which changes would probably be made sooner or later were Danzig, Austria, and Czechoslovakia. England was only interested in seeing that such changes were brought about by peaceful means.

To make this kind of suggestion to Hitler was dangerous, for it seemed to indicate that the British were thinking purely in terms of form rather than of strategy and interest; and, if that were true, why should he wait any longer? France seemed paralyzed by internal troubles and would be incapable of in-dependent action of any kind. The Fuehrer decided to liquidate Austria.

Before doing so, he carried through that basic reorganization of the armed forces which was designed to assure him of its absolute reliability (see p. 593). That done, he accused the Austrian government of violating the provisions of the Austro-German Pact of July 1936, started a violent press campaign against the Schuschnigg government, and in February 1938 summoned the Austrian chancellor to consultations at Berchtesgaden. By threatening to invade Austria in case of noncompliance, he browbeat Schuschnigg into agreeing to legalize the Austrian Nazi party, to fill the posts of minister of war, minister of finance,

"After the Anschluß" After a cartoon by the American cartoonist Fitzpatrick of the St. Louis Post-Dispatch, 1938.

and minister of the interior with pro-Nazis, to establish closer relations between the Austrian and German armies, and to submit to preparations for "the assimilation of the Austrian into the German political system."

This was the real end of the Austrian Republic, although it still had four weeks to live. Hitler began immediately to protest against imaginary violations of the new agreement. Schuschnigg belatedly sought to rally his people behind him, but with little success, for the Socialists and trade unions had too lively a memory of the events of February 1934 (see p. 599) to give him enthusiastic support. On March 9 the chancellor announced that, a week hence, there would be a plebiscite to determine whether the people desired to remain a "free, independent, social, Christian, and united Austria." This announcement infuriated Hitler, who let it be known that an attempt to hold the plebiscite would result in immediate German invasion. Schuschnigg was also informed that Hitler would no longer tolerate him as chancellor, and, resigning himself to what appeared to be inevitable, he gave up his office. Some momentary resistance was put up by the Austrian president, Wilhelm Miklas, but it was overcome by a trick doubtless calculated to appeal to Chamberlain's respect for legality. The pro-Nazi minister of the interior, Dr. Arthur von Seyss-Inquart, was instructed from Hermann Goering's office to assume Schuschnigg's functions and, immediately, to request that German troops be sent into Austria to help the government establish peace and public security, which were supposedly threatened by Red disorders. This was done; and in the course of the night of March 11 German troops invaded Austria, entering the capital the next day while Berlin newspapers carried the headline "German Austria Saved from Chaos." On March 13, Austria was made a province of the German Reich, and the process of *Gleichschaltung* got under way.

Hitler had been more worried about Italy's reaction to the *Anschluß* than about what other powers might do, and he was relieved when Mussolini, despite the strong anti-German reaction in Italy, gave him his blessing. "Please tell Mussolini," he said to Prince Philip of Hesse, "that I will never forget him for this. . . . I shall be ready to go with him through thick and thin—through anything." As for the Western democracies, the Fuehrer was beginning to believe them incapable of action, either political or military. He would have been strengthened in this conviction had he known of Neville Chamberlain's response to a Soviet note of March 17, 1938. The note proposed a meeting of representatives of the American, British, French, and Soviet governments to discuss means of collective action against new aggression. Chamberlain, who had accepted the *Anschluß* with no apparent qualms, turned down the proposal on the grounds that Great Britain could not accept "mutual undertakings in advance to resist aggression" and that the results of such a meeting would be "to aggravate the tendency towards the establishment of exclusive groups of nations which must . . . be inimical to the prospects of European peace."

Munich and Prague   Hitler's next target was Czechoslovakia, and he saw no reason to delay moving against that state. The instrument he chose for this purpose was the German minority in the Sudeten district (see p. 597). In March 1938, the leader of the Sudeten German party, Konrad Henlein, visited Hitler at Berchtesgaden and was instructed to begin an intensive agitation for special privileges and rights of self-government, always placing his demands so high that the Czech government could not afford to meet them, but not making a premature demand for anything like independence, since that might cause international complications. Henlein obeyed and, in April, submitted the so-called Karlsbad program to the Czech government, asking for what amounted to complete autonomy of the Sudeten area, the right of the German minority to adhere to the principles of National Socialism, and a revision of Czech foreign policy—presumably in the direction of severance of treaty relations with France and the Soviet Union.

The knowledge that a German campaign against Czechoslovakia was shaping up worried the French government, which was conscious of its treaty obligation to defend that country but aware that it was unsupported by a similar British pledge. In April the new prime minister, Édouard Daladier, and his foreign minister, Georges Bonnet, visited London and tried to persuade Chamberlain that an explicit British commitment was the best way to deter Hitler. Chamberlain refused to believe them. It would be a bluff that would not work, he said. Czechoslovakia was a bad risk; its other ally, the Soviet Union, had, thanks to the purges, neither the will nor the strength to support it, and Britain's military forces were incapable of doing so. He did not believe that Hitler wanted to destroy Czechoslovakia but, if he did, Chamberlain "did not see how this could be prevented." Someone said later that if Chamberlain had been writing a letter to the Czechs, his message would have been:

> Dear Czechoslovakyer
> I don't think he's going to attack yer
> But even if he does
> I'm not going to back yer.

The only practical course, he insisted, was to persuade the Czech government to make satisfactory concessions to their German minority and, simultaneously, to sound out Hitler concerning his idea of a just settlement.

The French finally agreed and, in so doing, tacitly admitted that they would not abide by their treaty. Henceforth, they engaged with the British in the hopeless task of persuading the Czechs to make concessions that would satisfy a minority that had been ordered by Hitler to set demands that could not be satisfied.

The urgency with which they pursued this task was increased in late May when the Czech government, alleging that it had received reports of German troop movements on the Bohemian border, called up their army reserves and manned their defensive rampart. In the sharp war scare that followed, the British and French governments made stiff representations in Berlin, warning Hitler of the grave consequences that would follow a German attack on Czechoslovakia. The German government protested its innocence and the crisis passed, but it left two results behind. The fact that the Western press hailed the affair as a German setback infuriated Hitler and led him to order his army to be prepared to invade Czechoslovakia no later than October 1. At the same time, the war scare frightened the French; rightist newspapers in Paris were now carrying articles with headlines reading "Do you want to die for Czechoslovakia?", and the mood of doubt and withdrawal that Sartre was to describe so brilliantly in his novel of 1938, *The Reprieve,* was beginning to grow. It also made Chamberlain more determined than ever that the Czech business must be solved, in the words of his ambassador in Berlin, by giving "Prague a real turn of the screw." His pressure upon the Czech government was successful in one respect. It forced the Czechs, in the first week of September, to grant virtually all of the original Karlsbad demands. To Henlein and Hitler this was embarrassing, for it forced them to come out into the open. Still, they had no intention of turning back now. On September 12, in an impassioned speech about the suffering of the German minority in Czechoslovakia, Hitler offered his support to "these tortured creatures." The following day, Henlein openly declared that the Sudetenland must be ceded to Germany.

Military experts have argued ever since 1938 about what might have happened if Czechoslovakia had been encouraged by Britain and France to resist and if war had come. It is, of course, impossible to answer this with any assurance. It should be noted, however, that German defenses in the west were unfinished and would not have withstood invasion, that Germany had insufficient troops to hold a western and an eastern front, that a Czech campaign would have been difficult in view of the size of the Czech army and the strength of its

Munich, 1938. From left: Chamberlain, Daladier, Hitler, Mussolini, and Count Galeazzo Ciano. (United Press International)

defenses, that even General Keitel believed (as he admitted during the Nuremberg trials) that "our means of attack against the frontier fortifications of Czechoslovakia were insufficient," and that other German generals were so sure of impending disaster that they were planning to attempt a *coup d'état* if Hitler insisted on war. Finally, despite Chamberlain's low opinion of Soviet strength and intentions, it seems likely that national interest would have dictated some kind of Soviet intervention on Czechoslovakia's behalf if the Western powers had undertaken to fight for that country. In view of all this, some British soldiers felt that the West should have risked war, despite British weakness in arms. General Archibald Wavell said later: "I believe that the Boches were also unready and that they made better use of the year's respite than we did."

But none of these things has any relevance to the actual course of events. Chamberlain was already privately well disposed to the idea of separating the Sudeten area from Czechoslovakia. He now flew to Berchtesgaden to persuade Hitler to give him time to arrange the separation. When this was granted, President Beneš of Czechoslovakia was forced to accept the loss of the Sudetenland by a plain intimation that he would receive no support if he refused.

Even after this, Europe had a narrow escape from war. At a subsequent meeting with Chamberlain at Godesberg, Hitler declared that the mere cession of the Sudetenland was not enough, adding demands for a triumphant entrance of German forces and the humiliating withdrawal of all Czech troops, leaving their installations intact. When these terms were submitted to the Czechs, they refused them indignantly and, in a last flicker of French resistance to Hitler, they were backed by Paris. But, as the tension mounted in the European capitals, Hitler—perhaps because he suddenly sensed a total lack of enthusiasm for war in Germany—held his hand and, in a personal letter to Chamberlain, promised to wait until a last effort was made to reach an agreement. The British prime minister reverted to an idea that he had long toyed with—that of a four-power conference to solve the Czech problem. He telephoned Paris and received eager approval; he telephoned Rome and received equally enthusiastic support from the Italian government, which was at this moment as fearful of a major war as were statesmen in London and Paris. The Duce undertook to make the proposal to Hitler, who accepted on September 28. The next day Hitler, Mussolini, Chamberlain, and Daladier gathered at Munich and, in short order, gave Hitler everything he had demanded at Godesberg, depriving Czechoslovakia of a third of its population, its most important industrial areas, and its only means of self-defense.

Chamberlain was convinced that results would justify these concessions to Hitler and he reacted to criticisms of the Munich agreement with irritation. "A lot of people," he wrote in October, "seem to me to be losing their heads, and talking and thinking as though Munich had made war more, instead of less, imminent." The very fact that Hitler had been willing to sign a new declaration of friendship with Great Britain, expressing the intention of avoiding the use of war in disputes that might arise between them, indicated, in the prime minister's opinion, that the appeasement policy had worked and that a new era of peace was about to open.

His optimism was not justified. Both Hitler and Mussolini regarded the Sudeten settlement as a Western capitulation and were encouraged to seek new conquests. At the beginning of September, Mussolini had told one of his aides that Czechoslovakia would be only a beginning for Hitler, that he would insist on a total revenge for Versailles, person by person and nation by nation; and he added: "It is better that it should happen with us rather than against us." The Duce seems to have decided therefore to collaborate. After Munich the Italians began to plan the seizure of Albania, which was consummated in April, and by the beginning of the new year the Fascist press had started a shrill campaign demanding that France be forced to cede Nice, Savoy, Tunis, and Jibuti to the new Italian empire.

Hitler, in the meantime, proceeded with the liquidation of what was left of Czechoslovakia. He encouraged all the centrifugal and disruptive forces that the shock of Munich released in that country, and gave financial support to Slovakian and Ruthenian separatist movements so that, even before the end of 1938, the rump state was virtually divided into three autonomous sections. Having got that far, the Fuehrer saw no reason to stop, and he returned to the tactics that had worked so well in the case of Austria. In January 1939 he summoned the Czech foreign minister and told him that the disorders in his country were a menace to German security and must be suppressed, ordering him at the same time to purge the Czech army of Jews and anti-Germans and to bring his country's foreign policy into conformity with Germany's. Two months later, as the Czech government tried vainly to restore some kind of order in a country torn by German conspiracies, he decided to strike. On March 14,

Joachim von Ribbentrop, Hitler's foreign minister, informed the Italian ambassador that:

> Our patience is exhausted. Intrigues have been spun with our enemies in the west. An attempt has been made to make Czechia once more a pawn in the European game. The Fuehrer intends to lance the abscess. The liquidation of this problem is of interest not only to Germany but also to the Axis. The present event is a useful preparation for a contest in another direction which will be necessary sooner or later and for the tasks which this will bring to the Axis powers jointly.

On the same day Hitler peremptorily ordered the Czech President, Emil Hácha, to come to Berlin. When he arrived, Hácha was put through a grueling night session, in which Goering and Ribbentrop threatened to destroy his capital immediately and literally forced him to sign an agreement "placing with entire confidence the destiny of the Czech people and the Czech country in the hands of the Fuehrer of the German Reich." On the following morning, German troops marched into Prague.

The Polish Pledge and the Duel for Russia   The Prague coup dispelled the illusions of all those who had persisted in believing that Hitler was interested only in reclaiming German territory for the Reich, and it marked the complete bankruptcy of the appeasement policy. Even Neville Chamberlain was disillusioned, horrified—as Rebecca West has written—by the discovery that he had been dealing all along with people who did not keep their word because they did not mind being revealed as liars and could not be made to suffer for their breaches of faith. Raging over the destruction of his hopes, the prime minister began belatedly building defenses against the possibility of new Axis aggression. A mutual assistance pact was concluded with Turkey; promises of support and protection were extended to Greece and Rumania; and, most important of all, the decision was made to protect the country that seemed destined to be Hitler's next victim, Poland. On March 31, 1939, Chamberlain announced that in the event

> of any action which clearly threatened Polish independence, and which the Polish government accordingly considered it vital to resist with their national forces, His Majesty's Government would feel themselves bound at once to lend the Polish government all the support in their power.

France, he added, had authorized him to say that it would do the same.

The question now was whether this would be enough to persuade Hitler to hold back and, if it were not enough, whether Britain and France could do anything to defend Poland. It seemed clear to many, and was pointed out in the House of Commons by both David Lloyd George and Winston Churchill, that the democracies' ability to deter or oppose Hitler effectively would depend upon how close their cooperation was with the Soviet Union. It proved difficult, however, to convince Chamberlain of this.

The prime minister had once written:

> I must confess to the most profound distrust of Russia. I have no belief
> whatever in her ability to maintain an effective offensive even if she wanted
> to. And I distrust her motives, which seem to me to have little connection
> with our ideas of liberty and to be concerned only with getting everyone
> else by the ears.

This fundamental suspicion of Soviet motives made it impossible for Chamberlain
to admit that the Soviets and the West might have a community of interest
in opposing Hitler. Thus, he had turned down the Soviet suggestion for a meeting
of British, French, Soviet, and American leaders after Hitler's invasion of Austria,
and had persistently slighted the Russians during the long Czechoslovakian crisis.
Despite the fact that the Soviet Union was allied to France and to Czechoslovakia,
its government was not consulted, nor was it invited to the Munich conference.
The Russians, who had been loyal supporters of collective security, even if for
reasons of self-interest, may be forgiven for being suspicious. Shortly after Mun-

ich, Stalin said: "One might think that the districts of Czechoslovakia were yielded to Germany as the prize for its undertaking to launch war on the Soviet Union."

Even after he had begun to build defenses against Hitler, Chamberlain was very hesitant about approaching the Russians. Not until mid-April did the British government make any move, and then it was only to suggest that the Soviet government might wish to cooperate in the defense of eastern Europe by giving a unilateral guarantee of the western borders of Poland and Rumania. This idea the Soviets rejected.

By this time recent Western policy had convinced the Russians, as they thought about the threat to Poland, that they must at least consider the advantages of a rapprochement with Germany. Immediately after Munich, a Russian Foreign Office official said to Robert Coulondre, the French ambassador: "My dear friend, what have you done? Don't you see that there is now no alternative to a fourth partition of Poland?" These words indicated that the idea of a German deal was already being canvassed.[4] By the beginning of the new year, Stalin seems to have decided to make some soundings in Berlin, without, however, closing the door to an arrangement with the West. In the months that followed, the Soviet Union had a dual policy: on the one hand, delicately hinting in Berlin of the possibility of an agreement on Polish and other affairs (the first such hint seems to have been dropped in February 1939); on the other, warning the Western powers that only a comprehensive eastern defensive league with specific military commitments by both the Soviet Union and the Western powers would succeed in deterring Hitler. In rejecting the British suggestion of a unilateral Soviet guarantee, Stalin proposed the conclusion of actual military and political conventions between the Soviet Union and the West.

In considering the Soviet suggestion, the Western powers immediately encountered some awkward questions. The Soviets insisted that no alliance system would be effective unless it provided for defense against indirect, as well as direct, aggression—the kind of subversion that had weakened Czechoslovakia before March 1939. They insisted also that they could not guarantee Poland and Rumania unless their troops were permitted to operate inside those countries if war came and unless joint staff talks began immediately. The British soon discovered that both the Poles and the Rumanians were opposed to having Red troops bivouacked amongst them, even for purposes of defense. The British were disinclined to put pressure upon them, showing a greater sensitivity to the feelings of lesser states in this case than they had in the case of Czechoslovakia in the previous year. As a result of this, between April and August 1939, no real progress was made in bringing the Soviet Union and the West together. Innumerable conversations were held with the French and the other states and counterproposals were drafted and submitted to the Russians, but a defense system did not come any closer to actuality.

Meanwhile, the Russians stuck to their terms and pursued their tentative

---

[4] Adam Ulam has suggested that they may have been designed to alarm the Western powers into seeking more formal ties with the Soviet Union.

soundings in Berlin. It cannot be said that they did not warn the West of the dangers of delay. One such warning was the dropping of Maxim Litvinov from the post of people's commissar for foreign affairs. Litvinov's name had been intimately associated with the policy of collective security. Vyacheslav Molotov, his replacement, was a rigid nationalist. Nor were all the warnings from the Russian side. On April 28 Hitler denounced the Nazi-Polish Pact of January 1934 and the Anglo-German Naval Agreement of 1935 in a furious speech, which, significantly, was absolutely silent with respect to the Soviet Union—a fact noted by the perceptive Coulondre, who sensed that Soviet-German talks must be getting under way. Also, on May 22, while the German press fulminated against Poland, Germany and Italy concluded a formal military alliance (the Pact of Steel), an indication that war might not be far away. On the following day, although this was not known outside Hitler's intimate circle (and was not disclosed to the Italians, who discovered only in August what Hitler's true objectives were), the Fuehrer announced to his chief advisers that Poland must be attacked "at the first suitable opportunity."

Chamberlain was not entirely unresponsive to these warnings. In June he decided to send a special emissary to Moscow to see if divergent points might be ironed out. But instead of choosing a man of undoubted stature (Eden volunteered to go), he sent the head of the Central Department of the Foreign Office, William Strang, a man with all of the necessary gifts except rank. This deficiency, as Molotov later admitted, offended the Russians and made them feel that the British were not serious. Strang was not successful in advancing the negotiations, and in July the Russians took another step toward Germany by agreeing to begin negotiations for a new economic agreement. They still did not close the door on the West. Indeed, in July they asked the British and French to send a military mission to Moscow to discuss the possibilities of defending Poland and the Baltic states. It is clear in retrospect, however, that Stalin was now pitting London against Berlin and that only quick and decisive action by the West had any chance of holding his support.

That decisiveness the Western powers did not show. In August they appointed military missions to go to Moscow, but the British mission was composed of a retired admiral and two generals who had no connection with strategical questions and, as the German ambassador in London noted, the mission seemed designed to find out the fighting value of the Soviet army rather than to make any agreement. Moreover, the missions traveled to Moscow by the slowest possible route, going by ship to Leningrad and then by rail to Moscow, instead of flying, as Chamberlain had always done when consulting Hitler, although this was at a time when the Germans had made up their minds that a deal with Russia must be reached and were working at top speed to that end. Finally, when the missions arrived on August 11, and were informed by Marshal Voroshilov that he was empowered to sign a military convention and that the time had come to put all their cards on the table, it turned out that the head of the British mission had no power to conclude agreements. Indeed, his credentials did not arrive until August 21, and by that time they were useless. The Germans had acted too quickly. On August 14, Ribbentrop proposed by wire that he fly to Moscow "to set forth the Fuehrer's views to M. Stalin [and] ... to lay the foundations for a final settlement of German-Russian relations." The Russians accepted on the following day, suggesting that the talks be concrete and center on the feasibility of a nonaggression pact. It took almost a week to settle the details, but, on August 21, the German radio was able to announce to a stupefied world that

> the Reich government and the Soviet government have agreed to conclude a pact of nonaggression with each other. The Reich minister for foreign affairs will arrive in Moscow on Wednesday, August 23, for the conclusion of the negotiations.

The public announcement made no mention of the secret agreement that had been signed at the same time as the innocuous pledge of friendship. This defined the boundary between the Soviet and German spheres of influence in eastern Europe "in the event of a territorial and political rearrangement." It assigned Finland, Estonia, Latvia, and Bessarabia to the Soviet Union and Lithuania to

German photograph of the signing of the Nazi-Soviet Pact. (Hoover Institution)

Rendezvous (1939). Appearing immediately after the conclusion of the Nazi-Soviet Pact, this is one of the British cartoonist David Low's masterpieces. From *Low's Autobiography*. (Simon & Schuster, New York, 1957).

Germany. In Poland, the boundary between the Soviet and German spheres was defined as the line of the Narew, Vistula, and San rivers. Questions of detail arising out of future political developments would be settled, the secret protocol said, "by means of a friendly agreement." To all intents and purposes this amounted to an alliance, and it removed any hesitations that Hitler might still have felt.

Three months before this time, in May 1939, an American newspaperman,[5] referring to the pending Soviet-Western negotiations, had written: "Consummate the alliance, say the Russians, and Mussolini would be negotiating in London and Paris within 24 hours. There would be peace. Fail to consummate the alliance, or water it down, or even parley too long and there will be war this year." It is, of course, possible that the Soviets would have turned to the Germans in any case, that their real desire was to remain at peace (a desire reinforced by the fact that serious fighting was going on between Japanese and Russian troops in Siberia at this time) and that they were finally convinced that even a Soviet-Western military alliance would not assure peace, especially since the

[5] John W. Owens of the Baltimore *Sun*.

British admitted in Moscow that they had only two divisions of troops to throw into action on the day of mobilization. Stalin said something of the sort to Churchill in August 1942. It remains difficult, however, to reject the thought that the long protracted negotiations and the deference to Polish and Rumanian feelings helped produce the debacle. The West had parleyed too long, and the Germans had won the Soviet Union for their own purposes.

The Coming of War   It is unnecessary to give a detailed account of the events of the week that followed the conclusion of the Nazi-Soviet Pact of Nonaggression. The important thing is that it convinced Hitler that he could now attack Poland without further hesitation. He may have felt that the British would now withdraw their pledge to Poland, enabling him to dispose of that country, and that he could then turn to his ultimate plans in eastern Europe, after solving the French problem as the occasion seemed to require. If this was the line of his thinking, he was disagreeably surprised.

On September 1, 1939, the German armies invaded Poland. The British immediately informed the German government that they would uphold their obligation to Poland unless the action were called off. When they received no reply, the British government, early in the morning of September 3, informed the Germans that unless they gave assurance by 11 A.M. that they would terminate hostilities forthwith, a state of war would exist between Germany and Britain as of that hour. Paul Schmidt, Hitler's interpreter, has written that, after he had translated the British ultimatum, "Hitler sat immobile, gazing before him. . . . After an interval that seemed an age, he turned to Ribbentrop, who had remained standing by the window. 'What now?' asked Hitler with a savage look."

It was too late now for questions of that nature. From the beginning, Hitler's foreign policy has been predicated on the assumption that it could probably be carried out successfully only by war. The Polish action had now touched off what was to be the greatest war the world had ever seen. Germany was better prepared for that conflict than any of the other European states, and its chances of attaining Hitler's most grandiose objectives were good. But the thought of what lay ahead momentarily daunted even so confident a man as Hitler, and there must have been many on September 3, 1939, as the British time limit ran out, who felt as Goering did when he said to a friend: "If we lose this war, then God have mercy on us!"

Chapter 28 WORLD WAR II

Before it was finished, the conflict that began when Hitler's columns sliced into Poland made even the war of 1914–1918 look like a small-time affair. In scope, it was much more truly a world war than the first contest, for, although Europe was, as in World War I, the major theater of operations, the importance of other areas and the magnitude of the battles fought in them was infinitely greater than in the earlier struggle, and the fate of Europe depended much more clearly upon the turn of events at places like El Alamein and Midway Island than it had ever done then. In another respect also its scope dwarfed that of World War I: namely, in the totality of effort and risk required of its participants. Something has been said above about the ways in which civilian populations were affected in that war (see p. 474). This time the mobilization of human resources and the controls placed upon the customary liberties of civilians were infinitely more rigorous, while the dangers to which they were exposed were proportionately greater. In the war of 1914 saturation bombing of cities and systematic extermination of whole populations were, after all, unknown, and nothing remotely like the holocaust of Hiroshima had ever been dreamed of.

In this great global conflict, the art of war was carried to its ultimate point of sophistication. To the armory of military combat World War I had introduced the submarine, the convoy system, the airplane, and the tank. The technique of using these weapons was vastly refined during the second war. The freeing of armor from the shackles that had bound it to the infantry in order to permit the full exploitation of its offensive capabilities, together with the development of close air support of ground troops, restored mobility to land warfare. The elaboration of strategic bombing techniques greatly enhanced the effects of the older naval blockade as a weapon of attrition. The war on the sea was revolutionized by the appearance of the aircraft carrier, the development of amphibious doctrine, the creation of specialized craft for ship-to-shore movement, and the use of electronic rays for the detection of submarines.

In no previous war had the resources of science been so completely engaged in devising new instruments of war or so productive in their results. A list of the discoveries and inventions of the war years would be long and would include, at the very minimum, such things as the various types of magnetic mines that were used by the opposing naval forces, as well as the different means devised to frustrate them (degaussing techniques and the creation of sound barriers, for example); the adaptation of radar to special uses, like the antisubmarine defenses made possible by the Braun scanning tube, which operated by means of high-frequency vibrations, and the equally remarkable evolution of the *Schnorkel* air mast, which enabled U-boats to recharge their batteries and replenish their air supply without surfacing for weeks on end; the Norden bombsight, which greatly improved the accuracy of high-level bombing, and the proximity fuse, a kind of electronic trigger which, when used in antiaircraft fire, made defense against air attack more effective; and, coming late in the war and pointing to a grimmer future, the jet aircraft, the liquid fuel rocket (even in 1945 not susceptible to interception), and the atomic bomb.

Finally—and this was partly the result of the invention of these ingenious new tools of war—no conflict in human history had been as destructive to life and property as this turned out to be. At least 17,000,000 men died on the battlefields of this war, while 18,000,000 noncombatants were killed in one way or another. Among the great powers, Russia, suffered most heavily: 6,115,000 military deaths and 14,012,000 military casualties, and civilian deaths in the neighborhood of 10,000,000. The Germans, who inflicted most of these terrible losses, suffered grievously themselves, with over 6,000,000 military deaths, 7,250,000 other casualties, 1,300,000 missing, and very heavy civilian losses. Almost 2,000,000 Japanese troops died of wounds or disease, while 78,000 civilians died in the atom bombing of Hiroshima alone, and almost as many in that of Nagasaki. In general, the casualties of the other major participants were much lower (357,116 British troops were killed, 369,267 wounded, and 46,079 missing), but in all cases they represented a crippling loss.

Almost as staggering as these totals, which, in military casualties alone, were double those of World War I, were the financial and material costs of the war. Military expenditures alone totaled more than a trillion dollars, and property losses were incalculable. Some of the scars were ineradicable—as long as they stand, the cities of London and Hamburg will bear visible testimony to the destructiveness of World War II—and much that was capable of repair could be put right only after years of effort. When hostilities ceased, the economic structure of Europe seemed completely shattered.

Less tangible but equally real was the political destruction wrought by the war. The strength of the European states was, indeed, so diminished that their future ability to assume the responsibilities that go with Great-Power status seemed questionable. This suggested that there might be a significant diminution of the once dominant role of Europe in world affairs.

THE INITIAL TRIUMPHS OF THE DICTATORS, 1939–1942

The Polish and Finnish Campaigns   The first revelation of the new mobility possible in war came in the Polish campaign. It took Hitler only a month to conquer Poland, and this was the result less of Germany's great superiority in numbers, firepower, air, and armor than of its coordinated tactics and the speed with which they were employed. The *Luftwaffe* led the way by systematically destroying the Polish air force on the ground and disrupting transportation facilities and communications. Divebombers were then directed against concentrations of Polish troops and against the towns and cities. As terror and disorder spread, German armored columns crossed the borders and cut their way into the interior, using the tactics of *Blitzkrieg*, which were later defined succinctly by one of Germany's most gifted commanders of armor, Erwin Rommel, as "the art of concentrating strength at one point, forcing a breakthrough, rolling up

BLITZKRIEG I – POLAND

———— German Mobilization Positions
·········· Polish Positions

0   50   100   150
Miles

and securing the flanks on either side, and then penetrating like lightning, before the enemy has time to react, deep into his rear." Into the gaping holes torn by these tank thrusts came the columns of motorized and nonmotorized infantry. There were no fronts in this kind of war—no main lines of resistance upon which the bewildered Poles could stand and fight and die. The enemy was on every side, and to stand meant to be encircled and strangled into submission, as 170,000 Polish troops learned at Kutno in the third week of the war. By September 21 western Poland had been completely overrun, and the only serious resistance was in Warsaw, which was holding on under ceaseless aerial bombardment. Meanwhile, Russian troops had occupied the eastern part of the country and eliminated any possibility of effective resistance there. In Warsaw the Poles fought on courageously until September 27 and then had to give in.

On the following day, Ribbentrop met with his opposite number Molotov and completed the fourth partition of Poland of which Coulondre had been warned in October 1938 (see p. 653). The eastern half of the country, comprising some fourteen million people, was joined to the Soviet Union. The industrial areas of the west were absorbed by Germany, and the area around Cracow was established as a separate "protectorate," ruled over by the Nazi Hans Frank, who was sentenced to death at Nuremberg in October 1946 for the cruelties committed in his satrapy. Although thousands of Poland's bravest sons escaped to fight in the British and French armies and to help defeat the *Luftwaffe* in the skies over London, and although a Polish government in exile was established in the British capital, their country was now subjected to long years of terror and exploitation.

While the Germans regrouped their forces, the Russians took another step forward. Perhaps remembering Germany's expansion in the Baltic lands during World War I, they extended their military control over Lithuania (defined as a Russian sphere in a recent revision of the secret agreement of August 23) and Estonia and Latvia by demanding the right to garrison them and establish military and naval bases there. At the same time, they pushed forward negotiations with Finland for border changes on the Karelian isthmus and the cession to Russia of a group of islands in the Gulf of Finland that could be fortified to improve the defenses of Leningrad. Here again the motive was fear of a future German attack (Stalin admitted to the Finnish ambassador in October 1939 that the Nazi-Soviet Pact would probably not last forever), and the Soviet terms, at least originally, were regarded by Marshal Mannerheim as being in the main acceptable. But the majority of the Finnish government were unimpressed by the Soviet insistence and, backed by a public opinion that was emotional and in part chauvinistic, took a rigid and unyielding position. The Soviets responded by fomenting border incidents and used these to justify an invasion that began on November 30.

In the outside world, the Soviet attack on Finland aroused universal disgust, which changed to satisfaction when the Finns fought the first five-pronged Russian assault to a standstill. The Soviet troops employed in Finland had no experience in the techniques of fighting in the snow or, for that matter, of storming pillboxes and reinforced concrete structures, and they lacked the proper equipment for either task. While their offensive was failing, the League of Nations brushed aside Soviet explanations of their action and, on December 14, 1939, expelled the aggressor from its membership, the only time in its existence that it took such action. This gesture of sympathy did not, however, bring material aid to the Finns, whose resources were soon strained to their limits. At the turn of the year, Stalin shook up the command of the northern army, put some of his best units and his most modern equipment into the fight, and concentrated his attack upon the Mannerheim Line facing Leningrad, instead of persisting in his attacks in north and central Finland. After that, the result was inevitable; and, on March 12, 1940, after submitting for a month to a bombardment that at times reached the intensity of that against Verdun in 1916, the Finns capitulated. They were forced to accept the original Soviet demands and to cede, in addition, the city of Viborg and the whole of the Karelian peninsula.

The Phony War   The Western powers had remained true to their pledge to Poland and, backed by the whole British Commonwealth, except Eire, had gone to war with Germany on September 3. The British sent all available trained combat troops to France (158,000 in the first five months of the war), instituted new training programs at home, began to assemble a large combat force in the Middle East, and appealed successfully to Australia and New Zealand to send troops into Egypt for the defense of the Canal.

On the other hand, despite the relative weakness of the German defenses in the west and the involvement of most of the Nazi forces in Poland, no truly offensive action was taken on the western front, the Allied armies making at most a few probing thrusts that lacked determination. The speed with which Poland was conquered and the curious lull that followed seemed to rob the conflict, if not of reality, then certainly of urgency. In French government circles, there was more enthusiasm for entering the war against the Soviet Union in Finland's behalf than for any action that might seriously annoy Hitler; and General Gamelin, the supreme French commander, neither pressed for more energetic action nor used the pause that followed the Polish campaign to give his conscripts combat training, allowing a degree of slackness in the armed forces that had fatal effects a few months later. In Great Britain, too, the war seemed remote. It is true there was no disposition to consider making peace with Hitler— and the Fuehrer's hints that he might be induced to negotiate elicited no response—but it was also evident that the British people had not yet faced up to the full implications of being at war.

In the winter of 1939–1940, the war effort of the West was for the most part confined to occasional air raids for the purpose of dropping propaganda pamphlets. There was, however, more serious action on the seas. The first naval successes of the war were won by German submarines. Leaving aside the torpedoing of the passenger ship S.S. *Athena* off the northwest coast of Ireland on September 3, an exploit that brought no honor to German arms, the sinking of the aircraft carrier *Courageous* on September 16 was an undoubted German triumph, and this was excelled on the night of October 13–14 when Lieutenant Prien took the German U-47 through the harbor defenses of Scapa Flow and avenged the internment of the German fleet in that port in 1918 by sending six torpedoes into *Royal Oak,* sinking her with a loss of 800 men, and escaping into the open sea.

The Royal Navy got a bit of its own back in December, when the cruisers *Exeter, Achilles,* and *Ajax* intercepted the pocket battleship *Graf Spee* off the coast of Uruguay and, by attacking as if they were destroyers, offset their disadvantage in range and firepower and so badly damaged the finest of the German capital ships that she had to put in to Montevideo for repairs. There, two days later, her capain destroyed her rather than face a renewal of the battle.

Despite this success, the British found themselves threatened, as in World War I, with the possibility of economic strangulation effected by the submarine. Winston Churchill said later: "This was the only thing that ever really frightened me during the war." British success in defeating this danger was partly due to the fact that Germany had not produced as many submarines before the war as the Anglo-German naval Agreement of 1935 (see p. 636) would have permitted it to do and had started the war with only fifty-seven U-boats, of which only twenty-two were equipped for Atlantic operations. Other factors were the aid given by the United States both before and after its formal entrance into the war, the successful use of statistical method and the principles of mathematical probability to reduce cargo-ship losses by the adjustment of the size and pattern of convoys, and—most important—the success of British scientists in devising tools of detection. Even so, it was not until the middle of 1943 that success seemed to be assured, and until then the economic pinch was severe.

The German Offensive in the West   The Nazi offensive had not yet made sufficient strides in the winter of 1939–1940 to awaken the peoples of Britain and France to the hard facts of war. Their enlightenment came in the spring, as a result of a series of German hammer blows in the west.

The first of these came in Scandinavia. In pursuance of their plans to impose a naval blockade upon Germany, the British and French had been concerned over the use of Norwegian territorial waters by German ships carrying Swedish steel from Narvik to home ports. They finally decided to stop German shipping and informed the Norwegian government on April 8, 1940 that they were sowing mines for this purpose. While they prepared to answer the expected Norwegian protests, Hitler gave them a tougher reply. On the morning of April 9, Nazi columns rolled across the undefended frontier of Denmark and seized the capital, German planes dropped parachute troops on the Norwegian towns of Oslo, Bergen, Trondheim, Stavanger, and Narvik, and German ships brought infantry into the more important Norwegian coastal towns. Unlike the Danes, the Norwegians fought back, and the coastal defense guns at Oslo sank the cruiser *Blücher* and damaged the pocket battleship *Deutschland,* the cruiser *Emden,* and a training ship. Nonetheless, the Germans made good their landings, seizing the capital (King Haakon and the government escaped to England) and setting up a puppet government under a man whose name became a byword for traitor throughout the world, Vidkun Quisling.

Caught completely unaware by this stroke, the British tried to rally by landing troop units at Andalsnes and Namsos on the Norwegian coast, but the forces

| Chamberlain | Greenwood | Halifax | | Sinclair | Duff Cooper | Alexander | Eden | | K. Wood |
| Churchill | Attlee | | Bevin | | Morrison | | Amery | | |

"ALL BEHIND YOU, WINSTON"

Cartoon by David Low, *London Evening Standard*, May 10, 1940. (Pictorial Parade, Inc.)

thrown into this desperate maneuver, without artillery or antiaircraft defenses, were cut to ribbons and had to be withdrawn after a month's desperate fighting. The sole tangible result of the British campaign in Norway was that it awakened the British people with a start and, incidentally, at long last, brought down the government of Neville Chamberlain. His remark at the outset of Germany's Scandinavian thrust, "Hitler has missed the bus!" exhausted the patience of even his close supporters. In May his policies were subjected to a scathing review in the House of Commons by Leo Amery, who ended his speech with the words of Oliver Cromwell to the Long Parliament: "You have sat too long here for any good you are doing. Depart, I say, and let us have done with you. In the name of God, go!" Two days later, the once arrogant and self-confident prime minister obeyed. His place was filled by the man who, after years in the political wilderness, was now to bring his great talents to a great task and to become the indomitable voice of Britain's defiance of the dictators and the inspirer of its victory over them. This was Winston Churchill.

He entered upon his assigned role in the darkest of circumstances, for on the very day of his appointment, German armies struck with full force in the

Low Countries, inaugurating the struggle that Hitler said in his order to his troops would "decide the fate of the German people for a thousand years."

Western strategists had long expected that when Hitler attacked he would violate the neutrality of Belgium and Holland, but this calculation did them no good. The two neutral governments persisted in hoping that they could dissuade Hitler from attacking them by avoiding joint military preparations. They had refused not only to cooperate with the British and French army commands but even to divulge their plans in the event that their hopes were disappointed. Already at a disadvantage in terms of numbers (Hitler had 140 divisions in the west, compared with their own 89), the British and French now had the problem of moving fast enough, once hostilities started, to prop up the Belgian and Dutch defenses before they collapsed.

They proved incapable of doing so. The German *Blitz* was even more spectacular in Holland than in Poland. The *Wehrmacht* started its invasion shortly after midnight of May 9–10 and, by the use of parachute troops, seized every important airfield and most of the strategic bridges by dawn. Armored columns were across the Maas before the Dutch plans to flood the area had been executed. Within four days, the backbone of resistance had been snapped, and a savage air raid on Rotterdam, which caused 30,000 deaths, led to the capitulation of the army on May 14. The Nazis were frustrated in their hope of seizing Queen Wilhelmina and her government, who escaped to England; but the country was theirs.

The attack on Belgium had started at the same moment as the one on Holland and was equally successful, although it took eighteen days instead of four. On May 11, German glider troops knocked out Fort Eben Emael, the key to Belgian defenses. On the same day armored forces crossed the Albert Canal and, by turning the Belgian flank, forced the first of a series of retirements. The Belgians were supported by the British Second Corps on the Dyle River, by the French Seventh Army in the north, and by the French Cavalry Corps on the Meuse. The maneuverability of these forces disappeared on May 13–14 when General Ewald von Kleist crashed through the supposedly impassable Ardennes and threw two armored corps across the Meuse north of Sedan. Corap's Ninth French Army was overrun, and Guderian, with three German armored divisons, raced for the coast, closely supported by motorized infantry. He reached it on May 23, and the whole Belgian army and its supporting French and British units were caught in a girdle that now tightened remorselessly.

An Allied plan to effect a break-out by concerted attacks from inside and outside the ring was frustrated by German pressure and by lack of vigor in the French command, which was already showing signs of the indecision that would contribute so powerfully to the complete collapse of the French war effort a month later. Inside the circle, the Allied forces were pushed slowly toward the coast. On May 27 the limit of Belgian resistance had been reached, and King Leopold II sued for an armistice and ordered a cessation of hostilities. For this he was bitterly criticized by his allies and by his own people, on the grounds that he had given insufficient warning to his allies. This is not wholly just. Communications were, at this time, far from perfect, as is shown by the fact that Leopold's allies had begun their evacuation before he approached the Ger-

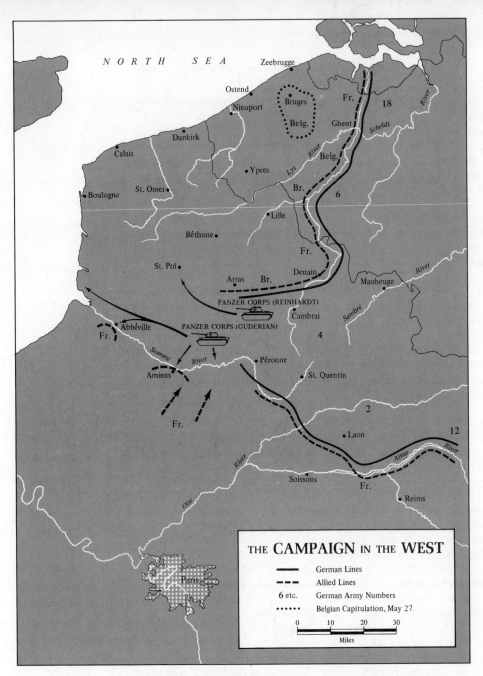

NORTH SEA

THE **CAMPAIGN** IN THE **WEST**

――――――― German Lines
- - - - - - - Allied Lines
6 etc.   German Army Numbers
· · · · · · ·   Belgian Capitulation, May 27

0   10   20   30
Miles

mans and had not succeeded in consulting him before doing so. But the Belgian capitulation created a wide gap on the northeastern flank and forced the British and French back upon the beaches of Dunkirk.

In his book *Other Men's Flowers*,[1] General Archibald Wavell wrote, "At Dun-

---

[1] *Other Men's Flowers* is an anthology of the poems Wavell liked and committed to memory. The selection of poems and the charming introductory notes will puzzle readers who have stereotyped notions about General Staff officers.

kirk the true spirit of our people flashed out like a sword from its sheath." Three hundred and thirty-eight thousand troops were extricated from the pocket by an amazingly miscellaneous armada of Royal Navy and private craft, including tugs, fire-floats, pleasure cruisers, and sloops. The courage of these seamen was not alone responsible for the "miracle of Dunkirk," however. It was possible only because the Germans pressed their attack with artillery and airpower rather than with armor and because the *Luftwaffe* made the fundamental error of concentrating on the beaches rather than on the evacuation craft. These errors permitted the rescue fleet to carry the bulk of the British forces and 139,000 French and Belgians to safety in England. Winston Churchill was doubtless right in warning the House of Commons that "we must be very careful not to assign to this deliverance the attributes of a victory. Wars are not won by evacuations." Even so, the importance of this remarkable operation should not be under-estimated. By bringing back the core of a professional army, it facilitated military recovery and expansion and saved for the future British army a large number of commanders who had learned more in the brief and shattering campaign in Flanders than they could have learned in years at staff schools. It simulta-neously awakened British pride in what they could accomplish even in defeat and gave them a new commitment to the struggle.

Unfortunately, it could do nothing to retrieve the situation in France, which now deteriorated swiftly. The French still had enough reserves to equal the enemy

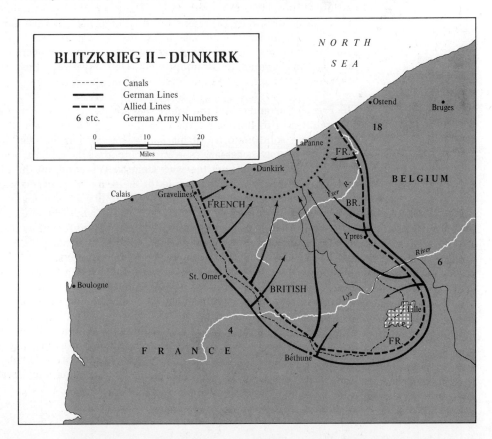

BLITZKRIEG II – DUNKIRK

- – – – – – –   Canals
- —————   German Lines
- – – – – –   Allied Lines
- 6 etc.   German Army Numbers

0   10   20
Miles

in numbers and as much armor and superior artillery; their only relative weakness was in the air. But French staff planners had never been able to think in terms of a truly mobile war; they had persisted in parceling out tanks and aircraft to ground formations instead of using them in concentration; their artillery was static rather than mobile; and they had no real battle plan. The speed of the German advance overwhelmed General Gamelin and, when he was relieved on May 19, his successor, the seventy-three-year-old Weygand, showed less vigor than the occasion warranted. Indeed, as the Somme front crumbled and the German armies wheeled to the south, the new commander tended to blame all his misfortunes on the British, while refusing to withdraw the unused divisions in the Maginot Line to bolster his defenses. The hope of making a stand was weakened by an incredible amount of administrative confusion. At a time when the French were insisting, unsuccessfully, that the British move the last of their fighter squadrons to France, they had 150 fighter planes in good condition at Tours while the pilots of Corap's army were sitting 30 kilometers away, complaining that they had nothing to fly. At a time when the French were pleading for British antitank guns, 520 new 20 mm antitank guns and 750 25 mm antitank guns were sitting in French depots, where the Germans found them when the fighting was over. With this sort of thing going on and the roads clogged with refugees, it is not surprising that the armies did not hold.

On June 10, the signs of collapse were so evident that Mussolini, who had, because of Italy's lack of preparedness, received Hitler's permission in September to remain neutral, now overcame the doubts of his generals and insisted upon declaring war on France. ("I need a few thousand dead," he is reported to have said, "so that I can attend the peace conference as a belligerent.") On June 14 the Germans entered Paris unopposed. Two days later they outflanked and breached the Maginot Line and pressed across the Loire.

The French Surrender and the Vichy Regime   The French government had meanwhile fled to Bordeaux. Viewing the rout, Prime Minister Paul Reynaud, backed by a solid majority of his colleagues, argued that the army should, if it were absolutely necessary, surrender, but that the government should go to North Africa and continue the war. General Weygand, on the other hand, declared that it would be dishonorable for the army to act in this way and insisted that the government must take the responsibility for seeking an armistice. He was unmoved by Reynaud's argument that this would violate an earlier pledge to the British not to seek a separate peace and unimpressed by pleas that Britain would fight on and win and that France must be at her side. He made it clear that he expected a British collapse almost immediately.

Raynaud, nevertheless, insisted on consulting the British. After some hesitation, they agreed on May 16 not to object if the French sounded out the Germans on terms, provided the French fleet were dispatched to British ports. Later in the day, the British government sought to recall that permission by proposing in its place that France and Britain unite as one nation, with joint citizenship and common policy and with joint responsibility for repairing the ravages of the war once it had been won. This revolutionary proposal had no result. In Bordeaux the supporters of an appeal to the Germans had grown in numbers and determination; the British declaration was regarded as an attempt to degrade France to the position of a dominion; Reynaud resigned in despair; and all parties turned to Marshal Pétain, the hero of Verdun, who now became head of the government and, on June 17, asked the Germans for armistice terms.

The agreement that the French were forced to sign was a harsh one. German troops were to occupy more than half of France, including Paris, all of the northern part of the country, and the whole Atlantic coast to the Spanish border. Occupation costs were to be borne by the French, who in the unoccupied zone were to maintain a regime friendly to Germany. The terms included provisions for the immediate surrender of German prisoners, the disbanding of the French army, and—and this was to cause serious misunderstanding between France and Britain—the concentration and demobilization of all French fleet units in ports under German or Italian control.

The Pétain government accepted these terms in return for a pledge that Germany would not use the fleet units in question. To make doubly sure, Admiral Darlan, the French naval commander in chief, in a secret signal on June 24, ordered his fleet commanders to scuttle their ships if the enemy tried to seize them by force. Unfortunately, the British government was not kept fully informed of these orders and assurances and regarded the possibility of German use of the French navy as a danger that must be eliminated. Consequently, on the night of July 2, a British naval force appeared off the roads of Mers-el-Kebir in Algeria, where the French Atlantic squadron (four cruisers, six destroyers, one carrier, four submarines, and smaller ships) was berthed, sealed off the harbor with magnetic mines, and then invited the French commander to join forces with them or take the consequences. The French commander, Admiral Gensoul, refused but sought to explain the nature of Darlan's order, adding personal assurances of his intention of obeying it. The British commander was under too great pressure from London to be content with his explanation and proceeded to destroy the French fleet in a bombardment that lasted only thirteen minutes and from which only one cruiser and three destroyers escaped.

Mers-el-Kebir caused a wave of anti-British feeling in Vichy, where the Pétain government was now stationed, and brought further discredit upon the Third Republic by making it possible to accuse it of having based its foreign policy on an alliance with a power that would attack defenseless French ships. This played into the hands of those who wished to destroy democracy and establish a totalitarian regime. Under the cunning leadership of Pierre Laval, what was left of the old French parliament now voted the Republic out of existence and vested full powers in Marshal Pétain. This octogenarian had long believed that the Republic was decadent and should be replaced and, with the help of an entourage filled with members of the *Action Française* and similar groups, he now established a regime that was strongly authoritarian in cast. Indeed, in the four years of its existence, the Vichy regime enacted some of the most repressive laws that France had ever known, made all citizens the subject of possible administrative sanctions, and excluded certain categories of Frenchmen (Freemasons and Jews, for example) from the protection of the laws. The individual liberty of even the most distinguished citizens was subject to restriction: André Gide was forbidden by the local head of the *Légion des Combattants* to deliver a lecture in Nice, on the grounds that it would not be fitting for "the triumphant champion of the spirit of pleasure" to speak in these times of sacrifice and suffering. Humbler persons were apt to suffer from appalling injustice. Foreigners who had volunteered for service in the Foreign Legion during the campaign of France were penned up in concentration camps in Africa and treated with a brutality that rivaled that of the Nazi camps at Dachau and Auschwitz.

In foreign affairs, Pétain himself, whose most marked characteristic was slyness, sought to keep wires open to both Berlin and London, so as to secure France's future whatever happened in the war. On the other hand, Pierre Laval, always the strongest man in Vichy, although his relations with the marshal were sometimes less than cordial, believed in wholehearted collaboration with Germany and, had he had his way, would probably have gone to war against Britain. The line that was followed was an equivocal one. The Vichy regime was accorded diplomatic recognition by the Western powers because of the obvious advantages that such recognition brought, but it won no affection either abroad or at home. The real France, to a growing number of Frenchmen, was represented by the resistance in the *Maquis* (or underbrush) and by those who fled to England to join the Free French movement of General Charles de Gaulle.

The Battle of Britain   After the fall of France, as after the fall of Poland, Hitler paused and put out feelers to the British; and once more he found no disposition to treat. He therefore began preparations for an invasion of the British Isles—an operation that was given the code name Sea Lion. Throughout the summer and the early fall of 1940, a great invasion fleet of barges was assembled at the coastal ports, and troops were trained for the amphibious operation. Many of Hitler's naval commanders, in particular, viewed all of these preparations with foreboding. They need not have worried. In the end, Sea Lion was abandoned, because the air battle that preceded it was lost.

After the war was over, some Russian officers asked the German general Gerd von Rundstedt what he thought had been the decisive battle of the war. Doubtless to their disappointment, he named the Battle of Britain, and there is much to be said for his answer. If the British had collapsed in 1940, the Germans would have been able to launch their Russian drive sooner and with stronger forces, and they might have taken Moscow in 1941. Moreover, a British collapse would have completed the deterioration of faith in democracy that had been growing ever since the mid-1930s and had by this time begun to make even some Americans believe that totalitarianism was the wave of the future.

The Battle of Britain was won by the RAF and by the people of London and the other industrial cities of Great Britain. They were helped, it is true, by German mistakes. When the *Luftwaffe* began its great assault in early August, its mission was to knock out the British air force and soften up England for the invasion. Despite the overconfidence of its commander Hermann Goering, it was neither trained for the kind of operations demanded of it nor supplied with a proper advance assessment of British strength or effective intelligence during the battle. Inconsistency of target selection and faulty coordination between the bombing and fighter arms were characteristic of German performance throughout the operation, and the *Luftwaffe's* best chances were lost by strategic errors, like the decision in early September to shift the attack from control stations and airfields to London and other cities—a decision made at the very moment when the airfield attacks seemed on the point of exhausting British resources.

On the other hand, the Battle of Britain deserves to be thought of in positive terms rather than as a victory by German default. It was won by the British, and won because of five things. The first was the possession of an effective radar net, which had been built up since 1934. The second was the heavy armament of Spitfires and Hurricanes, which bore the brunt of the fighting and outgunned the aircraft that they had to intercept (see p. 615). The third was the skill and the unpretentious gallantry of the British fighter pilots. The fourth was the fact that—thanks to Winston Churchill's refusal to commit the last of Britain's fighter planes to the battle of France in May—the RAF had enough planes to fight until the tide turned. The fifth was the spirit of the British people, who took the terrific pounding without panicking or calling for surrender.

Thanks to these things, Goering's offensive failed, at a cost from which the *Luftwaffe* never recovered. And when the failure was obvious, in the winter, Sea Lion was abandoned by its author. But the Battle of Britain accomplished more even than that. It put an end to doubts about Britain's will to fight on and inspired resistance movements in the Low Countries, Norway, and France with new hope. It aroused new enthusiasm for the British cause in the United States and made it easier for the administration of Franklin D. Roosevelt to win support for measures of aid to Britain. In September 1940, the United States, in return for a lease of naval bases in the West Indies and Bermuda, transferred fifty overage destroyers to the British navy, who put them to good use immediately. Simultaneously, the War Department released surplus material and weapons to the British army. Even more important than these measures of aid was the Lend-Lease Act of March 1941, by which Congress authorized the manufacture, sale, loan, lease, or transfer of war material to "the government of any country whose defense the President deems vital for the defense of the United States." The President was given discretion to make such arrangements without requiring repayment, if he so desired, and he proceeded to use his authority to bolster Britain's defenses.

Africa and the Mediterranean   The junior partner of the Axis had derived little personal satisfaction from his intervention in the last stages of the French campaign. Although collapsing everywhere else, the French had stood so firmly against Italian attacks on the southeastern front that, at one point, Mussolini had asked the Germans for transport planes to fly units over the line of resistance into the rear. The Germans had refused, and the campaign had ended with no laurels for Italy at all.

With Britain fully engaged in its fight for existence, however, Mussolini saw prospects of victory and spoils in Africa and, indeed, in the whole Mediterranean area. In August 1940, at the height of the Battle of Britain, he ordered the Duke of Aosta, with 200,000 Italian and native troops under his command, to advance from Eritrea and Italian Somaliland against British troops at the entrance of the Red Sea. Within two weeks, the British had been forced out of Somaliland. On September 14, the second stage of Mussolini's ambitious campaign opened.

An army of 250,000 under Marshal Graziani moved from Libya eastward into Egypt and forced the ill-armed, vastly outnumbered troops of General Sir Archibald Wavell to fall back on Mersa Matruh, the railhead on the way to Alexandria.

All might have gone well if the British had been willing to admit the danger of their position in the Mediterranean and to withdraw their fleet units entirely from that sea. But, under the leadership of Admiral Sir Andrew Brown Cunningham, who has been called the greatest English sailor since Nelson, they not only refused to do this but proceeded to raise havoc with Graziani's supply lines. Nor were they content with that. On November 11, 1940, a British task force had the temerity to steam into the Italian base of Taranto, where, using torpedo planes, they sank or severly damaged three battleships, two cruisers, and two auxiliaries and left the harbor in flames.

While the Duce reflected on this humiliation, Wavell made what was supposed to be a raid in force from Mersa Matruh in December. It developed into an Italian rout. Hitting Graziani's forward forces at Sidi Barrani, the mixed British, Indian, and Anzac forces took the town and its whole garrison after two days' fighting and then rolled over Bardia in Libya to Tobruk, moved on to Derna, and in February actually reached and captured Benghazi. Within three months the British had knocked out ten Italian divisions, taken 113,000 prisoners, captured 1300 guns and hundreds of tanks, and eliminated the threat to Suez. And, as if that were not enough, in January 1941 British forces from the Sudan conquered Eritrea, and a column from Nairobi reconquered all of Somaliland. In May the Duke of Aosta was crushed at Amba Alagi, and Ethiopia was liberated. The Duce's African empire was in ruins; and his navy, hard hit at Taranto, had suffered another grievous beating in March, when Cunningham caught it off Cape Matapan and sank three cruisers and three destroyers and severely damaged a new battleship.

So desperate did the plight of his partner seem by now that Hitler intervened. In April General Erwin Rommel appeared in North Africa and immediately struck back at the British in Libya. Within a week he had bypassed Tobruk, stormed Bardia, and forced Wavell to withdraw into Egypt. The Desert Fox, as he was soon called, was no Graziani, and with his coming the threat to Suez became very real again.

Greece and Yugoslavia   It was not from his African plight alone that Mussolini needed to be extricated. He had become enmeshed in more serious troubles in Greece. The idea of launching an attack upon Greece from Albania had been on the Duce's mind for some time, and—perhaps because he was resentful about the number of times he had been surprised by his ally—he decided this time to strike without consulting Hitler. In October 1940, therefore, he dispatched an ultimatum to the Greek government, charging it with unneutral behavior and other crimes and demanding the right to occupy certain strategic areas in Greece for the duration of the war. Without giving the Greeks a chance to reply, the Italians crossed the Greco-Albanian border on October 28 with 200,000 troops.

The British immediately offered their aid to the Greeks and brought troops across from Africa, beginning a process of draining Wavell's strength that was soon to be exploited by Rommel. But the Greeks were already in command of the situation. Mountain troops trapped the overconfident Italian invaders in the narrow mountain valleys and began to pound them with artillery. In the first week of November, the 3d Italian Alpini division lost 5000 men in the Pindus gorges; a week later, the whole invading army was being pressed back to the Albanian border; a month after that, having suffered frightful losses, they had been expelled from Greece and were in danger of losing Albania as well.

If Mussolini was cast down by these setbacks, his fellow dictator was infuriated, and for good reason. Hitler had never lost sight of his main objective, which was expansion toward the east; and, even while he pursued his onslaught against Britain, he had been using the resources of diplomacy to extend German domination over the quarreling Balkan countries, so as to be in an advanced position when the break with Russia came. In the twelve months that followed the conclusion of the Nazi-Soviet Pact, he had succeeded—to the dismay of the Soviet Union—in winning paramount influence over the governments of Hungary, Bulgaria, and Rumania. This he had accomplished by supporting the territorial ambitions of the first two and by granting a guarantee to what was left of Rumania after it had been forced, in July and August 1940, to cede a large part of its territory to Hungary, Bulgaria, and Russia. Rumanian territorial losses caused the abdication of King Carol, and the new king, Michael, was not only grateful for the guarantee of his fast-dwindling realm but actually requested Germany to send troops to help restore order. These forward strides, which brought the Germans an excellent jumping-off place for any future operations, far exceeded Russian gains in Rumania, from which they had exacted Bukovina and Bessarabia, and in Finland.[2] But the Russians had not dared utter more than formal protests, preferring to indulge in an appeasement policy that yielded far more territory to Hitler than Anglo-French appeasement had given him between 1933 and 1939.

These gains were all jeopardized by Mussolini's action in Greece, which began at a time when Hitler was preoccupied with western rather than eastern problems. For some time he had been under pressure from Admiral Raeder, the navy's chief, to make up for the failure of Sea Lion by striking a blow in the western Mediterranean, capturing Gibraltar and closing its straits. Raeder insisted that Britain, becoming stronger monthly as a result of American aid, must be subjected to new attacks and that the crucial strategical area for this was Africa and the Mediterranean. Hitler was sufficiently impressed by these arguments to meet with General Francisco Franco at Hendaye in October 1940 and to try to persuade him to agree to a joint Spanish-German campaign. He had no success. Indeed, he was so exhausted by the Caudillo's counterarguments in their long conversation that he said later he would rather "have three or four teeth yanked out ... than go through that again." It was not, however, Franco's verbal delaying action that put an end to the idea of a campaign against the straits of Gibraltar. It was the news, which came immediately after Hendaye, that Mussolini had invaded Greece and the subsequent disastrous development of that adventure. The British response especially worried Hitler, for their occupation of Crete and

[2] Especially in view of the fact that the Germans sent troops into Finland, presumably for protective purposes, in September 1940.

MEDITERRANEAN THEATER OF WAR

BAY OF BISCAY

FRANCE

SWITZERLAND

GERMA

Munich

Trieste

Venice

Pula

Genoa Bologna

Bilbao

Marseilles

Toulon

Livorno

CORSICA

Rome

Barcelona

Madrid

SPAIN

PORTUGAL

Lisbon

SARDINIA

Naples

TYRRHENIAN
SEA

MEDITERRA

Tangiers

Algiers

Bizerte

SICI

SPAN. MOROCCO

Oran

Bougie Bone

Rabat

ALGERIA

Tunis

Pantelleria

Ma

Casablanca Fez

TUNISIA

MOROCCO

Lampedusa

Mareth

Tripoli

0   100   200   300   400
Miles

LIBY

Lemnos and their troop landings on the mainland threatened the whole German position in the Balkans.

The Fuehrer, therefore, abandoned whatever plans he may have been considering for another blow in the west and prepared to liquidate the threat in Greece. At the beginning of the new year, he sent requests for troop transit to the governments of Bulgaria and Yugoslavia. On March 1, 1941, the Bulgarians signed a treaty of alliance and permitted German troops to enter Sofia and Varna.

The regency in Yugoslavia, which had become increasingly pro-German in its views (see p. 600), indicated its intention of doing the same later in the month.

This was regarded, however, as a shameful capitulation by the people of Yugoslavia, who were by nature courageous, combative, and independently minded. On March 27, 1941, with every evidece of strong public support, an army revolt deposed the regent Paul and put the young King Peter II on the throne. He immediately appointed an anti-German cabinet and would probably have sought to give aid to the victorious but now tiring Greeks had he been given more time. But Hitler was not generous with that commodity. In April 1941, his planes subjected Belgrade to one of the most terrific bombardments of the war; twenty divisions of his troops came tumbling through the mountains and seized all the principal cities of the country; the king and his government fled; the realm was divided into an independent Croatia, leaning toward Germany, and a Serbia under direct German military control; and the Nazi juggernaut rolled on toward Greece.

By this time, the British had put 56,657 trained desert troops, most of them Australians and New Zealanders, into the country. But they had to face an enemy of half a million men, who possessed, in addition, command of the skies and a great superiority in armor. The issue was decided in advance. The Germans moved with an incredible rapidity that made their containment impossible. The Greeks fought bravely but with far less spirit than they had shown against the Italians—perhaps because of weariness, perhaps because of the aura of invincibility that surrounded the gray columns that swept into their country. The British lost 15,000 troops trying to find a line that could be defended, and then were forced once more to retire by sea—this time to the island of Crete, whence they were expelled by bombing attacks and parachute drops in May.

The conquest of Crete gave Hitler an important base from which to harry Cunningham's fleet and Wavell's supply lines. It also gave him a jumping-off place for penetrating the oil-rich Middle East, an invasion that, if pushed in strength and in conjunction with increasing support for Rommel's operations in Africa, might have been disastrous for Britain. It is difficult to avoid the conclusion that Hitler's greatest strategical mistake was his failure to exploit these opportunities after the end of the Greek campaign. But once he had completed his domination of the Balkan area, Raeder's arguments meant little to him. His eyes and his mind were filled with visions of victory over Russia, and he now turned his armies to the east.

Hitler's Attack on Russia   The Fuehrer had, indeed, definitely decided on an invasion of Russia before his troops were actually committed in Greece. The directive for what was called Operation Barbarossa had been issued on December 18, 1940, and began with the words:

> The German Armed Forces must be prepared to crush Soviet Russia in a quick campaign even before the conclusion of the war against England. For this purpose the Army will have to employ all available units. . . .

Both Finland and Rumania were counted on as allies in this war, and both had already been transformed into German *places d'armes*. By February 1941 there were 680,000 well-equipped German troops in Rumania; and, during the preparations for the blow against Greece, they were increased in number, and units were sent to Bulgaria as well. This meant that German planes had command over the southwestern approaches to the Ukraine and the Caucasus, the richest agricultural and industrial areas in the Soviet Union. By May Hitler's preparations were well in hand, and the decision to attack waited only upon the end of operations in Greece and Crete. On June 22 the text of the declaration of war was handed to the Russians, and the German armies attacked along the whole front from Finland to the Caucasus. To Mussolini, Hitler wrote:

> Since I struggled through to this decision, I again feel spiritually free. The partnership with the Soviet Union, in spite of the complete sincerity of efforts to bring about a final conciliation, was nevertheless often very irksome to me, for in some way or other it seemed to me to be a break with my whole origin, my concepts and my former obligations. I AM happy now to be relieved of these mental agonies.

It is not improbable that his sentiments were genuine.

Once more the world witnessed an impressive demonstration of German power. Within ten days of the opening of hostilities, the *Luftwaffe* had won almost complete air supremacy, German armored columns were piercing and encircling the dazed Russian defenders, and Nazi legions had already captured 150,000 prisoners, 1200 tanks, and 600 big guns. The main German objective was the line Leningrad-Moscow-lower Volga, which would give Hitler control of the Ukrainian grain fields, the Donets mineral deposits, Caucasian oil, and command of the Baltic and Black seas. For a time it seemed that this line would be reached with ease. General von Leeb's army group in the north occupied Riga in the first week of fighting and, by September, was poised before Leningrad. In the center, General von Bock's army advanced 500 miles in the first month but was

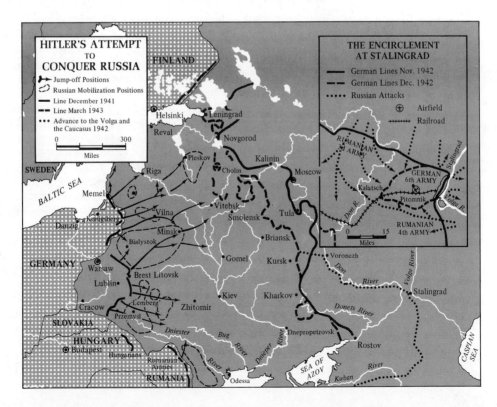

held up in front of Smolensk for almost three months by the most desperate kind of resistance. It was then reinforced and rolled on toward Moscow in October. In the south, Rundstedt's army group encircled Kiev and rushed on to the line Taganrog-Kharkov-Kursk in the same period, and in November Manstein invaded the Crimea and Kleist took Rostov-on-Don.

All three of these massive thrusts failed, in the end, to reach their objectives, although Bock's forces could at one time actually see the spires of the Kremlin outlined against the sky. The Russian winter, which had defeated Napoleon, defeated Hitler also by arriving three weeks early.[3] In late November the freezing cold immobilized German transport and armor and caused frightful suffering among the invading armies, who were ill-equipped for it and found it difficult to meet the counterattacks that Marshal Zhukov now mounted north and south of Moscow. German staff officers urged a general withdrawal to permit a regrouping for a spring offensive. Hitler refused, and was probably right in doing so, since a general withdrawal in these circumstances might have led to a dissolution of the whole battle line. There were some local retirements and then a general stabilization of the thousand-mile front.

The *Blitzkrieg* had failed, but not definitively. The Russians had lost over a million troops in prisoners alone, as well as an enormous amount of territory. Who could say that they would have the strength to withstand the new blows that would surely come in the spring?

THE JAPANESE OFFENSIVE

In September 1940 the Japanese government had entered a pact with Germany and Italy that bound the signatories "to assist one another with all political, economic and military means if one of the three Contracting Parties is attacked by a Power at present not involved in the European War or in the Chinese-Japanese conflict." This was designed primarily to induce the United States to be cautious in giving aid to the West. It did not oblige Japan to aid Germany if it attacked the Soviet Union, and, in April 1941, the Japanese and Soviet governments signed a pact by which each promised to maintain a benevolent neutrality if the other became involved in a war.

Japan, therefore, did not directly support the German drive when it started in June 1941. Nevertheless, six months later, it brought powerful aid, at least temporarily, to the German cause. By attacking the United States and Great Britain in the Pacific, Japan greatly reduced the possibility of these countries giving assistance to the Soviet Union, while weakening their resources for their own battles on other fronts.

Since the beginning of the European war, the ambitions of Japanese expansionists had grown rapidly. The fall of Holland and France and the absorption of Britain's energies in the European and Mediterranean theaters seemed an open invitation for Japan to lay its hands upon their Pacific possessions. As

---

[3] At the end of his career, Hitler blamed all this on Mussolini's Greek adventure. "I only failed by a short head," he said, "exactly five weeks . . . and I lost them because of the confidence I had placed in my dearest and most admired friend, Mussolini."

early as June 1940, the Tokyo government was pressing for special rights and bases in Indochina, and the Vichy authorities found it expedient to grant them air bases in Tonkin. These first concessions did not appease the Japanese but merely intensified their hunger. In July 1941 they moved troops into Indochina and Siam and began menacing motions in the direction of Burma, the Dutch possessions in Indonesia, and the British naval base at Singapore.

The United States government could not view with equanimity the further weakening of powers it was supporting with economic aid and military supplies in Europe; and, in any case, Washington had opposed Japan's Asian ambitions ever since 1931 and had, since the opening of the Japanese offensive of 1937, been giving all possible aid to the Chinese government of Chiang Kai-shek. The Roosevelt administration did not respond to British suggestions that it send the American fleet to Singapore; nor did it, on the other hand, follow the advice of those of its own members who wanted a rigid economic strait jacket imposed on Japan as early as 1940. Either of these lines, it was felt by the President and his chief military advisers, might precipitate a major Pacific war, which would seriously reduce the possibility of a democratic victory in Europe. Throughout 1940 and 1941, therefore, the United States government relied upon diplomatic representations accompanied by a gradual tightening of economic pressure (freezing of assets, embargoes on certain products, and the like), while at the same time holding staff talks with the British and the Dutch.

This policy did at least prevent hostilities for a long time, but it neither impressed the Japanese sufficiently to make them give up their aggressive designs nor weakened their resources for a war in any significant way. By the fall of 1941, the diplomatic positions of both sides had become rigid: the Japanese demanding a withdrawal of all embargo measures and of all aid to Chiang Kai-shek as the price of agreement, the United States refusing to lift any restrictions until the prewar situation was restored. This deadlock was resolved on December 7, 1941, when the Japanese fleet, in accordance with a carefully worked-out plan and without any warning, struck at Pearl Harbor in Oahu, where the bulk of the United States fleet was assembled, sank the battleships *Arizona, West Virginia,* and *Oklahoma,* severely damaged five other battleships, killed 2343 men, wounded over 1200, and virtually destroyed the striking force of the United States in the Pacific.

To the astonishment and dread of the democratic world, this shattering victory was succeeded by a long string of others. Guam, Wake, and the Philippines were conquered by Japanese task forces by March. A belated British attempt to bolster the defenses of Singapore was frustrated when their new 35,000-ton battleship *Prince of Wales* and the 32,000-ton armored cruiser *Repulse* were caught 150 miles from the base and sunk by naval torpedoes on December 10, 1941. A month later, Japanese forces systematically conquered the Malayan peninsula and, taking Singapore from the rear, forced it to surrender on February 15 with 60,000 troops. Simultaneously, Japanese columns invaded the Kra Peninsula in Burma, captured Moulmein and Rangoon, cleared the country of British and Chinese troops, closed the great Burma Road (the main supply line to China), and installed a puppet government. Finally, in mid-February, in the battle of the Java Sea, the Japanese fleet destroyed a mixed Allied force of five cruisers,

THE PACIFIC THEATER OF WAR

Japanese occupied areas after Dec. 7, 1941

Japanese occupied areas on Dec. 7, 1941

The Allies

Allied Advances

six destroyers, and a sloop under the command of the Dutch Admiral Helfrich and made possible the conquest of all of the Netherlands East Indies by March.

There was no reason to suppose at that time that further Japanese expansion could be checked. The confident aggressors were already looking toward Australia, and there were few barriers in their way. Moreover, a renewal of German activities could be expected as soon as spring came to Russia. All in all, the outlook for the democracies was distinctly unpromising.

THE TURN OF THE TIDE, 1942–1943

The Grand Alliance   As it happened, the aggressors had reached the peak of their power in the early spring of 1942, and they were never to be as strong and as close to victory again. Even before the end of 1942, there were signs that the democratic powers were regaining the initiative, and the year 1943 saw the definite beginning of a shift in the fortunes of this gigantic war.

The first order of business for the democratic powers, after the shock of Pearl

Harbor had passed, was the creation of an effective coalition to combat the forces of totalitarianism. The basis for this had been laid by the cordial cooperation between Franklin Roosevelt and Winston Churchill even before the formal entrance of the United States into the war, and by the immediate decision made by these statesmen in June 1941 that, despite their ideological differences with the Soviet Union, they must do everything in their power to help the Russians withstand the German onslaught. This informal collaboration was given a more public and dramatic form in January 1942 when the three major powers, with twenty-three others, issued the Declaration of the United Nations, pledging common action against the aggressor powers and expressing their adhesion to the principles of the Atlantic Charter, which had been formulated by Churchill and Roosevelt in a famous meeting on the high seas in August 1941. That charter had denied any desire for aggrandizement, territorial changes without the assent of interested populations, or infringements of sovereignty, and had expressed the intention of creating a world in which "all men in all lands may live out their lives in freedom from fear and want." The fact that these principles were not universally respected when the war was won is perhaps not as important as the fact that they helped to hearten men in the free world in 1942.

The coalition was not merely a matter of words. In the crucial period of the war, it provided for consultation and exchange of information between Hitler's chief adversaries; and it was always backed by the tremendous productive capacity of the United States, which had started, during its period of neutrality, to make itself the arsenal of democracy and was now tooled for the job.

To supply the fighting forces of this war was a difficult task; and a shortage of landing craft, to take only one example, could—and for a time did—mean that amphibious operations could not be conducted simultaneously in two theaters of war. But despite Hermann Goering's jeer that the United States "could make nothing except refrigerators and razor blades," these difficulties were overcome. American industry helped supply the force that finally broke Rommel's back in Africa and sent a constant stream of indispensable supplies to Russia. By the end of the war (according to Louis L. Snyder), the United States had produced 296,601 planes, 87,000 tanks, 2,434,553 trucks, 17,400,000 rifles, 315,000 pieces of field artillery, and 4,200,000 tons of artillery shells, among other necessities of war. Large amounts of these materials went to America's allies, under the aegis of Lend-Lease (which sent $4,750,000,000 of supplies to the Soviet Union alone in the course of the struggle); and all of it was used in the fight against the Axis powers.

The problem of maintaining supply lines was never easy. In the Atlantic, the effectiveness of the wolf-pack tactics of German submarines was finally overcome, as has already been indicated, by the refinement of convoy techniques and the perfection of underseas detection devices; and, in the Atlantic particularly, the security of shipping was attained by mid-1943. Supply routes in the Mediterranean were subject to heavy bombardment by land-based planes until the time of the Italian invasion, and this menace was even greater along the northern supply routes—the Murmansk run—to Russia. To circumvent the dangers of the northern passage, the western Allies developed an alternate route through the Persian Gulf and across Iran. Before it could be relied upon, however, British and Free French forces had to eliminate the threat posed by the collaboration of Vichy French authorities in Syria with the Nazis, as well by pro-Axis sympathies in Iraq and Iran. This was accomplished in mid-1941, and the Persian Gulf route was put into operation.

The Pacific War   Had Japanese aggression not been contained, it is possible that the Pacific war would, in time, have absorbed the greater part of the fighting energies of the United States, despite the general agreement of its staff planners that the main strategical effort should be in Europe. Even as it was, the heavy drain on American resources by Pacific needs severely limited possibilities of action in Europe.

Nevertheless, the helter-skelter retreat before Japanese might was checked in 1942 in three great battles. The first was a hard-fought engagement in the Coral Sea between Australia and the Solomon Islands, during which American carrier-based planes attacked a heavy Japanese fleet concentration, sank a carrier, four cruisers, and two destroyers, crippled seven other ships, and forced the enemy to retire northward. American losses in' this battle were not inconsiderable—the carrier *Lexington,* a destroyer, and a tanker—but the action succeeded in checking a possible thrust against the southeast coast of Australia. More important was the defeat of a Japanese attempt to seize the island of Midway in the central Pacific, in order to secure their outer defensive perimeter (Kiska-Midway-Wake-the Marshalls-the Gilberts-Fiji) and to acquire a jumping-off point for future thrusts into the Hawaiian group. In May 1942, the Japanese assembled a fleet of 200 ships, including eleven battleships, eight carriers, twenty-two cruisers, sixty-five destroyers, and twenty-one submarines, together with 700 planes, and advanced toward Midway in five tactical forces, hoping to entice the remnants of the U.S. fleet into a hopeless battle. On June 4 they launched their attack with a seventy-plane strike on the island. Forty of these planes were shot down by U.S. marine and army interceptors, and those that returned to their carriers were never flown again. For the Japanese fleet was now hit by naval aviation from two American task forces lying northeast of Midway and, in a four-day inferno of fire, suffered the greatest defeat in the history of the Japanese navy, losing 5000 men, 322 planes, four carriers and a heavy cruiser, and having at least six other fleet units disabled.

These naval encounters slowed the momentum of the Japanese drive but did not stop it. The Japanese high command still looked toward Australia and planned a great pincers movement against the subcontinent, the arms of which would extend from Port Moresby in New Guinea on the one hand and the Solomons chain on the other. But Japan's strategy was too ambitious for its resources and, by attempting to gain both these widely separated areas, it won neither. Under the command of General Douglas MacArthur, who had been forced to flee from beleaguered Bataan in the Philippines, Australian and American forces defeated Japanese attempts to cross the mountains and seize Port Moresby. In August 1942, the U.S. Marines anticipated the Japanese thrust toward the southern Solomons by making a daring landing on Guadalcanal and, through months of desperate fighting on the sea, in the air, and in the fever-infested jungles, made good their possession of this vital point.

These successes were the key to future victory. By the spring of 1943, Mac-Arthur's forces were beginning to move northward through the coastal swamps of New Guinea toward Salamaua and Lae, while allied amphibious forces advanced up the Solomons chain and seized the Russell Islands and Bougainville. It was not long before the main Japanese base in the southwest Pacific, Rabaul on New Britain, was being pounded into helplessness. By the middle of 1943 the Japanese dream of Pacific-wide empire was fading fast: the Allies had reconquered the southwest Pacific and the beginning of their island-hopping advance was not far away.

Western Europe   Throughout 1942 operations in western Europe were confined to a stepping-up of the Allied bombing offensive against German bases and installations in Norway and northern France and German industrial cities, and occasional raids to destroy or test defenses. The most daring of these last came early in March 1942 when a tiny British force carried by launches and torpedo boats crept into St.-Nazaire harbor on the Bay of Biscay, rammed HMS *Campbeltown* (one of the overage destroyers given to Britain in 1940) against the main locks, and blew her and the dry docks up. This raid immobilized *Tirpitz* (the last great German battleship after the torpedoing of *Bismarck* in May 1941), for, without an Atlantic port capable of servicing her, she did not dare leave Norwegian waters.

A second raid, less happy in its immediate results, was on Dieppe, staged by a force of 5000 troops, mostly Canadian, in August 1942. Western planners, thnking ahead to the future invasion to liberate Europe, felt it essential to try something on a scale sufficient to test landing equipment and techniques and throw light on what, in 1942, was considered the primary invasion problem—the seizure of a major port. The Dieppe raid, executed by a frontal assault on the port with infantry and tanks, combined with landings on the flanking beaches, was repulsed with heavy losses, more than a thousand men dying on the beaches and two thousand being captured by the Germans; but its long-run value was incalculable. It taught the Allies that the magnitude of the invasion task was much greater than they had thought and that attacks on open beaches were to be preferred to assaults on ports. Simultaneously, it deluded the Germans into believing that ports would be the primary Allied objectives, and this warped their defensive system to the Allied advantage.

North Africa: Crusader and El Alamein   The same months saw the rise and fall of Rommel's fortunes in Africa. The arrival of that energetic commander in April 1941 had retrieved sagging Axis fortunes, driven the British desert army back into Egypt, and isolated and bypassed the port of Tobruk, whose Australian garrison won the attention of the world by refusing to surrender despite a terrific and incessant bombardment from the air. Rommel was less concerned by the exertions of the "desert rats" in Tobruk than he was by the failure of Hitler and the OKW to give him the supplies he needed for a real offensive. It is generally believed, even by Rommel's foes, that if he had been given the three extra divisions of tanks that he kept asking for in 1941, he would have reached Cairo and the Suez Canal at the beginning of the next year and could then have rolled on to Basra and cut the flow of American supplies that were going to Russia by the Persian Gulf routes. The Allies were saved from that disaster by Hitler's preoccupation with the main offensive against Russia and by the failure of the supreme German staffs to take the African war seriously.

This is not all there is to it, however, for the British Eighth Army also played its part. In December 1941, Wavell's successor in the Middle East, General Auchinleck, launched a well-planned offensive against Rommel's lines and drove him all the way back to El Agheila, liberating Tobruk in the process. But Rommel, as Winston Churchill admitted in the House of Commons at the height of Auchinleck's "Crusader" operation, was "a daring and skillful opponent ... a great general," and he not only escaped the snares set before him but kept the bulk of his armor intact. By the late spring, he was moving forward again and, in May, he began the great counterattack that finally took Tobruk and rolled on into Egypt, past Sidi Barrani and Mersa Matruh, until he had reached El Alamein, only 60 miles west of Alexandria.

During this advance, however, his stocks of fuel had been seriously depleted, and he could expect no reliable replenishment, since Malta-based planes and ships were now seriously hampering his supply lines. His tanks were being knocked out of action by combat fatigue and by the harassing tactics of RAF fighter bombers, now using American-made shells. His pleas for aid were disregarded or met with empty promises.

This was fatal, for, under the methodical supervision of Lieutenant General Bernard Law Montgomery, the British Eighth Army had been gathering every ounce of available power for a death thrust. In the bright moonlight of October 23, 1942, it opened a massive artillery barrage upon Rommel's lines. Four hours later came the assault by the hand-picked Commonwealth troops, and Rommel's columns were thrown into a retreat that did not stop until the last of the haggard *Afrika Korps* laid down their arms in Tunis months later.

As they staggered toward that inevitable end, pursued by furious demands from Hitler to stand and die in their places, a great Allied invasion fleet bore down upon the Moroccan coast and began, on November 8, to land British and American troops at Casablanca, Oran, and Algiers. This was the long-planned Operation Torch, which, it was hoped—although in vain—would be unopposed by French garrisons. Unfortunately, the Americans did not make allowance for the sinuosities of Vichy politics and negotiated with the wrong people or put inadequate trust in the right ones to effect their purposes. There was, therefore, resistance at Casablanca, where thirteen French ships had to be sunk and 15,000 Americans and Frenchmen were killed, and at Oran, although not at Algiers, where pro-Allied conspirators seized the town. Hostilities were finally terminated on November 10 as a result of an arrangement made by the American Commander, General Dwight D. Eisenhower, with Admiral Jean François Darlan, commander of the French navy and former Vichy foreign minister. This decision was not popular in England and the United States, but it gave North Africa to the Allied cause and made any recovery by Rommel impossible.

In January 1943, at a conference at Casablanca attended by President Roosevelt, Winston Churchill, and Charles de Gaulle, the Allies announced to the world their intention of fighting on until the "unconditional surrender" of Germany,

Italy, and Japan. Privately, they agreed to intensify their air offensive against Germany and to push on the preparations for a cross-Channel invasion of the continent, to sustain the Soviet Union by providing the greatest possible volume of supplies, to keep the pressure on Japan—but not at the risk of slowing European operations—and, immediately, to start planning an attack on Sicily for the summer of 1943. This last operation conformed more to Winston Churchill's preference for peripheral operations than to the views of the Clausewitzian Americans, who wanted to concentrate all forces for a punch across the Channel. It was decided, however, that the time had not come for the main drive, and that a thrust into Sicily would secure the Mediterranean supply routes, divert German pressure from the Russian front, and knock Italy out of the war.

Hitler meanwhile had been making frantic attempts to hold on to North Africa by pouring reinforcements and supplies into the ports of Tunis and Bizerte. What might have won Cairo in 1941 or saved Rommel in 1942 was not enough to retrieve Axis fortunes in 1943. Rommel's tired forces and the levies flown across to Tunisia managed to mount an offensive in February that hit the inexperienced Americans at the Kasserine Pass and inflicted heavy losses on them. But they recovered from this jab quickly and, in March and April, in conjunction with Montgomery's veterans, they drove Rommel's troops to the tip of Cape Bon peninsula, where a quarter of a million of them finally surrendered in May 1943.

The Fall of Italy   With hardly a pause, the plans laid at Casablanca were carried out. In June aerial and naval bombardment began to soften up Sicily; in July a fleet of 3000 vessels launched the first major amphibious assault on Axis-held territory. Montgomery's Eighth Army and Canadian forces landed on the east coast and took the port of Syracuse. George S. Patton, the most dashing of the American commanders, landed in the south, took Marsala and Palermo, and then linked up with the British and drove the three German divisions to the sea. Here—in an imitation of Dunkirk—they managed to evacuate 60,000 men to the mainland. But Sicily was in Allied hands, after only thirty-nine days of fighting.

These events and the beginning of serious bombing of the Italian mainland (Rome was bombed for the first time on July 19 by 700 Allied planes) brought an abrupt end to the career of the man who had aspired to make the Mediterranean a Roman lake. Mussolini's popularity had long since evaporated. On April 1, 1943, Roberto Farinacci, one of the oldest of the party bosses, wrote to The Duce: "The unbelievable is happening. Everywhere, in the trains, the theaters, the air-raid shelters ... people are denouncing the regime, and not only this or that party figure, but the Duce himself. And the most serious thing is that no one reacts." Farinacci wanted a tightening up of the system and harsh measures against the dissidents. But it was too late for Mussolini to take this kind of advice, for opposition and conspiracy were rife even among his closest supporters. On July 24, 1943, the Fascist Grand Council, which the Duce had easily dominated in the past and which had not even met since 1939, convened itself and demanded that Mussolini hand over command of the army to the king. The next day, the Duce was told by Victor Emmanuel that he no longer desired him as premier. As Mussolini left the palace, he was arrested and interned. Later in the year, he was rescued in a daring coup by German agents and installed as head of a puppet government in the north. But he never regained a popular following and, when the total collapse came, he was captured and brutally murdered by Italian partisans.

Speedy action by the Allies in the days following Mussolini's fall might have brought all Italy into Allied hands. The protracted armistice negotiations that took place between them and the new government of Marshal Pietro Badoglio gave the Germans an opportunity to build up their defenses. Thus, when an armistice was finally signed on September 3, it did nothing to facilitate the Allied landings that began on the same day. The Eighth Army found comparatively little resistance to their landings on the Calabrian coast; but the assault of the U.S. Fifth Army at Salerno in September was met by four days of counterattack, which at times seemed likely to turn the landing into a debacle. This did not happen, but it was clear that the advance northward was not going to be easy.

Stalingrad and the Recoil in Russia   Even before these reversals had taken place, the tide had begun to turn against Hitler in Russia also. In the spring of 1942 he had resumed offensive operations along the whole front and, although he had no success in taking Leningrad or Moscow, his armies had made impressive gains on the southern front. But Russian resistance was hardening daily, partly as a result of American supplies and partly as a result of German behavior toward the Russian people. Alexander Dallin has written that, in the early stages of the Russian war, Germany "had a rare opportunity to appeal to the population of the Soviet Union ... [who were] potentially receptive to a skillful attempt to drive a wedge between the rulers and the people." Hitler failed utterly to take advantage of this. He is reported to have said in July 1941, "Russia is our Africa and the Russians are our Negroes," and he persisted in the years that followed in thinking of the Russian people as objects for enslavement or extermination. Russian prisoners of war, who might have been easily turned against their former masters, were treated with brutality or callous neglect and, by the Germans' own admission, the incredible number of 3,700,000 POW's died in German hands. Civilian populations were exploited or killed or turned over to the mercies of addlepates like Alfred Rosenberg or sadists like Erich Koch, the German commissar for the Ukraine, whom Stalin once described as "the chief of those blockheads in Berlin who reminded every man in the Soviet Union every day of what he had to fight against." German brutality, political obtuseness, and administrative inefficiency deprived them of the support of subject populations, the economic reserves that would have fed their war effort, and the aid of trained soldiers eager to change sides, and gave them, instead, the problem of coping with an aggressive and massive partisan movement that operated behind their lines.

As Hitler's difficulties in Russia mounted, he became increasingly suspicious of his generals, and his prejudice against operational flexibility and maneuver, his lack of sympathy for the troops, and his proneness to self-deception became dangerous. Nothing illustrates these qualities more strikingly than his conduct during the battle of Stalingrad. In August 1942 the German Sixth Army under General von Paulus reached and invested this industrial center on the west bank of the Volga and proceeded to attempt to pound it into submission. Despite the difficulty of keeping the city supplied (all food, clothing, and munitions had to be ferried across the river under German bombardment), the Soviet troops and the citizens of the city held out in the rubble of their homes, and were still holding out at the end of the year.

By this time, Hitler had set his heart on the capture of the city. On November 9 he said publicly:

> I wanted to get to the Volga and to do so at a particular point where stands a certain town. By chance it bears the name of Stalin himself. I wanted to take the place and, do you know, we've pulled it off, we've got it really, except for a few enemy positions still holding out.

Ten days after this speech the Russians smashed the front held by Germany's Rumanian ally northwest of Stalingrad; on November 20 they launched a successful attack south of the city, and, two days later, they closed the pincers and encircled the German forces (see map, p. 677).

One of General von Paulus' subordinates wrote at this time: "To remain where we are deliberately is not only a crime from a military point of view, but it is a criminal act as regards our responsibility to the German nation." It was nevertheless a crime insisted upon by Hitler, who flatly refused to countenance a break-out (which would have involved leaving the Volga and the city bearing Stalin's name) and who entrusted Goering with the task of keeping the Sixth Army supplied. Goering expressed every confidence in the *Luftwaffe's* ability to fulfill this mission; in fact, as any airman of competence could have seen, it was impossible. Yet, as his soldiers fought and starved and died, and as the Russian ring became so thick and strong that a break-in or a break-out was impossible, Hitler remained adamantly opposed to any withdrawal. But human resistance has limits. Paulus had begun the siege with 300,000 men. In the first days of February 1943, their ragged remnants, 123,000 officers and men, surrendered. Germany had suffered its greatest defeat as a result of the deliberate and callous indifference of its ruler to the fate of its sons.

In the same month in which the Sixth Army died, the Russians recaptured Rostov, Kursk, and Kharkov and, before their momentum slowed, they had won back 185,000 square miles of territory. The German offensive of 1943 was an attempt to regain this lost ground, and it failed badly. The fact was that the days of conquest in Russia were over. By the end of 1943 the Russians were back in Kiev (where the Germans had slaughtered the entire Jewish population before evacuation) and in Zhitomir, close to the old border of Poland.

THE ROAD TO VICTORY, 1943–1945

Problems of the Coalition   Once their armies had begun to press the Germans back, the Soviets became more difficult partners than they had been. Not that they had ever been the most comfortable of allies, for, conscious of the fact that their armies were carrying the brunt of the fighting on land, they had always been demanding in the matter of supplies and less than grateful when

Allied seamen braved the perils of the Murmansk passage to bring them. Moreover, they had kept up a drumfire of criticism against Allied failure to provide a second front in Europe—exasperating Churchill on one occasion into asking where they had been when the Allied front had borne the full weight of German aggression in 1940, and on another, when his ambassador in Moscow had supported the Russian request for a "superhuman effort" in the west, to reply tartly: "When you speak of a 'superhuman effort' you mean, I presume, an effort rising superior to space, time, and geography. Unfortunately, such attributes are denied us."

The Allied statesmen were for the most part, however, patient in the face of these attacks and tried to explain their own difficulties and to show their gratitude by the volume of their supplies. There was never any disposition on their part to undervalue the Soviet contribution to the war or the indispensability of Soviet cooperation in rebuilding the international system when the war was over. On the whole, their tactics seemed to work. In October 1943 the British foreign secretary, Anthony Eden, and the United States secretary of state, Cordell Hull, traveled to Moscow to hold talks with their opposite number, Molotov. After meeting Stalin, Eden noted that there was no recrimination about the past and that Stalin seemed to understand that the Allies were bending all their efforts toward an invasion of the continent, adding that "the confidence he is placing in our word is most striking." The talks ended with a pledge of joint action to defeat, disarm, and control Germany, to free Italy of fascism, to liberate Austria from its forced union with Germany, and to punish all Germans guilty of atrocities. With respect to the long future, the foreign secretaries spoke of the possibility of establishing a world organization.

All these pledges were reaffirmed in December 1943 at Teheran, where Roosevelt, Churchill, and Stalin had their first joint meeting. There the determination to establish a world organization with membership from all nations dedicated to peace was expressed more emphatically. Indeed, in the following year, at Dumbarton Oaks, Virginia, representatives of the three Allied powers and China held talks in an attempt to make more precise the nature and purpose of what was eventually to become the United Nations.

The Soviet Union's collaboration in these talks was gratifying. Less so was its growing interest in the postwar disposition of European territory. As in World War I, the Western powers had a tendency to wish to push political questions into the backs of their minds until the war was won. Not so the Russians, to whom war and peace were reverse sides of the same coin. As early as 1943, Stalin was evincing a desire to discuss the future eastern frontiers of Poland with some responsible Polish authority, an indication that he had his mind set on acquiring the eastern districts. And, as his troops advanced further, his interest in both the Baltic and those Balkan states that had fought on Hitler's side also began to awaken. There were obvious signs of future trouble here, although Allied statesmen tried very hard not to see them.

Italy from Salerno to the Fall of Rome   The year 1944 was one long slugging match in Italy with heavy Allied casualties. Attempts to restore the operational mobility that had been lost by the delay before Salerno were frustrated by the terrain and by the tenacity of the defense organized by the German supreme commander in Italy, Marshal Kesselring. Kesselring slowed the double-pronged advance of the British Eighth Army and the U.S. Fifth Army of General Mark Clark by building a strong defensive position called the Gustav Line, which had as its center the 1700-foot Monte Cassino, and which blocked the road through the Liri valley to Rome. To outflank the Gustav Line, the Allies on January 22, 1944, made another amphibious landing at Anzio on the coast 33 miles south of Rome. This met the most stubborn kind of German resistance, and the G.I.'s were pinned to the beaches and the adjoining slopes for four months before a break-out was effected.

To reduce pressure upon them, Clark had launched an attack across the Rapido River in front of Cassino at the time of the original landing. This was nothing short of disastrous and temporarily destroyed the 36th (Texas) Division as a fighting force. In February, another attempt was made to draw the Germans away from Anzio, when Cassino was assaulted by the 2d New Zealand and the 4th Indian divisions. It was during this second battle that the decision was made to bomb the Benedictine abbey on Monte Cassino, a decision that was subsequently much criticized in Allied countries and was heavily exploited by German propaganda agencies. To the troops on the spot this controversy would have meant nothing. They were sure that the Germans were using the abbey for observation purposes and expected and wanted the bombardment to be made. Unfortunately, when it came, it was not coordinated with a ground attack and served no useful purpose.

Cassino finally fell in April in a battle that might have been a masterpiece. Planned by Field Marshal Alexander, the supreme Allied commander in Italy, it was designed to smother Cassino by numbers and, at the same time, to suck in, encircle, and destroy the bulk of the German forces in Italy. It was preceded by diversionary amphibious feints and was then delivered with a massive force that effected its first objective and might have justified all the bloodshed and sacrifice that had gone before, if it had only been properly coordinated with the simultaneous break-out from Anzio. But at the very moment when Alexander's trap was closing on the out-generaled and broken Germans, General Clark detached his forces from the pursuit and sent them racing toward Rome. His desire to be first in the Eternal City prevented the destruction of the German Tenth Army.

This rather took the bloom off the triumphal entry into Rome in June, for it meant that fighting had to continue. When, a little later, seven Allied divisions were withdrawn from Italy to support the Normandy invasion by a landing in southern France, the prospects of an early end to the Italian war vanished completely.

Cross-Channel Attack   In the first days of June 1944, the BBC transmitters beamed to the forces of the French resistance the prearranged signal that indicated the start of the long-awaited invasion of France. They had chosen for the purpose two lines from Verlaine's *Chanson d'Automne*:

> *Les sanglots longs des violons de l'automne*
> *Blessent mon coeur d'une langueur monotone.*

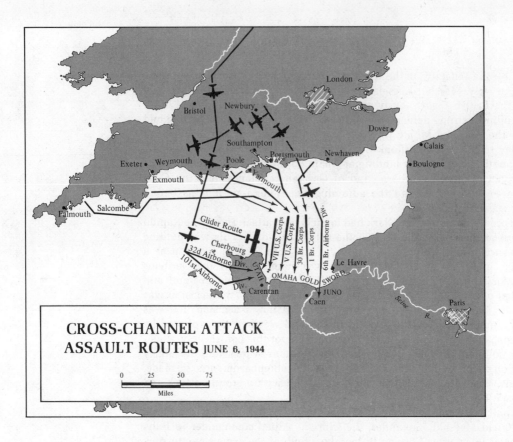

**CROSS-CHANNEL ATTACK
ASSAULT ROUTES** JUNE 6, 1944

In view of the violence that was to follow, one can hardly imagine more inappropriate words.

The preparations for Operation Overlord had been going on since 1942, and the forces that had been assembled constituted the greatest amphibious force in history. More than five thousand ships and landing craft were waiting to transport 150,000 trained men, 1500 tanks, and thousands of guns, vehicles, and supplies to the Normandy coast. They were supported by 12,000 planes, some of which had been systematically destroying bridges and access routes in order to seal off the invasion area from the interior, while others—transports and gliders—prepared to drop paratroopers and demolition teams well behind the beaches in order to complete that job. To facilitate constant supply for this immense host until such time as a major port could be seized, artificial breakwaters and docks—the so-called Mulberries—had been built in England and were ready to be towed across the Channel and installed along the beaches. D-Day was June 6.

Throughout the spring months, Field Marshal Rommel, brought to the west from Italy, had been applying his energies to the gigantic task of preparing for the blow that he knew was coming. He was confronted with a hopeless task. Hitler, with complete scorn for strategical principles, was insisting that every foot of land be held—in Russia, in Italy, in France—and his rigidity not only made tactical mobility impossible but deprived the western commanders of adequate forces with which to oppose the Allied thrust. As Rommel's chief of staff wrote later, the much advertised Atlantic Wall was "in its manning and armaments . . . no more than a thin line without depth or substantial reserves." Rommel did his best to improve the beach defenses by increasing the number of strong points and building elaborate underwater obstacles. But the Germans had no naval forces to help in repulsing a landing and, by this time, their air force had been shot out of the skies. And, as if this were not enough, the commanders in the west were constantly bedeviled by an incredible chain of command that left the power of decision, even in tactical matters, in the hands of the Fuehrer in Berlin.

All of these weaknesses played into the hands of the Allies when Overlord began and British and American forces poured onto the selected beaches between Caen and the Cherbourg peninsula on the Normandy coast. There was heavy initial resistance, especially on Omaha Beach where the U.S. 29th Division was pinned down by murderous fire, but there was no repetition of Anzio. Within five days the German defensive ring was broken. The Canadians and the British on the left were headed for Caen; the defenses on Omaha had been knocked out by aerial and naval bombardment; and the U.S. First Army was moving

American troops landing on Omaha Beach under heavy fire, June 6, 1944. (Official Coast Guard Photo)

inland. The sixteen Allied divisions had established a beachhead eighty miles long and twenty miles deep. By D-Day plus twenty, a million men were ashore; more were pouring in over the Mulberries near the British beach at Arromanches; and the German garrison in the great port of Cherbourg was preparing to surrender.

The Plot against Hitler   On July 20, 1944, at approximately 12:30 in the afternoon, Colonel Count Claus Schenk von Stauffenberg entered Hitler's conference hall at Rastenburg, while the Fuehrer and his staff were listening to a situation report, slid his briefcase under the table, and unobtrusively left the room. Five minutes later there was a terrific explosion. The windows of the wooden building were blown out, the roof partially collapsed, there was the sound of men screaming. Stauffenberg, standing at a safe distance outside, climbed quickly into a staff car and drove off to the airstrip, where a plane was waiting to take him to Berlin.

His action was the end result of years of planning and debate by a German underground that reached into every class of society and had as its leaders Prussian aristocrats, high-ranking civil servants, Socialist politicians and trade-union leaders, ministers of the gospel, diplomats, university teachers, and soldiers. Some of them had already died because of their participation in the conspiracy; some had risked their lives in attempts on Hitler's life that had failed; all were, by the middle of 1944, in great danger, for the Gestapo was, at long last, closing in on them. But their plans were ready. Hitler was to be killed; military authorities in Berlin and Paris were to seize power, arrest the other Nazi notables, set up a provisional government with General Ludwig Beck as head of state, and open negotiations with the western Allies. Stauffenberg's bomb was the first step in the chain of events that was supposed to lead to liberation from both tyranny and war.

But the bomb did not kill Hitler, and the news that it had not done so, relayed

Germans who died because of their resistance to Hitler. A series of stamps issued by the Federal Republic of Germany on the twentieth anniversary of the attempt on Hitler's life at Rastenburg.

quickly to Berlin, paralyzed the plotters with indecision and persuaded some of the troop commanders upon whom they had been counting to attempt to withdraw from the enterprise. These delays and hesitations were adroitly exploited by Joseph Goebbels in Berlin in such a way as to reassert Hitler's authority. The conspiracy collapsed; its leaders were arrested; and the immediate result was a series of ghastly public trials followed by the degradation and butchery of all who were suspected of complicity in the plot. July 20 had no effect on the course of the war. But it was a reminder that not all Germans were Nazis by conviction and that, in addition to the "other Germany" in exile, there had been an "inner emigration" into which those whose consciences had been revolted by Hitler's acts had withdrawn, not merely to ride out the storm but, in a great many cases, to risk their lives in making plans for the liberation of their country. The Bonn government annually commemorates this plot that failed, and it is just that it should do so.

The End of Nazi Germany   Speaking to his generals after the failure of the conspiracy, Hitler said:

> We'll fight until we get a peace that secures the life of the German nation for the next fifty or a hundred years.... If my life had been ended, I think I can say that for me personally it would only have been a release from worry, sleepless nights, and a great nervous suffering.... Just the same, I am grateful to destiny for letting me live, because I believe.

Uttered at a time when the Allied armies, spearheaded by Patton's tanks, were pouring through the gap at Avranches and beginning the sweep toward the Rhine, when the second Allied landing—this time on the southern coast of France between Toulon and Cannes—was only days away, when the RAF bomber command was dropping 25,000 tons of bombs nightly on German cities, and when Russian armies were pushing from Riga into East Prussia, encircling Warsaw, and approaching Bucharest, the Fuehrer's words might be taken only as a proof of deepening megalomania. What was there, after all, for him to believe in?

Hitler's conviction that he would win his war rested in part on faith in himself, on the belief that, somehow or other, like a second Frederick the Great, he would extricate himself from his difficulties by sheer force of will. But it is clear also that he was relying on two other things: upon new and more dreadful secret weapons and, most of all, upon a sudden dissolution of the coalition that opposed him. "Do you think," he said to his staff in January 1945, "that, deep down inside, the English are enthusiastic about all the Russian developments?"; and Goering answered comfortably, "They certainly didn't plan that we hold them off while the Russians conquer all of Germany. If this goes on, we will get a telegram in a few days."

Hitler's faith in this sort of resolution of his problem was disappointed. His scientists did invent wonder weapons, the most impressive of which was the V-2, a liquid-fuel rocket of about twelve tons take-off weight capable of carrying a one-ton warhead approximately 200 miles from its launching point. If the V-2 had been operational before D-Day, the Normandy invasion would have been

The Grand Alliance: Churchill, Roosevelt, and Stalin at Yalta in the Crimea, February 1945.
(United Press International)

infinitely more difficult. As it was, it came into use only in September 1944 and, although the Germans launched 1500 V-2s against England and 2100 against Antwerp, the swift advance of the Allies soon made it unusable. Other weapons—the jet plane, for instance—came too late to save Germany.

Nor was the dissolution of the enemy coalition to take place, at least until the war was over. At the very moment when Goering was talking about telegrams from London, the British and the Americans were preparing for their meeting with the Russians at Yalta in the Crimea, which took place in the first part of February 1945. Here Roosevelt, Churchill, and Stalin, in an atmosphere of cordiality, agreed upon the postwar control of Germany and the division of that potentially conquered country into zones of occupation. They also concluded agreements concerning the future world organization (setting April 25, 1945, as the date for a conference in San Francisco to begin the drafting of a charter), the postwar organization of eastern Europe, and the common pursuit of the war against Japan. In the course of these discussions, it was apparent that there were deep differences of view among the Allies, especially with regard to the boundaries and the government of postwar Poland, but these were overcome by Allied concessions to the Soviet point of view, granted in order to secure Soviet participation in the war against Japan. Nothing that was done at Yalta brought any comfort or hope to Hitler.

Moreover, the will of the German soldier was now broken. On the eastern front, it had been worn down by time, weather, and the relentless pressure of the Russian armies. In the west, the last flicker of hope and combativeness was snuffed out by the failure of the German offensive in the Ardennes at the end of 1944. This battle—known best in the west as the Battle of the Bulge—was a last desperate throw by Hitler, an attempt to crack the American lines by surprise, which would permit the German armor to cross the Meuse between Liège and Namur and to drive toward Antwerp. If this was accomplished, the supply and communications lines of Allied forces in the Brussels-Antwerp area could be cut, twenty-five to thirty Allied divisions could be destroyed and an Allied offensive against the West Wall could be delayed indefinitely. These hopes

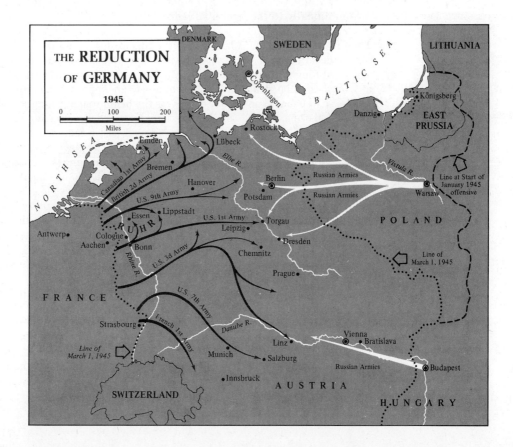

were not realized, although, for some days during the dark December of 1944, it appeared that they might be. The brunt of this last German punch fell on a thinly held sector of the American lines, manned by green troops, at a time when the reserve and supply system was muddled and weather was making air support impossible. The initial effect was shattering; confusion and panic reigned for days and as late as the beginning of January the issue was in doubt. In the battle around Bastogne, some battalions of the U.S. 17th Airborne Division suffered 40 percent casualties; and George Patton wrote, "We can still lose this war." But by the middle of the month, it was all over and the Germans never recovered. Now it was just a matter of time before the Allied victory was made final.

In March and April, Russian armies under Marshals Zhukov and Konev took Danzig and Vienna, overran Czechoslovakia, and pressed on toward Berlin. On March 7, by a stroke of luck, American forces seized the bridge over the Rhine at Remagen before it could be destroyed and upset the whole German defensive system along the river. In Italy, Allied forces took Bologna and crossed the Po. Mussolini, fleeing for safety, was caught and killed with his mistress on April 28 by Italian partisans. Hitler shot himself and his bride of one day in a bunker in Berlin on April 30. Three days earlier the western armies and the Russians had made their first contact in Saxony. On May 2 Berlin fell to the Russians. On May 7, the Third Reich, in the person of Admiral Karl Doenitz, surrendered unconditionally to the Grand Alliance.

The End of Japan   Victory over the remaining enemy was not long delayed. Since the latter part of 1943, the Allies had tightened the ring around Japan. The hard-fought victory of the U.S. Marines at Tarawa in November 1943, where, at a cost of 1100 dead and 2072 wounded, an apparently impregnable island fortress had been taken in four days, was the beginning of a long series of brilliant amphibious operations, which were characterized by amazing coordination of ground, naval, and aerial operations, as well as by the speed and economy of effort employed. Here the war attained its greatest degree of mobility, as the U.S. navy carried army and marine forces long distances, bypassing Japanese strong points and allowing them to die of inactivity, hitting at places where attack was not expected, and advancing by tremendous strides toward the very heart of the Japanese empire. Kwajalein was seized in January 1944 and with it control over the Marshalls; Eniwetok fell in February; in the same month the great Japanese naval base at Truk was pounded into helplessness; in June and July, Saipan and Tinian fell to marine and army forces; in July, American troops landed on Guam; in September, Pelelieu was in American hands, eliminating a threat to General MacArthur's flank as he now crossed, after a remarkable advance up the coast of New Guinea, to Leyte in the Philippines; in October, the great naval battle of the Leyte Gulf finished what was left of the offensive capabilities of the Japanese navy; in January 1945, MacArthur invaded Luzon; in February, in an epic battle, the Marines took Iwo Jima and provided an essential refueling base for B-29s returning from bomb runs on Tokyo; in April, the great island of Okinawa was invaded and systematically conquered by U.S. army and marine troops. Only by tracing this progress of American arms on a map of the Pacific can one appreciate the magnitude of the accomplishment.

Plans were now made for the invasion of the Japanese homeland, which was thought of in terms of simultaneous landings on the island of Kyushu and on the Tokyo plain. Considering the fanatical resistance shown by Japanese fighting men on Saipan and Iwo Jima and the suicide missions of Japanese pilots at Okinawa, the bitterest kind of resistance was expected. Even the prospective entrance of the Soviet Union into the war, which, it was hoped, would bottle up Japan's Manchurian armies, would not prevent serious casualties to the invading forces, which were expected to run as high as half a million men.

It was this calculation that led to the hard decision to use against Japan the weapon that had been devised by American and European scientists working in the United States since 1942. This was the atomic bomb, first successfully tested at Alamogordo Flats, New Mexico, in July 1945. Convinced that no mere warning would be effective in persuading the Japanese government to surrender and fearing the effects of an announced demonstration that might fail, the U.S. government (now headed by Harry S. Truman), backed by its Allies, decided that this terrible weapon must be used against Japanese cities. On August 6, 1945, two days before Russia declared war on Japan, the first atomic bomb was dropped on the city of Hiroshima, destroying the city and killing 78,000 people. On August 9 the second bomb was dropped, this time on Nagasaki in Kyushu, demolishing the torpedo yards and the great steel mill for which the town was noted, destroying the whole municipal area, and killing tens of thousands of people. On the following day, the Japanese government surrendered. The global war was over, although the formal armistice was not signed until September 2.

PART FIVE

SINCE 1945

GENERAL OBSERVATIONS

In March 1944, the Italian philosopher Benedetto Croce wrote in his diary: "We must not expect the rebirth of that world [the pre-1914 world], its revival and improvement, but we must expect an interminable sequence of clashes, and upsets and ruin due to revolutions and wars. . . . We must . . . get accustomed to living a life without stability . . . so repugnant to us who were men who labored, who set ourselves well-thought-out programs and carried them calmly through. Upon this scene, faltering at every step, we must do the best we can to live with dignity. . . ."

The pessimism that sounds through these lines was doubtless shared by the majority of reflective Europeans at the end of World War II, and certainly Croce's prognostications were proven correct in the first postwar years. For every member of the European community, these were times of political conflict and social and economic dislocation; and the problems of the individual parts were enormously complicated by the fact that the continent as a whole was sundered into two halves, separated by an institutional and ideological barrier.

The imposition of a vast dualism upon Europe was the result of the fact that the dissolution of the Allied wartime coalition for which Hitler had longed in vain finally took place. After three years, Western statesmen were forced to admit that the fellowship in arms that had led to the defeat of Germany and Japan was not going to be prolonged and that, far from wishing to promote the economic and political recovery of the war-shattered European countries, the Soviet Union was hoping to exploit misery and want in order to spread communism to the West. The Truman Doctrine, the Marshall Plan, and the establishment of the North Atlantic Treaty Organization were successive responses to what had become an obvious threat to the political freedom of Europe; the Warsaw Pact was the Soviet rejoinder, which indicated that the Soviet Union had no intention of relinquishing the control that it had won over the states of eastern Europe in the first postwar years, and which thus completed the establishment of what came to be known as the Iron Curtain, dividing the continent in two.

On the eastern side of this barrier, the presence of Soviet military power enforced ideological and institutional conformity and political and economic cooperation on the part of the lesser states. Yugoslavia alone succeeded in breaking away from the iron grip of this system and establishing an independent position, and this was largely due to accidents of geography. Hungary's attempt in 1956 to imitate its southern neighbor was crushed by Soviet armor; Czechoslovakia's hope of modifying the rigors of totalitarianism in 1968 was also frustrated by determined Soviet intervention.

Examples of centralization and unity of policy accomplished by the use or threat of force have not been infrequent in history and are never particularly impressive. A more notable postwar political development was the voluntary movement toward unification on the western side of the curtain. This, as we shall see below (p. 765), took various forms and involved grappling with many difficult problems; but, in view of the historical disinclination of the European states to any sacrifice of their sovereignty, its results were impressive.

While these developments were taking place, Europe's influence in world affairs suffered a radical diminution. This process had, to be sure, begun during the war of 1914–1918 and had been accelerated by the economic ills of the interwar period. Yet, until the outbreak of the second global conflict, Europe remained the center of world politics, and the decisions of the European powers determined the course of events in far-flung regions of the world. The long hard years that stretched from the Nazi capture of Warsaw to Hitler's suicide amid the rubble of Berlin changed all this in a fundamental way. They inflicted upon all European powers material and psychological damage so great that the resources necessary for their full political recovery were eaten up and even their desire for such recovery was exhausted. When the war was over, there was a tendency for some Europeans to view the transfer of power and responsibility to the United States and the Soviet Union with a resignation that was tinged with fear but also with satisfaction. Thus, *Punch* wryly discussed the positive advantages that might accrue from becoming a state of second, or even third, rank.

The changed position of the European states in the world was thrown into sharper relief by the loss of their colonial empires as a result of nationalistic movements in the Orient, the Near East, and Africa. These movements too had existed before the war, but they had been greatly encouraged by that conflict's demonstration in its first stages that white nations are not necessarily superior in military skill to peoples of different pigmentation. Postwar illustrations of this same truth, in Korea and Indochina, stimulated opposition to colonialism and forced concessions to it in British, French, Dutch, and Belgian dependencies. Once the process of liberation had started, it proceeded with a rush that defied all wartime expectations. By the end of

1965, African and Asian nations, most of which had won their independence after 1945, made up more than half of the membership of the Assembly of the United Nations—an organization, incidentally, that the European nations had learned, because of their reduced strength in comparison with the United States and the Soviet Union and for other reasons, to take more seriously than they had taken the League of Nations.

In the economic field, the postwar period began with the most dismal prospects for Europe as a whole. Trade was at a standstill; industry was paralyzed by wartime destruction and shortages of raw materials and fuel; agriculture was suffering from the lack of machinery, seed, and fertilizer; transportation and communications systems had been disrupted and in some cases largely destroyed by bombing; markets and distribution systems were hopelessly confused by the destruction of the Nazi empire, which had embraced most of the continent for five years; currencies were depreciated and credit facilities uncertain; food and fuel stocks were inadequate and promised to become dangerously so in the near future; and all problems were made doubly difficult by the demobilization of the armies and by the existence of millions of displaced persons who lacked the very necessities of life.

The recovery from these conditions was slower in eastern Europe than in the west, largely because the eastern countries had to defer in all basic matters to the Soviet Union and were denied opportunities open to the western countries, and also because their patron, suffering terrible physical and economic damage from the war, was in no position in the first postwar years to extend material aid to them. Yet even in Poland, where 38 percent of the country's wealth had been destroyed, as well as 85 percent of the city of Warsaw and 50 percent of the port installations of Gdynia and Gdánsk, and where all problems were complicated by the great postwar shifts of territory and population, recovery was steady; and in other parts of eastern Europe this was even more so. By the 1960s Western visitors to Budapest and Bucharest, while still conscious of the relative lack of consumers' goods, were likely to be impressed by the appearance of the cities and their inhabitants.

Progress in western Europe had been somewhat easier, since it was encouraged by loans from the United States; and assistance of other kinds increased after the implementation of the Marshall Plan in 1948. Once resumed, the economic development of the West was spectacular compared with the interwar period. Within a decade, the production of some countries reached three times the volume attained in the peak year of 1913; and this growth went hand in hand with increased personal income for all social groups, so that, in almost all countries, the real wages of industrial workers were double the prewar figure. Exactly how much the movement toward economic federation contributed to this would be hard to assess, just as it would be difficult to estimate how it was affected by the loss of Europe's overseas empires. In this last respect, it is worth noting, however, that living standards in both Belgium and the Netherlands rose after the loss of their colonies, which may indicate that managerial talent and technical skill are more important resources than Lenin supposed when he was writing his book on imperialism.

The economic recovery on both sides of the Iron Curtain and the relaxation of tension between Europe's two halves at the beginning of the 1960s were reflected in a growth of self-confidence that had some interesting political results. In western Europe, it caused a deceleration in the progress toward political union and the beginnings, in some countries, of a revival of nationalism. In eastern Europe also there was a loosening of the monolithic unity of earlier days and some manifestation of a desire not only for greater independence but also for closer contacts with the west. Among western intellectuals, there was much talk now of "a New Europe," and some of those who used the term were thinking less of the kind of political union that had been the objective of men like Robert Schumann, Alcide de Gasperi, and Konrad Adenauer than they were of the possibility, voiced by Charles de Gaulle, of a Europe of free fatherlands stretching all the way to the Urals.

About intellectual and cultural tendencies something will be said in the next chapter. It must be emphasized here, however, that these could not help but be affected by the division of Europe. The Iron Curtain represented a barrier to the free exchange of ideas, to mutual stimulation, and to scholarly and scientific collaboration that was extremely difficult to surmount. Not since the religious wars of the sixteenth century had two parts of Europe been so effectively sealed off from each other, and it was impossible to calculate the extent to which this hampered Europe's spiritual recovery from the war.

Yet barriers always seem to represent a challenge to human beings, and as the postwar years passed, there were many free spirits who labored to break down the physical and intellectual walls that divided mankind. This was nowhere more evident than in the field of established religion, where the suffering caused by World War II inspired a new spirit of tolerance and openness, which was reflected in a vigorous ecumenical movement and a new emphasis upon the churches' duty to work for international peace. The German Evangelical Church called upon its congregations to face up to their responsibility for the crimes committed during the war in the name of Germany and, by doing so, to take the first step toward atonement and reconciliation. The Roman Catholic church made an equally positive response to the daunting problems of the age. In his brief but inspiring pontificate, Pope John XXIII, a man of the people who instinctively sensed the yearning of the masses, urged the leaders of his faith, gathered together in the Second Vatican Council, to find formulations and programs that would be effective in the contemporary world and to bring Christians together in a socially creative brotherhood. His successor, Paul VI, typified the new spirit by becoming the first traveling pope of modern times, making unprecedented journeys to Jerusalem and India, in order to consult with leaders of his own and other churches. In October 1965, he flew to United Nations headquarters in New York, where he told the assembled delegates that their vocation was "to make brothers not only of some but of all peoples. . . . No more war! War never again! It is peace that must guide the destinies of all peoples and of all mankind!"

Chapter 29 THE RECONSTRUCTION AND THE EVOLUTION OF THE EUROPEAN STATES, 1945–1970

The Peace Treaties   As if recognizing that the transition from war to peace would be even more difficult than it had proved to be after World War I, the victorious powers made no attempt to hold a general peace conference. The territorial settlement was worked out on a piecemeal basis in many conferences and negotiations, some of which were successful in short order, while others finished their work, if they finished it at all, only after years of meetings. Twenty years after the cessation of hostilities against the Axis powers, the boundaries of a large part of Europe were still, from a legal point of view, mere *ad hoc* arrangements, without treaty sanction.

This was true, for example, of Germany. The general principles of a postwar settlement for Germany had been agreed upon by the Allies during the war, although they soon broke down in practice. With respect to territory, it had been decided at Yalta in February 1945 (see p. 694) that Germany would be deprived of certain of its eastern provinces, which would go to the Soviet Union and to Poland; and, at the Potsdam Conference of July and August 1945, Stalin, President Truman of the United States, and the new British prime minister, Clement Attlee, had defined the Polish grant as comprising the lands east of the Oder and Neisse rivers, the southern part of East Prussia (the rest of which went to the Soviet Union), and the former free city of Danzig. But there were

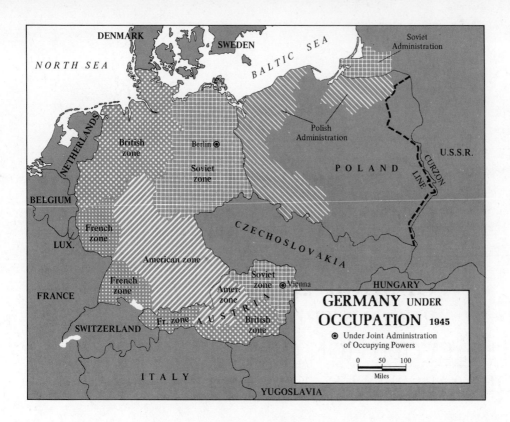

Labels on map: DENMARK, SWEDEN, NORTH SEA, BALTIC SEA, Soviet Administration, Polish Administration, British zone, Berlin, Soviet zone, POLAND, U.S.S.R., CURZON LINE, NETHERLANDS, BELGIUM, LUX., CZECHOSLOVAKIA, American zone, French zone, French zone, FRANCE, SWITZERLAND, Soviet zone, Vienna, Amer. zone, AUSTRIA, Fr. zone, British zone, HUNGARY, ITALY, YUGOSLAVIA

GERMANY UNDER
OCCUPATION 1945
⊙ Under Joint Administration of Occupying Powers
0   50   100
Miles

subsequent differences even on this aspect of the German settlement, for the Western powers insisted that the grant was provisional and could not be considered otherwise until it was legitimized by a formal German treaty. The Poles, who regarded their gains as compensation for the provinces west of the old Curzon Line (see p. 525), which they had had to cede to the Soviet Union, took the Potsdam grant to be definitive and, with Soviet backing, proceeded to act accordingly.

The decision to punish the German leaders who were guilty of crimes of aggression and of crimes against humanity, which had led to the death of six million people in countries occupied by Germany, aroused no great conflicts of view. In November 1945, an Inter-Allied Tribunal began the trials of the major war criminals. These lasted for over a year and led to the conviction of twenty-two defendants and the sentencing of eleven to death: Goering (who escaped execution by committing suicide), Rosenberg, Ribbentrop, Streicher, Seyss-Inquart, Frick, Frank, Kaltenbrunner, Sauckel, and Generals Keitel and Jodl. Aside from this, however, the Allies were soon divided on all aspects of their German policy.

In accordance with decisions reached as early as 1943 and made more precise at Yalta, the conquered country was divided into four zones, to be occupied and administered by Great Britain, France, the Soviet Union, and the United States. Berlin, lying well within the Soviet zone, was also divided into four zones; and an Allied Control Council, composed of four military commanders-in-chief with supreme authority, was established to direct affairs in the almost demolished capital. The basic assumption was that the occupying powers would carry out a rigorous policy of de-Nazification, demilitarization, dismantling of war industries, and re-education; that reparations would be paid by Germany in the form of capital equipment and external assets; but that, after the process of expiation and rehabilitation was reasonably complete, Germany would be reunited and its rights of sovereignty restored.

This system of four-power control was put into effect, but difficulties arose almost immediately. They were caused in the first instance by Soviet insistence upon taking reparations out of the current production rather than from assets. To the United States government, which had by this time recovered from the romantic wartime notion that Germany could be forcibly transformed into a purely agrarian state, and to the other Western powers, who had a more intimate knowledge of the interdependence of European national economics, Soviet policy seemed designed to prevent German recovery and, by spreading general economic depression, to promote communism. This impression was strengthened by the Soviet refusal to abide by its promise to share food stocks from its zone in return for reparations from the three others. Western protests were answered by Soviet demands for new rights—a share in the control of the Ruhr industrial area, for example—and conferences of the foreign ministers at Paris and Moscow in 1946 and 1947 proved powerless to solve the growing dispute.

"Down Barriers in Germany (August 1, 1946)." A cartoon by David Low on the fusion of the Western zones. (From *Low's Cartoon History,* Simon & Schuster, New York, 1953)

By 1948 the pretense of following a common policy was abandoned. To check growing economic distress, the Western powers introduced a currency reform in their zones that had the effect of creating two economic systems in the country. The Soviet government had already made it clear, however, that it would follow an independent economic line in its zone and, in June 1948, by cutting off access by land to the western sectors of Berlin, it showed that its ambitions went beyond the economic sphere. The Berlin blockade was defeated by an Anglo-American airlift that kept the western part of the city supplied until the Soviet Union lifted the restrictions in May 1949. Before that happened, the western powers decided to take steps to effect an economic and political fusion of their zones and to encourage the creation of an autonomous German government in the united territory, and the Soviet government had sponsored a People's Congress in Berlin to start the drafting of a constitution for eastern Germany. By the end of 1949, Hitler's Reich was divided into two Germanies, protected by rival power blocs, although the semblance of four-power control was maintained and a definitive German settlement continued to be a subject for negotiation.

Meanwhile, more progress had been made toward liquidating the state of war that existed between the Allies on the one hand and Italy and the other Axis satellite states on the other. Meetings of the foreign ministers in London and Paris in 1946 and 1947 laid the basis for a peace conference in the latter capital in July-September 1947, which succeeded in drawing up treaties with Italy, Bulgaria, Hungary, Rumania, and Finland. The treaty that posed most difficulties was the Italian one because of a long-standing Allied dispute over the future of Trieste and the thorny questions raised by the necessity of disposing of Mussolini's colonial empire. In the end, Italy was required to cede most of Venezia Giulia to Yugoslavia, including the scene of D'Annunzio's exploits, the port of Fiume (see p. 540). Trieste was made a free city under the supervision and guarantee of the U.N.'s Security Council (see p. 760) until 1954, when a compromise was reached between Italy, which regained the port city, and Yugoslavia, which acquired the surrounding territory.

The settlement of 1947 required Italy to pay $360,000,000 in reparations, to surrender the remains of its navy to the Allies, and to cede some coastal islands in the Adriatic to Albania, the Dodecanese Islands to Greece, and some trifling areas along its western frontier to France. The empire of Abyssinia, reconquered from the Duce by British troops in 1941 (see p. 672), had its independence confirmed, while Libya, Eritrea, and Somaliland, after remaining for another year in the hands of their British conquerors, were handed over to U.N. supervision.

Finland, which had made itself useful to German aims during the war, now paid for that with the loss to the Soviet Union of the northernmost province of Petsamo, some territory on the central Finnish-Soviet border, most of the Karelian peninsula, including Viborg, and (by fifty-year lease) a naval base in the Gulf of Finland, which the Russians subsequently abandoned. The other Axis satellites suffered in various degrees. Hungary was forced to cede territory to Czechoslovakia and to surrender Northern Transylvania to Rumania, which, in turn, had (as in 1940) to hand Northern Bessarabia and Bukovina over to the Soviet Union and Southern Dobrudja over to Bulgaria. The last-named state had no territorial losses but, like its neighbors, had to pay reparations to the victorious powers[1] and to submit to the reduction and control of its armed forces. All of these states, including Italy, had to guarantee human rights and fundamental freedoms to their peoples, to bring war criminals to trial, and (most significant, since it provided an excuse for subsequent Soviet attacks upon independent governments in eastern Europe) to agree to dissolve Fascist organizations and to keep Fascist elements out of public life.

Another significant feature of these treaties was that, while they provided for the withdrawal of Allied troops ninety days after they were ratified, the Soviet Union was given the right to maintain forces in Rumania and Hungary, on the grounds that they were necessary to make secure Soviet lines of communication to Austria, where the USSR had continued occupation duties. As in the case of the Polish acquisition of the Oder-Neisse lands, the Soviets came to regard the provisional grant as definitive and did not withdraw their troops after the end of the occupation of Austria.

The Allied foreign ministers had decided in their Moscow meeting of October 1943 that Austria should be restored as an independent state. The first of Hitler's victims had to wait until 1955, however, for the fulfillment of that promise. For a whole decade after the war, despite continuous negotiations, the former Allies were at odds on significant points, and Austria remained divided into four occupation zones, with its capital administered somewhat after the fashion of postwar Berlin.

In making a settlement with the last of the former enemy states, Japan, the European Allies left matters for the most part in the hands of the United States government. After a conference at Cairo in November 1943, President Roosevelt, Prime Minister Churchill, and Generalissimo Chiang Kai-shek had announced that Japan's conquests would be taken from it at the restoration of peace. The expectations of the Chinese government were doubtless modified by the subsequent decision of the Big Three at Yalta to restore to the Soviet Union the rights that Imperial Russia had enjoyed within the Chinese empire before 1905, including rights in Manchuria, joint operation with China of railroads in that area, and the lease of Port Arthur (see p. 416). The Soviet Union was further authorized to annex the southern part of Sakhalin Island and the Kuril Islands, and—at the subsequent conference at Potsdam—to occupy that part of Korea lying above the 38th parallel of latitude, the United States exercising similar rights in the southern half of that traditionally troublesome but strategically important country. Time was to bring all of these concessions into question, and they doubtless facilitated Communist conquest of the mainland, although they were by no means the only, or even the most important, reason for that. But they had been made to assure the entrance of the Soviet Union into the war against Japan, which, at a time when the effectiveness of the atomic bomb was unknown, seemed essential.

After the Japanese surrender, while the Soviet Union busied itself on the mainland, United States troops occupied Japan and a policy of demilitarization and democratization was instituted under the authority of General Douglas

[1] Bulgaria had to pay $70,000,000; Finland, Hungary, and Rumania, $300,000,000 each; Italy, $360,000,000.

MacArthur, the Supreme Allied Commander. In general, the evolution of Western policy toward Japan was much like that of the policy followed with respect to Western Germany. That is to say, as inter-Allied cooperation broke down and as communism conquered China, the United States pushed for a definitive settlement with Japan that would convert that country into a bastion against Communist influence. The American line was that the best way of effecting this result would be by concluding a separate treaty between Japan and the Western powers. In September 1951, after many difficult negotiations, the United States and Great Britain concluded the treaty, in which Japan accepted the loss of the territories taken from it. The question of Japan's relations with the Communist Chinese government on the mainland and Chiang Kai-shek's regime on Formosa and the settlement of reparations payments to the various powers were left to later negotiations between Japan and the interested parties. By separate treaty between Japan and the United States, American troops received the right to garrison bases in Japan for the purpose of protecting the country and contributing to the general security of the Far East.

The Soviet Union did not recognize these arrangements and did not end its state of war with Japan until 1956.

REBUILDING THE WEST

Socialist Britain   While these diplomatic arrangements were being made, the countries of Europe were once more making the painful effort to overcome the ravages of war. Once again the plight of the victors was almost as desperate as the vanquished. Great Britain, for example, had not only suffered far more physical damage than in World War I but had also virtually exhausted its foreign assets and stretched its economic resources to the breaking point. One discouraged Englishman, writing in the magazine *Horizon* shortly after the end of the war, said gloomily:

> The advantages which position, coal, skill and enterprise won for us in the nineteenth century have been liquidated, and we go back to scratch—as a barren, humid, raw, but densely over-populated group of islands with an obsolete industrial plant, hideous but inadequate housing, a variety of unhealthy jungle possessions, vast international commitments, a falling birthrate, and a large class of infertile rentiers or over-specialized middlemen and brokers as our main capital.

With these conditions, the British people proceeded to "cope"—a favorite British expression of the 1940s. Their first step toward coping was to retire Churchill from the prime ministership by bringing the Labour party to power in the elections of 1945. Churchill's defeat caused some consternation in the United States, where the behavior of the British electorate was considered to show a lack of gratitude to the great wartime leader. In reality, it had nothing to do with Churchill, whom the British people continued to hold in affection and admiration. The Labour party's victory of 1945, which gave it 390 out of 640 seats in the House of Commons, was a belated judgment on the ineffective social policy of the Conservative party during the 1930s and the expression of a determination to make economic democracy work in Britain. That fifty percent of the electorate were prepared to face up to the prospect of radical reform (it may be noted in passing that the Labour party had never before polled more than thirty percent of the vote) was probably due to two things: the Labour party's success since 1926 in convincing the middle classes that it was not a band of wild-eyed visionaries or Bolshevik egalitarians (see p. 610) and the basing of American troops in England during the war. The presence of Americans in Britain kept the social question firmly before the British common people. They saw that their American counterparts were better paid and better provided for and that they bore visible signs of having social advantages superior to those enjoyed in England; and the British determined that they should receive some of the benefits which G.I.'s seemed to take for granted.

In their six years of office,[2] the Labour government sought to satisfy these desires by an elaborate program of social reform and industrial reorganization. In 1946 a National Insurance Act went far beyond the Act of 1911 (see p. 299) by providing for health, old age, and unemployment insurance to be supported by weekly contributions by employers, employees, and the state. It was supplemented by the Industrial Injuries Act and, two years later, by the National Assistance Act, which was designed to supply the needs of the indigent who were not covered by the Insurance Act. A more revolutionary piece of legislation was the National Health Service Act, which gave free medical care (including hospital services, nursing care, and dental and other appliances) to all British subjects who registered for such coverage.

These benefits helped make up for the austerity of English life during the first postwar years, when financial stringency and an excess of imports over exports made it necessary for the government to prolong wartime rationing of food, fuel, and clothing and to restrict the amount of currency that British travelers could take out of the country. In time, the currency pinch was relieved by loans from the United States and the European Recovery Program, as well as by a new devaluation of the currency in September 1949. Despite the fact that relative prosperity returned to both trade and industry, the trade balance of the country remained unfavorable. Because of the exhaustion of its foreign assets by two world wars (between 1939 and 1945 Britain had to sell £1,118,000,000 of overseas investments), the country was forced to pay its way by exports, and only the virtual exclusion of consumers' goods from the domestic market could have corrected the imbalance.

The Labour government sought with some success to ease this problem with the second part of their program, which was designed to increase production by effecting the basic reorganization and modernization of British industry that had not been carried out in the interwar period (see p. 603). This was set in train by a series of measures that nationalized key industries with compensation for their former owners: the Bank of England, the cable and wireless services,

---

[2] The Labour party was re-elected to office in February 1950 when they won 315 seats to the Conservative bloc's 297 and the Liberals' nine. In the elections of October 1951, however, the Conservatives returned to power with 321 seats to Labour's 295.

and civil aviation in 1946; the coal mines, the canals and docks, and the road transport system in 1947; the electrical supply and gas works in 1948; and the iron and steel industry in 1951.

After the return of the Conservatives—and Churchill—to power in 1951, part of this program was undone. Steel was denationalized and road transport turned back to private hands, although both were made subject to supervision by government boards. Yet, however much Conservative speakers fulminated against Labour on the hustings and in Parliament, they found it difficult and inexpedient to return to the old private enterprise system. Whether they liked it or not, England had passed through a revolution—a cautious revolution perhaps, at least in its means, but one that nevertheless established the most fully elaborated social welfare state in the Western world and opened to the British common people prospects that had been denied them in the past. Nor was this a one-party accomplishment. At least one important contribution had been made to it by the National government before its demise in 1945. This was the Education Act of 1944, which raised the compulsory school age, made secondary education free, and provided free lunches to all children in primary and secondary schools. This basic law was supplemented after 1945 by an active program of school construction, by a state-supported program of adult education, and by increased attention to scholarship programs which provided equality of opportunity in higher education.

The Conservative willingness to accept, in modified form, the social program of the Labour party helped win back the middle class electorate that had abandoned the party in 1945. In the elections of 1955 and 1959, the Conservatives won commanding majorities in the House of Commons, the 1959 success being all the more impressive in view of their fumbling during the Suez Crisis of 1956 (see p. 778). The dissatisfaction and doubt caused by that debacle brought about the retirement of Anthony Eden, who had succeeded Churchill in 1955; but his place was taken by Harold Macmillan, a calm and tactful man who won the confidence not only of his riven party but of the electorate as a whole and retained it until the mid-60s brought new and intractable problems.

During the years of recovery, there was no tendency in Great Britain to reject the political heritage of the past nor was there any significant increase in political extremism. The war years had allowed the constitutional crisis of 1936 (see p. 643) to recede into the back of people's minds, and the fact that King George VI and his queen had shared the rigors of the blitz (and had even suffered a bombing of Buckingham Palace) had made the monarchy a more popular institution than it had been since the last years of Queen Victoria. When George VI died in February 1952, national mourning was sincere and deep, giving way very soon, however, to widespread rejoicing as the late king's daughter assumed the throne as Elizabeth II. In the trials that lay ahead for the country in its foreign and imperial relations (see pp. 776 and 782ff.), the queen was a symbol of the essential unity of the Commonwealth of Nations.

France: The Fourth and Fifth Republics   The first postwar government of France was organized by the Free French movement of General Charles de Gaulle, which, since 1940, had inspired resistance to the Axis both inside France and out. When the Allied landings were made in France in June 1944, what semblance of authority the Vichy regime (see p. 669) retained quickly crumbled. It is melancholy to observe that Vichy's leader, Marshal Pétain, now quite senile and apparently insensitive to the crimes committed under the shadow of his name (including political murders carried out even after the Allied landings), believed that he could still count on some form of Allied recognition. Indeed, he sent a message to General de Gaulle through a secret agent, informing him that he hoped to remain in power

> a few months with him in order to ensure the transition and consolidate the union which will come to birth through our mutual understanding. Then, as soon as possible, I want to go back and live in peace on my estate and finish my days in tranquility.

The hero of Verdun was denied the fulfillment of these wishes. His overtures were received with bleak indifference at de Gaulle's headquarters. Then, to Pétain's intense indignation, he was forced by the Germans, in August 1944, to take up residence at Sigmaringen in the Black Forest. When this part of Germany was occupied by American forces, the marshal voluntarily surrendered to the French government, but he was tried for treason and condemned to death, this sentence then being commuted to life imprisonment on a lonely island in the Bay of Biscay. There Pétain died in July 1951.

Meanwhile, General de Gaulle had entered liberated Paris. In September 1944, he appointed a temporary government of the French Republic which governed France in collaboration with the Provisional Consultative Assembly, which had been organized in Algiers in November 1943 and had crossed to France at the time of the Allied invasion. These provisional agencies gave direction to French affairs while the country was passing through the turmoil and dislocation of the liberation period, and they instituted the program of nationalization of mines, basic industry, and credit that was to play an important part in the country's economic recovery.

At the end of 1945, when more orderly conditions at last prevailed, elections were held for a National Assembly whose mission was to draft a constitution for the state. The discussions of this body soon indicated that most of the deputies desired to revive the constitutional system of the Third Republic, centering power in the legislative body and keeping the executive power weak. De Gaulle, who had been elected provisional president by the Assembly, objected strenuously to this, and in January 1946 he resigned his office in order to carry on a campaign against the proposed constitution. He was not successful in effecting more than minor changes, and the constitution was accepted by popular plebiscite in October 1946. It is worth noting, however, that, while nine and a quarter million people voted to approve the document, eight million voted no, and eight and a half million abstained, figures that gave few grounds for confidence in the longevity of the new regime.

The Fourth French Republic, which thus came into being, nevertheless lasted for twelve years and accomplished much for the country, especially in the economic sphere. Its success in this respect becomes very clear if we reflect that in 1947 the economy of the country was dislocated by a wave of strikes and social misery was so marked that the gloomier newspaper pundits of the West were predicting a Communist take-over by the end of the year. Ten years later, this threat had become very remote; the country was prosperous; and the minister of finance could boast, "In the domain of industry our country is holding a world record. It is in France that, from 1952 on, the most rapid rate of growth has taken place: 10 percent per year."

The reasons for recovery were many. Marshall Plan aid from the United States (see p. 765) played its part, especially in overcoming the crisis of 1947–1948. So did the nationalization decrees of the previous year. Much was accomplished by the systematic modernization of power resources, industrial equipment, and farm machinery, the last being particularly important, since at long last the old balance between agriculture and industry was beginning to break down, and there was a decided movement toward the urban centers, which the government, in the interest of industrial expansion, encouraged. Progress was accelerated also by state planning, the Monnet Plan of January 1947, for instance, setting production goals for the coal, power, steel, cement, agricultural machinery, and transport industries. Finally, the spirit with which the French people approached their job of rebuilding was one of confidence and energy, reflected, as Raymond Aron has written, in a substantial increase in the birth rate and in a positive desire for expansion that could be detected among the workers as well as among the entrepreneurs. Thanks to the operation of these forces, the gross national product increased by 49 percent between 1949 and 1957 and, in the same period, the population between the ages of 4 and 13 rose by 37 percent, agricultural production by 24 percent, production of industrial chemicals by 132 percent, the number of vehicles by 100 percent, the volume of investments by 142 percent, and so forth. This was perhaps inferior to progress made in the same period in West Germany, but it attested to the essential vitality of France.

Unfortunately, none of this admirable spirit and drive was to be detected in the working of France's political institutions. With parties on the right and the left that were enemies of the regime (de Gaulle's Reunion of the French People, RPF, on the one hand and the Communists on the other), government rested on uneasy combinations of Socialists, Radicals, members of the Catholic Popular Movement (MRP), and various kinds of conservatives. These coalitions were so frail that in the twelve years of the Fourth Republic, there were twenty-five separate governments.[3] As Aron has written, the deputy's life seemed to center around three ceremonies that recurred at intervals of three, six, or twelve months: an execution (the overthrow of a cabinet), a *fête* (a ministerial crisis), and a distribution of prizes (the composition of a new cabinet). He was so exclusively concerned with these crises that he rarely turned his eyes outward to see what was really going on in France and the world. In popular parlance, the Assembly came to be known as "the house without windows." That government was possible at all was due to the stabilizing influence of a bureaucracy of experts. It was in France that the most striking illustration was given of a growing

[3] In the fourteen years of the Weimar Republic, there were twenty-one.

tendency in post-World War II Europe—the growth of administration at the expense of parliamentary institutions.

Preoccupation with the game of politics was accompanied by what can fairly be described as an essential unwillingness to accept responsibility or even to admit that there was such a thing as responsibility to be accepted. In this new "republic of pals," no one was ever blamed for anything, and it was tacitly assumed in time of unpleasantness—as it had been tacitly assumed in pre-1914 Austria (see p. 362)—that these things "just sort of happened." Responsibility for France's unsuccessful postwar colonial policy (see pp. 786–787) was spread so thin that no one was thought of as being culpable in any way. When an occasional energetic minister arose who was willing to assume partial blame for a disaster—as René Pleven did in the case of the defeat of Dienbienphu in Indochina in 1954—or who sought to liquidate impossible situations and to impute responsibility for their existence—as Pierre Mendès-France did with respect to the Indochina war—he was considered by the ordinary parliamentarian to be violating the rules of "the system." This sort of thing, D. W. Brogan has written, doubtless "made for an amiable form of parliamentary life but destroyed the voter's sense that he was voting for anything or anybody in particular, or that his formal representatives, once they were elected, were responsible to him or to anybody." This led to a frustration of democracy and a gradual erosion of public confidence in the regime. It also caused behavior in foreign policy that exasperated France's allies (as in August 1954, when the Assembly, acting largely for reasons that had little to do with the issue at stake and out of a desire to overthrow one more government, destroyed years of inter-allied planning by voting against the European Defense Community [see p. 769]); and it led to fatal mismanagement of affairs in Africa and the Far East.

The mishandling of overseas affairs eventually aroused the opposition of a body that had refrained from intervention in politics since the Dreyfus case: the French army. It had fought bravely in Indochina, Tunis, and Morocco since 1945, with frightful losses—of its officers, the equivalent of a whole class of St. Cyr had died in Indochina—only to be forced in the end, by political decisions made in Paris, to withdraw from the contested ground. Its officers felt that this was a betrayal not only of the army but of the native levies that had fought with them. One lieutenant wrote:

> I thought of all those in Indochina who were massacred for having believed that France, having engaged them on its side, would not abandon them; of those in Tunisia, faithful to the end, but vanished without a trace since our departure; of those in Morocco. And once more I asked myself whether my comrades and I would not, one day, have on our consciences the deaths of all those whom we had rallied to our side and compromised forever.

The army officers feared another sell-out in Algeria, where civil war had been raging since 1954 (see p. 789). To prevent this, they seized power in Algeria in May 1958 and demanded that General de Gaulle be called to head the government.

The government in Paris gave way before the rapidly expanding revolt and entered into negotiations with de Gaulle, who proved to be willing to take political responsibility. He was empowered by the Assembly to submit a new constitutional reform to a popular referendum and, in September 1958, he did so. His draft constitution provided for a popularly elected Assembly and a Senate elected by indirect vote, but left their powers vague. Wide authority was vested in a president who would be elected for a seven-year term by an electoral college of more than 80,000 electors, or approximately one grand elector for each thousand inhabitants, representing all the peoples of the French Community. The constitution had a marked authoritarian tone; and the president was given much more power than that possessed by Clemenceau in 1917 or Poincaré in 1926, being rather comparable in authority to the prince president at the outset of the second Bonapartist regime (see p. 169). The ministers of state were still in theory responsible to the Assembly; in actuality, they became interpreters and agents of the will of the president. Even so, aside from the Communists and a small group around Mendès-France, there was no real opposition to this shift to the right, primarily because everyone was heartily sick of the Fourth Republic. In May, when it was being overthrown by the military coup, a journalist spoke of "the prodigious lack of interest of an entire people"; in September, the plebiscite on the constitution was approved in Metropolitan France by a majority of four to one and was subsequently approved by all members of the Community with the exception of Guinea, which, by its action, severed its connection with France.[4]

The Fifth Republic began its existence with an electoral reform that divided Metropolitan France into 465 single-member constituencies. In elections in November 1958, supporters of de Gaulle won a resounding victory, while the Communists, who had held about a third of the seats in the assembly since 1945, were reduced from 144 seats to 10, although their popular vote remained sizable. De Gaulle was elected president of the French Republic on December 21, 1958, by more than 62,000 of the electoral college votes, or 76 percent of the electoral college. He immediately buckled down to the task of seeking a solution for the troubled situation in Algeria. This proved to be a prolonged and laborious business; and it was not until the spring of 1962 that the president's patience was rewarded with a cease fire and an agreed settlement, which granted Algeria its independence (see p. 790). The course he had followed had alienated many of his previous supporters and, in January 1960 and again in April 1961, abortive insurrections led by disgruntled generals took place in Algeria. The violence characteristic of the Algerian conflict also communicated itself to France in the years before a solution was reached; violent crime and political terrorism both increased, and there were three attempts on the president's life in the course of 1962.

In the period that followed, concern was voiced among the moderate and leftist parties over the president's tendency to enhance the powers of his office

[4] The Community was defined as comprising thirteen states, which, in order of population, were: the French Republic (Metropolitan France, the Algerian and Saharan Departments, the Overseas Departments, and the Overseas Territories), Malagasy Republic, Sudanese Republic, Republic of the Upper Volta, Republic of the Ivory Coast, Republic of Chad, Republic of the Niger, Republic of Senegal, Republic of Dahomey, Central African Republic, Republic of the Congo, Islamic Republic of Mauretania, and Gabon Republic.

at the expense of parliament. His preference for deciding matters of foreign policy by himself, striking out on an extreme nationalist line without giving his opponents a chance to express themselves, and his proposal that the president be elected henceforth by direct popular vote rather than by the electoral college aroused the fear that the Bonapartist tendency was becoming stronger, while his condoning administrative violation of normal civil liberties during the Algerian troubles led one critic to charge that France was losing its soul.

The great majority of Frenchmen seemed, however, to be less worried about this. The country was prosperous. Population increased by 5,600,000 between 1946 and 1960; standards of living and health were high; production and trade were booming; and the balance of payments situation was healthy. Under these circumstances, the ordinary Frenchman became agitated about politics only when his special interest was affected and was inclined to leave the big issues to the president. De Gaulle, therefore, had his way for a time.

The Liberated States   Like France, the Low Countries, Luxembourg, Norway, and Denmark had suffered German occupation and the imposition of puppet regimes. In every case there were political and economic problems consequent upon the restoration of freedom and self-government. Belgium turned out to be the most fortunate of these states economically and the most troubled politically. Its economic recovery started almost immediately upon the arrival of Allied troops in the country in September 1944, for Antwerp became an important supply center for the last push against Germany. Economic progress was set back, at least temporarily, by the Battle of the Bulge (see p. 695) but was steady thereafter. Belgium was soon the most prosperous country in western Europe and was able to demonstrate the fruits of its recovery in the Brussels Exposition of 1958 and the New York World's Fair of 1964. Progress was encouraged by modernization of its industrial plant and by tariff agreements with the governments of the Netherlands and the Grand Duchy of Luxembourg, which formed the basis of the so-called Benelux Union of January 1948, later elaborated as the Benelux Economic Union on February 1958. This organization eliminated tariff barriers between the three participants and provided a common trade policy toward the outside world as well as a single labor market with free movement of workers among the three nations.

Politically, the most serious issues in postwar Belgium were the question of the status of the king, Leopold III, the colonial issue, and the always difficult language problem. Because of his surrender to the Germans in 1940, his supposed predilection for authoritarian rule, and his marriage to a commoner after the death of his wife, the widely admired Queen Astrid, Leopold had lost the support of many of his subjects. The fact that his new wife was a Fleming helped assure him of the Protestant vote, although it alienated those who resented the gains made by the Flemish movement during the German occupation. In 1950, a national referendum showed that 57 percent of the voters were prepared to tolerate Leopold's continued rule, but subsequent disorders encouraged by the Socialist opposition persuaded him to abdicate in favor of his son Baudouin, who ascended the throne in 1951.

Belgian politics thereafter were relatively quiet until 1960, when the decision to grant independence to the Congo and the subsequent troubles of that vast country caused attacks on the government for its alleged mishandling of the situation (see p. 795). Discontent over this issue waned rapidly when it was discovered that the loss of the Congo was not going to have the unfortunate economic effects that had been feared; and, in any case, the colonial question was superseded by the much thornier language controversy.

The concessions made to the Flemish nationalists in the interwar period (see p. 623) had never satisfied their leaders, whose ambitions grew during the war and were expressed in new demands for an outright division of the country along language lines into two autonomous states loosely linked with Brussels as the national capital. The demands of the Flemish nationalists, which inspired similar ones on the part of Walloon extremists, were opposed by the Socialist and Liberal parties, which held the balance of political power in the country, although they found it expedient to be conciliatory. Thus, in 1964, they passed a new linguistic law which made Flemish, a form of Dutch, the official language in the northern part of the country and French the legal language in the south, and stipulated further that both languages would be official in Brussels. The hope that this would end the perennial agitation was not, however, realized in the years that followed. The language problem caused government crises in 1965 and 1966 and was still unsolved when NATO moved its headquarters to Brussels in 1967.

The governments of Luxembourg and the Netherlands were restored without incident. In the latter country, Queen Wilhelmina, who had spent the war years in exile, was able to celebrate the fiftieth anniversary of her accession to the throne in her own capital, before abdicating in favor of her daughter Juliana. Parliamentary life was characterized in the Netherlands, as in Belgium, by the division of power between Catholic and Socialist parties, the latter showing a slight preponderance throughout the period. The political issue that caused the greatest amount of controversy in the period was the loss of Holland's empire in Indonesia (see p. 785), which caused some temporary economic dislocation but in the end seemed to aid rather than hurt the economy. Between 1958 and 1963, the country's gross national product increased by 34 percent and its exports by 50 percent, figures exceeded only by Italy and West Germany.

Both Denmark and Norway recovered rapidly from the economic effects of German occupation. As in the case of the Benelux countries, there was a tendency toward regional economic collaboration, although its effects were slow in being realized. In 1957 a Committee on Economic Cooperation, founded by the governments of Norway, Denmark, Sweden, and Iceland[5] ten years earlier and joined by Finland in 1956, submitted to its member governments a draft convention for a Nordic Customs Union with common tariffs against outsiders, a common market, and a labor and credit pool for members.

In both Denmark and Norway, politics was dominated in the first postwar years by the liquidation of those who had collaborated with the Germans, and, until people like Quisling were hunted down, tried, and executed, life did not return to normal. There was no disposition to change the monarchical institutions of the past, despite Communist attempts to undermine the idea of monarchy.

[5] Iceland became independent of Denmark in 1944.

In Denmark, Christian X resumed his throne and, when he died in 1947, was succeeded by his son, Frederick IX, a tall handsome man with a military bearing, who won the respect and admiration of his subjects. Norway too had a peaceful change of reign when, after ruling for fifty-two years, King Haakon VII died in 1957 and was succeeded by Olaf V. Predominantly an agrarian country, Denmark's strongest political parties were the Socialists and the Agrarians, and throughout the 1950s and 1960s it was the former of these that governed, generally in coalition with the Radical party. The principal political issue was that of agricultural prices, in the interests of which Denmark applied for membership in the Common Market in 1961, an application that was, however, withdrawn when Great Britain's bid for membership was declined. In Norway, the Workers party, which had first come to power in the 1930s, continued to maintain its parliamentary control in the first two postwar decades, and, under the able leadership of Einar Gerhardsen and Halvard Lange, carried out new experiments in economic democracy, particularly in the field of social insurance. In the elections of September 1965, however, the socialists lost almost six percent of their popular vote and were forced to yield power to a coalition of middle class parties, a development that did not slow the pace of social reform, a new wage-based pension plan coming into effect in January 1967.

The Western Neutrals   Five states of western Europe had remained neutral during World War II: Sweden, Switzerland, Eire (although thousands of Irishmen fought in British armies), Portugal, and Spain.

The first two of these neutral states profited greatly from the war, as a result of German orders and Allied pre-emptive buying programs that were designed to deny strategical materials to the enemy. The termination of hostilities gave rise to some fear that there would be grave economic dislocations. This was not borne out in fact, although wartime American generosity was replaced, in the case of Switzerland, by tariffs on certain products like watches and bicycles. Throughout most of the postwar period, Switzerland had full employment and, in addition, gave employment to foreign laborers; for the most part, it enjoyed export surpluses. In the case of Sweden, the loss of the important German market in the first years after 1945 was partly made up by a profitable economic agreement with the Soviet Union and, by the mid-1950s, the country's trading position was sound again. Relations with the Soviet Union were jeopardized in 1963 by the discovery that a former colonel in the Swedish air force, Stig Wennerstrom, had been serving the Soviet espionage arm for fifteen years, but this was smoothed over by a visit of Premier Khrushchev in June 1964 and a new trade agreement of February 1965 which provided for the exchange of Swedish industrial equipment, ships, and machinery for Soviet oil, coal, and coke.

The most important political development in Switzerland was the relaxation of wartime controls that had tended to increase the already strong tendency toward centralization of power in the hands of the federal government. In Sweden, as in other Scandinavian countries, politics centered around the expansion of social-insurance legislation at the insistence of the Socialist party, which, under the able leadership of Tage Erlander, exercised uninterrupted power from 1945 to 1970. In the 1960s it became clear that even a country as rich as Sweden and as committed to the welfare state principle was not immune to the problems that beset Sweden's larger neighbors (see pp. 733–744). When Olof Palme succeeded Erlander at the end of 1969, he announced that his government would seek to control technological progress so as to avoid unacceptable social consequences and to work for a greater degree of social equality and democratic participation in government. Sweden continued in the postwar period to be a monarchical country.

Eire, which had long occupied an ambiguous position within the British Commonwealth (see p. 611), broke its last legal ties to Great Britain in 1949 and assumed the title of the Republic of Ireland. In 1955, the country became a member of the United Nations (see pp. 760–763), and in 1960 an Irishman, Frederick H. Boland, served as president of its General Assembly, in which capacity he had some success in controlling the ebullitions of Premier Nikita Khrushchev and the discourtesies of some of the other Soviet-bloc leaders—angrily terminating one session at which a Rumanian delegate included the Irish people among those oppressed colonial peoples who deserved, in his opinion, to be liberated.

From popular wartime literature and from the motion pictures, one gets the impression that the people of Lisbon could have lived comfortably during the war if they had had no other income than the tips left by Axis and Allied agents and counteragents working in that capital. This is doubtless an exaggeration, but it is true that Portugal benefited economically from its neutral position. With the end of the war, however, the country suffered an appreciable slump, and the limping rate of agricultural and industrial production in the years that followed was quite incapable of keeping up with the increase of population, whose rate was one of the highest in Europe. The deterioration of economic conditions doubtless accounts for the unusual appearance of political opposition in the presidential elections that followed the death of Marshal Carmona (see p. 625) in 1951, and for sporadic manifestations by students and manual workers in the fifteen years that followed. None of this was strong enough to shake the regime, although the dictatorship of Salazar felt called upon to increase its vigilance with respect to subversion and to restrict individual political rights even further. Portugal became a member of the U.N. in 1955, but, in all essentials, even after Salazar's retirement in 1968, remained an authoritarian state.

So did Spain, where Franco had managed to resist all of the threats and blandishments of the Fuehrer and to retain the position of neutrality that he had taken at Hendaye (see p. 673), although he had permitted Spanish "volunteers" to fight on the Russian front in behalf of the Axis. This concession, and the memory of the Civil War, was enough to destroy any hope of reconciliation with the victor states in the immediate postwar years; and the nations meeting at San Francisco in 1945 (p. 760) banned Spain from membership in the U.N.[6] This vote became a bit of an embarrassment at a later date, when the Cold War led Western soldiers to ponder the importance of an Iberian redoubt and when the strongest of the NATO countries felt it necessary to have bases in Spain. If Spain remained for a time beyond the pale, there were lots of people willing to cross it in order to deal with its government, or, as was true of thousands of American tourists, to discover the bull rings and gypsy dances of Andalusia, the grandeur of the Basque provinces, and the primitive magnificence of the Costa Brava.

[6] Spain was admitted in 1955.

The money spent by these visitors and the American military assistance extended after 1953 helped to ease, but did not cure, the problems caused by the unhappy combination of a static economy and a rising birth rate. The discipline of dictatorship was also ineffective in coping with these. Politically, the regime remained much what it was at the end of the civil war, a Fascist state that tolerated none of the institutions of democracy. Opposition to the regime continued and even mounted as the years passed. In the Basque provinces, particularly, a liberal movement gathered weight within the clergy and began to press for social reform. In the late 1950s, workers in the mining districts, always a volatile element in Spanish politics, became increasingly restive, and in other trades as well illegal workers' committees (*comisiones obreras*) were founded in opposition to the government *syndicats*. By the middle of the 1960s these were linked in a loose federal system. Among the students, too, there was growing resistance. Indeed, the first clear gesture of opposition to the regime was made by the university students of Madrid in 1955, when they took the occasion of the death of Ortega y Gasset, the highly respected philosopher and known opponent of the Franco dictatorship, to stage a demonstration of protest against restrictions upon freedom of thought and civil liberties. It was firmly put down, but the spirit it expressed survived, and in 1967–1968, when the student protest movement assumed European dimensions (see pp. 742–744), mass meetings of Spanish students raised new demands for democratic reform.

As the years passed, the established order in Spain—the church, the army, and the business community—proved itself not entirely immune to modernization. Ideological zeal fell out of fashion, and the Falange (see p. 626) was progressively deprived of power and became a mere agency for administering the bureaucracy. The church lay order *Opus Dei,* in contrast, increased its influence in the educational system and in business, and in the latter sphere (although not in the former) showed an interest in progressive ideas and in overcoming Spain's economic parochialism.

By a law of 1947, Franco was made chief of state for life and was empowered, whenever he saw fit, to propose to the Cortes the name of his successor. On July 22, 1969, he did so, naming as the man best suited to carry on the work of the National Movement of 1936 the grandson of King Alfonso XIII, Prince Juan Carlos of Bourbon.

Italy and Austria   In most of the countries of western Europe, communism increased its strength as a result of the war[7]; but in none did it have as much

---

[7] The strength did not last in most cases, as is shown by the following table of Communist parliamentary strength in the first postwar years, reproduced from Hugh Seton-Watson's *From Lenin to Khrushchev* (New York: Frederick A. Praeger, 1960), p. 304:

    Britain: 1945, 2 seats out of 615; 1950, 1; 1951, none.
    Belgium: 1946, 23 seats out of 202; 1949, 12; 1950, 7.
    Holland: 1946, 10 seats out of 100; 1948, 8; 1952, 6.
    Denmark: 1945, 18 seats out of 148; 1947, 9, 1950, 7.
    Iceland: 1946, 10 seats out of 52; 1949, 7.
    Norway: 1945, 11 seats out of 150; 1949, none.
    Sweden: 1948, 8 seats out of 230; 1952, 5.
In France, as we have seen above the Communists continued to receive one third of the vote and the seats until 1958.

chance actually to take over power as it did in postwar Italy. Here both economic and political conditions were suitable to its growth, for the country was prostrate economically as a result of the fearful hammering it had received in the last stages of the war, and the collapse of fascism left a political vacuum into which the Communists (as the party least encumbered by a record of past mistakes of execution or omission) seemed likely to move. The Italian Communist party was a well-disciplined and organized body led by Palmiro Togliatti, who spent the war years in Moscow and returned to Italy in April 1944. In the first government of liberated Italy, Communists held the important ministries of justice and finance, and the party was supported by thousands of idealistic middle-class intellectuals who dreamed of a new *Risorgimento* led by the only truly revolutionary party.

This mood did not last. In June 1946, when a national referendum decided that the country should be a republic rather than a monarchy and sent the House of Savoy into exile, the elections to the Constituent Assembly of the republic gave the Communists only 19 percent of the poll, the united Socialist groups 21 percent, and 35 percent to the Christian Democratic movement, which was headed by Italy's ablest postwar statesman, Alcide de Gasperi. The subsequent dissolution of Socialist unity brought new strength to the Communists, who became the undisputed leaders of the working class, but their gains were matched by those that de Gasperi made by piecing together coalitions of the moderate Left and Center. In the winter of 1947–1948, the Communists made their big bid for power by fomenting nation-wide strikes and demonstrations and by building mass organizations in factories and among the peasants. Nevertheless, in the April 1948 elections, the first held under the new democratic constitution, the Christian Democrats, supported by the Catholic Church and exploiting the promise of American economic aid, won 48 percent of the vote as compared to the 32 percent won by the Communists and the left-wing Socialists. This made it clear that the Communists would not take over in the near future. De Gasperi became prime minister, a post he held until 1953. Luigi Einaudi, a distinguished economist, was elected president of Italy and served as such until he was succeeded in 1955 by the Christian Democrat Giovanni Gronchi.

Communism retained the support of a majority of the Italian working class and could generally count—at least until the great crisis of conscience that followed the events in Hungary in 1956 (see p. 752)—upon that of the left-wing Socialists led by Pietro Nenni. In their attacks upon the regime and its foreign policy, the Communists profited from the revival in the 1950s of neo-Fascist and monarchist groups. They profited, too, from the tendency of the younger leaders of the Christian Democratic movement after de Gasperi's death in 1954 to seek power at the expense of principle and to abandon faith in democracy in favor of an opportunism that increasingly avoided social reform in return for the support of the extreme right. This caused a major ministerial crisis, with widespread rioting in the country in 1960; and this was not solved until the left-wing Christian Democrats and other moderate parties rallied around de Gasperi's most gifted follower Amintore Fanfani. The *connubio* of the center and moderate left which he pieced together faced great difficulties in the economic field, complicated by over-population, poor educational standards (reflected in a rate of illiteracy that continued to waver between 10 and 30 percent and in a wholly inadequate popular understanding of scientific methods in agriculture and industry), and a shocking amount of organized crime, particularly in Sicily where the Mafia's influence was still paramount. Even so, it made some headway in solving them, thanks to Marshall Plan aid in the first postwar years and membership in the Common Market after 1957 (see pp. 765–766).

In Austria, the economic difficulties were as great as those being grappled with in Italy, but communism was able to make less headway there. This was largely because the Austrian Socialist party—unlike its Italian counterpart, which showed all the fissiparous tendencies of the years 1890–1922 (see p. 314)—evinced a courage and discipline that retained the loyalty of the Austrian working class. In the provisional government that was set up in Austria in April 1945 by the Soviet authorities, under the leadership of the veteran Socialist Karl Renner, the Communists played an important part and controlled the Ministry of the Interior. The hope that this might pave the way for Communist domination came to nothing; and, in the parliamentary elections of November 1945, the Communists won only four seats out of 163. Austrian politics, as before the war (see p. 598), was henceforth ruled by the Socialists and the old Christian Socialist party of Dollfuss, now purged of its authoritarian ideas and rechristened the People's party. The difference was that these two formerly hostile parties, which had both suffered at Hitler's hands and whose leaders had learned to understand each other while sitting in his concentration camps, no longer competed for power but collaborated in wielding it. In 1945 they formed a Great Coalition and for the next twenty years administered Austria in common, sharing executive and administrative offices and positions in the civil service.[8] The administrative task was not simple, for state control was carried further in the postwar period than in any country of the west. In 1945 the two-party government nationalized the banks and all heavy industry, and in the years that followed railroads, civil aviation, public utilities, radio and television, and the salt, tobacco, liquor, and match monopolies passed under government administration as well.

Although placed under four-power occupation, the Austrian government was recognized by the powers and permitted to conduct foreign affairs, which it did with vigor and adroitness under the leadership of Renner, its first president, and Leopold Figl and Julius Raab, federal chancellors from 1945 to 1953 and 1953 to 1961 respectively. Their success in ingratiating themselves with all of the occupying powers, without appearing to have a partiality for any, probably contributed to the breaking of the diplomatic log jam that led to the conclusion of the Austrian State Treaty of May 1955. By this, Austria became an independent,

[8] The first four presidents after 1945 (Renner, Körner, Schärf, and Jonas) were Socialists; the first four chancellors (Figl, Raab, Gorbach, and Klaus) belonged to the People's party. Each of these officials had a State Secretary of the opposite political persuasion. State agencies tended also to be divided: the officers of the army being predominantly People's party, the police Socialist, and so forth. This system, called by the Austrians *Proporz*, was not essentially changed during the years 1965–1970 when a Peoples Party government replaced the Great Coalition; and there was every indication that it would continue after a Socialist victory at the polls in March 1970 made Bruno Kreisky the country's first Socialist chancellor.

sovereign state with the boundaries of 1937. It was pledged to neutrality and promised not to enter military alliances or to permit the establishment of foreign military bases on its soil. *Anschluß* with Germany was forbidden.

Although the nature of the coalition and the acrobatics necessary to maintain it forbade daring social and economic experiments and left some problems (housing, for instance) virtually untouched, Austria's economic picture was bright compared with prewar years. After 1955 Vienna began to exert its customary fascination upon tourists, who were drawn particularly by the splendor of its museums and galleries, the excellence of its theaters, and the renascence of its musical eminence. At the same time, industrial production rose nearly 70 percent between 1953 and 1960 and was reflected in a rising standard of living. In commerce the government was as neutral as in other aspects of its foreign relations. Half of its trade was with members of the Common Market, to which it did not, however, belong; and it also steadily increased its trade with states of the eastern bloc.

Divided Germany   The course of political events in Germany until the year 1949 has already been sketched above, in connection with the postwar peace treaties (pp. 705-708). Economically, those same years were years of steady disintegration and mounting misery. By the decisions of Yalta and Potsdam, Germany had lost to the Poles an area that had supplied 25 percent of its food supply as well as much of its industrial coal. From that area, over twelve million Germans had been evicted and were now forced to live and seek work in western Germany, where food stocks were limited. The results were grim to observe. In 1947 Germany's greatest modern novelist, Thomas Mann, in his last major work, *Dr. Faustus*, wrote a moving comparison of the Germany of Hitler's time with the broken country that had emerged from the war.

> At that time [he wrote] Germany, with her cheeks feverishly flushed, reeled drunkenly at the height of her empty triumphs. . . . Today, girt round with demons, a hand over one eye, but staring with the other into horrors, she plunges from despair to deeper despair. When will she reach the bottom of the abyss? When, out of the ultimate hopelessness, will the light of hope dawn, a wonder that passes all belief?

Although Mann could not know it, the light of hope was not far away and the wonder was soon to be born. The fusion of the western zones by the Allies, after they had realized that they could not count on Soviet cooperation in promoting German stability, and currency reform in 1948 laid the basis for recovery. It was promoted, in the first instance, by Marshall Plan aid and, later, by the careful planning of German administrators, the austere taxation and subvention policy adopted by the West German government after its establishment, the thrift and industry of the average German, and—not least important—the fact that, unlike its neighbors, West Germany had no military expenses and was indeed forbidden to have any until 1955.

Progress, once under way, was remarkable. As early as 1953, West Germany held third rank, after the United States and Great Britain, among the nations participating in world trade. Five years later the country was exporting almost twice as much of its national product as Germany was in 1936 and importing two thirds as much as the United States; and between 1958 and 1962 its total exports increased by another 76 percent. German industry was producing two and a half times as much as before the war; the country was enjoying full employment; prices were stable; and the country had come close to balance of payments equilibrium. Moreover, West Germany had thus far escaped the kind of inflationary spiral that occurred in other countries as a result of continued labor-management disputes. This was due in large part to German labor's traditional lack of enthusiasm for strikes, the strong tradition of effective collective bargaining, the sense of joint responsibility which resulted from the share granted to labor in the management of industry (the so-called *Mitbestimmungsrecht*), and the success of the government's effort to persuade people not to make excessive demands on the economy.

The political recovery of Germany was almost as spectacular as the economic. This was the result of the growing recognition by the Western Allies that they would need German military strength in any trial with the Soviet Union; and it was due further to the ability of Germany's outstanding postwar statesman, Konrad Adenauer.

Germany's political development began with Allied authorization of the revival on the local level of party organization and activity. As early as 1946, state constitutional conventions were held, legislatures were chosen, and the first regional political parties appeared: the Social Democrats, taking up where the old party of that name had left off in 1933; the Christian Democrats (in Bavaria, the Christian Social Union), a party designed to appeal to both religious faiths but predominantly Catholic, like the MRP in France, the People's party in Austria, and the party of de Gasperi in Italy; the Free Democratic party, a liberal-conservative party standing for free enterprise; and the Communists, who never represented more than 10 percent of the voters in the western zones but flourished in the Soviet zone, where, in 1946, they merged with the Socialists to form the Socialist Unity party (SED), which in time became wholly Communist.

The decision of the Western Allies to unite their zones led to the convocation of a Parliamentary Council of delegates of the Western state governments in Bonn in September 1948. This body proceeded to draft the Basic Law for the Federal Republic of Germany, which was ratified by the state governments and went into effect in May 1949. The Basic Law provided for a bicameral legislature composed of an upper chamber or Bundesrat of thirty-eight members, representing the state governments, and a lower chamber or Bundestag, elected by a combination of direct and proportional electoral procedures by all persons who had reached the age of twenty-one. The Federal Republic had a president, elected for a term of five years by the lower house and representatives of the state governments, but he was given none of the prerogatives that had been misused by Field Marshal von Hindenburg in the 1930s. Real power was vested in the chancellor and the cabinet, who were freed from the perpetual insecurity of their Weimar predecessors (see p. 573) by a rule that prohibited the Bundestag from dismissing them unless it was prepared to elect their successors immediately—a stipulation that eliminated the lengthy cabinet crises of an earlier era.

The first Bundestag elections were held in August 1949 and led to the creation, by a narrow margin of votes, of a coalition government composed of Christian Democrats, Free Democrats, and the so-called German party (a conservative nationalist group), with Konrad Adenauer as chancellor. The Social Democrats, under their brilliant leader, Kurt Schumacher, formed the opposition, which was to be their role for the next decade and a half.

The new chancellor had entered politics before World War I, had been chief mayor of Cologne from 1917 to 1933, when he was dismissed by the Nazis, and had been an unsuccessful candidate for the chancellorship in 1926. In 1944, when he was arrested by the Gestapo, the warden of Brauweiler prison had said to him: "Now, please do not commit suicide. You would cause me no end of trouble. You're sixty-eight years old, and your life is over anyway." That official would have been astonished to know that his prisoner had almost twenty years of active political activity left to him and that he was to serve as chancellor of Germany for two years longer than Adolf Hitler.

It was under Adenauer's leadership that West Germany was transformed from a beaten foe to a respected ally. The chancellor did not concentrate his energies on the pursuit of national unity and the liberation of the seventeen million Germans in the Soviet zone, for these things seemed remote and impossible of achievement. Instead, he bent his efforts to reducing the restrictions still imposed on West Germany by the Allies, and he went about this task with a blend of realism and idealism. In November 1949, he negotiated the Petersberg Agreement with the Western powers, in accordance with which they put an end to the policy of dismantling German factories, and he accepted the Ruhr Statute of December 1948, which set up an international authority for that important industrial area. Although attacked at home for this concession, Adenauer believed that it was more than made up for by the termination of the ruinous dismantling policy and that this concession might, in any event, be productive of later advantage. In any case, he was no narrow nationalist, believing, indeed, that the time had come when Germany must rise above the nationalism of the past. The future lay, he believed, in collaboration between Germany and its neighbors, especially France, and the Ruhr Statute might be, as he said in a speech at Berne, "a promising starting point for general and comprehensive cooperation among the nations of Europe."[9]

In subsequent years, Adenauer always held before the eyes of his people the vision of a new Europe founded on such institutions as the Coal and Steel Community, the European Defense Community, the Common Market and Euratom (see p. 765). His devotion to these ideals not only won him continued support at home, as his electoral victories of 1953 and 1957 and 1961 showed, but convinced the Western powers of his reliability and helped persuade them that it was safe to relax the postwar controls on Germany. Their willingness to do so was prompted also by their desire, especially after 1950, for German military aid, and Adenauer shrewdly played to this by becoming an advocate of German rearmament within the Western alliance system. Despite opposition by the Socialists, sections of the German church, and university youth, he won a series

[9] The plan of internationalizing the Ruhr was not, in fact, implemented.

Konrad Adenauer, 1876–1967.
(German Information Center)

of parliamentary battles on this issue, finally obtaining Bundestag assent for the Federal Republic's entrance into NATO (see p. 769). This was accompanied by West Germany's reacquisition of untrammeled sovereignty.

Adenauer's policy with respect to the reunification of Germany was based essentially on the theory that close association of the Bonn Republic with the Western powers and the common pursuit of a "policy of strength" would persuade the Soviet Union to yield on contested points and give up its control of East Germany. As the years passed, there was little indication that this policy was going to succeed.

The Soviet Union had also sponsored a constitutional congress in its zone, and the work of this body eventuated in the proclamation of the German Democratic Republic in October 1949. This state had a president (Wilhelm Pieck, head of the German Communist party), a prime minister (Otto Grotewohl, head of the SED), and a popularly elected single chamber, but power was concentrated for the most part in the hands of the Politburo of the SED, which was directed by Walter Ulbricht. The Democratic Republic was organized on Soviet lines, and the policy of strict centralization eliminated all local agencies that might serve as centers of resistance to state power. Internal repression was heightened after the outbreak of riots against Soviet control in East Berlin and other German cities in June 1953. In 1955, the republic was recognized by the Soviet regime as a sovereign state, and thereafter the Moscow leaders took the line that German reunification could come about only as a result of negotiations between the two German governments. This was rejected by the Western powers, with a resultant stalemate.

A particularly dangerous issue in German affairs and in east-west relations generally was created by the anomalous position of Berlin. Situated a hundred miles within the Soviet zone and recognized by both German regimes as the natural capital of the country as a whole, Berlin continued to be split into a western sector, subsidized by West Germany and garrisoned by Allied troops, and an eastern sector under the control of the Democratic Republic and protected by Soviet arms. In November 1958, the Soviet Union announced that it intended

"Hunter with Prey." A West German view of Ulbricht, by Flora. From *Die Zeit,* August 24, 1962. Two days before this appeared, a young German named Peter Fechter was shot and allowed to bleed to death while attempting to escape to West Berlin.

to terminate the last vestiges of four-power control over the city and hand its rights over to the East German government. No date was set for this projected action, and the Western powers correctly interpreted the announcement as an attempt to frighten them into recognizing the East German regime; and they refused to enter into any Berlin talks except within the framework of a total German settlement. Although it repeated its ultimatum periodically, the Soviet government decided in the end not to give up its position in Berlin or to give Ulbricht control of the city's communications; and, after 1964, no further reference was made to the note of November 1958. On the other hand, the Soviets did authorize their German satellite to strengthen its position by an act that shocked the Western world and revolted the consciences of men everywhere. On August 13, 1961, in order to prevent the continuing flood of refugees from East Germany to West Berlin—a drain of energy and talent that was threatening their regime with economic collapse—the East German authorities began the construction of a wall which eventually ran from the external sector boundaries across the whole width of the city, dividing it into two parts. This barrier was manned with armed guards with orders to shoot anyone who tried to flee to the West. Soon such shootings, in the Bernauer Strasse and at other points along the wall, became almost daily occurrences. The sheer inhumanity of the action and its brutal disregard for the ties of family (West Berliners were henceforth denied access to the eastern part of the city on any pretext)[10] left Western governments incredulous, which may be the reason that they did not act positively in the first days of Ulbricht's grim operation. He was permitted to complete it uninterrupted.

After 1962, the Berlin question was in abeyance, but shootings and occasional confrontations of armed strength along the wall and Soviet harassing tactics

[10] Four years later, after much negotiation, visits were permitted at Christmas time and on other very limited occasions.

on the access routes were indications that the city could easily become a storm center again.

CULTURAL AND INTELLECTUAL TENDENCIES IN THE WEST

In the arts after 1945, the resilience of Europe's genius was as apparent as it had been in the years following World War I, although some of the results were less impressive than those of the earlier period and less original in conception. Much of European painting, for example, amounted to little more than skillful variations on the ideas of the interwar surrealists, cubists, and abstractionists. If there was a revolution in postwar painting, it came from America rather than Europe, when Jackson Pollock broke with the traditional view that a painting was the realization of an idea conceived in the mind of the artist and invented "action painting," in which pictures grow out of unpremeditated and spontaneous creative actions. For a time, Pollock found many followers in Europe, as did other American innovators of the op art and pop art schools, but there was little that was new in European painting for them to borrow in return.

Similarly, with respect to poetry, the springs of lyrical inspiration appeared to have dried up in all of western Europe. In Great Britain, there were no fresh voices after Dylan Thomas died in 1953; the best poets were those who had written their finest work in the 1930s: Louis Macneice, for example, and Hugh MacDiarmid, who was sometimes called the greatest Scottish poet since Burns, but who showed only occasional flashes of his lyrical power after 1945. The fault lay perhaps with the times, and it may be that, like the years after 1830, those after 1945 were better suited to prose than poetry. Certainly France fared no better in this respect than England, the few notable poets being relics of the interwar years: St. John Perse, Henri Michaud, René Char, and Paul Eluard, whose death in 1952 served to emphasize the dearth of qualified successors. In Germany, the defeat produced in Ingeborg Bachmann, Hans Magnus Enzensberger, and Walter Höllerer a group of young poets who recaptured some of the spirit of the expressionist activists of an earlier time, but they did not succeed any better than their contemporaries in other European countries in winning an international audience.

In contrast, European achievements with the novel, the drama, and the film were acknowledged in every part of the world. With respect to the first of these—if we except brilliant individual triumphs, like Giuseppe di Lampedusa's historical novel of the Risorgimento, *The Leopard* (1958), the unclassifiable novels of Max Frisch, *Stiller* (1954) and *Homo Faber* (1957), and Anthony Powell's multivolumed remembrance of things past, *The Music of Time* (1951 and continuing)—France and Germany provided the most interesting examples of new directions. The novel in France had always been closely associated with philosophy, and after 1945 this continued to be true, the novels of Sartre (*The Age of Reason,* 1947–1951), Simone de Beauvoir (*The Mandarins,* 1956), and Albert Camus (*The Plague,* 1947, and *The Fall,* 1956) all being inspired by, and helping to propagate, the existentialism that became so fashionable in the West in the first postwar years. Starting in the 1950s, as a deliberate reaction to the subjectivism and idealism of these writers, the "new novel" was born. Its authors—Alain Robbe-Grillet, Michel Butor, Nathalie Sarraute, and Claude Simon in particular—sought to exclude moral judgments from their writing and to portray the world with scientific accuracy, an approach that owed something to the new philosophy of structuralism, which will be touched on below.

Common to both the existentialists and the school of the *nouveau roman* was a lack of interest in politics and a disinclination to discuss social realities. In contrast, the postwar German novel was markedly political, which did not, however, militate against its esthetic qualities. The first postwar novelists (Hermann Kasack, Elisabeth Langässer, Bruno E. Werner) sought earnestly to deal with German responsibility for the recent holocaust; their successors—Uwe Johnson (*Conjectures about Jacob*, 1959), Martin Walser (*Half-Time*, 1960), Heinrich Böll (*Billiards at Half-past Nine*, 1959, and *The Clown*, 1963), Siegfried Lenz (*German Lesson*, 1968), and Günter Grass—combined narrative power with incisive social and political criticism. Grass's major novels (*The Tin Drum*, 1962, and *Dog Years*, 1963) were works of extraordinary epic sweep and stylistic virtuosity and won for their author an international renown comparable with that enjoyed earlier by Thomas Mann.

In the drama, two distinct but related schools developed. The influence of Bertolt Brecht upon Western dramatists was profound, despite the fact that he was on the other side of the curtain, working at the Theater on the Schiffbauerdamm in East Berlin. His brand of social realism and penetrating criticism was reflected in plays by the Swiss dramatists Max Frisch (*Andorra*, an analysis of anti-Semitism that deeply moved audiences in 1961) and Friedrich Dürrenmatt (The *Visit*, 1956, and *The Physicists*, 1962),[11] as well as the Germans Rolf Hochhuth (*The Deputy*, 1963, an excoriating attack upon Pope Pius XII for his alleged unwillingness to try to halt the persecution of the Jews, and *Soldiers*, 1969) and Peter Weiss (*Marat-Sade*, 1964). The English dramatist John Osborne, whose *Look Back in Anger* (1957) caused a sensation in his own country by the brutality of its assault upon accepted ideals of status and morality, owed little to Brecht in technique but certainly shared his lack of reverence for respectability and bourgeois virtues, which accounts for the success of his play in productions by university theater groups on the continent.

Less explicit in their social message were those dramatists whose work was collectively labeled the Theater of the Absurd, because, in the words of one of them, Eugene Ionesco, they agreed that human existence was "devoid of purpose" and that "cut off from his religious, metaphysical and transcendental roots, man is lost; all his actions become senseless, absurd, useless." This message was powerfully presented in plays that soon entered the repertories of theaters in New York, Tokyo, and Rio de Janeiro as well as those of the old world—Samuel Beckett's *Waiting for Godot* (1952), Ionesco's *The Chairs* (1952) and *Rhinoceros* (1959),[12] Arthur Adamov's *Ping-Pong* (1955), Harold Pinter's *The Caretaker* (1960),

[11] Brecht's influence is shown most clearly, perhaps, in a relatively unknown play of Dürrenmatt, *Frank the Fifth: Opera of a Private Bank* (1960), which in theme and treatment is strongly reminiscent of *The Three Penny Opera*.

[12] In *Rhinoceros*, which is at its most basic level about political conformism, all of the characters except one become rhinoceroses, and the protagonist is left, not entirely to his

Open City, directed by Roberto Rosselini, 1944–1945, a film about Italian resistance to fascism and national socialism. Here a priest, who has been a resistance leader, prepares to meet his death at the hands of a German firing squad. (Museum of Modern Art, New York. Film Stills Archive)

and Tom Stoppard's *Rosenkrantz and Guildenstern Are Dead* (1966), to mention only a few of the most outstanding.

Even more notable were the successes won by European film-makers, who were not so demoralized by the competition of television as American producers were and who were much less willing than they to compromise artistic values for the sake of commercial gain. In the first decade after the war, Italy was the center of a virtual cinematographic revolution as a group of brilliant directors—Vittorio de Sica, Roberto Rossellini, Cesare Zavattini, and others—probed the social effects of fascism and the problems of moral as well as physical recovery. And in the 1960s, such statements of social criticism as Federico Fellini's *La Dolce Vita* and Michelangelo Antonioni's *Blow-up* showed that Italian vitality was undiminished. Swedish films also aroused attention and respect, especially

---

own satisfaction, to make a stand for humanity. The play caused Sean O'Casey, the distinguished Irish writer of social and political drama, to observe tartly: "There is no fear of our turning into rhinoceroses, but there is a possible chance, if these playwrights get their way, of us all turning into Ionescos, a more terrible fate still."

those of Ingmar Bergman, whose screen plays dealt with the great themes of human dignity and frailty and the problems of life and morality, and whose films *The Seventh Seal* (1956) and *Wild Strawberries* (1957) were soon accorded the status of classics. In France, the late 1950s saw the emergence of the so-called new wave of films, beginning with Roger Vadim's *And God Created Woman,* which was followed by such notable works as François Truffaut's *The Four Hundred Blows,* Alan Resnais' *Hiroshima, mon amour* (which some critics claimed deserved to stand with *Potemkin* and *Citizen Kane* as one of the landmarks of world cinema), and Jean-Luc Godard's *Pierrot le fou, Alphaville,* and *La Chinoise.* Meanwhile, the British, thanks to actors like Alec Guinness, Peter Sellers, and Richard Attenborough, rediscovered the art of comedy in the film, which, in the United States, had been one of the casualties of television humor.

In music, it can be argued that the artistic achievement with the widest impact was that of the Liverpool singing group The Beatles, who took Europe and America by storm in the years 1963–1967 and laid the basis for a distinctive new art form, rock music, which became the *lingua franca* of the student generation.[13] In the field of opera, the Munich composer Carl Orff aroused enthusiasm in German critical circles with his trilogy *Antigonae* (1949), *Oedipus* (1959), and *Prometheus* (1968), although the dissonant primitivism of these works annoyed many who had been delighted with his earlier scenic cantatas, of which *Carmina burana* (1939) was the best known. Another German composer, Hans Werner Henze, won a wider audience with his *Prinz von Homburg* (1960), based on the play by Heinrich von Kleist, *Elegy for Young Lovers* (1961), and, in the tradition of the *opera buffa, Der junge Lord* (1965). In England, Benjamin Britten followed up his first success, *Peter Grimes* (1942), with two others, *Billy Budd* (1951) and *The Turn of the Screw* (1954). Britten's most widely admired work, however, was probably his *War Requiem* (1961), based upon the poems of Wilfred Owen, who died in the trenches in the first World War. To the student generation of the 1960s, intensely opposed to the war in Vietnam, this impressive work made an immediate appeal.

In musical performance, Europe quickly regained its prewar level of excellence, all major capitals vying for artists and orchestras, but with the German cities taking the lead, thanks to Herbert von Karajan's direction of the Vienna State Opera and the Berlin Symphony and to the brilliant work of the British choreographers John Cranko and Kenneth MacMillan with the ballet companies of Stuttgart and Berlin. A conspicuous exception was Paris, where the musical arts suffered from a lack of inspired direction and financial support by the state; and the inferior quality of performance in the French capital underlined its

---

[13] On June 12, 1965, it was announced that the Beatles were to be made Members of the Order of the British Empire. This elicited indignant protests from many people who felt the order was being cheapened. This was hardly justified, given the fact that William Mann, the music critic of *The Times,* in a long and serious review, had called John Lennon and Paul McCartney "the outstanding English composers of 1963," while a writer in *The Sunday Times* said they were "the greatest composers since Beethoven." Their services to their country were not, of course, purely musical. In 1964, the prime minister, Sir Alec Douglas-Home, called them "our best exports" and "a useful contribution to the balance of payments." This may, or may not, have influenced their inclusion in the honors list.

decline as a center of the arts, despite the efforts of de Gaulle's minister of culture, André Malraux, to restore its former pre-eminence.

About intellectual tendencies since 1945, as distinct from artistic ones, it is difficult to generalize. It is probably safe to say that, in contrast to the interwar period, there was a general retreat from ideology. This accounts for the popularity of variants of existentialism in the first decade after the war, for, despite Sartre's insistence that this philosophy necessitated commitment, the intellectuals who talked most about existentialism seemed to be interested in using it as an excuse for the privatization of their interests rather than as a moral imperative to social action. By the 1960s, much of the original excitement of existentialism seemed to have drained away, and the fashionable philosophy had become that of structuralism, whose leading spokesman—Claude Lévi-Strauss, Michel Foucault, Paul Lacan, and Roland Barthes—used the methods of psychoanalysis, anthropology, and linguistics to support a new deterministic view of life, in which human thought and action were controlled by a network of social and psychological structures that left little room for free will.

This bleak philosophy was hardly calculated to win converts in large numbers, and there were signs as the decade of the 1960s came to its end that European intellectuals preferred more pragmatic prescriptions. One such sign was the growing interest in the thought of Teilhard de Chardin, a highly unconventional Jesuit philosopher who died in 1955, leaving behind a corpus of work in which, in terms capable of appealing to non-Christians as well as to the faithful, he preached the immanence of God in all aspects of the modern world and expressed an optimistic belief in human progress through scientific discovery. Another was the appeal that the new technocracy exerted upon university graduates, especially, but not exclusively, in France—a growing interest in opportunities for practical work in the interest of modernization. And a third sign was the fact that rebels against the existing political and social system, while willing to borrow arguments from the structuralists when they were useful, refused to be bound by their intellectual discipline and placed their faith in inspired activism rather than the systematic procedures demanded by doctrine.

THE PROBLEMS OF AFFLUENCE

Great Britain: Macmillan and Wilson   As has been indicated above, the austerity that accompanied the process of repairing the ravages of the war came to an end in most countries of western Europe in the mid 1950s, and an economic boom began that profoundly affected the ordinary citizen's way of life and his attitudes toward politics.

This was markedly apparent in Great Britain. After long years of penny-pinching and making do, the country began rapidly to take on the characteristics of the "affluent society," to use the popular phrase of the 1960s. With full employment and a healthy economic growth rate, a consumers' boom took place, which was encouraged on the one hand by new mass advertising techniques and on the other by the breaking down of the last prejudices against instalment buying. This method of paying for goods was now used with increasing frequency, the total in one eighteen-month period mounting by as much as £300 millions.

Between 1955 and 1959, the number of families owning television sets rose from forty to over seventy percent, and the number of automobiles on English roads increased from three and a half million to almost five million and gave no indication of stopping there. Sales of refrigerators, washing machines, power lawnmowers, boats and camping equipment, and other luxury items went up proportionately and underlined the conclusion that the ordinary Englishman was living more comfortably and enjoying his leisure time more actively than ever before: as Harold Macmillan said, he had "never had it so good."

Politically, this redounded to the benefit of the Conservative party and, indeed, enabled it to survive the humiliation suffered at Suez in 1956 (see p. 778). In the wake of that affair, Harold Macmillan became prime minister. As a member of Eden's cabinet, he had been one of the strongest advocates of military action against Nasser's Egypt, but, once he was in office, the apparent success of his economic policies soon made people forget that. Macmillan was an incurable optimist who laughed at the timidity of the Labour party, still captive of the ration-book psychosis of the war years and their aftermath, and who overrode the doubts of his more orthodox chancellors of the exchequer. He facilitated the extension of credit to business by relaxing controls on bank lending and instalment buying; he increased purchasing power by lowering the income tax; and he used television skillfully to preach his philosophy of expansion. He was soon being referred to jeeringly by his opponents as MacWonder and Super-Mac, but the electorate was impressed and gave the Conservatives a lead of 107 seats over Labour in the general election of 1959, forty more than in 1955, a triumph that caused a sharp rise on the stock market.

Macmillan was to remain in office until October 1963, completing a term longer than any prime minister since Asquith (see pp. 299, 437). Yet long before his resignation, the bloom had faded from his early successes, which had, indeed, done nothing to correct some troubling basic problems. Although a lot of people in Britain were better off than ever before, great inequalities of wealth remained, and it was impossible to hide the fact that, in the race for affluence, the aged and the sick were left behind and that there was a lag in subsidized housing and in the building of hospitals, schools, and playgrounds. Moreover, no great progress was made toward alleviating the British disadvantage in balance of payments; as early as 1961, as a result of its own inflationary policies and the revaluation of the German mark, which took place in March, the government was confronted with a sterling crisis and was forced to raise the bank rate and call for a wage freeze. Popular reaction, reflected in by-elections, was unfavorable, which seemed to prove that there was no disposition on the part of the electorate to make sacrifices in order to secure the gains it had made. It is difficult to avoid the conclusion that this was at the root of much of Britain's economic troubles in the years that followed, when it became clear that the country was not keeping pace with its economic competitors. Because of its heavy overseas commitments and the burdens it had assumed by deciding to build nuclear weapons, effective remedial action would have been difficult in any case. It was made doubly so by the disinclination of British management to undertake the costs of conversion to more efficient methods of production and the stubborn resistance of the trade unions to the very concept of modernization—an attitude skillfully satirized in one of Peter Sellers's best films, *I'm All Right, Jack.*

Other issues contributed to the ending of the Conservative party's thirteen years of supremacy. The party's right wing was alienated by Macmillan's ambiguous policy in African affairs, accusing him of having yielded too easily to demands for the exclusion of the Union of South Africa from the Commonwealth because of its policy of *apartheid* (see p. 793) and of having dismantled the Central African Confederation to the detriment of the white population of Rhodesia (see p. 792). People in both parties who remembered Britain's palmier days resented what they felt, particularly after Macmillan's meeting with President Kennedy at Nassau in December 1962, to be a tendency to allow the Americans to dictate British defense policy (see p. 771) and were humiliated by General de Gaulle's abrupt refusal to agree to British membership in the Common Market (see p. 766) after months of patient negotiation and preparation of public opinion. Finally, in 1963, the party's prestige was shaken by revelations of *la dolce vita* in ministerial circles, in which the name of Minister of War John Profumo figured all too prominently. (It says much for the shift of values since Parnell's day [see p. 301] that it seemed to be Profumo's disingenuousness in his statements to the House of Commons about the affair that forced his resignation rather than his association with known prostitutes.) But in the last analysis what undermined Macmillan's government was growing awareness that his early boasts about economic progress had been bogus. The country seemed to want a change, and, when Macmillan retired because of illness in the autumn of 1963, his successor, Sir Alec Douglas-Home, was not able to develop enough Conservative strength to deny that desire, and the Labour party returned to power in October 1964 with a slim majority, which improved in new elections held two years later.

The new prime minister, Harold Wilson, made it clear at the outset that it was time for the country to face up to the realities of its situation, rid itself of unneeded ballast, and acquire the tools necessary for effective competition in the modern world. This involved a progressive withdrawal from Britain's imperial holdings east of Suez, a more modest view of her military potential, and, on the production front, an emphasis on technology. In the years that followed, the government sought with increasing difficulty to hold to that line. Unfortunately, its national plan made no provision for the outbreak of new crises or for failure of the social partners to cooperate. The Rhodesian crisis, which began in November 1965 (see p. 792), and the troubles that began between Catholics and Protestants in Northern Ireland in the summer of 1969 were costly distractions. The definitive end of the boom in 1966 confronted the government with new balance of payments problems, which it sought to meet with a devaluation of the pound in November 1967 and other measures intended to encourage production and trade. The effectiveness of these was reduced by a rising curve of industrial unrest, marked by an extraordinary number of wildcat strikes; and the government's attempt to discourage these by proposing controls merely caused widening criticism of the party leadership by the trade unions. There was no doubt at the end of 1969 that public confidence in the government was waning. In the spring of 1970 there were some superficial signs of a recovery of Labour's strength, but these succeeded only in misleading the opinion polls, which—when Wilson called for national elections in June—predicted that he would win. They were wrong. The Conservatives returned with a 30-seat majority, and Edward Heath became prime minister.

It seemed likely, nevertheless, that a mere change of government would not solve Britain's problems.

France: The Fall of De Gaulle   France's course during the years of de Gaulle's ascendancy was strikingly similar. The general began boldly in December 1958 with a series of financial reforms (including devaluation of the franc by 17.5 percent and acceptance of proposed tariff reductions by Common Market partners) that had immediate results in the improvement of the trade balance, the increase of gold and other reserves, and the halting of inflation. For the next four years, industrial production increased rapidly, over-all exports doubled and exports to Common Market members increased threefold, consumers' goods appeared and were purchased in abundance, and France acquired all those external evidences of affluence already discussed in the case of Great Britain.

As was also true in Britain, not everyone enjoyed the new prosperity. The economy remained uneven: agricultural income was always about thirty percent lower than that of industrial workers, and the latter were, in some trades, at the mercy of a system threatened by shortages of capital and productive invest-

De Gaulle, as seen on the cover of the German weekly *Der Spiegel* in 1967.

ment, lack of funds for research, and inflationary pressures. Like the economists around Harold Wilson, the young technocrats in de Gaulle's movement believed that France's future lay in technological innovation and modernization, but the funds for this were not easy to come by. As M. Servan-Schreiber pointed out in his best-selling book of 1968, *The American Challenge,* French entrepreneurs were too conservative to support basic research or gamble on novelty, and General de Gaulle's preoccupation with foreign affairs, and particularly his insistence on France's maintaining a nuclear capability, absorbed funds that might otherwise have been used for development.

As the de Gaulle regime continued in power, its paternalism became offensive to many Frenchmen. One sign of this was seen in the elections of 1965, when a coalition of all of the leftist parties with the Communists seriously reduced the general's parliamentary majority. This produced no immediate change, since neither parliament nor parties nor unions seemed capable of taking any initiative in politics. But even this negative result helped persuade many people that the state—in the later words of Jacques Chaban-Delmas—was becoming both "tentacular" and "stifling," that it was extending its influence into every part of national life in such a way as to discourage private enterprise and local and regional government. Despite the economic prosperity, moreover, society was as rigidly stratified as it had always been, and opportunities for social mobility continued to be made difficult by an educational system that allowed the bourgeoisie to maintain a virtual monopoly in the state *lycées* (or secondary schools) and kept the percentage of working class children who went to the university at about one percent, significantly lower even than the figure in West Germany.

The political, economic, and spiritual malaise induced by these circumstances reached its height in May 1968 and produced an explosion of dissatisfaction and indignation that began in the Sorbonne and spread rapidly to the industrial quarters of Paris. For weeks the comfortable French middle class was confronted with the disturbing spectacle of public buildings being occupied by self-styled anarchist cadres and open fighting between police columns and workers carrying red flags. The repercussions were profound.

Superficially, the days of May strengthened de Gaulle's grasp on power by giving him a victory in the elections that he called in their wake. In response to his appeal for support, thousands of shopkeepers, pensioners, functionaries, and businessmen poured into the Champs Elysées and the Place de la Concorde on May 30 to demonstrate for law and order and the general, and three weeks later they went to the polls and gave him a clear majority in the Chamber. But from that time onward, everything for de Gaulle ran downhill.

It is true that the events of May convinced him that his exclusive interest in foreign affairs had been a mistake and that there were other problems that demanded attention. But his attempts to deal with them alienated the very people who voted for him in June. To them the reforms that de Gaulle now approved— Edgar Faure's proposals for a more democratic educational system and René Capitant's plan to give workers participation in industrial decision-making— seemed to reward the rebels, whereas Prime Minister Couve de Murville's increase of the income tax on the higher brackets penalized the loyalists. They reacted, characteristically and traditionally, by shipping gold out of the country, with

"The Uprising," ca. 1848, by Honoré Daumier. (The Phillips Collection, Washington)

the result that in November 1968 a new devaluation of the franc was narrowly averted. The general's old magic now seemed to desert him, and in April 1969, when he submitted to the people a series of proposed constitutional reforms in the form of a referendum that was clearly a demand for a vote of confidence, almost fifty-three percent of those voting opposed him. He resigned the next day, leaving a host of problems unsolved and a void in politics that would not be easily filled, as his successor, Georges Pompidou, was to discover.

Italy and West Germany: The Political Malaise   The dilemmas of affluence were nowhere more apparent than in Italy and West Germany, both of which experienced what journalists called economic miracles but had difficulty in providing effective, let alone inspiring, political leadership. Italy's prosperity was made possible by a highly developed economic infrastructure (built but not exploited by the Fascists), a significant amount of state ownership of industry, a great reservoir of surplus labor, and the stimulation provided first by the

"The Days of May in Paris, 1968." (Jean-Pierre Rey from Liaison Agency)

Marshall Plan and later by membership in the Common Market. The gross national product increased by an annual average of 6.3 percent from 1952 to 1962, one of the best rates of growth in Europe; once the Common Market was in operation, industrial production rose by 107 percent in seven years, and foreign trade almost as much. At the same time, the discovery of new resources of natural gas gave Italian companies unlimited amounts of cheap fuel for the first time; a spirited investment program fostered industrialization in southern Italy, always a problem area; and a long-range program to increase livestock farming began to correct the imbalance in the agricultural situation that had been aggravated by Mussolini's policies (see pp. 548–550).

On the other hand, as in the case of France, Italy's administrative system was too centralized and too ill-financed and understaffed to handle the concomitant problems of affluence—the exorbitant real estate costs, inadequate schools, the spread of crime, and, inevitably, the shrinkage of real income as a result of inflation; and the country failed to produce leaders strong enough to face these problems and find solutions. The governing coalition of Christian Democrats, Socialists, and Republicans continued in office from 1962 until 1969, but only at the cost of continued crises and so many changes of leadership that Gronchi's successors in the presidency, Antonio Segni (1962–1963) and Giuseppe Saragat (1963–), found it difficult to find new prime ministers. The opportunism of the government parties, which has already been commented on (see p. 722). became so blatant that in July 1969 it caused the collapse of the coalition when the Socialist party, laboriously united in 1965 after twenty years of factionalism, split once more into fragments when it was discovered that certain of its leaders were holding secret negotiations with the Communists.

As a result, Italy found itself in the autumn of 1969 being ruled by a stopgap government that was incapable of pushing for constructive reforms, and, since nothing was done to correct this in subsequent months, strikes and work stoppages became so frequent and so general that there were times in the late spring of 1970 when the country seemed near collapse. The most obvious potential beneficiary of this situation was the Italian Communist party, which had carefully built up its strength since the days of its first postwar leader, Palmiro Togliatti, by constructive work at the local level. This, and the reputation for independence that the party gained by its criticism of the Soviet action in Czechoslovakia in August 1968 (see pp. 754–756), impressed an increasing number of nonradical voters.

A similar process of disenchantment had taken place in West Germany and can be dated from Adenauer's time. His last years in office had been marked by a decline in his personal prestige, caused in part by his failure to react strongly to the building of the Berlin wall but perhaps more by his stubborn refusal, from 1959 onward, to heed the wishes of those in his party who wanted him to step down in favor of a more vigorous leader. As Adenauer held on, new ideas and initiatives were postponed; an air of tentativeness settled over Bonn; and the authority of the government began to suffer throughout the country. This was not wholly corrected when der Alte—having crowned his life's work with the conclusion of the Franco-German treaty of friendship in January 1963—finally handed his powers over to Ludwig Erhard. A vigorous man who had played a key role in the Federal Republic's sustained record of economic growth, Erhard lacked Adenauer's charisma and his political sense. He was soon involved in intraparty feuds, while simultaneously being attacked by the left for a lack of attention to basic social reforms. In September 1965, he led the Christian Democratic-Christian Social coalition to a victory over the opposition, but by too slim a margin to shore up his position or to inspire confidence in the country as a whole.

Two events in the mid-1960s deepened the discouragement of German democrats who feared that the Bonn Republic might go the way of its predecessor thirty years earlier. The first was the emergence of the National Democratic Party (NPD), which was accused of being neo-Nazi in leadership and philosophy (a plausible charge, given the fact that twelve of its eighteen-member directorate had been active Nazis) and which showed greater strength in state elections than previous parties of this stripe. The second was the decision of the Social Democratic party, in late 1966, to enter a coalition government with the CDU-CSU and to accept as chancellor of the new combination Kurt-Georg Kiesinger, who had entered the National Socialist party in 1933 and remained a member until 1945. This decision led the novelist Günter Grass to write a vigorous protest to Willi Brandt, the leader of the Socialists, and to address a public letter to Kiesinger in which he asked:

> How are young people of our country to find arguments against the party that died two decades ago but is being resurrected as the NPD, if you burden the chancellorship with the still very considerable weight of your past?
>
> How are we to honor the memory of the tortured, murdered resistance fighters, of the dead of Auschwitz and Treblinka, if you, the accomplice of those days, have the gall to assume responsibility today?

Grass's anger did not deter the Socialists from entering the coalition, and it may be that, in doing so, they saved themselves from the discouragement and disunity that drained away the energies of the Socialist parties in France and Italy in these years. Their participation in the governing coalition gave them an opportunity for positive action, and Willi Brandt as foreign minister and Karl Schiller as minister of economics in particular made the most of this and displayed new initiatives that were not always to the taste of their coalition partners. The effect on the electorate was a positive one, and in the parliamentary elections of October 1969 the Socialists gained so many seats that they were able to form a coalition with the liberal or Free Democratic party and to take over the reins of government.[14] Kiesinger, who had campaigned on the slogan "It's the chancellor who counts!" (which reminded many unpleasantly of Adenauer's paternalism) went with his party into opposition, and Willi Brandt became

---

[14] Earlier in the year the Free Democrats had provided the votes to secure the election of Gustav Heinemann as the first Socialist President of the Republic. Theodor Heuss (1949–1959) had been a Free Democrat; Heinrich Lübke (1959–1969) was a member of the CDU.

the Bonn Republic's first Socialist chancellor. Since the NPD had failed to attract enough voters to qualify for representation in the Bundestag, the election results were hailed as a modest victory for democracy. Their effects were felt beyond the borders of Germany, in the first instance in Austria, where they appear to have contributed to the Socialist victory in the elections of March 1970, which made Bruno Kreisky chancellor of the republic.[15]

The Student Revolts   Only time would tell, however, whether Brandt's victory and policy would impress German youth. Certainly Grass had been right in his concern about their feelings. To the university generation the formation of the Great Coalition in 1966 had appeared to be a patent demonstration of the distorted values and the lack of idealism and principle that was characteristic of the affluent society, and they expressed their indignation openly and violently.

Reaction against what came to be called the sickness of society was not confined to German youth. In the last years of the 1960s, all parts of western Europe (and some of the Soviet satellite countries as well) witnessed demonstrations, riots, and rebellions on the part of young people. The centers of such activity were usually the universities, partly because they supplied ready audiences and bodies of followers, partly because their traditional liberties made agitation and inflammatory exhortation easier than it was on streets patrolled by police, and partly because the universities themselves were good examples of the need of reform. In Germany, for example, after a brief period of progress and innovation following 1945, the universities had reverted to the authoritarian pattern of the past, in which a stubborn professorate with full powers resisted change, in which overworked junior faculty and assistants had little voice in university governance and students none at all, in which curricula were out of date and classrooms overcrowded, and in which there was inadequate scholarship aid to attract students from working class families and no very apparent desire to increase it. Conditions in French, Italian, and Spanish universities were similar and, in most cases, far worse.

Student movements to correct these abuses began in Germany in 1965 and were encouraged by the success of similar movements at the University of California at Berkeley and other American universities. The European movement soon encountered stubborn resistance from faculties and ministries of education and, when this happened, its members tended to shift their attention from the university proper to society as a whole, to see in defects in the university structure reflections of the deeper ills of society and to argue that the university should be used as a base for guerrilla warfare against those institutions and activities that threatened democracy. By 1967 the student movement at the Free University of Berlin was not only pursuing its demands for a university reform that would give students and assistants a voice in all academic affairs but—at least this

---

[15] Like Brandt, Kreisky had spent the war years in Scandinavia, returning to Austria in 1945, and like him he was a moderate socialist who distrusted ideologues. There was another similarity. Both had sons who were prominent activists in the extra-parliamentary opposition in their respective countries.

was true of its more radical groups—was also attacking the government's tacit approval of the American war effort in Vietnam, as well as the right of the Berlin Senate to give a formal reception to the Shah of Iran,[16] the concentration of press power in the hands of the publisher Axel Springer, and the government's preoccupation with a new law on internal security. A year later similar movements were at work in all major German universities, as well as those of France (where May saw the rising at the Sorbonne) and Italy, and student agitations played their part also in the unrest in Warsaw and the troubles that prompted the Soviet take-over in Prague during the summer.

As the movement spread, it became at once more international (with linkages between various centers of action) and more heterogeneous, attracting self-styled Maoists and anarchists and nature cultists and a not inconsiderable number of what could be called the academic *Lumpenproletariat*—hangers-on who were working for no degree but postponing the time when they would have to adjust to another and colder society and paying for the privilege. (The increase in the number of people in graduate schools who were students in only the most formal sense was another of the products and problems of affluence.) At times the motivation of the movement seemed to be purely disruptive (in Germany between 1968 and 1970 its wrecking tactics became so blatant and so destructive of the teaching process that some of its early leaders left in disgust); at times its demands were trivial and self-defeating (as in Italian universities in 1969, where the only concrete demands put forward were for simpler courses and a less complicated

[16] In June 1967, a demonstration against the Shah during his visit to Berlin led to the death of a student, Benno Ohnesorg, and a subsequent radicalization of the movement.

A French cartoon illustrating the protest of youth against a society of affluence and waste. (Hoover Institution)

examination schedule). But, regarded as a whole, the student movement raised questions of the most fundamental importance about the nature of European society, the viability of its institutions, the values of its ruling class, and the direction of their politics. To refuse to take it seriously because its members were young and inexperienced, as some people did, was to miss the point entirely. After spending a year with student rebels in New York, London, Berlin, Paris, and Prague in 1968, the English poet and critic Stephen Spender argued that it was precisely because they were young and inexperienced that they were able to develop a more continuous and active awareness than other people not only of the threat of a nuclear holocaust but also of that of a computerized future in which all individuality would be snuffed out. The mass of concerned students, he wrote, were protesting against a society that seemed to invite the coming of the 1984 world envisioned by George Orwell; they were calling for a stand "against a society whose standards of behavior are determined by the exigencies of industrial planning, the domination of *things.*"

THE SOVIET ORBIT

The Soviet Union from Stalin to Brezhnev   If there were Russians who had believed, at the war's end, that the victory would lead to an era in which the wartime collaboration with the Western democracies would be perpetuated and the rigid domestic controls relaxed, they were soon disenchanted. The Soviet regime seemed to sense that any tendency in this direction could only weaken its authority over the Russian masses, a reflection that was probably strengthened by the fact that thousands of Soviet citizens and members of the armed forces had defected to the West during the war and that thousands more, whom the fortunes of war had brought under foreign control, had desperately resisted repatriation.

Stalin and his aides reverted, therefore, to the line of policy they had followed before World War II. They preached that the Soviet Union was ringed about by capitalist enemies, bent on the destruction of communism, and that they were being aided by unpatriotic Russians on the home front. In February 1946, Stalin restated the thesis that war was inevitable as long as capitalism existed; and simultaneously, under the direction of Andrei Zhdanov, who was now recognized as Stalin's probable successor, a virulent campaign began against those who had succumbed to the lure of bourgeois culture. Meanwhile, as part of the reindoctrination process to which Soviet society was subjected, the victory over Hitler was credited by the press solely to Soviet arms, and Soviet pre-eminence in every aspect of human activity became a matter of faith.

The ludicrous nature of some of these claims had the effect of making the outside world overlook or depreciate the real achievements of the Soviet Union in the postwar period. These were notable. From the devastation wrought by the war and the staggering losses of population and resources, the country recovered with impressive speed. New five-year plans introduced in 1946 and 1951 gave direction and impetus to the drive for rehabilitation and growth, while the "Stalin Plan for the Transformation of Nature," inaugurated in 1948, set out to reforest the southern steppes, modernize the network of canals, and harness the rivers for the production of electric power. By disregarding what would be considered in the west as minimal consumers' needs, the state was able to launch a weapons and nuclear program that matched that of the United States in magnitude and results, while at the same time it brought production of steel, coal, oil, and electrical power to levels that were sometimes twice what they had been in 1940. As for agriculture, the system of collectivization, which had in some respects been liberalized during the war, was tightened again and, in 1948 and 1949, was extended to the newly annexed provinces in the west. A new tendency toward the creation of larger collective units, urged particularly by Nikita Khrushchev, strengthened party control over agriculture, although its economic results were spotty. Indeed, the general rule seemed to be that the state's success in promoting peasant discipline was made at the expense of agricultural efficiency, the peasant having few incentives to improve his performance.

In March 1953, Joseph Stalin died, presumably of a heart attack, although there were inevitable rumors of palace revolutions and assassinations. Zhdanov, his putative successor, had died the year before, and his position as chairman of the Council of Ministers was assumed by Georgi M. Malenkov, whose chief associates were Lavrenti Beria, Vyacheslav Molotov, and, as party secretary, a man still little known outside the Soviet Union, Nikita S. Khrushchev. The tendency of the new regime in internal affairs was toward a relaxation of the program of agricultural collectivization and a new emphasis on the production of consumers goods. The Malenkov interregnum was, however, of short duration and was marked from the start by dissension within the hierarchy and friction between the Red Army and the secret police. This led to the arrest and execution of Beria in July 1953, and a purge of the Moscow, Leningrad, and provincial party organizations, carried out under the direction of the party secretary, whose star had started to rise. In December 1954, Khrushchev launched an attack in print upon Malenkov's industrial policy, and two months later the premier resigned.

Although he was succeeded by Nicholas A. Bulganin, the real power in Soviet affairs was now in Khrushchev's hand, and he dominated both domestic and foreign policy. He immediately repudiated Malenkov's new course in industry and embarked on a basic reorganization of the whole industrial bureaucracy as a means of increasing efficiency in all sectors, including consumers goods. He also continued the policy of enforcing the large-scale organization of agriculture. Emphasis was placed upon "overtaking and surpassing" the United States in the economic sphere, and progress toward this was sufficiently great to make the sharp rise in Soviet economic growth a subject of concern and political debate in the United States.

In 1957 and 1958, Khrushchev consolidated his personal power by effecting the removal of Malenkov, Kaganovitch, and Molotov, who were all considered to be his rivals, from the Presidium of the Party and by dismissing the most popular of the Red Army marshals, Zhukov, from the same body and from the Central Committee. This last stroke eliminated the possibility of the army assuming a dominant role in politics, a possibility much speculated about at the time of Beria's death. Khrushchev now felt able to dispense with Bulganin, who was dismissed in March 1958, at which time Khrushchev combined the offices of prime minister and party secretary in his own person and seemed to have won the kind of primacy over party and government that had once been exercised by Stalin.

Certainly Khrushchev acted as if he were free of any control. An ebullient and self-confident man, he asserted himself in every aspect of Soviet policy. In foreign affairs, he sought, as has already been indicated, to pressure the United States into major concessions in the German question; and his Berlin ultimatum, his torpedoing of the summit conference of 1960, and his outrageous shoe-banging performance at the meeting of the United Nations General Assembly in October of the same year were all studied forcing plays. When they did not succeed, and when doctrinal and other differences between the leadership of the Chinese Communist party and his own caused grave divisions in the Communist world, Khrushchev subtly altered his policy towards the United States and inaugurated a policy of conciliation. This was particularly true after the United States government had adopted a menacing attitude towards his most adventurous experiment in foreign policy—the building of missile sites in Cuba in 1962. Perhaps surprised by the firmness of American policy, the Soviet Premier agreed to dismantle the bases in return for an American pledge not to invade Cuba, which under Fidel Castro's leadership was a source of concern to American policy makers. In the subsequent period, relations between the two Great Powers became more amicable, and this was symbolized by the conclusion of agreements to cooperate in peaceful uses of outer space (December 1962), to establish the so-called "hot line" between the White House and the Kremlin as a safeguard against nuclear crisis (June 1963), and to ban all nuclear tests except those conducted underground (August 1963). As he warmed up to the United States, Khrushchev grew colder to the Chinese Communists and resentful of their imputations of doctrinal heresy, revisionism, and softness toward the West. In 1964, he invited a showdown with his Far Eastern critics by making plans for a world conference of communism at which, presumably, Soviet leadership would be demonstrated whether the Chinese and their allies attended or not.

On the domestic side, Khrushchev was as unorthodox and as freewheeling as he was in foreign affairs. In ideological questions he had a free and easy way and a proneness to offhand formulation that offended the party theorists, while in economic policy his nervous energy and his tendency to change direction abruptly and to start new programs before old ones were completed dismayed the organization men and disrupted progress. His adventures in agriculture were particularly unfortunate; and his emphasis on the production of more consumers goods, while popular in the country, was opposed both by heavy industry and by the army.

In 1964, the premier's critics began to close ranks, and it became apparent as they did so that he possessed the appearance but not the reality of the power once wielded by Stalin. On September 4, *Pravda* printed a memorandum of the late Italian Communist leader Palmiro Togliatti in which he criticized Khrushchev's plans for a world conference of communism. When this was followed by delicate intimations, also in *Pravda*, that the conciliatory policy toward the United States had gone too far and had needlessly exacerbated relations with Peking, it became clear that an internal struggle was taking place within the Soviet leadership. By mid-October it was resolved, and Khrushchev handed over his offices to Leonid N. Brezhnev and Alexei Kosygin and went into disgruntled retirement.

His successors were orthodox party bureaucrats who shunned the kind of impulsiveness that was characteristic of Khrushchev's style but also put an end to whatever faint hope there had been while he was in power of a lightening of the restrictions upon political and intellectual freedom. In domestic policy, experiments of any kind were discouraged, and a dull and leaden conformism settled upon the land. Stalin's name, which Khrushchev had dared to hold up to justifiable obloquy, was quietly rehabilitated, and echoes of his terror were heard in the trials and public degradation of persons charged with "cosmopolitanism," a favorite Stalin word for disloyalty to the Soviet Union. In foreign affairs, the new leaders avoided trouble with the United States and even took new steps toward arms control, with the ratification of the Nuclear Nonproliferation Treaty in 1968 and, in 1969, a ban on testing on the ocean floor and the beginning of comprehensive strategic arms limitation talks (the so-called SALT talks). This did not prevent them from giving substantial military aid to the North Vietnam government or from rebuilding the striking force of the Egyptian army after the debacle of 1967 (p. 780), policies hardly designed to win favor in Washington. Aside from this, their main preoccupation, was relations with China, and, as the possibility of conflict in the Far East grew, they became as anxious to maintain the loyalty of the satellites as they were that of their own people. This accounts in part for their most daring and brutal initiative in the foreign field, the invasion of Czechoslovakia in August 1968 (see pp. 754–756).

Eastern Europe: Finland, Greece, and the Czech Crisis of 1948   Between 1945 and 1948 almost a hundred million eastern Europeans were brought under Communist rule, as "people's democracies" were established in Albania, Poland, Rumania, Bulgaria, Hungary, Czechoslovakia, East Germany, and Yugoslavia. This represented a tremendous victory for the Soviet Union and fundamentally altered the balance of world power.

A word must be said first about the two countries at the extreme ends of this great belt of territory, Finland and Greece, for here Soviet ambitions were not realized. In Finland, the prospects of communism seemed good in the immediate postwar years. In the first coalition governments formed after 1945, the Communists played an important part and controlled the ministry of the interior, a vital position from which, in other countries, they often succeeded in infiltrating the police forces. This did not take place in Finland; the Communist minister was forced out of office in 1948; and the Socialist and Agrarian parties soon sapped the strength of the Communists so effectively that none of the Finnish governments after 1948 included Communist members. Inroads into trade unions were also checked by the Socialists; and communism in general was reduced from a threat to a nuisance. The Soviet Union was willing to tolerate this setback because control of the country was not essential to Russia. Finland was bound by the terms of the Soviet-Finnish Mutual Aid Treaty of 1948 and by the limitations placed on its armed forces by the peace treaty (see p. 708). It did not lie athwart the main routes to the west. Any attempt to exert control over Finland would alarm Sweden and possibly drive it into the arms of NATO. All of these things counseled restraint.

A victory of communism was more nearly achieved in Greece, where, as early as 1941, the Communists had an effective underground, the Greek Liberation Front (EAM), and a fighting force, the Greek People's Liberation Army (ELAS). When the British landed in Greece after the German evacuation in October 1944, EAM-ELAS had a strong position throughout the country and could probably have consolidated its authority if it had seized Athens before the British were in effective control. Fighting between the British and the Communists broke out in December, but did not go well for the Communists, who found it expedient to agree to disarm ELAS and to promise to rely on legal parliamentary means of extending their influence. These promises they repudiated a year later when they reopened the civil war and, thanks to Soviet and satellite aid, fought on for another three years. But American assistance to the non-Communist forces in Greece, and Yugoslavia's break with Moscow, which led to the closing of the Yugoslav-Greek frontier and prevented supplies being shipped to the rebels from that direction, finally broke the back of Communist resistance, after a conflict in which atrocities were committed on both sides and casualties amounted to almost 80,000 for the Communists and almost 50,000 for the government forces.

How definitive this victory was remained a matter of conjecture, however, for Greek politics was subject to periodic convulsions in the years that followed. The unrest was largely due to the extreme nationalism engendered by the Cyprus question (p. 774), and the domestic disaffection caused by growing inequality of wealth, and by increasing tension between conservative supporters of the monarchy and the democratic parties of the left. This was particularly true when King Paul I died, after sixteen years on the throne, in March 1964 and was succeeded by his son Constantine. This twenty-three-year-old monarch became almost immediately involved in a conflict with his prime minister, George Papandreou, over a number of constitutional issues, chief among which was that of control over the army. In July 1965, accusing Papandreou of attempting to infiltrate the military establishment by means of a left-wing organization called Aspida, headed by his son Andreas, the king dismissed his prime minister from office, an action that ushered in a confusing period in which stopgap governments rose and fell, sensational judicial proceedings were instituted against officers implicated in the Aspida plot, and strikes and riots jeopardized public order. Finally, in April 1967, on the eve of new elections, a group of army officers, acting in the king's name, seized power. It soon transpired that the king had not been consulted about the coup or the intentions of the new rulers, and when they celebrated their take-over by arresting and deporting parliamentary leaders, instituting a systematic persecution of persons loosely labeled as subversives and placing extreme restrictions on civil liberties, the king's displeasure hardened into opposition. In December 1967 he attempted a coup of his own, which was, however, a fiasco and led to his departure from the country. The military junta was reconstructed, with Colonel Gregorios Papadoupolos as prime minister, and began a program of repression marked by brutalities that were reminiscent of the excesses of Hitler and Stalin. That this tragic turn in Greek affairs contributed to the decline of NATO there can be no doubt (see pp. 772–773); that it portended graver things, in the form of new risings and, ultimately perhaps, a renewed attempt on the part of the Communists to seize power, many observers predicted. This may have been in the mind of Greece's most distinguished living poet, George Seferis, when he spoke somberly of "the precipice toward which the oppression that covers the land is leading us."

Communism's postwar conquest of the rest of eastern Europe followed a general pattern, although there were differences in detail from country to country. Its basis was generally a tacit or explicit agreement on the part of the West that the Soviets had a right to, or could be allowed, a commanding position in the country in question. Thus, in 1944, Winston Churchill, in return for a promise of Stalin's recognition of primary British interest in Greece and equality of interest in Yugoslavia, admitted on paper that the Soviets had a predominant interest in Rumania, Hungary, and Bulgaria. Thus, also, at Yalta, concessions were made to Soviet views on Polish affairs that were tantamount to acknowledging Soviet primacy of interest there, although Soviet assurances were given that, in all eastern states, principles of democratic government would be observed. In some countries—notably Albania and Czechoslovakia—no Western acquiescence was necessary, since the governments took the initiative in inviting the Soviet Union to assume an influential position in their affairs.

The next phase in the take-over was one in which the Communists participated in the local political process and entered into governments in coalition with the other parties, gradually acquiring control of the governmental apparatus and infiltrating and splitting the other party organizations, until such time as they were able to dispense with their partners.

After that came the period of *Gleichschaltung* during which the other parties were forced to fuse with the Communists (as was done in the case of the SED in East Germany [see p. 725]), political opposition in parliament, the press and public meetings were forbidden, political opponents and former political allies were liquidated, and a Soviet system was imposed on the country. In some cases (East Germany and Poland), these measures were facilitated by the menacing presence of Soviet troops; in others, they were promoted by more discreet means, like economic pressure and threats, such as those that compelled the Czechoslovakian government to withdraw from the Paris conference on the Marshall Plan in 1947 after it had accepted the invitation.

The first states to go Communist were Albania and Yugoslavia, both of which were conquered by Communist resistance movements that had risen during the war. In Bulgaria and Rumania, it was not until mid-1945 that the leaders of the non-Communist parties were isolated and driven from power and the deposition of the reigning sovereigns, Simeon of Bulgaria and Michael of Rumania, was accomplished. In Poland, whose political future had been the subject of interminable inter-Allied discussions during the war and especially at Yalta and Potsdam, the Communists showed their hand clearly only in 1947. In June of the same year they took over completely in Hungary; and, in February 1948, in a series of events that shocked the Western world into a new comprehension of the momentum of the Communist march, a Communist regime was established in Czechoslovakia.

The case of Czechoslovakia was, in one respect, special, for, of all the countries of eastern Europe, it alone was predominantly industrial, with a social structure similar to that of the highly developed states of western Europe and with strong middle class democratic parties. That the Communists were able to take over here was due to their superior tactics, the mistakes of their opponents, and the traumatic experience of the years 1938–1945 which deprived the Czech people of any real will to resistance.

The Czechs began the postwar period filled with good will toward the Soviet Union, and leaders like President Eduard Beneš, still hoping to make their country a bridge between East and West, were anxious to do nothing that might offend their great eastern neighbor. Popular gratitude for the liberation of the country was reflected in the strength shown by communism in the elections of 1946 and the share given to the Communists in government. When the Communists proceeded to exploit the sectional differences that had always plagued Czechoslovakia, to infiltrate police and local administration, and to resort to open lawlessness, the democratic parties resisted, effectively for a time. In February 1948, however, they committed the grave tactical error of seeking to force the Communist minister of the interior out of office by withdrawing their representatives from the cabinet without first making sure that they had the support of the president, the Socialists, or anti-Communist elements in the army and the police. The Communists persuaded President Beneš to accept the resignations, proceeded to foment agitations that threatened to make public order break down completely, and then, backed by armed factory workers and the presence of Soviet forces on the frontiers of the country, boldly seized power. In face of this, President Beneš and the democratic leaders simply gave in. Munich had left them with a fundamental distrust of the West, from which they now expected no assistance; and the country as a whole had had its powers of resistance exhausted during the war and was in no mood to support last-ditch stands. Twenty years later the story was to be different.

East Berlin, Poland, and Hungary, 1953–1956   Whatever may be said about the economic benefits that the extension of communism brought to the peoples of eastern Europe (and to some sections of society, these were doubtless real), there is no doubt that the Soviet Union profited greatly from it. As early as 1947, the satellite states were taking more than half of the Soviet Union's exports and were supplying over a third of its imports, besides paying reparations in kind which the Soviets could re-export. Strategically, the forward march of communism gave to the Soviet Union that protective *glacis* that its foreign policy had striven to establish since the 1920s, and gave it, moreover, in a much more solid· form than could have been attained by mere treaty arrangements.

It was impossible to hide from the rest of the world that this represented a new form of imperialism, which Soviet dialecticians had always maintained was a disease peculiar to capitalism. The imposition of Soviet economic and social forms upon captive peoples, with little regard for cultural or physical differences, and the systematic exploitation of their resources was clearly reminiscent of the worst abuses of European colonial expansion. As in the case of the older imperialisms, moreover, there now came disturbing "native risings" against the colonizers, although these proved to be less successful than some of those treated above (see p. 411). Even so, the demonstrations of 1953 in East

Germany—and particularly the rising of June 17 in East Berlin—were so serious that Soviet tanks had to be brought in to quell them, which they did with a thoroughness that revolted even people who had opted for communism. Soviet brutality prompted the brightest star in East Germany's literary firmament, Bertolt Brecht, to write a poem called "The Solution," which appeared in the West after his death:

> Nach dem Aufstand des 17. Juni
> Ließ der Sekretär des Schriftstellerverbandes
> In der Stalinallee Flugblätter verteilen
> auf denen zu lesen war, daß das Volk
> Das Vertrauen der Regierung verscherzt habe
> und es nur durch verdoppelte Arbeit
> Zurückerobern könne. Wäre es da
> Nicht einfacher, die Regierung
> Löste das Volk auf und
> Wählte ein anderes?[17]

Three years later in Poznan, Poland, armed clashes between factory workers and the police led to perhaps a hundred deaths and revealed widespread disaffection in that country, a lesson underlined in August 1956 when the three hundredth anniversary of the crowning of the Blessed Virgin of Czestochowa attracted over a million celebrants and turned into an antigovernment demonstration. The central committee of the Polish Communist party decided that concessions must be made to the popular temper, and the Polish thaw began. The veteran Communist Wladeslaw Gomulka, expelled from the committee in 1949 because of his nationalism and his independence, was reinstated as the party's secretary general. The Soviet government showed signs of blocking this, and Khrushchev paid a special visit to Warsaw in October with the apparent intention of browbeating the Poles into subservience. After intimations from Marshal Rokossovsky about the unreliability of the Polish army, however, and after he was satisfied that Gomulka would not attempt to detach Poland from the Warsaw Pact, he seems to have decided that it was wiser to yield to Polish wishes than to risk a widespread armed insurrection. In the years that followed, some of the features of the Stalin period were modified: forced collectivization of agriculture was ended, political prisoners were released, the powers of the secret police were curtailed. But it would be an exaggeration to describe the results of this, as one Polish writer described them, as amounting to "humanistic Communism in an independent Poland." Gomulka's concessions to the desire for liberalization were never permitted to jeopardize the party's control over the country or its tie to the Soviet Union, and the restrictions upon civil and

---

[17] After the rising of June seventeenth/ The Secretary of the Writers Union/ Had handbills distributed in the Stalin Allee/ Which read that the people had forfeited/ The confidence of the government/ And could win it back again/ Only by redoubled work./ Wouldn't it be easier/ For the government to dissolve the people/ And to elect another one?

intellectual freedom continued to be oppressive. Indeed, in the late 1960s they became more so, as a government-approved policy of "anti-Zionism" got under way—a policy that pandered to the antisemitism that had often been noted in Polish history and in this case was directed particularly against the intellectuals.

One of the reasons why Khrushchev held his hand in Poland in October 1956 was that he was confronted with even graver troubles in Hungary, where a full-scale revolution erupted in that same month. Starting as a movement of university students, it spread rapidly to the workers, the middle classes, and even the army and the police and took the form of stormy demonstrations in favor of the withdrawal of Soviet troops, the reconstitution of the government, the guaranteeing of basic civil liberties, and widespread social reforms. When crowds were fired on by the Hungarian secret police, fighting broke out and spread throughout the country; workers' soviets began to be organized, this time against the regime; Russian troops had to retire from Budapest; a popular government was formed under the leadership of Imre Nagy, who appealed to the U.N. for assistance in defending Hungary's independence and neutrality.

At the U.N. the representative of the United States said to the Security Council: "We can truly say to the Hungarian people: 'By your sacrifice you have given the United Nations a brief moment in which to mobilize the conscience of the world on your behalf. We are seizing that moment, and we will not fail you'." But the events in Hungary coincided with the crisis at Suez (see p. 776), and in the end the promises were unfulfilled. On November 4 Soviet armored columns entered Hungary and swept into the larger urban centers. In Budapest there was desperate resistance, but it was put down with brutal severity, and the gallant fight for freedom ended in a new wave of executions and proscriptions.

Order was quickly restored in Hungary. A new government was formed under an obedient satrap, Janos Kadar; and Nagy was seized in defiance of a safe conduct given him by the Yugoslav embassy and subsequently executed as an example to others whose loyalty to the Soviet Union might be wavering. Nevertheless, the Hungarian revolution left scars. Even within the Soviet Union, it shook the faith of many members of the party and seriously disturbed university youth, while in Communist parties in the West there were many defections. In eastern Europe these repercussions caused some serious second thoughts, and in Hungary itself, as the crisis receded into the past, the Kadar regime elected to go in for a cautious policy of liberalization. In 1963 a political amnesty freed many of those convicted of political crimes in 1956, and Lazslo Rajk, the rebel leader executed during the suppression, was officially rehabilitated in March 1964 on the fifty-fifth anniversary of his birth. There was also an improvement in relations between church and state, as well as some encouraging signs that advancement in the civil service no longer depended exclusively upon membership in the Communist party.

Yugoslavia   The only country in eastern Europe, aside from Finland and Greece, that succeeded in establishing its freedom from Soviet imperialism was Yugoslavia. Entering upon the postwar period with a strong native Communist movement that had already liquidated its domestic opponents and with the prestige that came from the exploits of its leader, Tito (Josif Broz), in the resistance against German occupation during the war, Yugoslavia proved unresponsive to Soviet desires for conformity of policy. Its increasingly open gestures of independence led to an open break with the Soviet Union in 1948, when Yugoslavia was expelled from the Soviet association of nations. Worse might have followed, for the Soviets had no hesitation about encouraging economic blockade and military depredations on the part of Yugoslavia's neighbors. But these measures, when tried, merely kindled the fires of Yugloslav patriotism and made it apparent that only a major military effort could hope to wipe out the Titoist defection, and that even this might not succeed, for Yugoslavia had a long coastline and the Western powers were obviously prepared to supply the heretic with weapons and food supplies. American generosity, in particular, in providing both financial and military assistance, helped stiffen Tito's resistance and make it successful.

Yugoslavia's defection was one of degree. The country remained Communist, and restrictions on free thought and expression were hardly less stringent than in the Soviet Union. Institutionally, Tito favored a certain amount of decentralization in order to give authority to men who were in touch with local problems. Agriculture was decollectivized, and various experiments with profit sharing were made in order to stimulate industry and the social services. These were sufficiently successful to contribute to the stability of the regime. After 1955, the Russians recognized this and tried to reach a *modus vivendi* with the Yugoslavs. Their efforts did not succeed in bringing Yugoslavia back into the Soviet orbit, but neither did Western aid succeed in detaching Tito from the world of communism. Yugoslavia had become a neutral state but—as a U.N. observer noted—one of those "positive neutrals," whose neutrality seemed to operate against the West and in favor of its former friends and associates in eastern Europe.

The 1960s: Rumania and Czechoslovakia   In subsequent years, two quite different forces encouraged the countries of eastern Europe to loosen, if not to break, their ties with Moscow. After the sharp deterioration of relations between the Soviet Union and Communist China set in, the Chinese gave at least verbal support to the satellite governments when disputes with Moscow arose. On occasion Gomulka benefited from this, and Albania was described as a Chinese ideological outpost in the Balkans. On the other hand, the industrial progress and material prosperity of the West strengthened the desire of eastern governments to break out of the restrictions of Soviet bloc economy, and Rumania led the way in seeking trade agreements with the United States and West European governments.

Rumania's differences with the Soviet Union began in the early 1960s, when the Russians sought to transform Comecon, their rather anemic answer to the Marshall Plan, into a centralized planning authority that would dictate the economic structures and programs of all of the satellite states. Claiming that this would destroy their program of industrial development and their chances of developing trade with the West, the Rumanians objected so strenuously that, in December 1962, Khrushchev, preoccupied with other problems, abandoned his plan. Encouraged by this victory, the Rumanians took advantage of the

Sino-Soviet differences to maneuver themselves into a position of neutrality between the antagonists and at the same time restored formal contacts with Albania and Yugoslavia, although both those states were rebels from the Soviet system. In February 1964, the Rumanian Foreign Office actually offered its services as mediator between the Soviet Union and China, something that was unheard of in Soviet bloc diplomacy. By 1965, the Rumanian government was openly criticizing defects in the structure of the Warsaw Pact (see p. 769), intimating that it might withdraw unless they were corrected, and even refusing to allow Warsaw Pact military maneuvers within its borders. In 1968, it refused to support Soviet policy in Czechoslovakia; and in March 1969, in Warsaw, it virtually torpedoed Soviet plans for a united front against China, arguing that in disputes between Communist states there should be no choosing up of sides.

It used to be said of Hitler that one of the few men who impressed him was Marshal Antonescu of Rumania, who did so by an arrogance that kept the Fuehrer off balance. It may be that Nicolae Ceausescu, the leader of the Rumanian Communist party, was following Antonescu's prescription when he made such notable departures from Soviet bloc orthodoxy as he did in the summer of 1969 when he received the President of the United States in his capital city with excessive cordiality, and perhaps the Russians were impressed against their will. It is more likely, however, that the Soviet leaders were willing, before 1968, to tolerate Rumanian gestures of independence as long as they did not try anything as drastic as attempting to withdraw from the Warsaw Pact and that, after that date, they had other reasons for caution.

The year 1968—like 1938 and 1948—was one in which Czechoslovakia stood in the forefront of world news, and what was happening there was of crucial importance to the Soviet leaders. Ever since 1948, the Czechs had lived in the shadow of Stalinist oppression, administered most recently by the state president and first secretary of the Czech Communist party, Antonin Novotny. His unimaginative economic policies were the despair of the business community, and his contempt for culture a heavy burden on intellectuals. It was the latter group that struck the first blow against the party boss, when, in June 1967, an oblique attack was made upon his repression of free artistic expression during the Fourth Congress of the Czech Writers Union. Four months later, the Slovakian Communist leader Alexander Dubcek—an able politician who was responsive to all of the currents of unrest in his country—made a more forthright and circumstantial assault upon the party leadership, with such effect that Novotny's position was fatally compromised. In January Dubcek became first secretary of the Czech party and under his leadership the party presidium was purged of Stalinist hard-liners; and a reform group took over and drafted a program that called for a new electoral law, freedom of speech and assembly, protection of citizens from arbitrary actions of the security police, the rehabilitation of the victims of Stalin, unlimited rights of foreign travel, freedom of choice of profession, and economic reforms.

These events caused consternation in party headquarters in all east European capitals and, from May until August, there were repeated conferences between the Warsaw Pact powers, intended to bring the Prague reformers to their senses. Neither these, nor a visit by Kosygin to Prague in late May, nor Soviet troop maneuvers in Czechoslovakia in the early summer, daunted Dubcek and his

"Of course, Mr. Dubcek, we've had to bring a few lady stenographers, one or two secretaries and some tea boys . . ."

A British comment on the first stages of the Soviet takeover in Czecho-slovakia. (Cartoon by Cummings in *Daily Express,* London, August 1968)

colleagues, who were becoming more confident and uncompromising as the months passed and who were unresponsive even to the warnings of friendly visitors like Marshal Tito, who came to Prague early in August and was apparently shocked by the atmosphere of rebellion in the city. Close on Tito's heels came Ulbricht, a man who was highly sensitive to what was going on in Prague, since it could hardly help but affect his own position in East Germany. After talking with Dubcek, he continued on his way to Moscow, and what he told his hosts there about the Czech leader's mood seems to have confirmed the Soviets in their assumption that Dubcek was seeking independence for his country and consequently must be considered a counter-revolutionary; and this led them to give the green light to the soldiers, who had long demanded it. On the night of August 20, Soviet armor crossed Czech borders and advanced on Prague and Bratislawa, supported by East German units (who goose-stepped across Wenceslas Square as their Nazi predecessors had done in March 1939) and contingents from Poland, Bulgaria, and—reportedly with reluctance—Hungary. The world witnessed the first invasion of a Communist state by others of the same political persuasion.

The Czechs fought back gallantly with the means at their disposal—mass demonstrations and strikes and individual acts of heroism and desperation—but the Soviets were determined to stamp out the threat to the unity of the Eastern bloc, and they were implacable. Dubcek and other reformers were spirited off to Moscow and might never have been allowed to return had not the aged president of the state, Ludvik Svoboda, threatened to commit suicide unless they were released. The Soviets gave way on this point but insisted on a restructuring of the presidium of the Czech party, and once this began the hopes of the reformers were systematically destroyed.

Dubcek tried to pretend that this was not so, but, thanks to the maneuvering of Gustav Husak, who was placed in the presidium by the Soviets late in August, he was soon deprived of allies and left with no recourse but the dangerous one of appealing to public opinion against the occupying power. The Soviet military actually seemed to wish that he would do so. Infuriated by the mass demonstrations that followed the self-incineration of the student Jan Palach in January 1969 and by renewed disorders in March, the Soviet government on April 1 threatened to impose a military regime on the country and held back only when Husak promised that "the leadership of the Czechoslovak Socialist Republic [was] strong enough to restore order by itself." Two weeks later Dubcek, who had been allowed for the sake of appearances to retain his post as first secretary, was relieved of it; press censorship was made more rigorous; "anti-socialist elements" were declared responsible for disturbances of the public order since August; and the purge of the party began. By the autumn of 1969 the Czech spirit of resistance was still strong enough to inspire demonstrations in the streets on the anniversary of the Soviet invasion, but the pro-Soviet faction now had firm control of the instruments of power, and Dubcek, deprived of his post in the party presidium in September, was threatened with Khrushchev's fate—that of becoming an "un-person."[18]

This cursory account gives no real sense of the shock that the events of August 1968 and the renewed threat of April 1969 caused throughout the Western world, particularly to those who were ordinarily sympathetic to the Soviet Union. This was part of the price that the Soviet government had to pay for what they considered to be a necessary operation. It is understandable that they should have been reluctant to repeat the exercise again soon, particularly with Sino-Soviet relations as uncertain as they had become.

Science and Culture   Within the bloc, the intellectual and scientific progress made after 1945 was impressive. The governments of the Soviet Union and the satellite states lavished attention and support upon education, being particularly solicitous about the training of specialists who were needed in the economic, scientific, and engineering sectors of state activity. Soviet achievements in technical training certainly equaled those of the West in this period, and their effort in the field of foreign language training, to take one example, dwarfed anything being done, or even contemplated, in the United States. Soviet accomplishments in missile and rocket research and in cognate fields were particularly notable, and the successful launching of the first earth satellites in 1957 had a stunning impact on world opinion, causing some pessimistic Western observers to fear that supremacy in science had been lost irretrievably by the non-Communist

---

[18] Over the objections of the ultra-conservatives, Husak managed to get him the post of Minister to Turkey, but he was deprived of this and expelled from the party in the early summer of 1970.

world. By 1965, this fear had proved to be groundless, thanks to the notable achievements of Western scientists in rocketry and space travel, but the excellence of Soviet science was universally acknowledged.

The political uses to which the Soviets put their success with the *Sputniki* of 1957 illustrated an important truth about Communist support of research and development. Generally speaking, the Soviet and satellite governments gave their backing primarily to intellectual and scholarly activities that promised to increase state power or to advertise it. Thus, in addition to the obviously important or dramatic scientific activities, the performing arts were generously provided for, and those troupes from the Communist countries that were permitted to show themselves at the Brussels Exposition of 1958 and on similar occasions dazzled Western audiences.

In the creative arts, on the other hand, results were not so happy. For Soviet music, the cinema, and the pictorial arts, the great age had been the midtwenties—a period in which the experimental theater of Vsevolod Meyerhold flourished, when Pasternak and Mayakovsky were writing their best poetry, and when any number of vigorous prose works rolled from the presses, such as Fedin's *Cities and Years,* Leonid Leonov's *The Badgers,* and the grim and unforgettable sketches in Isaac Babel's *Red Cavalry.* But with the coming of Stalinism, and particularly when Zhdanov was acting as a kind of tsar of culture, such talents shriveled and died. It was now held that the role of the Soviet artist was to glorify the state and that failure to do so would not be tolerated. Mayakovsky committed suicide in 1930; the composer Shostakovitch, bitterly attacked by *Pravda* in 1936, came close to doing the same; Meyerhold, accused in 1937 of consistently producing anti-Soviet plays, was arrested in 1939 and died in a concentration camp during the war; Babel stopped writing—"So long as I don't publish anything, all they can do is call me lazy. But once I do a storm of serious and dangerous accusations is going to descend on my bald head."—but he was arrested nevertheless and died in a concentration camp. Outstanding figures like the musician Prokofiev and the film director Eisenstein were also abused and persecuted and had to go to humiliating private Canossas in order to expiate their sins.

The war years brought some relief to Soviet artists by loosening the ideological straitjacket that had been put on them; but the return of peace restored censorship and conformism. The state once again reserved the right to decide what was good art or bad and, in many cases, dictated both theme and treatment to writers. The result was apt to be dreary, if not banal. Commenting on "Socialist realism," a young Russian, who preferred to remain unnamed, wrote in 1959 that, since the theme of all Soviet novels was the Revolution, all of the endings had to be happy, although sometimes it was the technical processes rather than the human characters that survived.

> The reader gradually learns that, in spite of all break-downs, the machine-tool will be set to work, or that the kolkhoz "Victory," despite wet weather, is amassing a rich harvest of maize; and he closes the book with a sigh of relief, feeling that we have taken one more step toward communism.

From top left. Soviet Writers: Vladimir Mayakovsky, 1893–1930. Isaak Babel, 1894–1939. Aleksandr Solzhenitsyn, 1919– . Boris Pasternak, 1890–1960.

To an even greater extent than was true in the Russia of Nicholas I, criticism of the regime, even if it were indirect or referred to superficial aspects of Soviet life or governmental practice, was subject to punishment. This was shown all too clearly by the treatment accorded Boris Pasternak's novel *Doctor Zhivago,* which had a merited success throughout the Western world in 1957 and 1958 and won its author a Nobel prize but was banned in the Soviet Union, Pasternak being forced publicly to decline the honor paid him. Pasternak's most gifted successor, Aleksandr Solzhenitsyn, was treated even more meanly. After 1963, his published works, like *A Day in the Life of Ivan Denisovich* (1962), an account of life in one of Stalin's labor camps, disappeared from book stores and public libraries, and his longer works, *Cancer Ward* and *The First Circle,* which were triumphantly hailed in Western Europe and the United States, were not allowed to be published in his own country. Indeed, in November 1969, this most distinguished of modern Russian novelists was formally expelled from the National Writers Union. Other writers were even less fortunate. In 1966, Yuri Daniel and Andrei Sinyavsky were sentenced to five years of hard labor because works of theirs that appeared abroad were judged to be anti-Soviet propaganda.

The effect of this sort of thing on Soviet literature can be imagined. After he defected to the West in 1969, the novelist Anatoly Kuznetzov described how his works had been disfigured by state officials before being granted the right of publication. "But," he added, "they also deformed my whole life. I couldn't speak on the telephone; I practically stopped writing letters; and I saw an informer in every one of my acquaintances. I began to ponder: What sense is there in such a life at all?"

The state of the other arts was, by Western standards, deplorable, painting perhaps worst of all, particularly after Khrushchev had made clear his detestation of anything that smacked of abstraction. As for music, according to the American correspondent Henry Kanim, both the Bolshoi Opera and the Ballet had by the 1960s become museums of outdated styles, and a conductor, asked if he saw any possibility of mounting a performance of Alban Berg's *Wozzek*, replied sadly, "We haven't even reached Wagner and Strauß yet!"

Chapter 30 EUROPE AND THE WORLD: PROBLEMS AND PROSPECTS

THE UNITED NATIONS

Establishment and Institutions   Worn out by the long war and conscious that the future might not be free of international crisis, the weary peoples of Europe and their governments reacted with enthusiasm and hope to the creation of the organization that, in 1945, replaced the old League of Nations, which had passed out of existence six years before. Discussion of the necessity of a new world organization had begun early in the war, and planning in detail began at Dumbarton Oaks in 1944 (see p. 688). Although there was considerable wrangling at the subsequent Big Three conferences at Yalta and Potsdam (see p. 705) over questions of voting procedure and membership, agreement on all contested points was finally reached. The San Francisco Conference, which met in April 1945, completed the task of drafting and adopting the Charter of the United Nations in June.

The new organization was not intended to be a world government, for it recognized the sovereign rights of its members and was specifically forbiddden to "intervene in matters which [were] essentially within the domestic jurisdiction" of member states. Its declared purposes were rather to maintain peace and security, to develop good relations among nations, to promote the solution of economic, social, and other problems by international action, and to provide a forum at which the opposing views of its members might be reconciled.

To effect these purposes, the United Nations was provided with a number of different bodies of a representative, executive, and consultative nature. Like the League of Nations (see p. 502), it had an Assembly in which all its members had equal rights of representation and a Council (now called the Security Council)

UNESCO Headquarters, Paris. A general view of the Secretariat and Conference buildings. The statue in the plaza (foreground) is by Henry Moore. The buildings occupy a seven-and-a-half acre site made available by the French government. Plans for the headquarters were prepared by Marcel Breuer (U.S.), Pier Luigi Nervi (Italy), and Bernard Zehrfuss (France), and were approved by a panel of noted architects consisting of Lucio Costa (Brazil), Walter Gropius (U.S.), Le Corbusier (France), Sven Markelius (Sweden), and Ernesto Rogers (Italy). Eero Saarinen (U.S.) was also consulted. (UNESCO/Dominique Lajoux)

with more restricted and preferential membership. The General Assembly was given the authority to discuss all questions falling within the scope of the Charter, the right to appoint numerous standing and special committees, and the additional right to make recommendations to member states and to the Security Council. The Council, which was composed of five permanent members (the United States, the Soviet Union, China, Great Britain, and France) and six others elected for two-year terms by the Assembly, was designed to give direction and leadership to the work of the organization as a whole and to use its authority to deal swiftly and effectively with threats to the general peace. Its decisions on procedural matters were made by simple majority vote, but in all other questions the majority had to include the five permanent members. In short, every permanent member had the right of veto on most important issues.

This provision was written into the Charter in order to protect the interests of those powers with the greatest responsibilities, and it was not believed, by the Western powers at least, that the veto right would be abused. When the coming of the Cold War proved the frailty of this assumption of Great-Power cooperation, the work of the Security Council was hampered and at times paralyzed. As a result, the General Assembly achieved an importance that was probably not intended by the founders of the United Nations. In November 1950, the Assembly adopted a resolution stipulating that when lack of unanimity made it impossible for the Council to meet a threat to the peace, an emergency meeting of the General Assembly could be called at the request of a majority of its own members or of seven members of the Security Council and could make recommendations for collective action in the cause of peace, even to the point of recommending the use of military force. This broadening of the Assembly's mandate caused as many problems as it solved, and by the end of the 1960s the larger powers were inclining to the Soviet view that there should be a "return to the Charter." This promised to bring a clarification of the Council's prerogatives and a reduction of the Assembly's political powers.

Another body that gradually expanded its functions was the Secretariat, which was established to carry out administrative and technical tasks under the direction of a secretary general elected for a five-year term by the Assembly on the basis of recommendations made by the Security Council. In the 1950s and the first years of the following decade, when the U.N. was called upon to send troops to preserve peace in the Near East and the strife-torn Congo, the secretary's tasks increased in number and variety, and he was frequently required to act more as a diplomat than as a mere administrator. His growth in stature also reflected and reinforced that of the General Assembly, which tended to regard him as its spokesman and leader.

An important agency of the U.N. was the Economic and Social Council, whose mission was to contribute to the elimination and control of international friction by initiating studies in the area of social, health, and educational needs. This body, composed of eighteen members elected by the General Assembly without preferential treatment for Great Powers, had the right to appoint its own committees and worked through a network of such bodies, chosen for special tasks or work in specific areas. It maintained liaison with older organizations like the International Monetary Fund and the World Bank and supervised the establishment and functioning of new "specialized agencies," like the World Health Organization and the United Nations Educational, Scientific and Cultural Organization (UNESCO), to mention only two of the most important.

Other organs of the U.N. were the Trusteeship Council, which supervised the administration of territories whose peoples had not yet won full self-government (former mandated territories, former enemy colonies, territories handed over to the U.N. by their former administrators), and the International Court of Justice, which replaced the old Hague Court and was established in the same place. A special body set up in 1953 was the International Atomic Energy Agency (IAEA), which, despite its virtual autonomy, was required to report upon its activities to the U.N.

In the deliberations at San Francisco fifty states participated. The enemy powers were excluded, as were such neutrals as Spain, Portugal, Eire, Sweden, and Switzerland and one allied state, Poland, because it did not possess a government that was recognized by all the Great Powers.[1] Under pressure from the Latin American states, the United States government agreed to seek admission for Argentina (at that time, a country with a dictatorial regime) and succeeded in gaining it by promising the Soviet government to support the admission of two of Russia's provinces, the Ukraine and Byelorussia, as members with full rights and privileges. Membership was subsequently made available to other countries, provided they were "peace-loving states," recommended by the majority of the Security Council (with all permanent members either approving or abstaining), and backed by a two-thirds majority of the Assembly. The greatest changes in membership were those that followed the creation of the new independent states of Africa at the end of the 1950s. In 1970 there were 126 members,of which more than 60 were African and Asian states.

The U.N. Record, 1945–1970   When statesmen gathered in San Francisco in June 1965 to celebrate the twentieth anniversary of the United Nations, they did so with less enthusiasm and hope than was evident twenty years earlier, and nothing that happened in the next five troubled years lightened their somber mood. It was all too clear that the organization had not lived up to the idealistic expectations of its original supporters: it had failed to restrain the national ambitions of its members; it had been powerless to prevent Soviet aggression in eastern Europe or Indonesian aggression in Malaya; its peace-keeping activities had achieved no result in the Congo or in Vietnam; it was affected by acute financial embarrassment because of the refusal of some of its members to share the costs of peace-keeping operations, like that in the Congo, of which they disapproved; and its role in the Arab-Israeli dispute in the years 1967–1970 had been wholly ineffective. Too often the organization seemed to take the word for the deed. As Angie E. Brooks of Liberia said in her first speech as president of the Assembly in September 1969:

> We have sometimes failed to realize that neither oratory nor agreements between delegations, nor even resolutions and recommendations, have had much impact on the course of affairs in the world at large. . . . We have lacked, and do lack in this respect, a sense of reality. The sad fact is . . . that . . . we have not achieved the strength with which the Charter in its totality has endowed us.

Yet this was only one side of the picture. Even in the field of interstate conflict, the U.N.'s setbacks were matched by successes. It had, after all, voted to resist the attack on South Korea in June 1950 and had sent an expeditionary force which had finally gained its declared objective (see p. 767). It had also done important work, through its ability to mobilize public opinion, in defusing conflicts and promoting solutions. In this respect, its role in the Suez crisis of 1956 was notable (see p. 776) as was its intervention in Cyprus in 1964 and in the hostilities that erupted between India and Pakistan in 1965.

[1]Poland was admitted to U.N. membership in October 1945.

A cartoon by Illingworth from *Punch*, June 9, 1965. (© *Punch*, Ben Roth Agency)

Aside from this, it should not be forgotten that—in the words of Secretary of State of the United States Dean Rusk—"almost seventeen of every twenty U.N. employees and nearly ninety-three cents of every U.N. dollar are engaged in economic, social, and technical enterprises." On the basis of policy decisions made by the General Assembly and implemented by the Economic and Social Council, sixteen specialized agencies had done revolutionary work to improve world health standards, combat illiteracy, provide vocational training in under-developed countries, find new water supplies for arid areas, and formulate programs of irrigation, flood control, navigation, and hydroelectrical develop-ment, like the projected Mekong development plan of the Flood Control Bureau of the U.N. Economic Commission for Asia and the Far East. Given a chance of implementation, this last project might aid in the attainment of a viable political settlement in Southeast Asia, for it would bring great advantages to Laos, Cambodia, and both Vietnams.

It is possible that under the idealistic leadership of Secretary Dag Hammarsk-jöld, who died in Africa while seeking a solution to the Congo problem, the U.N. overcommitted itself in the political field. Hammarskjöld's successor, U Thant of Burma, was more modest in his expectations; and he was inclined to the view that, in a world in which resurgent nationalism reduced the U.N.'s ability to act effectively in the interest of peace, priority should be given to the job of combat-ing world poverty as the quickest route to world order.

THE DEFENSE OF WESTERN EUROPE

Challenge and Response   In the first years after the war, the states of western Europe had been unwilling to rely exclusively upon the U.N. for the defense of their security. They were threatened, indeed, by one of its charter members, the Soviet Union, which had the power to block any interference by the Security Council in its designs. The countries of the West were compelled, therefore, to seek other means of protection.

They had, it should be noted, faced up to the threat of Soviet imperialism reluctantly and slowly, clinging to the hope of collaboration with Russia and deferring the sacrifices necessary for effective opposition as long as possible. Perceptive observers saw the danger early and dutifully reported it. George Kennan, the United States chargé d'affaires in Moscow, wrote home in February 1946, "We have here a political force committed fanatically to the belief that with [the West] there can be no permanent *modus vivendi,* that it is desirable and necessary that the internal harmony of our society be disrupted, our traditional way of life be destroyed, the international authority of our [states] be broken, if Soviet power is to be secure." It was not, however, until 1947, when the Soviet threat to Greece and Turkey became obvious and pressing that the Western states prepared for a real defensive effort. The enunciation of the Truman Doctrine in March 1947, in which the United States government promised economic aid to Greece and Turkey and support to "all free peoples who are resisting attempted subjugation by armed minorities or by outside pressure," and the presentation of the Marshall Plan in June of the same year, promising American support for any European recovery effort that was undertaken by collaborative means, put an end to hesitation and to the mood of resignation that had reigned in more than one European capital since 1945 and stimulated a vigorous movement toward European integration.

This took several forms. On the political level, it led in 1949 to the establishment of the Council of Europe, a consultative body that eventually had sixteen members who found it a useful agency for the exchange of views and the establishment of common policy in areas of particular concern to the European states. On the economic level, it led, after the announcement of the Marshall Plan and the approval by the United States Congress of a total sum of financial aid to Europe, to the establishment of an Organization for European Economic Cooperation (OEEC) in April 1948. This body, which was designed to define the specific needs of the separate states requiring Marshall Plan aid and to draw up a long-term plan for European recovery, contributed greatly to the speed with which Europe got back on its feet. The OEEC also laid a foundation for other forms of economic cooperation; and, in the next decade, it was followed by such agencies as the European Coal and Steel Community (ECSC), formed to stimulate the production of coal and steel by reducing trade barriers, the European Atomic Energy Community (Euratom), set up in order to promote joint exploitation of the peaceful uses of atomic energy, and the European Economic Community (Common Market), which was founded in January 1958 with the purpose of eliminating all economic barriers among its members, facilitating the movement of workers, capital, and services among them, and giving them a common trade policy toward the rest of the world. The difficult problems that confronted these organizations were many, but the will to overcome them was strong, and their very creation showed a recognition of interdependence that had been lacking in Europe since the free-trade era of the 1860s. Indeed, the majority of the members of the Common Market (France, West Germany, Italy, and the Benelux countries) repeatedly sought to widen their association by adding new members (agreements providing for eventual membership were concluded with Greece in 1962 and Turkey in 1963) or by making special arrangements with other organizations, like the European Free Trade Association (Britain, Austria, Denmark, Sweden, Norway, Switzerland, and Portugal), which was founded in 1960. The movement of integration suffered a setback in January 1963 and again in November 1967 when General de Gaulle used his considerable authority to block British entrance into the Common Market but, after his departure from office in 1969, the issue was revived. Its resolution was complicated by difficult problems affecting currency, agricultural prices, and Great Britain's special relation to the Commonwealth. Meanwhile, both the EFTA and the Common Market brought solid advantages to their members, and membership in the latter organization played a significant role in the economic boom enjoyed by France and Italy in the 1960s.

The Birth of NATO and the Korean War   Significant as these developments were, it was considered of greater urgency to erect some kind of military barrier against the possibility of a westward surge of Soviet imperialism. Recognition of this need was behind the conclusion in March 1948 of the Treaty of Brussels, by which Great Britain, France, Belgium, the Netherlands, and Luxembourg committed themselves to common defense in case of an attack upon the European territory of any of their number. But even when this step had been taken, it was realized that the states of Western Europe would not succeed in raising very impressive military forces, at least in the foreseeable future, unless they received American assistance.

This, however, was not long delayed. In March 1948 President Harry S. Truman endorsed the purposes of the Brussels Treaty, and in June the United States Senate—acting in the wake of the Communist take-over in Czechoslovakia and during the Soviet blockade of Berlin (see p. 708)—adopted the so-called Vandenberg Resolution, which, while affirming that it was the policy of the United States to achieve international peace and security through the U.N., stated that the United States must also contribute to the maintenance of peace "by making clear its determination to exercise the right of individual and collective self defense under Article 51 [of the Charter] should any armed attack occur affecting its national security." This revolutionary identification of national security with collective action—revolutionary because it flew in the face of inherited American prejudice against entangling alliances—made it possible for the United States government to throw its support behind the Brussels powers. This assumed tangible form in the conclusion of the North Atlantic Treaty, which was signed in April 1949 by the five Brussels powers, Denmark and Norway (traditionally neutral powers whose reluctance to join a power bloc was overcome by the Czech coup), Iceland, Italy, Portugal, Canada, and the United States, and was subsequently ratified by their governments. By this treaty, the signatories agreed that an armed attack upon any one of them in Europe or North America would be considered as an attack upon them all and would be resisted by all of them by such action as was deemed necessary, "including the use of armed force," this being coordinated whenever possible with parallel action by the U.N. Upon this mutual guarantee, the North Atlantic Treaty Organization (NATO) was built.[2]

Although political and economic functions were envisaged for the new organization, or at least alluded to in the basic treaty, NATO was from the beginning a primarily military body, intended by its very existence to deter new Soviet aggression and to resist it if it came. How feasible this was, at least for the time being, was problematical. At the time of NATO's organization, there were in all Western Europe only about a dozen divisions of ground troops (including what was left of the United States army in Europe) backed by a few hundred planes. In contrast, the Russians were reported to have at least twenty-five divisions in the satellite states and many more at home, as well as thousands of operational aircraft. The Western governments, therefore, were called upon to enact the legislation and vote the funds that would make possible the raising of forces numerous and well armed enough to deny to the superior Soviet numbers a quick and easy victory, while giving their own countries the time for full mobilization.

The drive toward this objective was given impetus in June 1950 when the North Korean Communists drove across the 38th parallel and invaded South Korea. The background of this event lies properly beyond the scope of a book that is devoted primarily to European history. It was bound up with the postwar collapse of Chiang Kai-shek's attempts to maintain his government on the mainland of China, despite the great volume of American aid and advice that had been lavished upon him, and the systematic conquest of China by the Chinese Communists under their leader Mao Tse-tung, which was completed in 1949 and restricted Chiang's power to Formosa and neighboring islands. These events gave confidence to communism elsewhere in the Far East, not least of all in North Korea, where Soviet agents had remained after the withdrawal of Russian troops at the war's end. There had been frequent conflict between the two Korean regimes and several border incidents, but what ensued now was a full-scale war.

The United States government determined without hesitation to resist the breach of law and despatched troops and planes to Korea from General Douglas MacArthur's headquarters in Japan to reinforce the local garrisons and the South Korean army. It also sought the sanction of the U.N. for its actions and, despite Soviet resistance to this (and in part because of a tactical error on the part of the Soviets in absenting themselves from the Security Council at the time of a crucial vote), received it. Thus, the war became an international effort with the objective of resisting the initial aggression and restoring the status quo, and British, Canadian, Australian, Turkish, and other U.N. troops participated in it before it was over, although the bulk of the U.N. force was supplied by the United States.

This, in itself, created some difficulties, for, if the great majority of those in

[2] To the original twelve members, Greece and Turkey were added in 1952 and West Germany in 1955.

the U.N. who had favored resistance regarded this as a limited war, many Americans were impatient with this idea and demanded, in the press, in Congress, and in public debate, that there should be a total solution. This insistence increased when the first overwhelming enemy drive was at last beaten to a standstill in the very outskirts of the southern port of Pusan, and when the counteroffensive began and—thanks to a brilliant amphibious operation at Inchon on the west coast, where MacArthur's forces and the U.S. Marines stormed ashore behind the enemy lines—drove the North Koreans back to the 38th parallel. General MacArthur shared the view that wars should end in total victory, and he ordered his armies to advance across the parallel and to move north to the Yalu River. This action brought Chinese Communist "volunteer forces" into the fight; and, striking hard at a gap that had appeared in the U.N. lines during the rapid advance, they routed American forward units and changed the whole complexion of the war. It now became a dogged seesaw conflict that went on until a truce was finally patched up in the summer of 1953 which restored the situation of 1950. By that time, the United States suffered about half as many casualties as it had in World War II.

The heated controversy that embittered American politics during the last years of this conflict, which led to charges of inefficiency and treason against the Democratic administration and compelled President Truman to dismiss General MacArthur for what amounted to insubordination, need not concern us here. It is important to note, however, that, in refusing to expand the war into an all-out conflict with China, as some of its critics seemed to desire, the Truman Administration was holding to the belief that the critical strategic area in the struggle against communism was Europe. It shared the fear of its European allies that an attack similar to that of the North Koreans might be launched at any moment from the eastern satellite states, where the Russians were known to be encouraging the raising of military forces.

These fears had a direct and important effect upon the development of NATO's strength and operational plans. The fear of imminent attack stimulated the efforts of the European states to increase their military strength quickly and persuaded the United States government to let Europe share the results of its own mobilization for the Korean war. It also made it seem necessary for NATO planners to think in terms of a "forward strategy," so that, if an attack from the Soviet orbit actually came, it would be checked as far to the east as possible, thus eliminating the dismal prospect of an easy Soviet conquest of Western Europe, followed, possibly, by a re-liberation of the devastated continent by Western armies. These considerations led in the last months of 1950 to a reorganization of the NATO forces (which, among other things, placed American and French troops in Germany under NATO), the creation of a Supreme Command under General Dwight D. Eisenhower, the sending of additional American forces to Europe (four new divisions in 1951), the admission of Greece and Turkey to NATO (although their memberships did not become effective until 1952), and—not least important—the decision, in principle, to authorize the rearmament of Germany.

This last proposal was one that, not unnaturally, raised grave doubts in many minds in countries that had suffered under Nazi invasion and occupation; but, especially after a NATO Council meeting in Lisbon in February 1952 had set the level of forces required for a forward strategy at ninety-eight divisions, to be available within thirty days of the outbreak of a war, a German contribution to European defense was seen to be inevitable for economic and other reasons. The French government, which had the greatest original hesitation about rearming the Germans, was forced to see the logic of this, but nevertheless proposed that, as a safeguard against danger, the European army should be organized as an integrated force, in which there were no national units of more than battalion strength. This was the famous project of a European Defense Community (EDC) which involved the NATO governments in laborious negotiations until August 1954, when the French Assembly, in a highly fractious mood, rejected it out of hand—an event, incidentally, that is said to have contributed to the death of that zealous champion of European unity. Alcide de Gasperi. (see p. 722).

This caused a crisis of major proportions within the alliance, although it was finally overcome by patient diplomacy in which the British took the lead (and U.S. Secretary of State John Foster Dulles did important work behind the scenes). In return for a British promise not to withdraw their forces from Europe without the concurrence of the Brussels powers, the French government agreed to amend the Brussels Pact, create out of it a Western European Union (WEU) with Germany and Italy as new members, and permit Germany to join NATO. By the London and Paris agreements of December 1954, ratified in the following spring, West Germany was admitted to NATO and authorized to raise an armed force of 500,000 officers and men as a contingent in the NATO line of battle.

The Soviet Union countered these moves in May 1955 by organizing its satellites in a military league known as the Warsaw Pact.[3] It simultaneously began a skillful propaganda campaign that was designed to slow German rearmament by intimating that the Bonn government's membership in NATO would be a permanent barrier to German reunification. This was not without effect in West Germany, the Socialists in particular arguing that new negotiations with the Soviet Union on the German question should precede any implementation of the London and Paris agreements. Socialist opposition was not strong enough to block Bonn's adhesion to NATO, since there was a good deal of evidence that the German question was not negotiable. When it was actually discussed in 1955 at a summit meeting in Geneva, which was attended by President Eisenhower, Prime Minister Eden of Great Britain, and the Soviet leaders Bulganin and Khrushchev, and at a subsequent meeting of Soviet and Western foreign ministers, Eastern and Western views proved to be wholly irreconcilable, not because of the armaments issue but because the Western governments wanted reunification of Germany by means of free elections, while the Soviet Union argued that the most expeditious means of approaching the problem would be by direct negotiations between the two German governments.

[3] Its members were the Soviet Union, Albania (until 1961, when its diplomatic ties with Moscow were broken off), Bulgaria, Czechoslovakia, the German Democratic Republic, Hungary, Poland, and Rumania. Rumania has, on occasion, refused to cooperate in Warsaw Pact maneuvers (see p. 754).

NATO from 1955 to 1970   In the years that followed, NATO was subjected to trials that left it weaker than it was in the period immediately after the outbreak of the Korean war. Stalin's death in 1953 led to a thaw in East-West relations that reached its height at the summit meeting of 1955, which produced a euphoria similar to the one that followed Locarno (see pp. 510–511) and led to as much talk about the "spirit of Geneva" as there once had been about the "Locarno spirit." The inevitable result was a relaxation on the part of the states of Western Europe, which now showed no urgency about meeting the force levels set at Lisbon. Their performance was, indeed, so disappointing that, in its meeting of December 1954, the NATO Council authorized its commands to plan their operations on the assumption that they would be free to use nuclear weapons supplied by the United States in the case of an attack. Tactical nuclear weapons were to make up for numerical deficiencies in the deterrent force. Since the Russians would presumably have nuclear weapons too, this rationale was not entirely convincing to some Western Europeans, who were further concerned over the probable effects of atomic bombardment in a highly urbanized area like their own. After the December decision, therefore, as NATO became increasingly dependent upon nuclear weapons, both tactical and strategical, there was mounting public criticism of its operational plans.

The strength of NATO forces was further weakened by France's Algerian troubles (see p. 789), which necessitated the withdrawal of all but two of France's divisions from the NATO battle line; and the organization's internal cohesion was threatened by two crises in the Near East. Troubles on the island of Cyprus in September 1955 led to sharp differences between the British and Greek governments on the one hand and the Greek and Turkish governments on the other (see p. 774), all of which made for disharmony in the alliance. More serious was the Suez crisis of November 1956 (see p. 776), which led to a situation in which the United States government associated with the Soviet government in censuring the actions of its British and French allies before the U.N. Security Council. This might have led to the total collapse of NATO had it not been for the subsequent Soviet threats to rocket bomb London and Paris. These threats and the blood-letting in Hungary served as a healthy reminder to the NATO partners that the Soviet menace was still real and pressing, and at the Paris meeting of the NATO Council in December 1956 steps were taken to solve differences and strengthen the alliance.

In the subsequent period, Western Europe witnessed the opening of the Space Age, ushered in by the Soviet success in launching the first earth satellites (the *Sputniki*) in October 1957; it saw both the Soviet Union and the United States make great advances in the building of intercontinental missiles, which promised one day to eliminate the need for strategical bombers with human crews; and it suffered a continuing campaign of Soviet threats and blandishments designed to weaken the unity and will of the alliance. In the spring of 1960, for example, the capture of an American espionage plane (the U-2) inside Russian territory led the Soviet government to warn several NATO members that future use of their bases for such purposes would invite the gravest of reprisals. Two years later, the Soviets reached boldly into the heart of the Atlantic area and began to build a base of their own, a missile-launching site in Fidel Castro's Cuba.

The Launching of the Soviet Sputniki in October 1957. The patient surrounded by the rocket fragments is the United States. He is covered by placards announcing impending American space triumphs. Above his head, a diagnosis reads: "Altitude Sickness complicated by Cosmic Feebleness and Yellow Journalism Fever." By Boris Efimov in *Krokodil*. Compare the passage in Aleksandr Solzhenitsyn's novel *The First Circle* (1968) in which Khorobrov describes the role of the political guidance officer in the rocket crew, "when our people start on the first flight to the moon," and Pryanchikov answers, "Ilya Terentich! Let me assure you, it won't be that way . . . Americans will be on the moon first."

Atomic blackmail was not as successful here as in the Suez crisis. The United States government reacted promptly and firmly, and the Soviets found it expedient to retreat.

The Cuban crisis of October 1962 marked the beginning of an easing of relations between the two superpowers, and the result of this, as usual, was a dangerous degree of relaxation and disarray within the NATO framework. This was accompanied by the appearance of serious strategical differences between the allies. In December 1962, at a meeting in Nassau, President Kennedy and Prime Minister Harold Macmillan reached an agreement by which Great Britain abandoned its program for the construction of Skybolt missiles in return for American Polaris

Charles de Gaulle's campaign against NATO and SEATO. A West
German view by Flora. From *Die Zeit,* June 11, 1965.

missiles to be used in British nuclear submarines. These vessels were then to
be assigned, along with British bombers, to a joint NATO multilateral force—an
American project designed to prevent the proliferation of nuclear force among
the allies, to reward the Germans for their outstanding contribution to NATO's
ground forces (twelve almost complete divisions by 1962) by granting them a
share in nuclear planning, and (not the least consideration) to maintain American
control over the alliance's nuclear capacity.

The Nassau agreement was criticized in England as a surrender of independence in military affairs, and this contributed, although it would be difficult
to say exactly how much, to the Conservative party's decline (see p. 735). It
had more serious repercussions in France. On January 14, 1963, President Charles
de Gaulle announced that France would not accept Polaris missiles or participate
in the multilateral fleet. Moreover, with a plain intimation of his disenchantment
with NATO, *le grand Charles* expressed the belief that traditional alliances were
for all practical purposes obsolete and should be replaced by national nuclear
deterrents. Finally, as we have seen (p. 766), he caused general consternation
by vetoing Great Britain's projected entry into the Common Market.

These decisions were not as irresponsible as they appeared to some English
and American observers. De Gaulle sensed that a historical shift was taking
place and that the American dominance in the Western world, so pronounced
in the 1940s and 1950s, must now give way to a relation of equality among the
United States, the Soviet Union, and a free, united, and strong Europe. France's
role was to lead Europe to this kind of unity and strength and to advance her
own grandeur by doing so; but this must not be accomplished at the cost of
submerging France's identity in the kind of political union desired by the Americans and the smaller members of NATO. A confederation of free fatherlands
would suffice. As for the exclusion of Great Britain from the Common Market,
it was apparently guided by the belief that, as long as the British continued

to defer to the Americans in strategical matters and the Commonwealth in economic ones, they were not European enough to qualify for membership.

The general had the strength of his convictions and, in 1966, he effected France's military (but not political) withdrawal from the alliance. In addition to necessitating the transfer of NATO's headquarters from Paris to Brussels, this caused serious losses in manpower, logistical support, and strategical depth, which the other members found it difficult to repair in the years that followed. Their efforts to do so were given urgency in August 1968, as they had been in 1948, by Soviet aggression in Czechoslovakia, and they were not entirely unsuccessful. On its twentieth birthday, in April 1969, NATO was, at least on paper, a formidable organization which in the event of war could call upon a deterrent force of fifty-four divisions in the European theater plus about fifteen independent brigades—about 800,000 ground troops in all—and could support them with about 3500 tactical aircraft, a nuclear stockpile of 7000 tactical warheads and about 2250 delivery vehicles, and the ships and weapons of allied naval commands in the Atlantic, the English Channel, and the Mediterranean. On the other hand, not all of the units were at full strength (it was difficult, for example, after the military coup in Greece in 1967 (see p. 748), to estimate how strong or reliable the Greek contingent was) and not all of the members of the alliance were willing to make them so. In April 1969, the Canadian government announced that it would reduce the strength of its contingent (an inappropriate and discouraging birthday gift for the organization), and, responding to what appeared to be a ground swell of neo-isolationism induced by the Vietnam war, some American congressmen began to argue that the United States must follow the Canadian example. Despite events in Czechoslovakia, many people in Western Europe also, including a large proportion of academic youth, regarded NATO as an expensive anachronism, a circumstance that made its future problematical.

EUROPE AND THE NEAR EAST

The European Stake   The period that opened in 1945 was one of great changes in the Near East. This was an area in which the European states had been interested throughout the whole period covered by this book, and during that time they had invested time, money, technological skill, and political effort in the lands at the eastern end of the Mediterranean. Whether the strategic importance of the Near East was as great to the Western powers as it once had been was, in these days of long-range strategical bombers and intercontinental missiles, at least debatable, although no NATO commander would have admitted for a moment that bases in Turkey were an insignificant contribution to Western defense or that a growth of Soviet influence in the area would have negligible strategical results. As for its economic value to the West, there was no doubt whatsoever. Western European industry and transportation systems were heavily dependent upon the rich oil deposits of the area and would be exposed to danger if these were denied to the West.

The Western powers were therefore anxious to retain their position in the Near East. Because of the explosive nationalism that affected the peoples of the area, however, and because of their own tactical mistakes and the ability of the Soviet Union to exploit them, they lost ground very perceptibly.

Greece and Turkey   Western European strength in the area was, for one thing, weakened by grave differences between Great Britain and Greece, despite the services of the former to the Greek cause during the war and the first years that followed it, and between Greece and Turkey, despite their mutual membership in NATO.

The Anglo-Greek conflict arose in the island of Cyprus, which had been acquired as a British base in 1878 by Disraeli, who thought of it as the "key to western Asia" (see p. 256). British government of the island, during its days as a protectorate and, after 1925, as a crown colony, was benevolent and efficient and probably satisfactory to most of its Greek and Turkish inhabitants. Nevertheless. Cyprus had long been an objective of Philhellene aspiration, and the Greek church and a significant number of educated Greeks on the island worked long and faithfully for *Enosis* (union of Cyprus with Greece). In the early 1930s an outburst of prounion feeling led to so much disorder and material damage that the government had to arrest its leaders and send them into exile. In the 1950s a more systematic movement began under the leadership of Michael Mouskos, Archbishop Makarios III; and, starting in 1954, a guerrilla movement directed by George Grivas carried on a campaign of terrorism that was intended to win international sympathy and support for *Enosis*. It proved to be so bloodthirsty in its methods and so indiscriminate in its choice of victims that it had the opposite effect. In addition, it alienated the Turkish minority on the island, who took to anti-Greek terrorism on their own account; and this led to riots against the Greeks in Istanbul in September 1955 and to the bombing of the Turkish consulate in Salonika in reply.

British patience and the pressure of world opinion finally led to a provisional solution in 1959. Cyprus would achieve independent status, with the Greek and Turkish inhabitants administering their own affairs and with British strategical interests guaranteed, but with *Enosis* permanently denied. This settlement worked reasonably well until 1964, when it was denounced by Makarios. New fighting broke out between Greeks and Turks, and the U.N. was forced to intervene and to act as guarantor of the constitution. By that time, Greece's energies were so distracted by the internal troubles that led to the military coup of 1967 (see p. 748) that its government was in a weak position to play a role in Cyprus. The troubles there continued nonetheless to poison relations among NATO's Eastern partners.

Turkey's strength as an ally was cast in some doubt by the occurrence of serious internal troubles in 1959 and 1960. The one-party system that had obtained in the country after Kemal's revolution (see p. 499) had begun to break down before World War II; and, in 1946, a new party, the Democratic party, was founded and, four years later, was swept into power by a large majority. Under the prime ministership of Adnan Menderes, this party played an active role in rebuilding an economy that had been badly shaken by the war, in modernizing the transportation network, and in increasing agricultural production. The regime nevertheless showed a growing inattention to the laws of sound finance, and its mistaken belief that its deficits would be made good by the United States Treasury soon involved it in credit shortages, inflation, and social distress. To still its critics, the Menderes government used increasingly authoritarian methods.

Political opponents were jailed with little provocation, and, when student demonstrations took place in the spring of 1960, the police invaded university precincts without authorization, mishandled the rector when he protested, and acted with the utmost brutality against unarmed crowds.

By the early fall of 1960, a good part of the Turkish populace had had enough of Menderes, and a military coup led to the arrest of the prime minister and most of his cabinet, all of whom were tried for offenses against the state, and three of whom, including Menderes, were executed. The officers who engineered this were loud in their protestations that the *Putsch* was intended to restore respect for law and would make no difference in Turkey's commitment to NATO, and this was generally borne out by the civilian regime of Ismet Inonu, which took over from the military in 1961 and remained in office until February 1965. There was, however, little stability in the country, and the Justice party, which replaced the liquidated Democratic party and which came to power in October 1965 and confirmed its control of the National Assembly in the elections of October 1969, was increasingly critical of its Western allies. It in turn was the target of violent demonstrations in the universities, which were so destructive of public order that, by the summer of 1970, informed observers saw the possibility of a new military intervention in politics.

The Problem of Israel   Ever since World War I, many of the political troubles of the Arab world had centered around the problem of the Jews in Palestine and the conflicting promises made to them and the Arabs by the Western powers (see pp. 472 and 501). These assumed a new intensity after 1945. In that year the British announced that they planned to give up their mandate over Palestine and referred the long-vexed problem to the U.N. The U.N., responsive to the needs of homeless Jewish refugees in central and eastern Europe, accepted a plan in November 1947 for the partition of Palestine and the establishment there of a Jewish state, an Arab state, and an internationalized city of Jerusalem. Partition proved difficult to implement. When the Jews proceeded, in the spring of 1948, with the establishment of an independent republic in Palestine with its capital at Tel Aviv, they were attacked by military forces raised by the Arab League (Egypt, Syria, Lebanon, and Iraq), and disorderly fighting went on until the beginning of 1949. The Arab forces were ill-trained, badly led, and greatly inferior to their antagonists. When U.N. mediators, with great difficulty, finally arranged a truce, the new Israeli republic was given the greater part of Palestine.

Israel had made good its claim to statehood, was recognized by the U.N., and was admitted to U.N. membership in May 1949. For the next seven years, under the leadership of its prime minister, David Ben Gurion, it concentrated on its domestic tasks. Its population grew threefold in this period, as refugees came to the homeland from all over Europe. These immigrants had to be trained in the skills that would make for survival in a hard land and to be given the tools with which to earn their livelihood. For this and for various cooperative enterprises, the Israelis depended upon foreign loans, German reparations, and collections among Jewish communities abroad; but the United States, in particular, was generous, and the new republic made remarkable progress.

It was a progress with which the mounting indignation of its Arab neighbors kept pace. The Arab League had not accepted its setback as definitive. It exploited the grievances of the Palestinian Arabs, who had fled into neighboring lands where they lived in squalor and penury, and it began to organize terrorist gangs from the more active elements of these dispossessed people and to encourage border affrays. The new Egyptian regime was particularly active in these enterprises. The Israelis, scenting the imminence of another attack from that quarter, accelerated the training program of their armed forces, following procedures that later won the unstinted admiration of Western military observers. One of them, S. L. A. Marshall, wrote later:

> Both in the reserve and in the active army, training is more rigorous, puts heavier emphasis on field combat exercises, and makes heavier demand on the physical powers of the individual than in the United States Army.

The results of this preparation were evident in the campaign in the Sinai desert in 1956.

Egypt and the Suez Crisis of 1956   During the first postwar decade, Egyptian politics was marked by a frenetic nationalism that exceeded in violence even that of the years before 1936. This feeling, which was directed particularly at the remnants of British influence in Egypt, especially their rights in the Sudan and at the Suez Canal as defined in treaties of 1899 and 1936, became so virulent that in 1951 it defeated an Anglo-American plan for a Middle East Command based in Egypt and allied to NATO. When this proposal was submitted to the Egyptian government, they did not give it even the courtesy of careful study, replying obliquely by denouncing the two aforementioned treaties.

The importance of Egypt in any strategical plan for the defense of the Near East made the Western governments persist in their efforts to reach an agreement with Cairo. The deterioration of Egypt's internal situation seemed to favor their cause, for, after a military revolt had overthrown King Farouk's government and replaced it with one led first by General Naguib and then, in 1954, by Colonel Gamal Abdel Nasser, who became president and prime minister, it appeared that a political-military arrangement would be possible. At this stage of his career, Nasser seemed to be pro-Western in his views and was well regarded in Washington, whence he received substantial financial assistance and a promise to support the construction of a dam at Aswan, a project upon which the new dictator had set his heart. With Britain, Nasser concluded a new treaty in 1954, by which the British agreed to withdraw their troops from the Canal Zone within two years, on condition that they would have the right of re-entry in case of an external threat to Egypt's control of the Canal and that the Egyptian government would continue to respect the Convention of 1888, which guaranteed freedom of transit on this important international waterway. The Sudan question was also regulated, that country being given the choice of union with Egypt or independence, the second of which the Sudanese chose in 1955.

These signs of Egyptian friendship with the West were transitory. Nasser's insistent demands for military aid were refused by the West, which feared that any weapons sent him might be used against Israel. The Egyptian leader turned immediately to the Soviet bloc and, in September 1955, concluded an agreement for the delivery of arms, ostensibly with Czechoslovakia but in reality with the Soviet Union. The failure of the West to retaliate effectively encouraged him to go further. He began to stimulate anti-Western propaganda in other Arab countries, to give aid to the rebels in Algeria (see p. 790), and to negotiate for the establishment of relations with Red China, while at the same time being exceedingly arrogant in his negotiations with the United States government for the financing of the High Dam at Aswan. Nasser's attitude irritated John Foster Dulles, the American secretary of state, who was already deeply concerned over the multiplying contacts between Nasser and the Soviet bloc. As he later said in a press conference, "The Egyptians, in a sense, forced upon us an issue to which I think there was only one proper response. That issue was, do nations which play both sides get better treatment than nations which are stalwart and work with us?" He decided that they should not and, in July 1956, announced that American aid for the dam would be withdrawn.

Nasser regarded this as an attempt to humiliate him and his country, and he retaliated by seizing the Suez Canal Company in defiance of international conventions and of his own recent assurances to the British.

At this point, all semblance of unity within the Western alliance broke down. The British and French governments felt that firm action should be taken to make Nasser give up the canal and that, if he would not recognize some form of international administration of the canal, then the West must be ready to use military force to compel him to give way. Anthony Eden, foreign minister at the time, wrote to President Eisenhower:

> The seizure of the Suez Canal is, we are convinced, the opening gambit in a planned campaign designed by Nasser to expel all Western influence and interests from Arab countries. He believes that if he can get away with this, ... his prestige in Arabia will be so great that he will be able to mount revolutions of young officers in Saudi Arabia, Jordan, Syria, and Iraq. (We know that he is already preparing a revolution in Iraq, which is most stable and progressive.) These new Governments will in effect be Egyptian satellites, if not Russian ones. They will have to place their united oil resources under the control of a united Arabia led by Egypt and under Russian influence. When that moment comes, Nasser can deny oil to Western Europe and we here shall all be at his mercy.

The United States government might have been more responsive to this appeal had it not been for the fact that the country was in the throes of a presidential campaign in which the incumbent administration was using the settlement of the Korean war as an argument for its return to office. It was definitely opposed to the use of force to solve the Egyptian problem and preferred to let matters drift rather than to take any course that might in the end make forceful intervention necessary. It did not, however, make its position entirely clear to its allies. Its statements were so ambiguous that the British and French began to suspect it of a deliberate lack of candor, if not of a desire to deceive. Since Soviet and Yugoslav votes in the Security Council made any useful action by the U.N.

unlikely, the frustration of the two European powers mounted and finally led them to take rash and ill-considered action.

The steady increase in the number and intensity of incidents on the Arab-Israeli border and the growing evidence of Egyptian preparations for a full-scale war had by the beginning of October 1956 convinced the Israeli government of the necessity of taking steps to forestall possible disaster. They communicated their concerns to the government of Guy Mollet in France, which in turn suggested to the British that an Israeli attack across the Sinai peninsula would give the British and the French a pretext for intervening and seizing the canal. Eden, who was by this time, according to close associates, almost pathologically intent on overthrowing Nasser, agreed; and, even before he had persuaded his cabinet to go along, promised the Israelis, who were still not committed to action, that the Western allies would give appropriate support to their operations and that the British would destroy the Egyptian air force. With this assurance, the Israeli army, on October 29, invaded the Sinai peninsula, a fortified area about half the size of Nevada, held by an enemy with superiority in numbers, equipment, and munitions, and in a campaign that lasted just about a hundred hours proceeded to smash all its fighting units, capture all of its defensive positions, and force it to flee in wild and humiliating panic back across the canal into Egypt.

The planned British and French operation to seize the canal with their military forces was not so brilliantly staged and ended in a damaging setback. Logistical difficulties (compounded by Eden's failure to give his military commanders sufficient advance warning of Israeli intentions), lack of complete determination, and political interference in tactical matters blunted the power and speed of a thrust that might otherwise have succeeded. The United States government separated itself from its allies and joined in a U.N. demand for a cease-fire. This pressure, combined with liberal and leftist opposition at home, forced the British and French to call off the operation. The Soviet Union improved the occasion by sending ambiguous threats to the two Western European capitals, but, although Moscow subsequently claimed—and, in some quarters, received—credit for having solved the Suez crisis, it was the split in the NATO alliance and the action of the U.N. that actually did so and saved Nasser from the consequences of his policies by restoring to him all of the territory seized by his antagonists, while leaving him master of the canal.

The Other Arab Lands   In the subsequent period, the fears expressed in Anthony Eden's letter to President Eisenhower seemed on the point of being realized. Nasser's influence was now at its height and was exercised in other capitals beside his own. It grew rapidly in Syria and made possible the fusion of that country with Egypt in a new United Arab Republic in February 1958. Five months later, it had even more dramatic effects in Iraq. This former British dependency had remained on good relations with Great Britain and, under its long-time prime minister Nuri as-Said, had in 1955 joined the Baghdad Pact, a mutual defense arrangement of which Britain, Turkey, Pakistan, and Iran were also members and the United States a close associate. This tie, and Nuri as-Said's foreign policy in general, had been under bitter attack from Cairo since that time, and Nasser had done what he could to spread subversion inside Iraq. All

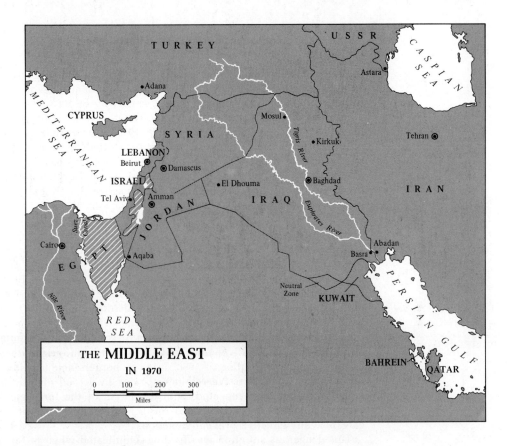

THE **MIDDLE EAST**

IN 1970

0   100   200   300

Miles

of this came to a head on July 14, 1958, when a group of army officers led by
General Karim el-Kassem suddenly seized power in Baghdad. King Faisal II and
his brother were brutally slain; Nuri as-Said was hunted down and dispatched
in the same manner; and a one-party dictatorial government, similar to that
in Cairo, was set up. Iraq severed its ties with the Baghdad Pact.

So meteoric was Nasser's rise that some of his neighbors became alarmed.
Young King Hussein of Jordan, who had been distancing himself from the British,
the traditional protectors of his territory,[4] now appealed to them for assistance
in restoring order in a country torn by nationalist plots, and the British responded
by sending a force from Cyprus. Similarly, the pro-Western regime of Camille
Chamoun in Lebanon requested the protection of the United States against
possible invasion by Arab nationalists, and in July 1958 a force of United States
marines was airlifted into the country and remained there until the threat had
passed.

Despite appearances, Nasser's position in the Arab lands never became a
dominant one. Given the chronic political instability of the Middle East, this
was hardly possible. In the twenty years following 1949, there were eight suc-

---

[4]According to one of Eden's aides, it was Hussein's dismissal of his military adviser, Sir
John Glubb, in March 1956, that convinced the British prime minister that Nasser's influence
was becoming so great that he must be destroyed.

cessful and five unsuccessful revolts in Syria; in Iraq there were thirty-nine known military plots between 1958 and 1965 (Karim el-Kassem, who took power by force in 1958, was deposed in the same way in 1963); Yemen, which was allied with Nasser in 1958, after a revolt that overthrew the pro-British ruling house, was waging war against him in 1965 as a result of the ousted ruler's return; in Jordan, King Hussein constantly shifted his position in response to the fluctuating strength of Palestinian nationalism, British pressure, Nasserism, and other forces at work in his country; and even in Egypt stability was adventitious, and two Muslim Brotherhood plots to assassinate Nasser were discovered in the early 1960s.

The Arab-Israeli War of 1967   It appeared that the only constant in Arab politics was hatred of Israel, and a second dramatic outburst of this in 1967 showed the weakness and the strength of Nasser's position. After 1956 there had been some relaxation of the tension between Israel and Egypt, facilitated by the presence of a U.N. emergency force on their joint frontier. Israel's relations with Jordan and Syria, however, steadily deteriorated, in part because of the activity of Arab terrorist groups which attacked Israeli settlements from sanctuaries across the border, in part because of Israeli-Syrian disputes over water rights on the Jordan River and activity in the demilitarized zone established on their common frontier in 1956. In 1962, border incidents involving Syrian artillery fire led to massive retaliatory raids by Israeli air power and armor, and this pattern was repeated, with escalation of the force employed, in the years that followed. This alarmed the U.N. Secretariat, but it was unable to galvanize any effective preventive action.

This dangerous situation was further complicated when in January 1964, the Arab League founded the Palestine Liberation Organization, which was designed to regain the lost lands of the Palestinian refugees. Under the leadership of Ahmed Shukairy, a perennial agitator who was fond of proclaiming his intention of utterly destroying the state of Israel, this body began to train a liberation army in the Gaza Strip and Syria, and the number of border incidents again increased in number and violence. Syrian efforts to divert the waters of the Jordan also increased tension, and, by 1967 war was being talked about by both sides as inevitable.

There is some evidence to indicate that Nasser did not want a renewal of hostilities, since he was conscious of the weakness of his armed forces, despite the material and technical assistance they had been receiving from the Soviet Union. But his hesitations elicited bitter reproaches from the Jordanians and from the Syrians, with whom his relations had been uncertain since 1961, when the union of 1958 had been dissolved. Doubtless feeling that his position would be threatened if he did anything else, Nasser associated himself publicly with their hard line toward Israel and with the wild mouthings of Shukairy. Moreover, in May 1967, as the Israelis became menacing in their turn and their chief of staff Itzhak Rabin threatened to send an expeditionary force to Damascus and overthrow the Syrian government, Nasser took two steps of fateful import. First, he requested the withdrawal of the U.N. emergency force, a request with which U Thant—with perhaps more legalism and less foresight than the occasion required—immediately complied. Second, he sent forces to occupy the Strait of Tiran and reimposed the blockade of the Gulf of Aqaba, which he had been forced to lift in 1956. This posed a clear threat to the Israeli port of Elath, and, since the Israeli government had made it clear that measures of this kind would be considered a sufficient cause for war, Nasser's action, considering its consequences, must be described as foolhardy.

The consequences were grave indeed. The Israeli army command had long expected another round with the Arabs; their troops were in top condition, physically and morally; and their plans were in order. On Monday, June 5, 1967, at 7:45 A.M., Israeli fighter-bombers attacked ten Egyptian air bases simultaneously and in repeated strikes, at ten-minute intervals for almost three hours, destroyed the Egyptian air strength that had been painfully built up since 1956. Later in the morning, after it had attacked Haifa, the Syrian air force was wiped out in retaliatory raids, and later in the day the Jordanian and Iraqi forces suffered crippling losses. All told, the Israeli pilots put 416 Arab planes out of commission and won complete command of the air. Meanwhile, three Israeli armored columns invaded the Sinai peninsula and proceeded to smash the Egyptian forces assembled there with an expedition and ferocity that exceeded that of 1956. Before this operation was secured, Jordanian forces, which attempted to relieve the pressure on the Egyptians by attacking the border settlements, were overwhelmed by a combined assault that battered and demoralized it and swept into the old city of Jerusalem, an object of Israeli longing for decades. Finally, on Friday of this crowded week of battle, two Israeli infantry columns penetrated the Syrian defense perimeter between Tel Fakar and El Kuneitra and, with trifling losses, cleared the Golan plateau and had Damascus at their mercy. Arab resistance was at an end.

It says much for Nasser's hold on his people and those of the other Arab lands that, despite the completeness of the Israeli victory and despite his ignominious attempts to escape responsibility for it by attempting to blame it on American and British collusion with Israel, he did not lose his office. Indeed, when he attempted to resign on June 9, his proposal was rejected by the Egyptian cabinet and there were popular demonstrations in his favor. As time passed, his position was shored up by a curious shift in world opinion, caused in part by the one-sidedness of the Israeli victory and also by the understandable reluctance of the Israelis to surrender their territorial gains, as they had done in 1956. In the West, a not inconsiderable number of people began, almost unconsciously, to think of Israel as the villain of the piece. This encouraged the Arab states to be obdurate in their refusal to negotiate directly with Israel on questions rising out of the war, and this in turn confirmed the Israelis in their opposition to concessions.

The result of the six days' war, therefore, was not peace but preparations for new conflict. By the summer of 1970 Israeli units in occupied territory were engaged in intermittent fire fights with Arab bands; Palestinian guerrillas were using Lebanese and Jordanian territory for raids against Israel; Nasser was once more talking of war and saying "we have to go along a road covered with blood"; the U.N. had proved itself powerless to affect the deteriorating situation; and there was a general feeling that unless the United States and the Soviet

Union could agree jointly to forbid new action and to regulate the military aid that each of them was giving to the opposing parties, a renewal of full-scale fighting could not be postponed indefinitely. The fragility of the situation was increased by the outbreak of fighting between Palestinian guerillas and government troops in Jordan in the late summer of 1970 and, while attempts were being made to end this, by the sudden death of Nasser in September.

Iran   A seesaw political battle between the Soviet Union and the West was waged in Iran in the postwar period. In the first years after the war, Soviet military incursions in Azerbaijan were terminated after firm intimations of reprisals on the part of the West. In the early 1950s, Western interests within the country were severely shaken by the rise of a fanatical nationalist prime minister, Mohammed Mossadeq, who by his nationalization of the British oil refineries and by other actions reduced the administration and the economy of the country to a shambles and presented the powerful underground Communist party with an excellent opportunity for a coup. This they did not seize, perhaps because they had no instructions from Moscow, and in August 1953 Mossadeq was overthrown by General Zahedi.

After this, the Shah returned from abroad, established an authoritarian regime of his own, and purged the military and civil services of the large number of Communists who had managed to infiltrate them. Iran then moved in the Western camp once more, joining the Baghdad Pact in 1955. The country still had grave economic and social problems, however, and the opportunities afforded communism were great. To the European youth movement of the 1960s, the Iranian regime became a symbol of imperialism and totalitarianism (see p. 743).

THE PASSING OF THE EUROPEAN EMPIRES

India, Pakistan, and Burma   In these years that saw the retreat of the European powers from the great empires that they had built in the eighteenth and nineteenth centuries, perhaps the most impressive, because the most symbolic, of all the withdrawals was that of the British from India. In contrast to later examples of the relinquishment of colonial domains, this was marked for the most part by good sense and political intelligence, and in consequence much evil was avoided.

The decision to liquidate the British Raj was a direct result of the war, which deprived the British people of the means and the inclination to oppose what had come to be regarded even before 1939 as inevitable. The problem confronting the Labour government was how to withdraw without plunging the subcontinent into civil war. Internal dissension was complicated not only by the tension between the Indian Congress party and the Moslem League but also by the growth of communism, especially in the city of Calcutta but also in Kashmir and the far south. Moreover, a solution had to be found with speed, for the British government had decided during the war to stop recruiting for the Indian civil service, and, by 1947, it was clear that the reduced bureaucracy could not administer the country for many more months. In addition, the British people were firmly opposed to further military commitments in India.

The task of breaking the deadlock between the parties in India was entrusted to Lord Louis Mountbatten, who succeeded Lord Wavell as viceroy of India in February 1947. By a remarkable job of personal diplomacy, Mountbatten was able, within seventy-three days of his arrival in India, to persuade the leaders of the Congress party and the Moslem League to agree on a plan for the creation of two states, India and Pakistan, the partition of the Punjab and Bengal and the division of the Indian army between them, and the grant of Dominion status to both of them in order to provide a maximum of administrative and constitutional continuity during the transfer of power.

This achievement, which was facilitated by the good sense shown by the Hindu leader Jawaharlal Nehru and the head of the Moslem League, Mohammed Ali Jinnah, was merely the beginning of Mountbatten's work. The administrative problems involved in implementing the plans were of staggering complexity. The partition of the Punjab and Bengal led to unrest and eventually to the migration of some nine million people, which was accomplished at a heavy human cost; among the Sikhs, who suffered most from partition, there were outbreaks

of violence; there were difficulties among the Indian princely states, which were called upon to accede to India or to Pakistan; and, after Independence Day (August 15, 1947), there were serious differences between the Indian and Pakistani governments with respect to the eventual disposition of the important states of Junagadh, Kashmir, and Hyderabad. And always those who dealt with these problems and disputes were aware, as one of them wrote later, that "the crust upholding order from the depths of chaos [was] dangeroulsy thin" and that the forces of fanaticism might render all their efforts meaningless.

Nevertheless, by the middle of 1948, when Mountbatten had completed his mission, most of the problems were in hand, the country was calm, and the two new states were functioning effectively. One reason for this, perhaps, was the assassination of Mohandas Gandhi by a young provincial newspaperman in January 1948, a senseless act that shocked the nation and sensibly diminished Hindu-Moslem strife.

In the years that followed, Nehru sought to maintain a position of neutrality for India in the global struggle between communism and the democratic world; and, although this often irritated statesmen in Moscow and Washington, it brought tangible economic benefits from both sides. This policy of balance made it possible for Nehru to perform useful services as a mediator during the Korean war and the Indochina crisis of the 1950s. On the other hand, it did not protect the Indian government from attacks from Communists on the home front, in the state of Kerala, or from the more serious menace of Chinese communism on the northeastern frontier, where numerous armed incursions by the Chinese took place.

In May 1964, Nehru died of a heart attack, leaving to his successor Shastri a host of unsolved problems. The one that became most immediately critical was the Kashmir question. In this province, a series of brushes between India and Pakistani troops led, in September 1965, to an ugly war, characterized, for the first time since Korea, by large-scale tank battles and aerial bombardment of cities. The struggle was, nevertheless, inconclusive, and both sides accepted the U.N. Security Council's call for a cease-fire in September 1965. Four months later, availing themselves of the good offices of the Soviet Union, the two countries signed a "no-war" agreement.

After his death in January 1966, Shastri was succeeded as prime minister by Indira Gandhi, who maintained her ascendancy in Indian politics for the next four years despite serious food shortages and religious strife.

At the same time that the British effected their withdrawal from India, they recognized the independence of Burma, whose freedom had been proclaimed during the war by Japan, in an action the reversal of which was considered to be impractical and undesirable. The grant of independence was made on January 4, 1948, and was accompanied by an Anglo-Burmese treaty that gave Great Britain the right to maintain military missions, but not bases, in the country. Burma's internal history was troubled, and its policy of economic nationalization was promoted by authoritarian methods, including suppression of civil liberties and the closing of universities.

Indonesia, Malaya, and Southeast Asia   Events soon showed that Japan's wartime conquests of other colonial areas had destroyed the prestige of the

INDOCHINA AND
SOUTHEAST ASIA IN 1970

European powers and stimulated nationalist movements that now successfully
resisted their return. This was particularly true in Indonesia, where the Dutch
colonial empire had been overrun by the Japanese in the first weeks after Pearl
Harbor.

When the war was over, the British undertook the task of reoccupying the
main Indonesia centers until such time as the Netherlands government had re-
established itself and reorganized its colonial service. Eventually, this led to an
unfortunate difference of view between the allies, for the British tended to cooperate with the Indonesia republic that had been organized in August 1945 by
the Javanese nationalist leader Achmed Sukarno, whereas the Dutch were opposed to all republican movements in their former domains and set out to
destroy them. Despite British attempts to bring the two parties together, bitter
fighting raged throughout 1947, as the Dutch sought to blockade republican centers and force their submission. U.N. intervention, although at first indignantly
repudiated by the Dutch, succeeded in arranging a conference at The Hague in
1949, where it was decided to establish a United States of Indonesia as a sovereign
state united in partnership with the Netherlands and recognizing the Dutch
crown. This lasted, with much friction among the partners, until February 1956,
when Indonesia unilaterally abrogated the treaty and elected to go to its own
way in what Sukarno called "guided democracy."

Communism had been a force in Indonesia since the 1920s, and Sukarno's attempt to collaborate with the Communists in his first government after 1956 aroused fears in the West of a general drift of this strategically important area into the Soviet bloc, a development that would represent a direct threat to the British position in Malaya and even to Australia. In general, Sukarno tended to follow a neutral line, seeking to propitiate the left and the nationalists by nationalizing Dutch plantations and expelling Dutch colonists, but preferring not to alienate conservative elements by a decided Communist orientation. At the meeting of the U.N. Assembly in the autumn of 1960, Sukarno associated with the neutralist block composed of Nehru, Tito, Nasser, and Kwame Nkrumah of Ghana in urging new contact between the leaders of the United States and the Soviet Union. In the next five years, however, he became violently anti-Western in his tone and actions, repudiating American aid from which he had benefited, withdrawing from the U.N., generally following the Red Chinese line in his policy, and vowing to destroy the Malaysian Federation.

The postwar course of events in the Malayan peninsula had been a tangled one. The British had wanted to avoid what had happened to the Dutch in Indonesia and had tried patiently to create a Malayan Union with equal rights of citizenship for Malays, Chinese, and Indians and the reduction of the powers of the Malay sultans. When this plan foundered on the opposition of the Malay population, they went over to a federal scheme that assured continued Malay supremacy. Communist insurrections began in 1948 and continued with great intensity for the next four years and at a lesser pitch thereafter. The British sought to combat this with military action on the one hand and, on the other, by encouraging a sense of Malayan nationalism so that the country might soon become independent. Between 1955 and 1963 this policy appeared to be successful, and in the latter year Malaya joined with the former British colonies of Sarawak and North Borneo to form the Federation of Malaysia. This initial success was put in jeopardy in August 1965 by the secession of Singapore from the federation, an action that seemed to foreshadow its complete disintegration and possible conquest by Sukarno. But such is the complexity of East Asian politics that the threat from Indonesia was simultaneously eased because of the sudden eruption of serious internal troubles in Sukarno's country, where fighting broke out between the Communists and the army. When it transpired later that Sukarno himself had been involved in the Communist plot, he was forced to surrender his power to General Suharto, the minister of war, who became acting president in March 1967 and president in the following year. Relations between Indonesia and Malaysia improved in consequence, and Indonesia returned to the U.N.

The most disastrous retreat of a European colonial power in this area took place in Southeast Asia, and there, as in the Near East, the violence of nationalism, the tactical disarray of the Western allies, and Communist skill in exploiting this all played their part.

Once more the delayed influence of Japan's wartime successes was felt here. The Japanese occupation authorities had encouraged the growth of a native revolutionary movement; and, in August 1945, this organization, the Vietminh party, deposed the pro-French ruler of Annam, Bao Dai, and established an independent republic, Vietnam, which embraced northern Annam and Tonkin and was presided over by Ho Chi Minh. Meanwhile, the French returned to the area, reasserted their authority in Laos, Cambodia, and Cochin China, and organized these separate states into a Federation of Indochina within the French Union. They sought to induce Ho Chi Minh to join the federation and, had they been willing to grant a large measure of self-government to Tonkin, Annam, and Cochin China, they might have succeeded, for Ho Chi Minh, while a Communist, was pro-French and anti-Chinese in his views. But the French insisted that Cochin China, the wealthiest of the regions and the one with the largest city, Saigon, remain separate and under their control. The negotiations broke down and war began between the French, who sought stubbornly and unrealistically to put Bao Dai back on the throne of a united Vietnam, and the Vietminh forces, supported by many local patriots who were not Communists but had no place to turn.

This war reached its height after the outbreak of the conflict in Korea had dramatized the struggle between communism and the democratic world and had persuaded the United States Congress to extend economic and military assistance to France and to the Bao Dai regime in Vietnam. The local French commanders gradually made their way, against strong guerrilla opposition, into Northern Vietnam; but, in 1954, they overextended their lines of communication and were trapped by superior enemy forces at a place called Dienbienphu.

At this stage of affairs the French government, on April 23, 1954, appealed to the United States for aid, apparently arguing that unless it was forthcoming immediately, all Indochina would fall. This sensibly agitated Washington, and some off-the-cuff statements by administration spokesmen made it appear that the United States was prepared to intervene. This was not strictly true. The United States government had already decided against the commitment of any ground forces in Indochina. Admiral Radford, the chairman of the Joint Chiefs of Staff, and Secretary of State Dulles seem to have convinced themselves, however, that intervention by air power alone would save the situation, but they wanted the collaboration of the RAF in any strikes planned. After much discussion, the British government decided that this was an irresponsible plan that would not save the French situation at Dienbienphu and might very well bring the Chinese Communists into the war, and they declined to cooperate. No action was therefore taken, and Dienbienphu fell, not without causing recriminations among the allies and leaving a public impression of Western disunity and unwillingness to make good on threats delivered and promises made. The situation in Indochina was regulated at a conference at Geneva whose meetings extended from April until July 1954 and which finally divided Vietnam between French and Vietminh forces at the 17th parallel and made provisions for future elections for a united government.

The United States government was unwilling to leave matters at this point and, in a special conference convoked at Manila in September 1954, Secretary Dulles won the approval of Great Britain, France, Australia, New Zealand, Pakistan, Thailand, and the Philippines for a new South Asia Defense Treaty. The organization that was subsequently set up to implement this was known as SEATO, and its members were pledged to take collective action to meet Communist aggression in Southeast Asia. SEATO never developed NATO's strength, however; in areas like Laos and Cambodia, where communism made inroads between 1954 and 1960 and where politics became a confused struggle between rightist, Communist, and neutralist forces, the British and French distrusted the tendencies of American policy. Thus, when the United States, at a meeting in Bangkok in March 1961, called on the allies to take collective action in the disintegrating Laotian situation, they proved unwilling to do so.

In Vietnam, the 1954 settlement was violated by both sides; the government of South Vietnam deciding that it would be dangerously unrealistic to hold elections for union on the date set, the North Vietnamese violating the letter of the agreement by encouraging and supporting subversive forces (the so-called Vietcong) in southern territory. Here again SEATO could concert on no effective policy, the French favoring a neutralist solution for the whole area, the Americans holding to a policy of forceful containment. As a result, the United States had to operate independently and assumed increasing influence in South Vietnam, so that, by the end of 1965, its efforts to protect a faltering and ineffective regime against unremitting Vietcong pressure had led it to open air operations against the insurgents' supply lines and to commit ground forces to the anti-Communist effort. Gradually and almost without realizing it, the United States had become involved in a war which became increasingly destructive and increasingly dangerous, since the possibility of an expansion of the war to include other powers and of an escalation that could reach nuclear proportions was never far away. This was a worrying thought to European governments that were allied with the United States and feared involvement against their will, and they were not reassured by President Johnson's decision, after increasing the troop investment in Vietnam to 510,000 men without visible sign of success, to seek peace by negotiation, particularly since the talks that began between the United States and North Vietnam in Paris in 1968 had made no apparent progress a year later. By the fall of 1969, the Vietnam issue was dividing Europeans almost as much as it divided Americans. The leaders of the Labour party in Great Britain and the Social Democratic party in West Germany were being criticized by their left-wing followers for failing to take a stand against American policy in Southeast Asia, and the name Ho Chi Minh had become a rallying cry for the European student movement.

North Africa   The French setback in Indochina had profound effects upon France's empire on the other side of the world, particularly in North Africa. In both Tunisia and Morocco nationalist movements had been active since 1945, but they had been met by an inflexible policy of repression. This became impossible after the blow given French prestige in Southeast Asia, and the Mendès-France government, which had courageously faced up to the necessity of accepting defeat in the Far East, now took the initiative in North Africa as well.

The leader of the nationalist movement (*Néo-Destour*) in Tunisia was Habib Bourguiba, who had been in imposed exile from his country since the end of 1951. In July 1954 he was brought to France for consultation; and, in the same month, Mendès-France announced, in a speech at Tunis, that the protectorate would be given complete internal independence. Negotiations for this purpose continued after the Assembly had overthrown Mendès-France; and, in May 1955, a Franco-Tunisian agreement was signed, and Bourguiba was allowed to return to his country. His moderate policy after he had assumed the leadership of the Tunisian government invited new concessions. In March 1956 Tunisia became virtually independent by a new agreement which acknowledged its right to maintain its own armed forces and carry on its own foreign policy, while giving France certain military and naval rights in the country.

Similar concessions had to be made in Morocco. The French had been particularly high-handed in this protectorate in the first postwar years, as if believing that the Moroccans should be willing to forego political ambitions in view of the undeniable economic advantages that they derived from their association with France. During the period when General Juin was resident of Morocco in the late 1940s, the French not only sought to break up all independent political movements but, when the sultan, Sidi Mohammed ben-Yusuf, showed his support of the objectives of the chief nationalist party, the *Istiqlal,* forced him in 1953 to hand his powers over to a joint Franco-Moroccan Council and deported him to Madagascar. This action was widely resented and united all sections of the Moroccan people against French rule, a fact the French themselves were forced to admit after two years of terrorism and disorder. In November 1955, the government acknowledged that the deposed sultan was the rightful ruler of Morocco; and, in the spring of 1956, negotiations were begun that eventuated in the grant of Morocco's independence later in the year.

These belated French concessions might have led to a fruitful and mutually advantageous cooperation between France and its former protectorates if it had not been for the continuation of the Algerian war, which, not unnaturally, attracted the sympathies of Moroccans and Tunisians and led to French charges that the rebels were being supported from the soil of their neighbors.

The Algerian war began in November 1954 when the *Front de libération nationale* (FLN), a nationalist, terrorist organization richly supplied with leaders trained in Egypt and Iraq, began an armed insurrection that rapidly won support among the Algerian Moslems, although part of this, it must be admitted, was induced by fear of the consequences of loyalty to the French authorities. The European colonists (*colons*), on the other hand, had been established in Algeria for a longer time than in the neighboring protectorates; their economic stake was greater; and their resistance to concessions to the opposition was stronger. It was largely their fear of a governmental drift toward a Tunisian or Moroccan solution that prompted the May 1958 rising in Algiers, which was also supported, as we have seen (p. 715), by an army that felt it had already been too frequently the victim of governmental concessions.

The fighting in Algeria was carried on with great savagery on both sides and, as the war continued, this aroused concern in France, where churchmen expressed horror at the inhumane methods used in the fighting, and student and trade union demonstrations called for a negotiated peace. President De Gaulle's own thinking ran in the same direction, to the indignation of the *colons* and many of his original supporters. His search for a moderate solution derived greater urgency from the fact that the rebels themselves leaned increasingly on aid from the Communist world. In October 1960, Ferhat Abbas, premier of the so-called Algerian Provisional Government, said in an interview in Tunis, "I was told in Peiping and Moscow a few days ago that Communist support will be greater this year than last, and still greater next year than this year." He went on to say: "They said also that, because we are fighting colonialism, there is no need to look for any other ideological bond. Our Chinese and Soviet friends recognize frankly that we are not Communists, and they ask no engagement whatsoever from us." This self-confidence led to the breakdown of the first talks which were held between the provisional government and the French in 1960 and in 1962; but at the beginning of 1962 there was greater willingness to treat on both sides, and the negotiations that led to Algeria's independence in July 1962 were begun.

When the new Algerian government took shape, the strong man who emerged was not Ferhat Abbas but Ahmed Ben Bella, who in March 1962 returned from six years in French prisons and subsequently became president of the Algerian Republic. In the three years that followed, Ben Bella became a leading figure in African politics, courted not only by France and the United States but by the Soviet Union and Red China as well, and establishing a close political relation with President Nasser of the UAR. It came as a decided surprise, therefore, when, in June 1965, as representatives of various nations were gathering in his capital for a conference of Afro-Asian powers, Ben Bella was deposed and thrown into prison on charges of treason by a former henchman, Colonel Houari Boumé-dienne. The fall of this would-be Caesar was a blow equally to the Red Chinese, who had hoped to use him, and to those French intellectuals who had considered him a heroic figure.

In 1967 Boumédienne was one of the strongest supporters of the Arab effort against Israel, and after the debacle, he was as unregenerate and uncompromising as the Syrians.

Sub-Sahara Africa   The retreat of the European powers from the holdings they had acquired in sub-Sahara Africa in the last years of the nineteenth century was general and, in some cases, precipitate, and was marked by the emergence of unprecedented problems. Only Portugal was virtually unaffected by nationalist movements, perhaps because of the poverty and backwardness of its colonies.

British policy varied from area to area. In West Africa, where there were no large non-African communities and where the social development of the Africans was well advanced, the British gradually yielded authority and broadened the basis of self-government. In both the Gold Coast and Nigeria, popularly elected assemblies were authorized by the early 1950s; in March 1957, after some tribal difficulties were overcome, independence was granted to the Gold Coast, which took the name Ghana; and, in the autumn of 1960, Nigeria became an independent nation as well. Both states became members of the U.N., where the Ghanaian leader, Kwame Nkrumah, became a prominent member of the neutralist bloc for a time. In 1966, he suffered a fate not uncommon in the new Africa and was overthrown by a military coup. Nigeria's influence in U.N. circles was also of short duration, for in 1967 the country was torn by a protracted and wasting civil war caused by differences between tribes. In view of the staggering loss of life suffered from starvation and disease before this Biafran conflict came to an end in 1970, Nigeria's political and economic prospects were decidedly unpromising.

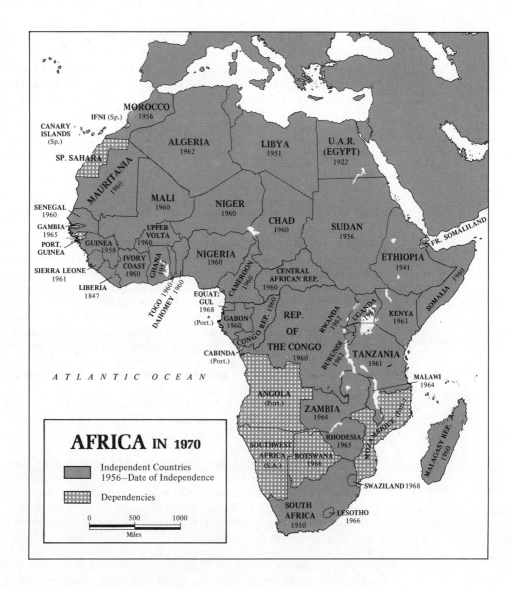

AFRICA IN 1970

Independent Countries
1956–Date of Independence

Dependencies

0   500   1000
Miles

IFNI (Sp.)
CANARY ISLANDS (Sp.)
MOROCCO 1956
SP. SAHARA
MAURITANIA 1960
ALGERIA 1962
LIBYA 1951
U.A.R. (EGYPT) 1922
SENEGAL 1960
GAMBIA 1965
PORT. GUINEA
GUINEA 1958
MALI 1960
NIGER 1960
CHAD 1960
SUDAN 1956
FR. SOMALILAND
UPPER VOLTA 1960
IVORY COAST 1960
GHANA 1957
NIGERIA 1960
CENTRAL AFRICAN REP. 1960
ETHIOPIA 1941
SOMALIA 1960
SIERRA LEONE 1961
LIBERIA 1847
TOGO 1960
DAHOMEY 1960
EQUAT. GUI. 1968 (Port.)
GABON 1960
CAMEROON 1960
CONGO REP. 1960
REP. OF THE CONGO 1960
RWANDA 1962
BURUNDI 1962
UGANDA 1962
KENYA 1963
CABINDA (Port.)
TANZANIA 1961
ATLANTIC OCEAN
ANGOLA (Port.)
ZAMBIA 1964
MALAWI 1964
MOZAMBIQUE (Port.)
SOUTHWEST AFRICA (S.A.)
BOTSWANA 1966
RHODESIA 1965
MALAGASY REP. 1960
SWAZILAND 1968
SOUTH AFRICA 1910
LESOTHO 1966

In African colonies where there were large white populations, the British were slower to make concessions, and this often alienated native intellectuals, drove them into extremist movements, or persuaded them to seek the aid of communism. In Kenya, this was true of the brilliant Jomo Kenyatta, a London-trained sociologist, who was alienated by the treatment he received in his own country from Europeans, turned to Moscow for aid and advice, and returned to Kenya in 1946 to become the leader of the Kenya Africa Union (KAU). This body worked for agricultural reform and was not ostensibly revolutionary; but Kenyatta was regarded by members of more militant native organizations as their natural leader. Other native intellectuals, including some of Kenyatta's associates, supplied leadership for the notorious Mau Mau movement, and it was due to their organizing abilities that the antiwhite rebellion started by it in 1952 resisted attempts at suppression by trained European troops for four years. This protracted struggle, which was marked by unparalleled savagery, made the European colonists more hostile to the independence movement, which nevertheless persisted, and was successful in December 1963, when Kenya was declared a republic. In the next five years, Kenya was one of the most stable and progressive of the African states, but even it was not immune to the general tendency to violence. In July 1969, one of its most gifted and vigorous politicians, the minister for economic development Tom Mboya, was shot and killed by a fanatic; and in the wake of this tribal tensions burst forth, particularly between Mboya's Luo tribe and the Kikuyu, who had played a leading role in the rebellion of the 1950s.

In the Central African Federation (formed in 1953 from Northern Rhodesia, Southern Rhodesia, and Nyasaland), the policy followed by the government also showed hesitation about yielding to native demands. One writer described the predominant European view as an abstract willingness to give rights to civilized Africans, combined with a conviction that few would become civilized and that very few must be given the opportunity to do so. There were indications in the late 1950s that this attitude would be productive of trouble, especially in Nyasaland, where an overwhelmingly African population was held under control by drastic security laws; but where the pressure was greatest, the British government gradually gave way. In July 1964 Nyasaland became the republic of Malawi and three months later Northern Rhodesia was transformed into the Republic of Zambia. Only Southern Rhodesia continued as a self-governing colony of the crown, and not for long.

In 1965, reacting to attempts by the British government to persuade Rhodesian authorities to liberalize the constitution in order to give greater voting strength to the black population, the prime minister Ian Smith issued a unilateral declaration of independence. This the British refused to accept and they sought, by protracted negotiation, to stay Smith's heedless course. This was to no avail, for the prime minister was strongly supported by his white constituents, who, in June 1969, by a three to one landslide, accepted a Smith-proposed constitution which went so far in restricting the civil rights of black subjects that U Thant, the Secretary-General of the U.N., angrily described it as "the product of the kind of racism which is abhorrent to the vast majority of mankind." The British government now severed all formal diplomatic contact with Rhodesia and closed down its mission in Salisbury. In March 1970 the process of separation was completed when the government in Salisbury announced that Rhodesia was now a republic.

In general, both major parties in England suffered from the course of Rhodesian affairs, for Macmillan was criticized for the original breakup of the Central African Federation and Wilson for mishandling the negotiations with Smith.

The situation was even more critical in the Union of South Africa, where the resistance of the white population to concessions to the natives hardened and interracial tension mounted steadily in the postwar years. This was largely the result of the rise of a new Nationalist party which rejected the moderate conservatism of General Hertzog (see p. 614) and called for a definite breaking of the connection with Great Britain, the establishment of a republic, and a more radical approach to native problems. Under the leadership first of Dr. Daniel

Malan and then of Dr. Henrik F. Verwoerd, this party won a majority in the elections of 1948, maintained and strengthened it during the next decade, and was strong enough by the autumn of 1960 to win parliamentary assent for the transformation of the country's status to that of a republic. The following year, because of its racial policies, the new state was excluded from the British Commonwealth at the insistence of Nigeria and other members. This was because the Nationalist party followed a policy, fashioned by Verwoerd, of *apartheid*, which called for a rigid separation of the native and European cultures. Presented as a means of saving the Bantus from a false and corrupting Europeanization, *apartheid* was in sharp contrast to prevailing economic tendencies, for the growth of industrialism, upon which South Africa's future to a large extent depended, promoted the integration of Bantu and European. In practice, *apartheid* seemed to be little more than a doctrine of racial superiority that appealed to lower class Afrikaners who were afraid that integration would force their already low standard of living even lower. Since it was an entirely negative system of policy, it could be made to work only by force; and by the 1960s clashes between the police and native demonstrators had become frequent and bloody.

The spiral of violence in South Africa claimed the life of Verwoerd himself, for in September 1966 he was murdered in parliament by a mentally deranged drifter. His successor, John Vorster, showed more appreciation for the inconsistencies of *apartheid* and less insistence upon its strict implementation.

In the colonies of West and Equatorial Africa, the French proved to be more foresighted than they had been in other parts of their empire. The new French constitution of 1958 recognized the political development of the colonies, which had been actively supported and encouraged by French administrators, and allowed the territories to choose between complete independence and membership in the French Community either individually or in federation. The greatest number voted for the second alternative (see p. 716), the significant exception being Guinea, which through its leader Sekou Touré announced the intention of forming a union with Ghana as a nucleus of a future union of West Africa. Like Nkrumah, Touré became one of the new "positive neutrals" at the U.N. Assembly of 1960, tending in his sympathies toward the Soviet bloc.

The swift progress of the French colonies toward independence was probably the chief cause of the emergence in 1960 of the most explosive situation that had arisen in Africa since the Mau Mau troubles. This was the Congo problem. Until the end of the 1950s, this great Belgian possession was apparently quiet and prosperous, without a ripple of racial tension or a discernible sign of a nationalistic movement of any importance. In 1955, King Baudouin had spoken, during a trip to the Congo, of "leading the natives to lead themselves ... though with the right of the colonizers to remain"; and in 1956 the Belgian Socialist party had formulated a long-term program for independence "in progressive stages." But even the warmest supporters of Congolese independence were thinking in terms of a thirty-year evolution.

The problem became immediate, however, as a result of two things: General De Gaulle's visit to Brazzaville, only three miles away from the Congolese capital, to offer a referendum on independence to the peoples of French Equatorial Africa; and the Brussels Exposition, in which some of the pavilions were manned by young Congolese who saw the outside world for the first time. By October 1958, under these influences, the Congo's first political parties had been born; and in January 1959 the first serious troubles erupted in the Congo, with four days of riot and destruction in Leopoldville.

This shocked the Belgian government, and the king announced on January 13, 1959, that the Congo would be given independence "without fatal delay . . . but without unconsidered haste." In view of the unrest in the country and the rapidly expanding ambitions and growing rivalry of native leaders, a clear statement of the government's intentions and its proposed procedure and timing would have been advisable; but the government could not agree on these vital matters. The result was that ambiguity led to increased Congolese importunity, and the latter to an ill-considered Belgian announcement that independence would be granted on June 30, 1960.

When that day came, it became immediately clear that the Congo had neither the trained leaders nor the unity of will to make independence effective. Almost immediately, the country was paralyzed by anti-Belgian demonstrations, rapine and pillage, tribal warfare, political dissension, and, inevitably, Communist subversion. By the end of 1960, the overhasty withdrawal of the Belgians from their colonial empire had created one more major threat to world peace, and the years that followed were years of changing governments, armed insurrections, attempts at subversion by the Soviet Union and Red China, periodic massacres of white settlers, and an inconclusive U.N. intervention which immersed that organization in financial difficulty. Not until a military regime had been imposed by General Joseph D. Mobutu, did the Congo begin, at the end of the 60's, to have prospects of order and solvency. This political solution was not uncommon in the new Africa. In 1970 three-fourths of the continent's 345 million people lived under one-party political systems or military rule.

EUROPE IN THE 1970s

The Dead Past and the Dangerous Present   In 1912 the French poet Guillaume Apollinaire wrote some melancholy lines in which he appeared to look to the future with foreboding and to the past for meaning and assurance.

> . . . détournant mes yeux de ce vide avenir
> En moi-même je vois tout le passé grandir
> Rien n'est mort que ce qui n'existe pas encore
> Près du passé luisant demain est incolore
> Il est informe aussi près de ce qui parfait
> Présente tout ensemble et l'effort et l'effet[1]

As the world entered the 1970s, there were doubtless Europeans who shared that feeling. It is likely, however, that most of those who did so were over fifty

[1] Turning my eyes from this empty future/ I see the whole past well up in myself/ Nothing is dead except that which does not yet exist/ Compared with the shining past tomorrow is without color/ It is also bereft of form compared with that which perfectly/ Presents as a unit both the effort and its result. "Cortège. A M. Léon Bailly", *Alcools* (1913).

and comprised a declining and unrepresentative portion of the whole. For the majority there was nothing very shining about a past that, as they remembered it, had until very recent years been filled with violence, deprivation, and sudden death. Understandably, there was little desire to return to those conditions, but neither was there any disposition to hanker after a more remote past, in which, according to the history books, a secure and prosperous Europe had ruled the globe. For such vanished splendors there seemed to be little nostalgia. Few Belgians regretted the loss of the Congo, which had never, in any real sense, belonged to them anyway; and in England the dismantling of the Empire did not leave behind it any tendency to idealize it, for it was seen now less through Kipling's kind of vision than through that of J. A. Hobson (see p. 401). It is significant that, throughout Western Europe, the parties and leaders that turned their eyes backward made little headway with voters, a fact demonstrated equally by De Gaulle's ultimate failure to lead France back to an older nationalist tradition and the defeat and decline of the authoritarian NPD in Germany.

About the future there was concern, as was natural in an age in which man's ingenuity in devising new weapons threatened to outrun his capacity to regulate their use. Some modest progress, to be sure, had been made in the latter regard. The Eighteen Nation Disarmament Committee, which had been holding meetings at Geneva since 1961,[2] had with great patience and persistence created the conditions for negotiation on substantive problems, and the conclusion of the Non-Proliferation Treaty in 1969 offered some hope that headlong competitive nuclear arming could be restrained until effective arms limitation agreements came into being.[3] But as nuclear technology became more sophisticated, as atomic bombs gave way to ballistic missiles and they in turn to multiple individually targetable reentry vehicles (MIRV's), the nuclear powers seemed to be nearing the point where their weapons systems would cease to be susceptible to inspection and where the hope of controlling the arms race would become futile. It was this prospect that gave a special urgency to the SALT talks that began in the autumn of 1969 (see p. 747).

There was food for pessimism here and also in the fact that no controls had been devised for the production and sale of conventional arms. Wherever there was a possibility of war around the world, this aggravated the danger. In the spring of 1970, to take only one example, Soviet military aid to the Arab states and French shipments of jet planes to Libya were contributing to the tension in the Middle East and were encouraging the Israeli government to take counter-measures that threatened to destroy the delicate balance of peace.

[2] The Eighteen Nation Committee on Disarmament, which meets at the Palais des Nations in Geneva, was created in 1961 under a joint agreement between the United States and the Soviet Union. While it is not a United Nations body, it reports to the General Assembly and to the Disarmament Commission and is serviced by the UN Secretariat. Membership is made up of five NATO nations (the United States, Canada, Italy, the United Kingdom, and France), five from the Warsaw Pact (Bulgaria, Czechoslovakia, Poland, Rumania and the Soviet Union), and eight nonaligned nations (Brazil, Burma, Ethiopia, India, Mexico, Nigeria, Sweden, and the United Arab Republic).

[3] The nuclear states signatory to the treaty (the Chinese Socialist Republic was not a signatory) undertook not to transfer nuclear weapons into the national control of nonnuclear states, while the latter agreed not to manufacture such weapons.

There were, to be sure, combustible materials enough in the world, not only in the Middle East, but in South East Asia, and along the Chinese-Soviet border, and in half a dozen African states. A conflagration in any one of these places could hardly leave Europe unaffected, despite its retreat from its former empires in the wake of the second World War. There was, moreover, always the possibility that once a fire had started it would not stop burning until it had consumed the very framework of western civilization.

Nor were all the problems political and military ones. At the beginning of the 1970s, Europeans, like Americans, were beginning to realize that, perhaps because of their preoccupation with politics, they had overlooked other matters that required urgent attention. It was necessary now, they discovered, to face up to the ultimate consequences of industrialism and to do something to cope with the problems of bigness, with population pressure, with menaces to the ecological balance, and with the varied threats to individual freedom—and to individuality itself—in a necessarily computerized society.

The Future   All of these dangers were perceived, but at the beginning of the new decade they had not deadened the spirit or weakened the will of the peoples of Europe. There was something exhilarating about living in a world in which the rate and degree of change were so great that Adolf Hitler was beginning to seem as remote as Charlemagne. Caught up in this vital movement, Europeans betrayed little of the cultural despair to which they had been prone in earlier transitional periods. On the contrary, their mood was curiously, almost defiantly, optimistic and characterized by impatience with old forms and procedures and answers, willingness to experiment and to take risks, and commitment to the idea of a new European society.

This was the prevailing spirit of the movement of youth on both sides of the Iron Curtain, as strongly felt, if not always as openly manifested, in Warsaw and Prague as in Berlin and Paris. This marked the style of the new breed of political leaders who, in both the east and the west, seemed eager to escape from the Cold War psychosis and the ideological rigidities of the past and willing to go unorthodox ways and to take new initiatives, like that which led to the agreements of August 1970 in which the Soviet and West German governments renounced the use of force in relations with each other. And certainly this mood was detectable in the marked revival of hope in the possibility of progress toward European union which was expressed in the speeches of the delegates to the conference of the Common Market at The Hague in December 1969. Despite the daunting problems that faced them on all sides, Europeans marched into the 1970s with their minds open to new ideas and their eyes fixed on new visions of the future.

BIBLIOGRAPHY

"The Reader" by Ernst Barlach.
(Staatliche Museen, National
Galerie, Berlin)

BIBLIOGRAPHY

The lists that follow are intended to be suggestive rather than exhaustive and for that reason have been kept short. They can be supplemented from other sources, notably from the 1961 revision of the *Guide to Historical Literature,* prepared by specialists on various fields under the sponsorship of the American Historical Association, from such useful compilations as Lowell J. Ragatz, *A Bibliography for the Study of European History, 1815–1939* (1942; supplements 1943, 1945) and Alan Bullock and A. J. P. Taylor, *A Select List of Books on European History 1815–1914* (1957), and from the excellent bibliographical essays in the volumes of the series *The Rise of Modern Europe,* edited by William L. Langer.

The selection of titles has been made with an eye to the needs and interests of undergraduate, rather than advanced, students. Emphasis has been placed upon recent historical literature, although not to the exclusion of older works that have stood the test of time. No attempt has been made to list individual works of art and music.

GENERAL WORKS

Among the older single-volume histories of the nineteenth century, Eduard Fueter's *World History, 1815–1920* (1920) and Benedetto Croce's *History of Europe in the Nineteenth Century* (1933) are still provocative but are less satisfactory in their treatment of social forces than such recent works as Peter Stearns, *European Society in Upheaval: Social History since 1800* (1967) and Eugene and Pauline Anderson, *Political Institutions and Social Change in Continental Europe in The Nineteenth Century* (1968). Of the general works dealing with shorter periods, the three volumes of the *Cambridge Modern History* (1902–1912) that treat the years since Napoleon are out of date but include chapters on domestic history that have not been superseded. The *New Cambridge Modern History* has four

Bibliography

volumes on the nineteenth and twentieth centuries: *War and Peace in an Age of Upheaval, 1793–1830,* edited by C. W. Crawley; *The Zenith of European Power, 1830–1870,* edited by J. P. T. Bury (1960); *Material Progress and World-Wide Problems, 1870–1898;* edited by F. H. Hinsley (1962); and *The Era of Violence, 1898–1945,* edited by David Thomson (1959) (2d ed., *The Shifting Balance of World Forces, 1898–1945,* edited by C. L. Mowat, 1967). These include good chapters on intellectual history, science, and military affairs, in addition to their chapters on politics and economics. In the *Rise of Modern Europe* series, five of the projected volumes on the modern period have been completed: F. B. Artz, *Reaction and Revolution, 1814–1832* (1934); William L. Langer, *Political and Social Upheaval, 1832–1852* (1969); R. C. Binkley, *Realism and Nationalism, 1852–1871* (1935), a brilliantly executed volume; C. J. H. Hayes, *A Generation of Materialism, 1871–1900* (1941); and Gordon Wright's comprehensive and balanced *The Ordeal of Total War, 1939–1945* (1968). A provocative Marxist survey of the first part of the period is E. J. Hobsbawm, *The Age of Revolution: Europe, 1789–1848* (1964).

Among the general histories of economic development, S. H. Clough and C. W. Cole's *An Economic History of Europe* (1941) and Bowden, Karpovich, and Usher's *An Economic History of Europe since 1750* (1937) are outstanding, W. Ashworth, *A Short History of the International Economy, 1850–1950* (1952), is useful; A. Birnie, *An Economic History of Europe, 1760–1939* (rev. ed., 1951), includes good sections on unionism and social legislation; W. A. Lewis, *Economic Survey, 1919–1939* (1949), is an authoritative treatment by a brilliant scholar. Michael Tracy, *Agriculture in Western Europe: Crisis and Adaptation since 1880* (1964) is a solid and authoritative study. On income, population, and technological change, see *The Cambridge Economic History of Europe,* VI: *The Industrial Revolutions and After,* edited by H. J. Habakkuk and M. Postan (1966), particulary for David Landes's essay on technology in Western Europe and Alexander Gershenkron's study of agrarian problems and industrialization in Russia. On the entrepreneurs, see Charles Morazé, *The Triumph of the Middle Classes (Les Bourgeois Conquérants)* (1966).

General accounts of foreign affairs include Sir Charles Petrie, *Diplomatic History, 1713–1933* (1947); R. W. Seton-Watson, *Britain in Europe, 1789–1914* (1937), which is more comprehensive than its title suggests; Lord Strang, *Britain in World Affairs* (1961), an interesting historical survey by a former Permanent Under-Secretary in the Foreign Office; A. J. P. Taylor, *The Struggle for Mastery in Europe, 1848–1918* (1954), sometimes a bit sweeping in its judgments; R. J. Sontag, *European Diplomatic History, 1870–1932* (1933), a fine account whose later chapters are in need of revision; Hajo Holborn, *The Political Collapse of Europe* (1951), brief but illuminating; and L. C. B. Seaman, *From Vienna to Versailles* (1956), slapdash but occasionally rewarding. An extended discussion of internationalist theories and organization, as well as of the evolution of the state system in the nineteenth and twentieth centuries, is to be found in F. H. Hinsley, *Power and the Pursuit of Peace: Theory and Practice in the History of Relations between States* (1963). Broader in scope and essential for an understanding of the general preoccupation with power in this period is *The Responsibility of Power,* edited by Leonard Krieger and Fritz Stern (1967), essays in honor of the late Hajo Holborn. Some provocative essays are to be found in

Bibliography

Studies in Diplomatic History and Historiography in Honour of G. P. Gooch, edited by A. O. Sarkissian (1961) and in Sir Charles Webster, *The Art and Practice of Diplomacy* (1962).

The important part played by war in the history of the period is dealt with in E. L. Woodward, *War and Peace in Europe, 1815–1870* (1931). More detailed and comprehensive are Theodore Ropp, *War in the Modern World* (1959), which has excellent bibliographical notes; Gordon B. Turner, *A History of Military Affairs in Western Society since the Eighteen Century* (1953), a collection of carefully selected readings; J. F. C. Fuller, *A Military History of the Western World,* vol. III (1956), by one of Britain's leading military experts; Viscount Montgomery of Alamein, *A History of Warfare* (1968), a handsome illustrated survey; *Makers of Modern Strategy: Military Thought from Machiavelli to Hitler,* edited by Edward Mead Earle, Gordon A. Craig, and Felix Gilbert (1943); and *The Theory and Practice of War,* edited by Michael Howard (1965). Howard has also edited a volume of essays on civil-military relations, *Soldiers and Governments* (1957). On the same subject, see Alfred Vagts, *A History of Militarism* (1937) and Gordon A. Craig, *War, Politics and Diplomacy: Selected Essays* (1966).

National political histories are listed in the appropriate sections below. *European Political Systems,* edited by Taylor Cole (new ed., 1959) is a useful book which, while emphasizing the recent period, includes historical background on the evolution of institutional forms in the principal European states. Of the general works dealing with political ideas and movements, C. J. H. Hayes, *The Historical Evolution of Modern Nationalism* (1931), treats one of the explosive forces of the age with brevity and authority. J. H. Hallowell's *Main Currents of Modern Political Thought* (1950) is a solid introduction, and M. Oakeshott's *Social and Political Doctrines of Contemporary Europe* (1939) a useful compilation of doctrinal statements. R. Kirk, *The Conservative Mind from Burke to Santayana* (1953), is well written and illuminating. Peter Viereck, *Conservatism Re-Visited: The Revolt against Revolt* (1949), is essentially an attack on the philosophy of liberalism, which finds its classical exposition in Guido Ruggiero, *European Liberalism* (1927), a comparative study. H. Marcuse, *Reason and Revolution: Hegel and the Rise of Social Theory* (1941), and J. L. Talmon, *Political Messianism: The Romantic Phase, 1815–1848* (1960), are learned and original studies. H. W. Laidler, *Social-Economic Movements: An Historical and Comparative Survey of Socialism, Communism, Cooperation, Utopianism and Other Forces of Reform and Reconstruction* (1944), is a valuable reference work which includes succinct summaries of doctrine and of the contents of basic socialist texts.

In the field of intellectual history, George L. Mosse, *The Culture of Western Europe* (1961), is always interesting and perceptive, although occasionally tendentious. Jacques Barzun, *Classic, Romantic, Modern* (new ed., 1961), warmly defends romanticism against its critics. Isaiah Berlin, *The Hedgehog and the Fox* (1953), is a brilliant essay on Tolstoy, which nevertheless manages to range over the whole intellectual history of the nineteenth century. A challenging intellectual history of the recent past is H. Stuart Hughes, *Consciousness and Society: The Re-Orientation of European Social Thought, 1890–1930* (1958).

The whole range of intellectual activity is treated in J. T. Merz, *A History of European Thought in the Nineteenth Century* (4 vols., 1896–1914), which is

Chapter 20   War and European Society, 1914–1918

The most satisfactory single-volume histories of military operations are C. R. M. F. Crutwell, *A History of the Great War, 1914–1918* (2d ed., 1936), Sir James Edmonds, *A Short History of World War I* (1951), B. H. Liddell Hart, *The War in Outline, 1914–1918* (1936), Cyril Falls, *The Great War, 1914–1918* (1959), and, most recently, Hanson W. Baldwin, *World War I: An Outline History* (1962).

Night Bombardment, World War I. (Bettmann Archive)

Bibliography

These can be supplemented with L. Stallings, *The First World War: A Photographic History* (1933, and new ed., with additions to text, 1964), *The American Heritage History of World War I* (1964), which has fine illustrations and a lively text by S. L. A. Marshall, and A. J. P. Taylor, *World War I: An Illustrated History* (1964), which discusses the military events in their political context, which is infrequently done in the works cited above. Paul Guinn, *British Strategy and Politics, 1914–1918* (1965), is also valuable for this reason, as is Sir Llewellyn Woodward's magisterial *Great Britain and the War of 1914–1918* (1967). See also A. J. P. Taylor, *Politics in Wartime* (1965). Among the many books on the role of the United States, E. R. May, *The World War and American Isolation, 1914–1917* (1959), is outstanding.

The number of accounts of single campaigns and of biographies and memoirs is enormous. Some notable items are John Terraine, *The Western Front, 1914–1918* (1964), a collection of essays, and W. S. Churchill, *The Unknown War* (1931), a history of the campaigns on the eastern front; Barbara Tuchman, *The Guns of August* (1962), and John Asprey, *The First Battle of the Marne* (1962), on the opening phase of the war; Alan Moorehead, *Gallipoli* (1956), and Trumbull Higgins, *Winston Churchill and the Dardanelles* (1964); Geoffrey Bennett, *The Battle of Jutland* (1964); Georges Blond, *Verdun* (1964), and Alistair Horne, *The Price of Glory: Verdun, 1916* (1962); Leon Wolff, *In Flanders Fields: The 1917 Campaign* (1958), a powerful indictment of the British command; John Williams, *Mutiny 1917* (1962), and R. M. Watt, *Dare Call It Treason* (1963), on the French mutinies of 1917; and Barrie Pitt, *1918: The Last Act* (1962). On individuals, see, among others, A. Duff Cooper, *Haig* (1935), and John Terraine, *Ordeal of Victory* (1963), the latter a somewhat excessive defense of Haig against his critics; Victor Bonham-Carter, *Soldier True: The Life and Times of Field Marshal Sir William Robertson* (1963); Brian Gardner, *Allenby* (1964); Karl Tschuppik, *Ludendorff: The Tragedy of a Military Mind* (1932); and J. W. Wheeler-Bennett, *Wooden Titan: Hindenburg* (1936). Critical but overstated accounts of military leadership are Correlli Barnett, *The Swordbearers* (1963), on Moltke, Jellicoe, Pétain, and Ludendorff; and Alan Clark, *The Donkeys* (1961), on British leadership in 1915. On air warfare, see Frederick Oughton, *The Aces* (1960), Andrew Boyle, *Trenchard* (1962), Sir John Slessor, *The Central Blue* (1957), and Douglas Robinson, *The Zeppelin in Combat* (1962). C. E. Montague, *Disenchantment* (1922), and Siegfried Sassoon, *Memoirs of an Infantry Officer* (1930), convey a sense of the excitement and the disillusionment felt by participants, and Ernst Jünger, *Storm of Steel* (1929), describes the *Frontkämpfer* mentality. T. E. Lawrence, *Seven Pillars of Wisdom* (1935), an account of the Arab revolt, has become a minor classic, and can now be supplemented with Cyril Falls, *Armageddon, 1918* (1964), an account of Allenby's last campaign. A refreshing new look at Turkey's role is given in Ulrich Trumpener, *Germany and the Ottoman Empire, 1914–1918* (1968). Brian Gardner, *German East* (1962), tells of the war in East Africa and the exploits of Lettow-Vorbeck. The social changes effected by the war on the home front are treated in Élie Halévy, *The Era of Tyrannies* (Eng. ed., 1965). Frank Chambers, *The War behind the War* (1939), A. Mendelssohn Bartholdy, *The War and German Society* (1938), Gerald D. Feldman, *Army, Industry and Labor, 1914–1918* (1966), a solid and rewarding study, W. Chamberlain, *Industrial Rela-*

Bibliography

tions in *War-Time Great Britain* (1940), Caroline Playne, *Society at War* (2 vols., 1934), Arthur Marwick, *The Deluge: British Society and the First World War* (1965), and A. Fontaine, *French Industry during the War* (1927); while wartime politics is discussed in Lord Beaverbrook, *Politicians and the War, 1914–1916* (1928) and *Men and Power, 1917–1918* (1956); Roy Jenkins, *Asquith* (1964); A. J. P. Taylor, *Politics in Warfare and Other Essays* (1965); *The Kaiser and His Court*, edited by Walter Görlitz (1964), the diaries and letters of Admiral von Müller, the chief of the Kaiser's naval cabinet; Marvin L. Edwards, *Stresemann and the Greater Germany, 1914–1918* (1962), good on the circumstances of Bethmann Hollweg's fall; Klaus Epstein, *Matthias Erzberger and the Dilemma of German Democracy* (1959); Hans W. Gatzke, *Germany's Drive to the West: A Study of Germany's Western War Aims* (1950); Fritz Fischer, *Germany's Aims* (1968); Z. A. B. Zeman, *The Breakup of the Hapsburg Empire, 1914–1918* (1961), which deals principally with the nationalities problem as it developed during the war; Arthur J. May, *The Passing of the Hapsburg Monarchy, 1914–1918* (2 vols., 1966); Gordon Brook-Shepherd, *The Last Habsburg* (1969), based on the papers of Charles I's consort Zita; and two books by Jere King on the civil-military problem in France, *Generals and Politicians* (1951) and *Foch versus Clemenceau* (1960).

Useful guides are Cyril Falls, *War Books: A Critical Guide* (1930), and Eugene Löhrke, *Armageddon: The World War in Literature* (1930).

Chapter 21   The Peace Treaties and the Search for Collective Security

H. W. V. Temperley, ed., *History of the Peace Conference* (6 vols., 1920–1924) is the standard work. Organization and procedure are described in F. S. Marston, *The Peace Conference of 1919* (1940), and in the memoir of the man who was in effect the general secretary of the Council of Four, Lord Hankey, *The Supreme Command: At the Paris Peace Conference, 1919* (1963). A summary of the aims and achievements of the conference and a comparison with the Congress of Vienna by two participants, C. K. Webster and H. W. V. Temperley, is reprinted in *From Metternich to Hitler: Aspects of British and Foreign Policy*, edited by W. N. Medlicott (1936). Harold Nicolson's *Peacemaking 1919* (1939) is a brilliant impressionistic view by a man who served on the British delegation. Paul Birdsall, *Versailles Twenty Years After* (1941), is a balanced reassessment which carefully analyzes some of the most difficult problems of negotiation. An important and illuminating book is Arno J. Mayer, *Politics and Diplomacy of Peacemaking: Containment and Counterrevolution at Versailles, 1918–1919* (1968), which shows the extent to which fear of Bolshevism determined the decisions of the conference. Unfavorable views of the economic clauses of the treaty are to be found in John Maynard Keynes, *The Economic Consequences of the Peace* (1920), a famous book in its day, and the first volume of W. S. Hancock's *Smuts* (2 vols., 1962, 1968), and the same author's *Four Studies of War and Peace in this Century* (1962). Keynes's conclusions have been attacked in E. Mantoux, *The Carthaginian Peace* (1952). Other problems rising out of the treaties are discussed in C. A. Macartney, *National States and National Minorities* (1934); Alfred Cobban, *National Self-Determination* (1944); Ivo J. Lederer, *Yugoslavia at the Paris Peace Conference* (1963); Arnold Wolfers, *Britain and France between the Wars: Con-*

flicting *Strategies of Peace* (1940); P. Wandycz, *France and Her Eastern Allies, 1919–1925* (1962), a solid book based on unpublished Polish materials; W. M. Jordan, *Great Britain, France and the German Problem, 1918–1939* (1943), which is particularly enlightening on disarmament and arms control; Harold Nicolson, *Curzon: The Last Phase* (1939), which has good accounts of some postwar conferences, including Lausanne, on which see also Lord Kinross, *Ataturk* (1964); and, from the voluminous Stresemann literature, Henry L. Bretton, *Stresemann and the Revision of Versailles* (1953). The story of the League and its troubles is told in F. P. Walters, *A History of the League of Nations* (2 vols., 1952); but see also Sir Alfred Zimmern, *The League of Nations and the Rule of Law* (1936), and Viscount Cecil, *A Great Experiment: An Autobiography* (1941). Good surveys of the postwar period are G. M. Gathorne-Hardy, *A Short History of International Affairs, 1920–1939* (4th rev. ed., 1950), and E. H. Carr, *The Twenty Years Crisis* (2d ed., 1956). A standard work, based on available printed documentary series, is the volume edited by Gordon A. Craig and Felix Gilbert, *The Diplomats, 1919–1939* (1953).

Chapter 22   The Russian Revolution and the West, 1917–1933

The most extensive history, indispensable for all students of the period, is E. H. Carr, *History of Soviet Russia* (7 vols., 1950 and continuing). This work now includes three volumes on the period 1917–1923, one on the so-called Interregnum 1923–1924, and, for the period 1924–1927, one on domestic politics, one on economics, and one, in two parts, on foreign policy. Shorter surveys of the whole period are Donald Treadgold, *Twentieth Century Russia* (1959), Hugh Seton-Watson, *From Lenin to Khrushchev* (2d ed., 1960), and Louis Aragon, *A History of the U.S.S.R.: From Lenin to Khrushchev* (1964), a quasi-official history by a fellow-traveler who has had the cooperation of Soviet authorities and has written an anti-Stalin history. Theodore Von Laue, *Why Lenin? Why Stalin? A Reappraisal of the Russian Revolution, 1900–1930* (1964), is a provocative analysis.

On the origins and course of the revolution, see Colin Wilson, *Rasputin and the Fall of the Romanovs* (1964), the latest book on the "holy devil" and unfortunately an often silly and inaccurate one; George Vernadsky, *The Russian Revolution, 1917–1921* (1932); Alan Moorehead, *The Russian Revolution* (1958), popular and oversimplified; and Joel Carmichael, *A Short History of the Russian Revolution* (1964). N. N. Sukhanov, *The Russian Revolution, 1917: A Personal Record*, edited by Joel Carmichael (1953), is an abridgment of the seven-volume memoir by a leading nonparty theoretician who witnessed the revolution and participated in the government. Recent biographies of Lenin are Robert Payne, *The Life and Death of Lenin* (1964), which is inclined to go beyond the evidence, as in its claim that Stalin murdered Lenin; Stefan T. Possony, *Lenin: The Complete Revolutionary* (1964), which makes good use of the secret police files and emphasizes Lenin's acceptance of German subsidies; and Louis Fischer, *The Life of Lenin* (1964), a detailed account by a former journalist who spent fourteen years in the Soviet Union and knew many of Lenin's associates. See also Angelica Balabanoff, *Impressions of Lenin* (1964), by a former associate who broke with him for moral reasons. The most satisfactory biography of Trotsky is the three-volume work by Isaac Deutscher, *The Prophet Armed: Trotsky, 1879–1921* (1954), *The Prophet Unarmed: Trotsky, 1921–1929* (1959), and *The Prophet Outcast: Trotsky, 1929–1940* (1963). Deutscher has also written *Stalin: A Political Biography* (1949). John S. Reshetar, Jr., *A Concise History of the Communist Party of the Soviet Union* (1960), is a useful guide. On the Comintern, aside from Carr, see Franz Borkenau, *The Communist International* (1938), Stefan T. Possony, *A Century of Conflict: Communist Techniques of World Revolution* (1953), James W. Hulse, *The Forming of the Communist International* (1964), which emphasizes departures from the original conception of the organization, and Victor Serge, *Memoirs of a Revolutionary, 1901–1941* (1963), by a former agent. On the Red Army see the first volume of Deutscher's biography of Trotsky, as well as the study of D. Fedotov White (1944), the symposium edited by B. H. Liddell Hart (1956), and John Erikson, *The Soviet High Command* (1962). The origins of Soviet diplomacy are treated in Arno J. Mayer, *Political Origins of the New Diplomacy, 1917–1918* (1959), and its course in George F. Kennan, *Soviet Foreign Policy, 1917–1941* (1960) and *Russia and the West under Lenin and Stalin* (1961), in Robert D. Warth, *Soviet Russia in World Politics* (1963), in Louis Fischer, *Soviet Foreign Relations, 1917–1941* (1969), by the former journalist and confidant of Chicherin, and in the solid but overlong survey by Adam B. Ulam, *Expansion and Coexistence: The History of Soviet Foreign Policy, 1917–1967* (1968). For more detailed treatment of shorter periods or of special subjects, see especially George F. Kennan's two volumes on Soviet-American relations, *Russia Leaves the War* (1956) and *The Decision To Intervene* (1958); Richard H. Ullman, *Intervention and the War: Anglo-Soviet Relations, 1917–1921* (1962) and *Britain and the Russian Civil War, 1918–1920* (1968); W. P. Coates and Z. K. Coates, *A History of Anglo-Soviet Relations* (1945); Malcolm D. Carroll, *Soviet Communism and Western Opinion, 1919–1921*, edited by Frederick B. M. Hollyday (1965); Louis Fischer, *The Soviets in World Affairs* (2 vols., 1930), on the Chicherin period; and *Russian Foreign Policy*, edited by Ivo J. Lederer (1962), on special aspects and agencies.

The best book on the purges is Robert Conquest, *The Great Terror: Stalin's Purge of the Thirties* (1968). See also Geoffrey Bailey, pseud., *The Conspirators* (1960), David J. Dallin, *From Purge to Coexistence* (1964), and, for the atmosphere of the time as felt by a young man, Wolfgang Leonhard, *Child of the Revolution* (1958). Victor Alexandrov, *The Tukhachevsky Affair* (1964), is interesting but often weak in documentation.

Of unfailing interest are the memoirs of Ilya Ehrenburg, now available in English translation, *Men, Years, Life* (5 vols., 1963–1965).

Chapter 23   The Rise of Italian Fascism

On fascism in general, see Ernst Nolte, *Three Faces of Fascism* (1966), studies of the Italian and German movements and of the Action Française, Francis L. Carsten, *The Rise of Fascism* (1967), S. J. Woolf, ed., *The Nature of Fascism* (1968), and "International Fascism, 1920–1945," *Journal of Contemporary History*, I, 1 (1966).

Bibliography

Benito Mussolini, *My Autobiography* (1938), gives the dictator's approved version of what he stood for, and Luigi Villari, *The Awakening of Italy* (1924), is an account by an ardent admirer and Fascist propagandist. More balanced and critical accounts are Gaudens Megaro's admirable *Mussolini in the Making* (1938), H. W. Schneider, *Making the Fascist State* (1928), and A. Rossi [Tasca], *The Rise of Italian Fascism, 1918–1922* (1938). G. A. Borgese, *Goliath: The March of Fascism* (1938), and G. Salvemini, *The Fascist Dictatorship in Italy* (vol. I, 1938), are openly hostile. Useful analyses of the practice of fascism are H. Finer, *Mussolini's Italy* (1935), M. T. Florinsky, *Fascism and National Socialism* (1935), W. Ebenstein, *Fascist Italy* (1939), and James Meenan, *The Italian Corporative System* (1945). P. Monelli's *Mussolini* (1953), an intimate life that sees the Duce as a petty bourgeois, is more perceptive than the biographies of Christopher Hibbert (1962), Laura Fermi (1961), and Roy MacGregor-Hastie (1962) but far less comprehensive and authoritative than Ivone Kirkpatrick, *Mussolini: A Study in Power* (1964). This gives a thorough treatment of the early years and of the Matteotti crisis but concentrates almost exclusively on foreign affairs after 1925. An interesting short sketch is to be found in Luigi Barzini, *The Italians* (1964). Federico Chabod, *A History of Italian Fascism* (1963), is by a distinguished Italian scholar and is particularly good on the early years. S. W. Halperin, *Mussolini and Italian Fascism* (1964), is an excellent short guide, as is Elizabeth Wiskemann, *Fascism in Italy: Its Development and Influence* (1969). Note should also be taken of the book by Christopher Seton-Watson listed under Chapter 13.

Chapter 24   The Republican Experiment in Germany

Good surveys of the period are to be found in R. T. Clark, *The Fall of the German Democracy* (1935), S. W. Halperin, *Germany Tried Democracy* (1946), and Erich Eyck, *History of the Weimar Republic* (2 vols., 1962–1963), none of which deals, however, with cultural or intellectual tendencies. The background and events of the revolution are given in A. J. Berlau, *The German Social Democratic Party, 1914–1921* (1949), Hans Gatzke, *Germany's Drive to the West* (1950), a history of wartime politics which shows why an explosion was inevitable, Harry Rudin, *Armistice 1918* (1944), which gives the situation at the time of the military collapse, Richard M. Watt, *The Kings Depart: The Tragedy of Germany at Versailles and the German Revolution* (1969), a popularized account, Eric Waldman, *The Spartacist Rising of 1919 and the Crisis of the German Socialist Movement* (1958), Alan Mitchell, *Revolution in Bavaria: The Eisner Regime and the Soviet Republic* (1965), both sound accounts, and J. W. Wheeler-Bennett, *Wooden Titan* (1936) and *The Nemesis of Power: The German Army in Politics, 1918–1945* (1953), which discuss the important role of the army during the revolution. On the latter subject, see also Craig, *Politics of the Prussian Army* and H. J. Gordon, Jr., *The Reichswehr and the German Republic, 1919–1926* (1957). The early political history of the republic is discussed in A. Rosenberg, *History of the German Republic* (1936), Werner Angress, *Stillborn Revolution: The Communist Bid for Power in Germany, 1921–1923* (1963), Klaus Epstein, *Matthias Erzberger and the Dilemma of German Democracy* (1959), Lewis Hertzman, *DNVP: Right Wing Opposition to the Weimar Republic* (1963), Count Harry

Bibliography

Kessler, *Walther Rathenau* (1928), and the chapter on Rathenau in James Joll, *Intellectuals in Politics* (1960). Hindenburg's role in domestic politics finds its first full-length treatment in Andreas Dorpalen, *Hindenburg and the Weimar Republic* (1964). On Stresemann, see Antonina Vallentin, *Stresemann* (1931), Hans Gatzke, *Stresemann and the Rearmament of Germany* (1954), and Henry A. Turner, *Stresemann and the Politics of the Weimar Republic* (1963), which discusses Stresemann's vain attempt to get party support for his policies. Rathenau, Stresemann, and Bruening are discussed in Craig, *From Bismarck to Adenauer* (rev. ed., 1965). M. J. Bonn, *Wandering Scholar* (1948), throws light upon the inflation years, P. Kosok, *Modern Germany* (1933), on problems of justice and education, Klemens von Klemperer, *Germany's New Conservatism* (1957), and Fritz Stern, *The Politics of Cultural Despair* (1961), on the intellectuals of the right, and Robert Waite, *Vanguard of Nazism: The Free Corps Movement* (1952), on one of the most pressing threats to social peace. S. Kracauer's *From Caligari to Hitler* (1947) is a psychological history of the German film that is illuminating on social relations. The cultural and psychological atmosphere of the republican period is admirably captured in Peter Gay, *Weimar Culture: The Outsider as Insider* (1968). On other aspects of the culture of the time, see Hans M. Wingler, *The Bauhaus* (1969).

The republic's relations with the Soviet Union are discussed in Gerald Fréund, *Unholy Alliance* (1957), E. H. Carr, *German-Soviet Relations between the Two World Wars* (1951), and Ruth Fischer, *Stalin and German Communism* (1948), by a former German Communist leader.

Chapter 25   The Crisis of Democracy: Central and Eastern Europe

On the depression and its impact, see J. K. Galbraith, *The Great Crash, 1929* (1955), Robert Sobel, *The Great Bull Market: Wall Street in the 1920's* (1968), a not entirely convincing account, and Paul Einzig, *The World Economic Crisis, 1929–1932* (1932). On its political effects in Germany, see the general works listed under Chapter 24, and, on Bruening's attempt to overcome them by diplomacy, the admirable book by Edward W. Bennett, *The Diplomacy of the Financial Crisis, 1931* (1962).

On the rise of National Socialism, Adolf Hitler, *Mein Kampf* (1939), gives the Fuehrer's own account, which is supplemented by *Hitler's Secret Conversations*, with an introduction by H. Trevor-Roper (1953), Hermann Rauschning, *Hitler Speaks* (1939), and *The Speeches of Adolf Hitler*, edited by Norman Baynes (2 vols., 1942). On Hitler, August Kubizek, *The Young Hitler I Knew* (1955), is a fascinating account by a friend of his youth; Konrad Heiden, *The Fuehrer: Hitler's Rise to Power* (1944), is dated but still useful; and Alan Bullock, *Hitler: A Study in Tyranny* (rev. ed., 1964) is a masterful brief biography. The evidence concerning the event that helped Hitler consolidate his power is analyzed, not very convincingly, in Fritz Tobias, *The Reichstag Fire* (1963). William Shirer's *The Rise and Fall of the Third Reich* (1960) is strongest on foreign affairs after 1938. The technique of domestic conquest is well described in Theodor Eschenburg and others, *The Path to Dictatorship* (1966), and in the brilliant study of William Sheridan Allen, *The Nazi Seizure of Power: The Experience of a Single*

Germany in the 1920s. "Jazz-Orchester und Shimmy-Tanz" by Karl Arnold. (Berliner Bilder, 1870–1932)

German Town, 1920–1935 (1965). Franz Neumann, *Behemoth: The Structure and Practise of National Socialism* (1944), is especially informative on economic organization, on which see also Jürgen Kuczynski, *Germany: Economic and Labor Conditions under Fascism* (1945), C. W. Guillebaud, *The Social Policy of Nazi Germany* (1939), and Burton H. Klein, *Germany's Economic Preparations for War* (1959). The social origins of the ruling class are analyzed in Daniel Lerner et al., *The Nazi Elite* (1951), and party organization and structure in Sigmund Neumann, *Permanent Revolution: The Total State in a World at War* (1942). David Schoenbaum, *Hitler's Social Revolution: Class and Status in Nazi Germany, 1933–1939* (1966), is an original and authoritative account of the collapse of the traditional social order under the impact of National Socialism. On Hitler's principal lieutenants, see R. Manvell and H. Fraenkel, *Hermann Goering* (1962) and *Himmler* (1965), and Ernest K. Bramsted, *Goebbels and National Socialist Propaganda*

(1965), a comprehensive and original study with a fine section on the creation of the Fuehrer myth. See also Z. A. B. Zeman, *Nazi Propaganda* (1964), and Oron J. Hale, *The Captive Press in the Third Reich* (1964). Nathaniel Micklem, *National Socialism and the Roman Catholic Church* (1939), is a basic study. Guenter Lewy, *The Catholic Church and Nazi Germany* (1964), accuses the church leadership of not standing up to the challenge. The best accounts of the growth and activities of the S. S. are G. Reitlinger, *The S.S.: Alibi of a Nation, 1922–1945* (1957), and Heinz Höhne, *The Order of the Death's Head* (1969); on the Gestapo, see the books of Edward Crankshaw (1956) and Jacques Delarue (1964). German accounts of the period include Hanna Vogt, *The Burden of Guilt* (1965) and the fascinating memoirs of Albert Speer, *Inside the Third Reich* (1970).

On the countries to the east, see Hugh Seton-Watson, *Eastern Europe between the Wars, 1918–1941* (1945), and C. A. Macartney and A. W. Palmer, *Independent Eastern Europe* (1962). The political history of Austria is told in Julius Braunthal, *The Tragedy of Austria* (1948), which includes some correspondence between Mussolini and Dollfuss, Joseph Buttinger, *In the Twilight of Socialism* (1953), valuable for its insight into socialist disunity, Malcolm Bullock, *Austria, 1918–1938: A Study in Failure* (1939), and Charles Gulick's lengthy and detailed *Austria from Habsburg to Hitler* (2 vols., 1948). See also Gordon Brook-Shephard, *Prelude to Infamy: The Story of Chancellor Dollfuss of Austria* (1962), which is sympathetic to its subject and stresses Italian pressure upon him, and the first chapters of Jürgen Gehl, *Austria, Germany and the Anschluss, 1931–1938* (1963), good on competing factions within Austria. G. E. R. Gedye, *Betrayal in Central Europe* (1939), is an account of the failure of democracy in Austria by a perceptive British journalist. On Poland, see Joseph Rothschild, *Pilsudski's Coup d'Etat* (1966); on Bulgaria, the same author's *The Communist Party of Bulgaria* (1959); on Rumania, Henry Roberts, *Political Problems of an Agrarian State* (1951).

Chapter 26   The Crisis of Democracy: Western Europe

British politics in the postwar period are covered clearly and concisely in D. C. Somervell, *British Politics since 1900* (1950), and social history is treated informally, but with great insight, in Robert Graves and Alan Hodge, *The Long Weekend, 1918–1939* (1939). Lord Beaverbrook, *The Decline and Fall of Lloyd George* (1962), is a lively account of the Welsh Wizard's last years of power. Reginald Pound and Geoffrey Harmsworth, *Northcliffe* (1959), throws interesting light on the politics of these years. The problems of industry and labor are discussed in Charles P. Kindleberger, *Economic Growth in France and Britain, 1851–1950* (1964), G. D. H. Cole, *A History of the Labour Party from 1914* (1948), and Alan Bullock, *The Life and Times of Ernest Bevin*, vol. I, *The Trade Union Leader, 1881–1940* (1960), which includes an excellent account of the general strike. On the crisis of 1931, see Harold Nicolson, *King George the Fifth: His Life and Reign* (1952); R. Bassett, *Nineteen Thirty One Political Crisis* (1958); Philip Viscount Snowden, *An Autobiography* (2 vols., 1934); Robert Skidelsky, *Politicians and the Slump* (1967), a study of the Labour government and its fall. The abdication crisis is treated in Lord Beaverbrook's *The Abdication of King Edward VIII*

(1965), a slashing attack upon Stanley Baldwin, and, more reliably, in Brian Inglis' *Abdication* (1966), and John W. Wheeler-Bennett's *King George VI: His Life and Reign* (1955).

Perceptive biographies are those on Stanley Baldwin by G. M. Young (1952) and, more flattering and more comprehensive, Keith Middlemas and John Barnes (1970), Colin Cross, *Philip Snowden* (1966), and Keith Feiling, *Life of Neville Chamberlain* (1946). Hugh Dalton's sparkling memoirs, *Call Back Yesterday, 1887–1931* (1953) and *The Fateful Years, 1931–1945* (1957), throw much new light on the politics of these years, as do the diaries of the cabinet secretary and intimate of Lloyd George and Baldwin, Thomas Jones, *Whitehall Diary, 1916–1930,* edited by Keith Middlemas (2 vols., 1969) and *A Diary with Letters, 1931–1950* (1954). Entertaining and engrossing are *The Diaries and Letters of Harold Nicolson, 1930–1939,* edited by Nigel Nicolson (1966). England's failure to rearm is discussed in John F. Kennedy, *Why England Slept* (1940), and B. H. Liddell Hart, *Memoirs,* (2 vols., 1965). On the whole period, see A. J. P. Taylor, *English History, 1914–1945* (1965).

On Britain's relations with the dominions, see especially Nicholas Mansergh, *The Commonwealth Experience* (1969), a most informative volume. On the Irish question, see Eoin Neeson, *The Civil War in Ireland, 1922–1923* (1966) and *The Life and Death of Michael Collins* (1968).

The problems of France are analyzed in the volumes by D. W. Brogan cited under Chapters 3 and 14, in Edward Mead Earle, ed., *Modern France* (1951), and in Alexander Werth, *The Twilight of France, 1933–1940* (1942). Aspects of the political struggle receive detailed treatment in Peter J. Larmour, *The French Radical Party in the 1930s* (1964), John T. Marcus, *French Socialism in the Crisis Years, 1933–1936: Fascism and the French Left* (1958), Charles A. Micaud, *The French Right and Nazi Germany, 1933–1939* (1943), the volumes on the Action Française listed under Chapter 14, and the somewhat sensational book by Louis Ducloux, *From Blackmail to Treason: Political Corruption and Crime in France, 1920–1940* (1958). Four books about the extreme left are valuable: Robert Wohl, *French Communism in the Making, 1919–1924* (1967), describing the early love affair of the French left with Bolshevism, Alfred J. Rubin, *Stalin and the French Communist Party* (1962), Charles A. Micaud, *Communism and the French Left* (1963), and David Caute, *Communism and the French Intellectuals, 1914–1960* (1964), the last dealing with the dilemma of the party intellectual. More provocative and incisive than the last is H. Stuart Hughes, *The Obstructed Path: French Social Thought in the Years of Desperation, 1930–1960* (1966). Works on individual politicians include Loise Elliott Dalby, *Léon Blum: Evolution of a Socialist* (1963), James Joll, *Intellectuals in Politics* (1960), on Blum, Rudolf Binion, *Defeated Leaders: The Political Fate of Caillaux, Jouvenel, and Tardieu* (1960), and Hubert Cole, *Laval: A Biography* (1963). R. D. Challener, *The French Theory of the Nation in Arms, 1866–1939* (1955), treats the military problem.

Events in the lesser states are covered in works cited earlier. The rise of fascism in some of them is discussed in *The European Right,* edited by Hans Rogger and Eugen Weber (1965). The background of the Spanish civil war is treated in Frank E. Manuel, *The Politics of Modern Spain* (1938), E. A. Peers, *The Spanish Tragedy* (1936), Gerald Brenan, *The Spanish Labyrinth* (1943), Sir Charles Petrie,

Bibliography

King Alfonso XIII and His Age (1963), a work by one who knew and talked with Alfonso about the events of his reign, and the first twelve chapters of Gabriel Jackson, *The Spanish Republic and the Civil War, 1931–1939* (1965), which brings forward much new material. See also Stanley G. Payne, *Politics and the Military in Modern Spain* (1967).

   A general work of importance, with essays on France, Great Britain, Sweden and Spain, among others, is Adolf Sturmthal, *The Tragedy of European Labor, 1918–1939* (1943).

Chapter 27   The Road to War, 1933–1939

   In addition to the works cited under Chapters 21, 25, and 26, the following should be noted: A. J. P. Taylor, *The Origins of the Second World War* (1961), a brilliant but willful treatment which rather plays down Hitler's responsibility and denies that his policy was marked either by consistency or desire for war; R. A. C. Parker, *Europe, 1919–1945* (1968), which has a good critique of the Taylor thesis; G. Salvemini, *Prelude to World War II* (1953); L. B. Namier, *In the Nazi Era* (1952), selected essays; John W. Wheeler-Bennett, *Munich: Prologue to Tragedy* (1948), which is more comprehensive than the title suggests, and Laurence Lafore, *The End of Glory: An Interpretation of the Origins of World War II* (1970). Aspects of British policy are treated in Winston S. Churchill, *The Gathering Storm* (1948); *The Memoirs of Anthony Eden: Facing the Dictators, 1923–1938* (1962), a rewarding volume; the biographies of Neville Chamberlain by Keith Feiling (1946) and Iain McLeod (1961); J. R. M. Butler, *Lord Lothian* (1960); A. L. Rowse, *All Souls and Appeasement* (1961); Martin Gilbert, *The Roots of Appeasement* (1966); Martin Gilbert and Richard Gott, *The Appeasers* (1963); D. C. Watt, *Personalities and Politics: Studies in the Formulation of British Foreign Policy in the Twentieth Century* (1965); and, most illuminating, *The History of the Times*, vol. IV, part 2, *1921–1948* (1952). William Scott, *Alliance against Hitler* (1962), is the basic work on the Franco-Soviet Pact, now supplemented by Geoffrey Warner, *Pierre Laval and the Eclipse of France, 1931–1945* (1969). France's relations with Great Britain receive detailed attention in A. H. Furnia, *The Diplomacy of Appeasement: Anglo-French Relations, 1931–1938* (1960). Elizabeth Wiskemann, *The Rome-Berlin Axis* (1949), is good on the origins and development of the friendship between the two dictators; and this account can now be supplemented by Ivone Kirkpatrick's *Mussolini* (1964). Max Beloff, *The Foreign Policy of the Soviet Union* (2 vols., 1947), is somewhat dated but still useful, but see the works cited under Chapter 22, and Marshall D. Shulman, *Stalin's Foreign Policy Reappraised* (1963). Roman Dibicki, *Foreign Policy of Poland, 1919–1939* (1963), by a former Polish diplomat, is good on the period immediately before the war, as is Anna M. Cienciala, *Poland and the Western Powers* (1968), which stresses the role of Colonel Beck.

   On the Spanish war, the most comprehensive study is that of Hugh Thomas, *The Spanish Civil War* (1961); others are Robert Payne, *The Spanish Civil War* (1962), James Cleugh, *Spanish Fury* (1962), which is pro-Nationalist in sympathy, and Gabriel Jackson, *The Spanish Republic and the Civil War* (1965), which emphasizes politics more than military operations. Dante A. Puzzo, *Spain and the*

Great Powers, 1936–1941 (1962), stresses the liberal and democratic nature of the Popular Front and is critical of British policy. David T. Cattell, *Communism and the Spanish Civil War* (1955) and *Soviet Diplomacy and the Spanish Civil War* (1957), and Ilya Ehrenburg, *Men, Years, Life,* vol. IV, *The Eve of War, 1933–1941* (1963), deal with the Russian role in Spain, the last written by a man who was personally acquainted with the brutal inconsistencies of Soviet policy. On the *Anschluß,* in addition to the works cited under Chapter 24, see Gordon Brook-Shepard, *Anschluß: The Rape of Austria* (1963); and, on the final crises, Keith Eubank, *Munich* (1963), and L. B. Namier, *Diplomatic Prelude, 1938–1939* (1948).

Memoirs are too numerous to list.

Chapter 28   World War II

The best over-all view is Gordon Wright, *The Ordeal of Total War, 1939–1945* (1968). The diplomatic history of the war is found in W. S. Churchill, *History of the Second World War* (6 vols., 1948–1953), *The Memoirs of Anthony Eden: The Reckoning* (1965), Sir Llewellyn Woodward, *British Foreign Policy in the Second World War* (1961), W. L. Langer and E. Gleason, *The Challenge to Isolation* (1952) and *The Undeclared War* (1953), which emphasize the American side, Robert E. Sherwood, *Roosevelt and Hopkins: An Intimate History* (1948), the fine volumes of Herbert Feis, *Churchill, Roosevelt, Stalin: The War They Waged and the Peace They Sought* (1957) and *Between Peace and War: The Potsdam Conference* (1960), and others too numerous to cite.

The best single-volume histories of military operations are J. F. C. Fuller, *The Second World War: A Strategical and Tactical History* (1949), Basil Collier, *A Short History of the Second World War* (1961), and Brigadier Peter Young, *A Short History of World War II* (1966). Chester Wilmot, *Struggle for Europe* (1952), is also notable. In the British official *History of the Second World War,* edited by J. R. M. Butler (1956 ff.), six volumes are devoted to "Grand Strategy." Strategical planning is discussed in two volumes in the series *The United States Army in World War II,* prepared in the Office of the Chief of Military History, Department of the Army: M. Matloff and E. M. Snell, *Strategic Planning for Coalition Warfare, 1941–1942* (1953), and M. Matloff, *Strategic Planning for Coalition Warfare, 1943–1944* (1959). Two interesting books on the turning points in the war are *Command Decisions* (1959), prepared by the Office of the Chief of Military History, and *The Fatal Decisions* (1956), edited by S. Freidin and W. Richardson, a series of essays by German generals. Supplementing the latter volume is B. H. Liddell Hart, *The Other Side of the Hill* (new ed., 1951), which is based on interviews with captured officers. The early campaigns of the European war are well described in Telford Taylor, *Sword and Swastika* (1952), *The March of Conquest* (1958), and *The Breaking Wave* (1967). The fall of France is treated by Major General Sir Edward Spears, *Assignment to Catastrophe* (2 vols., 1954), and J. Benoist-Méchin, *Sixty Days That Shook the West* (1963), Guy Chapman, *Why France Collapsed* (1968), and William L. Shirer, *The Collapse of the Third Republic* (1969), all of which treat politics as well as military affairs; essentially military studies are Colonel A. Goutard, *The Fall of France* (1959), General

Bibliography

André Beaufre, *1940: The Fall of France* (1968), and Alistair Horne, *To Lose a Battle* (1969). What followed in France is the subject of two excellent studies: Robert Aron, *The Vichy Regime* (1958), and Adrienne Hystier, *Two Years of French Foreign Policy, 1940–1942* (1958). See also the books on Laval by Hubert Cole (1963) and Geoffrey Warner (1968). American policy toward Vichy finds delicate treatment in W. L. Langer, *Our Vichy Gamble* (1947), and Robert Murphy, *Diplomat among Warriors* (1963). Aspects of the resistance movement are trated in *The Complete War Memoirs of Charles De Gaulle* (1964), which Stuart Hughes has called "the greatest literary classic of the Second World War." Dorothy Shipley White, *Seeds of Discord: De Gaulle, Free France and their Allies* (1964), and Milton Viorst, *Hostile Allies: F. D. R. and De Gaulle* (1965). On the liberation, see Robert Aron, *De Gaulle before Paris* (1963), an abbreviated version of his untranslated history of the liberation, and Willis Thornton, *The Liberation of Paris* (1963).

The battle of Britain is the subject of Walter Ansel, *Hitler Confronts England* (1960), Peter Fleming, *Operation Sea Lion* (1957), Constantine FitzGibbon, *The Blitz* (1957), and Drew Middleton, *The Sky Suspended* (1960), which deals with air operations, while problems of the civilian front are discussed in the second volume of Alan Bullock's biography of Ernest Bevin (1967) and in the second volume of Harold Nicolson's memoirs, *The War Years, 1939–1945* (1967). See also Harold Macmillan, *The Blast of War, 1939–1945* (1968). Books on the sea war and the Mediterranean theater are numerous and include *A Sailor's Odyssey: The Autobiography of Admiral Viscount Cunningham* (1951), Raymond de Belot, *The Struggle for the Mediterranean* (1951), Donald Macintyre, *The Battle for the Mediterranean* (1963), which is based on German and Italian as well as British sources, *The Rommel Papers*, edited by B. H. Liddell Hart (1953), Desmond Young, *Rommel: The Desert Fox* (1950), and John Connell's fine biography of Wavell (1965). See also Donald S. Detwiler, *Hitler, Franco, and Gibraltar* (1963). For the impact of the war on Italian life and politics, see Kirkpatrick's *Mussolini*; F. W. Deakin, *The Brutal Friendship: Mussolini, Hitler, and the Fall of Italian Fascism* (1962), a work of superb scholarship; and Charles F. Delzell, *Mussolini's Enemies: The Italian Anti-Fascist Resistance* (1961), an original and authoritative work.

On the war in Russia, see particularly Paul Carell, *Hitler Moves East, 1941–1943* (1965), which gives a good picture of the rigors of the ground war, and Alan Clark, *Barbarossa: The Russian-German Conflict, 1941–1945* (1965), a strategical account which is more favorable in its judgment of Hitler's military talent than most studies. Political aspects of the war in Russia find treatment in G. L. Weinberg, *Germany and the Soviet Union, 1939–1941* (1954), Alexander Dallin, *German Rule in Russia, 1941–1945* (1957), an admirable and frightening study, and G. Reitlinger, *House Built on Sand* (1960). For the Russian home front, see Alexander Werth, *Russia at War, 1941–1945* (1964), a correspondent's book that is too long and often inaccurate and inadequately documented, and the fifth volume of Ilya Ehrenburg's memoirs, *The War, 1941–1945* (1964).

The air war against Germany is analyzed in Noble Frankland, *The Bombing Offensive against Germany* (1965), and David Irving, *The Destruction of Dresden* (1964). No adequate description of life in Germany during the war exists, but see

Ernest Bramsted's *Goebbels* (1965) and the rich literature on the resistance, particularly Hans Rothfels, *The German Opposition to Hitler* (rev. ed., 1962), and
Gerhard Ritter, *The German Resistance: Carl Goerdeler's Struggle against Tyranny* (1959), and, most recently, Harold C. Deutsch, *The Conspiracy against
Hitler in the Twilight War* (1968).

Brilliant accounts of single battles or campaigns are to be found in David
Divine, *The Nine Days of Dunkirk* (1959); Fred Majdalany, *The Battle of Cassino*
(1957) and *The Battle of el Alamein* (1965); the books on El Alamein by Michael
Carver (1962) and C. E. Lucas Phillips (1962); Heinz Schröter, *Stalingrad* (1958);
Harrison Salisbury's account of the siege of Leningrad, *The 900 Days* (1968);
Martin Blumenson, *Anzio: The Gamble That Failed* (1963); Gordon A. Harrison,
Cross-Channel Attack (1951); Eversley Belfield and H. Essame, *The Battle of
Normandy* (1965); Cornelius Ryan, *The Longest Day* (1959); and the studies of the
battle of the Ardennes by John Toland (1959) and John Eisenhower (1969). Mar-
shal Vasili I. Chuikov, *The Fall of Berlin* (1967), should be read together with
Erich Kuby, *The Russians and Berlin, 1945* (1960), and Cornelius Ryan, *The Last
Battle* (1966).

Two interesting strategical critiques are Samuel Eliot Morison, *Strategy and
Compromise* (1958), and Trumbull Higgins, *Winston Churchill and the Second
Front* (1957).

Memoirs are too numerous to list.

Chapter 29 **Reconstruction and the Evolution of the European States to
the Mid-1960s**

Barbara Ward, *Faith and Freedom: A Study of Western Society* (1954), and
T. H. White, *Fire in the Ashes: Europe in Mid-Century* (1953), are both critical
appraisals of the first decade of European recovery. For later developments, the
special issue of *Daedalus: Journal of the American Academy of Arts and Sciences* (Winter, 1964), entitled "A New Europe?" is indispensable, as is Walter
Laqueur, *Europe Since Hitler* (1970). On Great Britain see, in addition to works
already cited, David Thomson, *England in the Twentieth Century* (1964), Hugh
Dalton, *High Tide and After: Memoirs, 1945–1960* (1961), Randolph S. Churchill,
The Fight for Tory Leadership: A Contemporary Chronicle (1964), the third vol-
ume of Harold MacMillan's memoirs, *Tides of Fortune, 1945–1955* (1969), Anthony
Sampson, *MacMillan: A Study in Ambiguity* (1967), and Max Nicholson, *The
System: The Misgovernment of Modern Britain* (1967). On France, Gordon Wright,
The Re-shaping of the French Democracy (1948), is still useful, while his *Rural
Revolution in France* (1964) is a thorough and original study of the change in
attitude and organization of the peasantry. The final chapters of David Thomson,
Democracy in France (4th rev. ed., 1965), give a clear and useful survey of the
political history of the Fourth and Fifth Republics. See also Philip M. Williams,
Politics in Post-War France (2d ed., 1958). The changeover of 1958 is treated in
James H. Meisel, *The Fall of the Republic: Military Revolt in France* (1962), John
Steward Ambler, *The French Army in Politics, 1945–1962* (1966), and, with more
attention to the long developing dilemma of the French army, in Paul-Marie de
la Gorce, *The French Army: A Military-Political History* (1963). On De Gaulle's

Bibliography

republic see Raymond Aron, *France: Constant and Changing* (1960), E. S. Furniss, *France, Troubled Ally* (1960), and the studies of Dorothy Pickles (1962), Roy C. Macrides and Bernhard E. Brown (1960), and Philip M. Williams and Martin Harrison (1960) and, on the general himself, Aidan Crawley, *De Gaulle* (1969), a full-scale biography. *In Search of France* by Stanley Hoffmann, Charles P. Kindleberger, Lawrence Wylie, Jesse R. Pitts, Jean-Baptiste Duroselle, and François Goguel (1963) is a profound and provocative volume dealing with every aspect of contemporary French life. An indispensable economic and social survey of the years from 1945 to 1968, with excellent chapters on education and the arts, is John Ardagh, *The New French Revolution* (1968).

On Germany, Ralf Dahrendorf, *Society and Democracy in Germany* (1968), is basic. J. F. Golay, *The Founding of the Federal Republic of Germany* (1958), and Alfred Grosser, *The Federal Republic of Germany: A Concise History* (1963) are enormously useful. On foreign policy, see Karl W. Deutsch and L. Edinger, *Germany Rejoins the Powers* (1957), and Hans Speier and W. P. Davison, *West German Leadership and Foreign Policy* (1957), both studies of mass opinion and elites; and on the reunification problem, see Frederick H. Hartmann, *Germany between East and West* (1965), and Ferenc A. Váli, *The Quest for a United Germany* (1967). Paul Weymar's *Adenauer* (1957) is an official biography; for other views, see Gordon A. Craig, *From Bismarck to Adenauer* (rev. ed., 1965), and Richard Hiscocks, *The Adenauer Era* (1966). Aspects of the Berlin problem are treated in W. P. Davison, *The Berlin Blockade* (1958), Jean Edward Smith, *The Defense of Berlin* (1964), Deane and David Heller, *The Berlin Wall* (1964), and Philip Windsor, *City on Leave: A History of Berlin, 1945–1962* (1963).

A massive study of rightist movements in the Federal Republic is Kurt B. Tauber, *Beyond Swastika and Eagle: German Nationalism since 1945* (2 vols., 1967). Developments in the German Democratic Republic are discussed in John Dornberg, *The Other Germany* (1968), and David Childs, *East Germany* (1969).

On Italy, see Serge Hughes, *The Rise and Fall of Modern Italy* (1967), a survey of politics from 1890 to the 1960s, with the emphasis on the postwar period.

On Eastern Europe and the Soviet Union, in addition to works already cited, see John A. Lukacs, *The Great Powers and Eastern Europe* (1953), Hugh Seton-Watson, *The East European Revolution* (2d rev. ed., 1952), Robert Lee Wolff, *The Balkans in our Time* (1956), an admirable survey, Hubert Ripka, *Eastern Europe in the Post-War World* (1961), Stephen Fischer-Galati, ed., *Eastern Europe in the Sixties* (1963), and Zbigniew K. Brzezinski, *The Soviet Bloc: Unity and Conflict* (2d rev. ed., 1961). For special problems, the following are reliable: William B. Bader, *Austria between East and West, 1945–1955* (1966); Josef Korbel, *The Communist Subversion of Czechoslovakia* (1959); *The Czech Black Book,* edited by Robert Littell (1969), on the events of August 1968; Robert Rhodes James, ed., *The Czech Crisis 1968* (1969); Richard Hiscocks, *Poland: Bridge for the Abyss* (1963); Paul E. Zinner, *Revolution in Hungary* (1962); and Kenneth Young, *The Greek Passion* (1969), which despite its rather uncritical acceptance of the Papadopoulos regime, is the most intelligent book in English on Greek politics and puts the events of 1967 in historical perspective. Ernest J. Simmons, ed., *Through the Glass of Soviet Literature* (1962), and Harold Swayze, *Political Control of Literature in the U.S.S.R.* (1962), discuss the state of the arts in the Soviet Union. Ideological questions are discussed in Robert C. Tucker, *The Soviet Political*

Mind (1963), and Richard Löwenthal, *World Communism: The Disintegration of a Secular Faith* (1964), and political ones in Edward Crankshaw, *Khrushchev: A Career* (1964). Recent and perceptive is (An Observer) *Message from Moscow* (1969).

Chapter 30   Europe and the World: Problems and Prospects

E. P. Chase, *The United Nations in Action* (1950), C. M. Eichelberger, *UN: The First Ten Years* (1955), and J. Maclaurin, *The United Nations and Power Politics* (1952), are still useful. More recent works are John G. Stoessinger, *Financing the United Nations System* (1964), an assessment of the limitations of executive action by the U.N., Alvin Rubenstein, *The Soviets in International Organizations* (1964), Hugh Foot, *A Start in Freedom* (1964), C. M. Eichelberger, *UN: The First Twenty Years* (1965), and Conor Cruise O'Brien and Feliks Topolski, *The United Nations: Sacred Drama* (1968), highly critical of the organization's performance.

On NATO and the defense of Western Europe, Lord Ismay, *NATO: The First Five Years, 1949-1954* (1955), is a useful guide to organization and functions, which should be supplemented by the essays in Klaus Knorr, ed., *NATO and American Security* (1959), and the fine essay by James E. King, "NATO: Genesis, Progress, Problems" in *National Security in the Nuclear Age* (1960), edited by Gordon B. Turner and R. D. Challener. An important book from the Center of Strategic Studies, Georgetown University, is *NATO in Quest of Cohesion,* edited by Karl H. Cerny and Henry W. Briefs (1965). W. O. Henderson, *The Genesis of the Common Market* (1962) is important. See also F. Roy Willis, *France, Germany and the New Europe, 1945-1967* (rev. ed., 1968).

Two books by Hugh Seton-Watson are valuable guides to world politics in the most recent period: *From Lenin to Khrushchev: The History of World Communism* (1960), and *Neither War Nor Peace: The Struggle for Power in the Post-War World* (1960). *The Politics of Developing Nations* (1960), edited by Gabriel A. Almond and James S. Coleman, Paul Seabury, *The Rise and Decline of the Cold War* (1967), and Louis J. Halle, *The Cold War as History* (1967), should also be consulted.

The events that led to India's independence are described in Alan Campell-Johnson, *Mission with Mountbatten* (1953), B. N. Pandey, *The Break-up of British India* (1969) and H. V. Hodson, *The Great Divide* (1969). Lucian W. Pye, *Guerrilla Communism in Malaya* (1956), and R. H. Fifield, *The Diplomacy of South East Asia, 1945-1958* (1958), discuss some of the problems of the former colonial powers in one part of the world. The crisis of 1954 in Indochina is discussed in Bernard Fall, *Street without Joy* (1963) and *Hell in a Very Small Place* (1966), Jules Roy, *The Battle of Dienbienphu* (1964), Robert Scigliano, *South Vietnam: Nation under Stress* (1963), and Philippe Devillers and Jean Lacouture, *Indochina, 1954* (1969), which includes the fullest available account of the Geneva conference. Both that crisis and the Suez crisis of 1956 are treated in *Full Circle: The Memoirs of Anthony Eden* (1960), with bitter criticism of United States policy. On Suez, Herman Finer, *Dulles over Suez* (1964), and Terence Robertson, *Crisis: The Inside Story of the Suez Conspiracy* (1964), are interesting, but it is difficult to assess the value of the sources used. More reliable is Hugh Thomas, *The Suez Affair* (1966). Anthony Nutting, *No End of a Lesson* (1967), is an insider's story, highly critical of Eden. An account sympathetic to Nasser is Kennett Love,

Bibliography

Suez: The Twice-Fought War (1969); more balanced is Bowyer Bell, *The Long War: Israel and the Arabs since 1946* (1969). See also Nadav Safran, *From War to War: The Arab-Israeli Confrontation, 1948–1967* (1969). Among the many books on the war in Algeria, see C. L. Sulzberger, *The Test: De Gaulle and Algeria* (1962), Dorothy Pickles, *Algeria and France* (1963), Alfred Grosser, *French Foreign Policy under De Gaulle* (1965), David Schoenbrun, *The Three Lives of Charles De Gaulle* (1968), and Jean Lacouture, *De Gaulle* (rev. ed., 1968).

The basic work on Africa is the now famous guide by Lord Hailey, *An African Survey: A Study of Problems Arising in Africa South of the Sahara* (rev. ed., 1966). Colin Legum, ed., *Africa: A Handbook to the Continent* (rev. ed., 1966) is an excellent reference guide to the politics of the new nations, which includes essays on changing cultural patterns and the role of the United Nations.

Finally, the world's preoccupation with the dangers caused by the weapons revolution is reflected in Herman Kahn, *On Thermonuclear War* (1960), which includes brilliant and original reassessments of problems of the wars of 1914–1918 and 1939–1945, in Thomas Schelling, *Arms and Influence* (1966), and in the rich literature on arms control. A good introduction to the last subject is Gerald Holton, ed., *Arms Control* (Special Issue of *Daedalus,* Fall, 1960).

Europe from the moon. (NASA)

INDEX

Index

Index

Index

Index

Index

Index

Gervinus, George Gottfried, 57
Gestapo (secret police), 692
Ghana, 790, 793
Gibraltar, 644, 673
Gide, André, 246, 456, 457, 669
Gilbert, William Schwenck, 247
Gill, André, 320
Gilson, Etienne, 459
Gioberti, V., 190
Giolitti, Giovanni, 314–315, 468, 469, 539–540, 543, 545
Girardin, Emile de, 81, 82
Gladstone, William Ewart, 225–230, 249, 287, 290–291, 295, 300–301, 408, 409, 411; Ireland and, 229–230; reforms of, 228–229
Gläser, Ernst, 451
Gleichschaltung, 587–591, 632, 633, 647, 749
Glinka, Michael, 62
Glubb, Sir John, 779*n*
Gneisenau, A. W. Neidhardt von, 9, 47
Godard, Jean-Luc, 732
Goderich, Lord, *see* Robinson, F. J.
Goebbels, Paul Joseph, 579, 591, 692
Goering, Hermann, 579, 586, 590, 646, 651, 657, 670, 671, 681, 687, 693, 694, 706
Goethe, Johann Wolfgang von, 61–62
Gogol, Nicholas, 60, 61, 231
Goltz, Colmar von der, 624
Gömbos, Julius, 600
Gomulka, Wladeslaw, 751, 753
Goncourt brothers, 180
Gooch, G. P., 406
Gorchakov, Prince, 166, 252, 255
Gordon, Charles, 411, 419
Görgey, Arthur, 140
Göttingen Seven, 57, 59
Gough, Sir Hugh, 483
Gounod, Charles François, 149, 246, 326
Graham, Sir James, 115
Gramont, Duke of, 236
Grand Alliance (1813), 11, 13, 14
Grandi, Dino, 542, 543
Grand National Consolidated Trades Union, 107, 108
Grass, Günter, 730, 741, 742
Graziani, Rodolfo, 672
Great Britain, 25; affluence, problems of, 733–736; Agadir crisis and, 441; agriculture in, 93; Anglo-Russian agreement, 433–435; army reforms, 296; arts in (1815–1848), 119–121; Balkan wars and, 443; Battle of Britain, 670–671; Boer War, 420–422; Bosnian crisis and, 439–440; Chartism, 108–110, 116; colonialism, 9, 121, 221–224; Commonwealth of Nations, 614; Corn Laws, 5, 93, 98, 111–115, 224, 225; Crimean War, 156–157, 221; democracy in, 301–302, 602–615; depression of the 1930s, impact of, 610–611; economic conditions after 1815, 91–97; education in (1815–1848), 118–119, 228–229; Egypt and, 258, 402, 408, 612; Europe and, 614–615; franchise, broadening of, 286–287; from 1815 to 1848, 91–122; from 1866 to 1871, 221–230; from 1871 to 1914, 286; general strike (1926), 607–610; German question and, 507–508; Great Reform Bill, 6, 28, 100–104; House of Commons, 101, 103, 104, 105, 109, 113, 227, 297, 299, 300; House of Lords, 102, 103, 113, 294, 297, 299; imperialism and, 400–404, 411, 412, 414, 415, 611; India and, 222–223, 613–614, 782–784; industrial development in, 5, 262; Ireland and, 229–230, 300–301, 611–612; League of Nations and, 504; liberalism, revival and relapse of, 294–300; National Insurance Act (1911), 299, (1946), 711; navy reforms, 296; Near East postwar problems of, 612; non-intervention policy, 221–224; Parliament, 94, 97, 98, 99, 100, 102, 104, 105, 106, 107, 108, 109, 111, 116, 226, 294, 299; party politics (1866–1871), 224–226; Polish pledge and, 651; politics, post-World War I, course of, 604–607; postwar differences with France, 503–505; rebuilding of (1945–1970), 710–712; Reform Act (1867), 226–228; reform movement (1820–1832), 97–104; religion in (1815–1848), 116–118; revolutions of 1848 and, 153–156; slavery, abolition of, 105, 121; social conditions after 1815, 91–97, 113–116; socialism in, 710–712; Spanish Civil War and, 642–643; Statute of Westminster, 614; trade union movement in, 106–108, 203–294; United States and, 223–224; Vienna Settlement and, 15; World War I and, 461–486; World War II and, 659–698
Great German (*Großdeutsch*) party, 133
Greece, 377–379, 443, 499, 552, 765; communism in, 748; Cyprus and, 774; democracy in, retreat of 600; from 1945 to 1970, 747–749; revolution of the 1820s, 23–27; World War I and, 469–471; World War II and, 672–674
Grégr, Edward, 366

Index

Grévy, Jules, 323, 330
Grey, Sir Edward, 103, 110, 295, 432, 437, 439, 441–442, 445, 447
Griboedov, Alexander, 60
Grieg, Edvard, 246
Grillparzer, Franz, 61, 139
Grimm, Jakob and Wilhelm, 57
Grisi, Carlotta, 90
Grivas, George, 774
Groener, Wilhelm, 556–557, 558, 577, 582
Gronchi, Giovanni, 722, 740
Gropius, Walter, 454, 455, 761
Grosz, George, 563
Grotewohl, Otto, 727
Grün, Anastasius, 61
Grünne, Count, 197, 373
Guadalcanal, 682
Guam, 412, 679, 696
Guderian, H., 665
Guérard, Albert, 175
Guesde, Jules, 330, 331
Guinea, 411, 716, 793
Guinness, Alec, 732
Guizot, François, 34, 75–76, 83, 84, 124
Gulbransson, O., 357
Gustavus V (Sweden), 308
Gyulai, Franz, 197

Haakon VII (Norway), 308, 663, 719
Hácha, Emil, 651
Haggard, H. Rider, 245, 408
Hague Conference (1929), 572
Haig, Sir Douglas, 296, 480
Haile Selassie I, 637
Haldane, R. B., 295, 296, 437, 442, 443
Halévy, Elie, 297
Halifax, Lord, 645
Haller, Karl Ludwig von, 37, 48, 56
Hammerskjöld, Dag, 764
Hammond, J. L. and B., 93
Hanover, 45, 46, 54, 56, 57, 131, 213, 214
Hansemann, David, 45
Hansen, Theophil, 370
Hapsburg monarchy, 186, 215–216
Hardenberg, Karl August Prince von, 14, 16
Hardie, James Keir, 292, 293
Hardy, Thomas, 245
Harkort, Friedrich, 45
Harney, G. J., 109
Hart, Basil Liddell, 614
Hartwig, 443
Hasenauer, Karl, 370
Hatzfeldt, Countess Sophie von, 346

Hatzfeldt, Paul, 428
Hauptmann, Gerhart, 245, 354, 355
Hauser, Arnold, 245, 454
Haussman, Baron G. E. B., 175, 181
Hazlitt, William, 119
Heath, Edward, 736
Hegel, Georg F., 7, 9, 48, 271, 273
Heidegger, Martin, 459
Heine, Heinrich, 62, 67, 149
Heinemann, Gustav, 741n
Heisenberg, Werner, 453
Hejaz, 472, 499, 501
Helfrich, Conrad E. L., 680
Helgoland, 15, 411, 426
Helmholtz, Hermann, 9
Helmholtz, Ludwig, 354
Hemingway, Ernest, 481
Henlein, Konrad, 597, 647, 648
Henry IV (Navarre), 321
Henry V (France), 321
Hentsch, Richard von, 463
Henze, Hans Werner, 732
Herriot, Edouard, 619
Hertzog, General James Barry, 614, 792
Hervé, Gustave, 476
Herzegovina, 252, 256, 373, 377, 438, 497
Herzen, Alexander, 43, 79, 130–131, 163, 280
Herzl, Theodore, 367
Hess, Rudolf, 196, 578, 579, 585, 590
Hesse, Hermann, 456, 457
Hesse-Cassel, 45, 56, 214
Hesse-Darmstadt, 55, 131, 219
Hetairia Philiké, 24
Heuss, Theodor, 137, 741
Himmler, Heinrich, 579
Hindemith, Paul, 572
Hindenburg, Oskar von, 583
Hindenburg, Paul von, 465, 466, 467, 476, 482, 573, 577, 582–583, 587, 592, 725
Hindenburg Line, 480, 483
Hiroshima, Japan, 658, 659, 697
Hirsch-Duncker Unions, 269
Hitler, Adolf, 368, 454, 484, 486, 494, 495, 508, 537, 568–569, 571, 578–594, 596–601, 623, 701, 754; appointment of, 581–586; armed forces subordinated to, 592; Austria invaded by, 645–647; Beer Hall Putsch of, 569; consolidation of power by, 586; Czechoslovakia invaded by, 647–651; first years (1933–1935), 633–636; foreign policy, 630–633; Munich Agreement, 650; Mussolini and, 639–640, 647; Nazi-Polish Pact (1934), 634; Nazi-Soviet

Index

Index

Index

Index

Omdurman, battle of, 419
Open Door Note, 416
Operation Overlord, 690–691
Orange, House of, 18
Orange Free State, 422
Orff, Carl, 732
Organisation du Travail, L' (Blanc), 80
Organization for European Economic Co-operation, 765
Orlando, Vittorio, 487, 488, 490, 545
Orpen, Sir William, 491
Orsini, Felice, 184, 185, 186, 195
Ortega y Gasset, José, 625, 721
Orwell, George, 148n, 604, 744
Osborne, John, 730
Osborne Judgment, 294
O'Shea, William Henry, 301
Oskar I (Sweden), 308
Oskar II (Sweden), 308
Osman Pasha, 252
Otto I (Greece), 27, 377
Ottoman Empire, 23, 163, 164, 165, 379
Oudinot, Nicholas Charles, 169, 191, 192, 203
Owen, Robert, 107–108, 275, 283, 292
Owen, Wilfred, 732
Owens, John W., 656n
Oxford Movement, 117

Pakistan, 783–784
Palach, Jan, 756
Palacký, Frantisek, 138, 366
Palermo, Sicily, 127, 191, 198
Palestine, 32, 499, 501, 613, 725
Palestine Liberation Organization, 780
Pallavicino, Georgio, 195
Pall Mall Gazette (London), 222
Palme, Olof, 720
Palmerston, Viscount (Henry Temple), 28, 29–30, 31, 33, 34, 121, 153–155, 157, 159, 209, 221, 224, 226; Far East and, 223
Panama affair (1892), 331
Pan-Germanism, 598
Pan-Slav Congress, 138, 217
Pan-Slavism, 252, 366
Panzini, Alfredo, 539
Papadoupolos, Gregorios, 748
Papal States, 30, 165, 186, 188, 190, 195, 200
Papandreou, George, 748
Papen, Franz von, 584, 585, 586, 588, 592
Pareto, Vilfredo, 315, 453
Paris, 65, 77, 124–127, 133–134, 171–172, 175–176, 183, 316–319, 326; Conferences; (1814), 12; (1815), 19 (1856), 163–165

Paris Peace Conference (1919), 488; Eastern Europe settlement, 496–499; German settlement, 492–495; Near East settlement, 499–501; procedural questions, 489–492; revision, machinery for, 501–502
Parliament, British, *see* Great Britain
Parma, 18, 30, 186, 195, 197, 198
Parnell, Charles Stewart, 300, 301
Paskévitch, I. F., 31
Pasternak, Boris, 387, 757–758
Pasternak, Leonid, 387
Pasteur, Louis, 146
Patton, George S., 685, 693, 696
Paul, Regent (Yugoslavia), 675
Paul, St., 459
Paul I (Greece), 758
Paul VI, Pope, 704
Paulus, Friedrich von, 686, 687
Pavlov, I. P., 386
Pearl Harbor, Japanese attack on, 679, 680–681
Pedro V (Portugal), 311
Peel, Sir Robert, 97, 98, 99, 100, 112–113, 116, 224, 225, 226
Peel, Sir Robert (the Younger), 249
Péguy, Charles, 246, 333, 334, 335, 338
Pellico, Silvio, 187
Pelloutier, Fernand, 282
Pelloux, Luigi, 313, 314, 315
People's Will, The, 388
Perovsky, Sophie, 388
Perry, Matthew, 415
Perse, St. John, 729
Persia, 417, 434
Persigny, Jean Gilbert, Duke of, 171, 172, 175
Pestel, Paul, 41, 42
Pétain, Philippe, 335, 480, 621, 669, 670, 713
Peter I (Serbia), 377
Peter II (Yugoslavia), 600, 675
Peterloo, massacre of, 97
Peters, Carl, 404, 409
Petersberg Agreement (1949), 726
Petit Journal, Le (Paris), 245
Petlyura, 524
Pfizer, Paul, 58–59
Philip of Hesse, Prince, 647
Philippe Egalité, Duke of Orleans, 76
Philippine Islands, 310, 413, 418, 679, 682, 696
Photius, Archmandrite, 40
Picasso, Pablo, 454, 456, 642
Picquart, Georges, 333
Pieck, Wilhelm, 727

Index

Reform Club, 104

Reformed Church (France), 86

Réforme, La (Paris), 125

Reggio, Italy, 200

Reichspartei (Free Conservatives), 342

Reinhardt, Walter, 563

Reinsurance Treaty (1887), 260, 426–427

Religion, 150; freedom of, 133; in France, 84–86; revival of, 8; under absolutism, 59–60

Remarque, Erich Maria, 486

Renan, Ernest, 179

Rennenkampf, P. K., 465, 466

Renner, Karl, 723

Renoir, Jean, 622

Renoir, Pierre Auguste, 181

Rerum Novarum, 343

Resnais, Alain, 732

Respighi, Ottorino, 247

Rethel, Alfred, 125

Revisionism, 283–284

Revolutions of 1848, 6, 123–142, 153–155; in Austria, 127–130, 215; in France, 124–127, 133; in Prussia and the German states, 130–133, 135

Rexists, 623, 624

Reynaud, Paul, 668, 669

Rheinische Zeitung, 271

Rhigas, 24

Rhineland, 17, 45, 48, 124, 205, 495, 504, 572; invaded by Hitler, 638

Rhineland Pact, 509, 510, 552, 571

Rhodes, Cecil J., 404, 405, 411, 421, 428

Rhodesia, 405, 411, 735, 792

Ribbentrop, Joachim von, 651, 654, 661, 706

Ricardo, David, 105

Richelieu, Duke of, 70

Richter, Eugen, 343

Riff war (1925–1926), 618, 625

Rigault, R., 318

Rike, Rainer Maria, 245, 355

Rimbaud, Arthur, 326, 418

Rimski-Korsakov, Nicholas, 62, 246

Robbe-Grillet, Alain, 730

Robertson, Sir William, 296

Robinson, F. J., 97, 98

Rocque, Colonel de la, 619

Rodin, Auguste, 332

Roehm, Ernst, 579, 585, 592

Roentgen, Wilhelm Konrad, 354

Rogers, Ernesto, 761

Rokossovsky, Konstantin, 751

Romagna, 197, 198

Roman Catholic Church, 8, 48, 50, 60, 150; in France, 84–85, 336–338; in Great Britain, 100, 116, 117

Romanticism, 7–8, 61, 86–87, 89, 119, 148, 149

Rommel, Erwin, 660, 672, 673, 681, 683–685, 690–691

Roon, Albrecht von, 206

Roosevelt, Franklin D., 671, 679, 681, 684; Cairo Conference, 709; Teheran Conference, 688; Yalta Conference, 694

Roosevelt, Theodore, 424

Rose, Sir Hugh, 222

Rosebery, Lord, 403

Rosenberg, Alfred, 579, 686, 706

Rossi, Pellegrino, 191, 192

Rossini, Gioacchino, 149

Rostow, W. W., 262

Rothschild, Baron, 263

Rotteck, Karl von, 58

Rouher, Eugène, 178

Rozhdestvensky, Z. P., 394, 424, 431

Rückert, Friedrich, 61

Rude, François, 89

Rugby School, 118

Ruhr, 508, 566

Ruhr Statute (1948), 726

Rumania, 25, 27, 184, 255, 373, 443, 469, 497, 498, 673, 676, 747, 749; democracy in, retreat of, 600; differences with Soviet Union, 753–754; post–World War II settlement, 708

Rumanians, 139, 217, 374–375

Rundstedt, Gerd von, 670, 678

Rusk, Dean, 764

Ruskin, John, 403, 404

Russell, Lord John, 35, 100–101, 103, 105

Russell, W. H., 160–161

Russia, 5, 27, 37–40; agrarian problem, 382–383; under Alexander II, 230–234, 386–389; Anglo-Russian agreement, 433–435; Balkan states and, 443; Bosnian crisis and, 438–440; Bolshevik revolution, 517–519; Bulgarian crisis, 258–260; civil war in, 520–524; colonialism, 9–10; constitutional experiment in, 395–397; Crimean War, 156–167; Decembrist revolt in, 40–42; economic conditions (1871–1914), 382–386; emancipation of serfs in, 151; foreign trade, 385–386; Franco-Russian Alliance, 426–427; from 1871 to 1914, 381–397; imperial expansion, 230–231, 414–416, 425; industrial development, 263,

Index

Index

Index

Index